African Americans in Conservative Movements

Louis G. Prisock

African Americans in Conservative Movements

The Inescapability of Race

Louis G. Prisock
Rutgers University
Piscataway, NJ, USA

ISBN 978-3-319-89350-1   ISBN 978-3-319-89351-8   (eBook)
https://doi.org/10.1007/978-3-319-89351-8

Library of Congress Control Number: 2018938327

Cover design: Jenner Images/Getty Images

Printed on acid-free paper

This Palgrave Macmillan imprint is published by the registered company Springer International Publishing AG part of Springer Nature
The registered company address is: Gewerbestrasse 11, 6330 Cham, Switzerland

Dedicated to my loving parents
Dorothy S. Prisock
and
Louis G. Prisock Sr. (1921–2016)

ACKNOWLEDGEMENTS

Growing up I can remember my mother often reminding me that as we make our way through life we must never forget that our achievements are the combination of our individual talents and efforts and the interventions of others. It is now I would like to recognize and offer thanks to the many individuals who played a role in helping me reach this goal. I'd like to first offer thanks to the wonderful editors at Palgrave who took me through the various steps in making my manuscript become an actual book. To my editor Mary AL-Sayed, I want to thank you for believing in my project, patiently answering all of my questions, providing sound advice, and staying on top of me to meet all of the necessary deadlines. Next I'd like to thank my professors in the sociology department at Drexel University, Drs. Elizabeth Petras and Julia Hall for exposing me to the intellectual power of sociology through their teaching and support given to me outside of class. My biggest thanks goes to my mentor Dr. Douglas Porpora, had I not taken his Wealth and Power course my senior year my life path would have been very different. Dr. Porpora saw something in an opinionated lanky twenty something student and asked if I would be interested in pursuing a career in sociology. My life was forever changed after that day as I decided I was better suited to be in a classroom than a corporate office. Doug, as I now call him, never waivered in his support and encouragement while I was navigating my way through graduate school. There were times when I doubted I would finish but Doug had enough faith and confidence in me to see me through to the end. Even after I completed graduate school and began working as an assistant professor Doug has always been, and continues to be, that encouraging and calming force that has kept me steady through the many ups and downs during my academic career. I cannot offer enough thanks to Doug for being the reason I am an academic and scholar today. I need to offer thanks to the many people at University of Massachusetts, Amherst who played a role in getting me to this moment in my career. First, I want to thank my other mentor and dissertation advisor Dan Clawson for the support, patience, and direction he provided me while I was a graduate student in the sociology department. To say Dan went the extra mile to see me get to the finish line and acquire my Ph.D. is an understatement. Dan provided the right amount of encouragement, support, and tough love to help mold me into a budding sociologist. In addition, Dan provided me with valuable opportunities such as working as an editorial assistant when he was the editor of the journal *Contemporary Sociology*. I learned the value of being a book author, the complexity and competiveness of the academic publishing landscape, and how the book review process works. Many thanks go out to Dan for him believing in me when at times I did not. I want to thank Michael Lewis for his support and providing me with the opportunity to be his research assistant on two occasions, experiences I will always remember. I also want to thank Michael for the many enlightening conversations we had in his office about the state of the academy, the direction sociology was headed as a discipline, race in the United States, and the usual guy stuff like sports. Thanks goes out to Suzanne Model for her helping me discover, through taking her class, an interest in social stratification. Deirdre Royster was instrumental in making this book a reality when she helped me shape the random ideas I had about black conservatism into a dissertation project. Thanks to my graduate school colleagues Ingrid Seaman and John O'Connor, two of the smartest sociologists I had the pleasure of befriending, thank you both for enriching my experience at UMASS and helping me get through the program. Thanks goes to Prof. John Bracey in the African American Studies department for his excellent guidance as a member of my dissertation committee. I would be remiss if I did not give a special thank you to Dean Robinson of the Political Science department. Dean has been my dear friend who I have been blessed to know for over twenty-five years, during the time of our friendship I have benefitted greatly from the intellectual insights Dean put forth during the many conversations we have had on black politics in America. I owe a debt of gratitude to the wonderful people at Hampshire College, the place where I first honed my teaching skills. A big thank you goes out to Margaret Cerullo, Amy Jordan, Mike Ford, Carolee Bengelsdorf, Kristen Luschen, and Mary Bombardier for your support and encouragement. A much deserved thank you goes to Marlene Gerber Fried for inviting me to participate in her annual Reproductive Rights conference; it was there I first presented my ideas on the black anti-abortion movement. The positive feedback I received from attendees helped me sharpen my analysis, which I present in Chapter 3 of the book. I must also thank three talented and wonderful students I had the privilege of teaching while at Hampshire, my mentoree Marika Dunn, Alex Kreit, and Jessica Nelson, you three have added to my academic career in more ways than you will ever know. At Mount Holyoke College I must thank Lucas Wilson, Preston Smith, and Amy Martin for their guidance and mentorship during my time there. When I arrived at Colgate University I did not realize the impact my stay there would have on me as a person and academic. I cannot say enough about my former colleagues in the Sociology and Anthropology department. It was a pleasure and honor to have worked with Rhonda Levine, Christopher Henke, Carolyn Hsu, Janel Benson, Meika Loe, Paul Lopes, Nancy Ries, Michelle Bigenho, Mary Moran, Jordan Gerber, Anthony Aveni, and Allan Maca. At my current home Rutgers University I must thank my Africana Studies department colleagues Edward Ramsamy, Kavitha Ramsamy, Melanye Price, Kim Butler, Brittany Cooper, and Walton Johnson for their support. A special thanks goes to Gayle Tate for her valuable suggestions on how I could improve my analysis on black conservatism. I'd also like to offer thanks to my American Studies colleagues Allan Isaac, Nicole Fleetwood, Sylvia Chan-Malik, Louis Masur, Andrew Urban, and Jefferson Decker for their encouragement. To my family, sister Natalie Prisock-Lockett, brother in law Le Andrew Lockett, nephews Brandon and Ryan Elliott, cousins Martin Brown, Wallace and Jody Prysock, and sister-in-law Sandra Stephens thank you all for the love and care you have given me over the years. To my parents there are not enough thanks I could adequately provide to express how much I greatly appreciate the many valuable and wonderful contributions you have made to my life. I am very lucky to say I had two role models and heroes who helped shaped me to be the person I am today. Although dad you have gone home please know I continue to work hard to live up to the model you set for me as a man and father. Last but definitely not least I must offer the biggest thanks to the two most important ladies in my life Michelle Stephens and Alexandria Stephens Prisock. Michelle, little did we know when we met almost twenty years ago at Mount Holyoke College the path our lives would take us on. I thank you for being my inspiration as a scholar, you are the epitome of academic excellence and without you I do not think I would have been able to go as far as I have in my career. You have been a wonderful life partner providing love and care while putting me in check when the time called for it; I will always cherish our time together. I could not have asked for a better mother to our daughter, it is a pleasure to watch you help Alexandria become a strong and secure woman of color. To my wonderful daughter Alexandria you give me so much joy, watching you grow up before my eyes into this compassionate, intelligent, informed outspoken person warms my heart. You are the greatest gift God has ever bestowed on me.

CONTENTS

CHAPTER 1

Introduction—Race: The Achilles Heel of a Movement

While working on this book I remembered a conversation I had with a white female friend of mine, who identifies as conservative in her political and social beliefs. My friend expressed befuddlement on why there was not more excitement from African Americans toward retired neurosurgeon Benjamin Carson's attempt to capture the Republican nomination. Carson after all represented everything that African Americans hold dear: he held a strong belief in God and family, recognized and promoted the importance in education, and rising up from very humble beginnings and overcoming such constraints like poverty and racism to become the pre-eminent neurosurgeon in the world. Plus, according to my friend, white conservatives like her found his life story inspiring and admirable because Carson's life narrative was one that Americans of all colors could look up to. As my friend pointed out, the interest and popularity Carson had with white conservatives like her not only illustrated their ability to embrace people of color but also show that one can be color blind. "When I listen to Dr. Carson speak I don't see race or that he's a black man, I see an American who exemplifies what America is all about." What my friend did not understand was while African Americans have looked up to Carson for the way he has lived his life and being the best in a field African Americans are not normally associated with, thus helping to dispel the pernicious stereotypes about the alleged intellectual and cultural inferiority of blacks, the various positions Carson has taken on issues, particularly those pertaining to race, often makes some African Americans feel that Carson does not speak to, or acknowledge,

© The Author(s) 2018
L. G. Prisock, *African Americans in Conservative Movements*,
https://doi.org/10.1007/978-3-319-89351-8_1

the realities they have faced. Carson's biting criticism of President Obama, the racial protests on America's college campuses, or the Black Lives Matter movement gives the impression to some African Americans that he is really speaking to white conservatives who find him appealing. Because of this the times Carson has taken his conservative peers to task for not addressing the issue of racism does not register as strongly with African Americans as it could or should (Chattanoga 2015). This is illustrative of the challenge African American conservatives face in attempting to make headway and cultivate significant support among their black peers. Because the positions and opinions African American conservatives hold puts them in line with a movement that is looked at by many African Americans with suspicion, a number of African Americans are leery about African American conservatives' claim they speak in the best interests of their community. On the other hand African American conservatives have to be mindful of not being positioned as the "token" conservative of color, by their white peers, who functions as a shield against criticisms from the left of racism, or as a "racial mascot" as argued by legal scholar Sumo Cho (1998) thus falling prey to the accusations by some African Americans of "uncle Tomming for the white man."

Racism has always been a thorn in the side of American conservatism, much of it due to the various oppositional stances that conservatives have historically taken on such issues as abolishing slavery, school and societal racial integration, and the Civil Rights movement. As conservative journalist Matt Lewis states, "I think it's fair to say that we on the center-right have been defending ourselves and our movement against charges of racism for so long that we've forgotten that, well, our side has some racists" (Lewis 2015).

The conflict among conservatives over the popularity of Donald Trump's nativism, the open support Trump received from white supremacists, and the debate among conservatives around issues like the legitimacy of the confederate flag and race and police brutality, are all instances of what I term "the inescapability of race." By this I refer to the continuing presence, power, and influence of race in highly racialized societies like the United States. Because race thoroughly permeates every social, political, and economic aspect of American life, ideologies such as color blindness cannot adequately address the realities of race. In fact, color blindness obfuscates the various ways in which race operates to create inequalities and an unjust social hierarchy. The main argument of this book is, while the presence of conservatives of color (such as African

American) within the conservative movement highlights the increasing acceptance of diversity by conservatives, various conflicts between African American conservatives and their white counterparts also illustrates the tenuousness of this diversity, and the ways that conservatives are prone to the inescapability of race.

African Americans in Conservative Movements sociological concern is not simply African American conservatives themselves; its greater focus is on their *relationships* to African Americans and conservatives writ large. A half-century ago, an African American would have been shunned and condemned by a significant fraction of the conservative movement—just as gay and lesbian conservatives are disparaged in many circles today. Today, the conservative movement actively seeks out African Americans and works to give them visibility, a practice culminating in 2009 with the election of the first African American, Michael Steele, to head the Republican Party.

The shift in conservatism that made possible, and perhaps necessary, the rise to prominence of African Americans, was the result of a concerted campaign and ideological process that continues to naturalize and cloak the constructed nature of their inclusion. An intentionality and purposefulness shapes the ways in which African American conservatism has been made to appear as a natural phenomenon, both to white conservatives and to black Americans as a whole. From World War II to the end of the 1960s, most conservatives openly allied with segregationists. The diversification of the Right both signals the political mainstreaming of American conservatism and illustrates the fluidity of conservatism as a movement and ideology.[1]

Chapter 2 charts the transformative process by which American conservatism, in the mid-twentieth century, shed its overtly racialist skin to create a conservatism that would be more palatable for mainstream political consumption and help facilitate the diversification of the movement. This new conservatism, in a sharp break with the past, both embraced the notion of color blindness and used it in a racially coded discourse, or "dog whistle" political discourse, a term coined by legal scholar Ian Haney Lopez (2014),[2] to frame a new more populist, movement.

In this context, color blindness refers to the philosophy, articulated by many conservatives, wherein the guiding principle of human relations is to evaluate a person's merits based on their individual characteristics (kindness, morals, values, talents, etc.) and not on their space within a racial category. This approach is best captured by the conservative co-optation of Dr. Martin Luther King's famous call that African Americans, "not be judged by the color of their skin, but by the content of their character." Embedded in the color-blind philosophy is the belief that the best approach to racial inequality is not to strive for equal outcomes; instead, it aims to make equal opportunities available to all. This approach confers the rights of equal treatment and fairness under the law to the individual, and disregards the notion of affording privileges based on racial categories. While the concept carries a veneer of noble intentions, it elides or overlooks the important role of social structures in maintaining and replicating racial inequality.

Chapter 3 continues the historical narrative started in Chapter 2. I provide a brief examination of the concept of color blindness, a concept whose origins go back to the founding of this nation. I pinpoint the seventies as the period that saw the creation of a conservative infrastructure or network of institutions—in the popular media, the public sphere, think tanks, and the organization of intellectuals—that brought together very different groups of New Right leaders, neoconservative intellectuals, and ministers of the religious right. This intellectual infrastructure helped to establish the contemporary discourse of color blindness within the right-wing community and, later, throughout the mainstream public. This new conservative movement seeded by the events of the 1950s and finding full bloom in 1980 with Ronald Reagan's election to the White House, finds itself in crisis today. Chapter 3 concludes by discussing how the movement, both in spite of and because of its vehement opposition to affirmative action and other forms of racial liberalism, actively recruited African American intellectuals, politicians, and ministers in violation of its own color-blind principles. Some of these figures have had a troubled relationship with the movement, as conservatives continue to take positions, engage in actions, and treat individual African Americans in ways that pose challenges for African American conservatives. African American conservatives have also had strained relations with the rest of the African American community, and their relationship to grassroots social movements and black churches, frames much of the discourse of both the chapter and the book as a whole.

The structure of the book shifts, as the focus of the remaining five chapters is not a linear chronological examination of the various areas where black conservatism is articulated and acted upon. Where Chapters 2 and 3 serve to both contextualize and historize the transformation of the movement's racial conservatism; Chapters 4–8 focuses on black conservatism as a multi-faceted and manifold social and political formation that manifests in various and differing realms, and frequently changes shape according to its context.

Chapter 4 begins with the groups that are most unlike those conservatives cultivated from the top-down by Republican and conservative white elites: Those that organize from the bottom-up in response to the issue of abortion. I argue that a different strand of black conservatism intersects with, and deviates from, the "traditional" black conservatives who are recruited and organized by the broader white conservative movement. One of the significant deviations in the conservative black social movements, such as the black anti-abortion movement, is the abandonment of a color-blind philosophy. I argue in Chapter 4 that race, racism, victimization, and conspiracy are central components that frame the black anti-abortion activist movement. In Chapter 5, I continue my examination of black conservative social movements with an analysis of the anti-gay rights and school choice movements. Like their pro-life counterparts, African American conservative activists in the anti-gay rights and school voucher movements fully embrace the use of race within their discourses and are comfortable in pointing out the racism of their white conservative peers, as illustrated through a profile on Annette "Polly" Williams, one of the influential founding members of the African American school voucher movement.

Chapter 6 describes the dilemma of black conservative politicians who find themselves positioned as a captured minority within the Republican Party. Their influence rests more in the ideological realm, as operatives who legitimize the notion of color blindness, than as representatives of a black constituency or deliverers of black votes. I detail the racial controversies and Republican Party pushback faced by Michael Steele and Herman Cain to explain the mazes that African American conservatives must navigate to hold their place at the GOP table. I also analyze the role of African Americans in the Tea Party, and explain how black Tea Party members solidify the Tea Party movement as, what scholar Lisa Disch calls, a "white citizenship movement" while also reinforcing in their white counterparts the notion that scholar Laurie Balfour calls "racial innocence." Chapter 7 explores the parallel struggle of black intellectuals and academics that are often identified as the go-to spokespeople for a broader set of black conservative values. I analyze and challenge the positions of two influential black intellectuals, John McWhorter, Shelby Steele, and an up-and-coming pundit named Kevin Williamson. I also examine the career of prominent former conservative intellectual Glenn Loury and Loury's conflicts with his white counterparts.

Chapter 8 points to perhaps the most potentially effective form of black conservatism taking shape at the end of the twentieth century and the beginning of the twenty-first: An increasingly well-funded black religious right. Under the auspices of such doctrines as the prosperity gospel, black conservative ministers are arguably doing more than any African American politician or movement to promote within the black American population a commonsense support for capitalism, through a discourse that leaves unchallenged and helps maintain ideologies of whiteness in American society. I conclude the book by providing an overview of where African American conservatism stands in the early part of the twenty-first century. This includes probing the strengths and weaknesses of African American conservatism, and its possible avenues for growth.

Because of the inescapability of race, African American conservatives will continually find themselves facing challenges from multiple fronts. While their advocacy of color blindness will align them with their white peers, it will continue to produce little traction among African Americans, as it does not speak to the lived experiences of many blacks in the United States. On the other hand, if African American conservatives place race and, particularly, racism more to the forefront of their perspective on America, they risk losing the support of their white conservative counterparts by impeding the movement's efforts to envision America as a nation that finally transcended race.

Notes

1. See historian Patrick Allitt's, *The Conservatives: Ideas & Personalities Throughout American History* (2009) for an excellent historical account of the fluidity of American conservatism. Allitt demonstrates how, at times, conservatism could be at odds with itself around such issues as democracy and inequality, and the extent to which during its trajectory in American history it has been in constant motion, never stagnant or rigid.
2. According to Lopez, dog whistle discourse is one that is not specific to one political perspective as it can be used by both the right and left and is applicable to a variety of issues targeting many different audiences.

REFERENCES

Allitt, Patrick. *The Conservatives: Ideas and Personalities Throughout American History.* New Haven, CT: Yale University Press, 2009.

Chattanoga, W.W. "Speaking Truth to Obliviousness," uploaded June 24, 2015, http://www.economist.com/blogs/democracyinamerica/2015/06/ben-carson-race, accessed July 14, 2016.

Cho, Sumo. "Redeeming Whiteness in the Shadow of Interment: Earl Warren, Brown, and a Theory of Racial Redemption." *Boston College Third World Law Journal,* vol. 19, no. 1, 1998: 73–170.

Lewis, Matt. "Twitter's Right-Wing Civil War: For a Not-Insignificant Portion of the Online Right, a New Form of White Nationalism Is Taking Root—And It Coincides with the Rise of Donald Trump," uploaded July 28, 2015, http://www.thedailybeast.com/articles/2015/07/28/twitter-s-right-wing-civil-war.html, accessed September 4, 2015.

Lopez, Ian Haney. *Dog Whistle Politics: How Coded Racial Appeals Have Reinvented Racism and Wrecked the Middle Class.* New York: Oxford University Press, 2014.

CHAPTER 2

Beginnings: The Subtleties of Race in Conservative Politics

BLACK CONSERVATISM LEGACY

While in this chapter my analysis of American conservatism and its relationship to blacks begins in the middle of the twentieth century, I should point out that the relationship conservatives have had with blacks has been both long and complex going back to beginnings of the United States. In fact, according to historian Rhett Jones, the origins of black conservatism can be traced back to the black Creole culture of the eighteenth century (Jones 2002). From slavery straight through to the Civil Rights movement era and beyond conservatives have expressed their opinions and beliefs about race, and the nation's "race problem," during these same periods there were blacks who articulated conservative beliefs about the society blacks lived in and, more importantly, the actions blacks needed to take to achieve racial equality in America. I point this out so as not to give the impression that the contemporary cohort of black conservatives I examine in this book are the alpha and omega of black conservatives in the United States. When in 1991 a relatively unknown law professor, Anita Hill, accused, then candidate for the Supreme Court, Clarence Thomas of sexual harassment the fascination and curiosity espoused by the media to blacks articulating a conservative point of view made it seem that it was the first time the nation had been exposed to black conservatism. Yet, there is

© The Author(s) 2018
L. G. Prisock, *African Americans in Conservative Movements*,
https://doi.org/10.1007/978-3-319-89351-8_2

a rich history of black conservatism in the United States. From prominent black conservatives such as Booker T. Washington and his accommodationist politics typified in his famous Atlanta Exposition speech where he advocated for the acceptance of racial segregation by stating, "In all things that are purely social we can be as separate as the fingers, yet one as the hand in all things essential to mutual progress," (Washington 1904: 240). To journalist George S. Schuyler who shifted from advocating socialism to becoming an ardent anti-communist providing strident criticism of the civil rights movement, a movement he thought was communist-influenced (Williams 2007). There are lesser known black conservatives that have contributed to the legacy of black conservatism in America, such as abolitionist James Forten a free black born in Philadelphia on September 2, 1766, who turned his skills as a sailmaker into a personal fortune and used his wealth to garner political status in the city. Forten was deeply patriotic, advocated integration, and a firm believer in the black Protestant ethic (Bracey 2008: 11–12). Black conservatism has not been devoid of contributions by black women, Zora Neale Hurston, anthropologist and writer associated with the Harlem Renaissance movement, was an ardent individualist who did not believe one needed to get pride in oneself through the achievement of an individual of the same race, to Hurston pride came from within not from without in racial symbolic identification:

> "Racial pride is not a luxury I can afford…I *do* glory when a Negro does something fine, I gloat because he or she has done a fine thing, but not because he was a Negro. That is incidental and accidental. It is the human achievement which I honor." (Hurston 1942: 248)

Of course the most prominent black female conservative is the former Secretary of State Condoleezza Rice who served in both George Bush Sr. and George W. Bush's administrations. Although much of black conservatism has been focused on individuals and groups that espouse Christianity, we must not forget the decades of work the Nation of Islam has been doing in black communities across the nation preaching their racial, social, and economic conservatism as the road to freedom and salvation. In the end, it is important to remember that black conservatism is a multidimensional diverse phenomenon that runs the span of eras (slavery to present day), racial politics (integrationist to separatist), religion (Christianity to Islam), and patriot to racial nationalist. In the next section, I outline the linear timeline of American conservatism racial reconfiguration in the mid-twentieth century, and it is this conservatism that today's black conservatives belong to, support, and as I illustrate throughout the rest of the book challenge.

THE NATIONALISTS VERSUS THE MULTINATIONALISTS

During the 1950s and 1960s, conservatism was seen as a relatively weak, almost fringe-like, movement in the United States. Liberal historian Richard Hofstadter labeled conservative adherents as "pseudo conservatives," borrowing the term from theorist Theodore Adorno. According to Hofstadter, paranoia, antagonism, and alienation were what fueled those who took on this political mindset:

> The restlessness, suspicion and fear manifested in various phases of the pseudo-conservative revolt give evidence of the real suffering which the pseudo-conservative experiences in his capacity as a citizen. He believes himself to be living in a world in which he is spied upon, plotted against, betrayed, and very likely destined for total ruin. (Hofstader 1964: 43, 45)

The mood of some conservatives was rather reserved and pessimistic. According to Clinton Rossiter, American conservatives had drifted further away from their bearings in the English conservative tradition of Edmund Burke and conservatism had become nothing more than a "thankless persuasion." As Rossiter saw it, American conservatives were hopelessly putting together a combination of ideas and beliefs that only faintly resembled the best legacy of conservative thought. Additionally, this general disorganization was allowing extreme visions to blossom. Rossiter expressed concern that the faction with the most influence during the fifties was the "ultraconservative" or "professional haters" groups such as the John Birch Society and Gerald L.K. Smith (Rossiter 1962: 168).[1]

Echoing these themes, William F. Buckley, Jr. argued that American conservatives would not be in a position to adequately challenge the liberal establishment until they had addressed weaknesses within the conservative movement. Buckley argued that these weaknesses were related to an excessively pessimistic outlook, too much concern with "crassly materialist positions," an inability to control extremes within the movement, and a failure to "put its theoretical house in order" (Buckley 1959: 161). Conservatism failed in the political arena, according to Buckley, because of its inability to effectively persuade the society at large that the welfare state was not an asset but a surrender of freedom. Part of this failure was due to the lack of control the right wing had over the Republican Party. Conservatives were frustrated not only by the hegemonic hold Franklin D. Roosevelt and his New Deal agenda had over the nation but also by their inability to put forth a viable conservative candidate from the Republican party to counter Roosevelt and the Democrats.

When Roosevelt died while in office in 1945, conservatives saw this as their opening to regain the White House and put a stop to the buildup of the welfare state. Their sense of opportunity increased even more with the outcome of the 1946 mid-term elections as Republicans took both Houses of Congress for the first time in sixteen years. Coming into the election year of 1948 conservative hopes were high, for Vice President Harry Truman looked very vulnerable in the eyes of many on the Right. Truman's Fair Deal agenda did not seem to be capturing the hearts of the American public to the same degree as Roosevelt's New Deal. This was in part due to the fact that Republicans in Congress had stymied most of Truman's Fair Deal agenda by voting down many aspects of it. There were also signs of internal strife within the Democratic party: During the 1948 presidential convention, a group of Southern Democrats, led by Governor Strom Thurmond of South Carolina, stormed out of the convention in protest against the civil rights positions in the Democratic party's plank. The walkout led to Thurmond's running as a third-party candidate, his platform a protest against the position claimed by the Democrats. Thurmond's party, the National States Rights Party, was dubbed the "Dixiecrat party." Thurmond's run would be a chilling harbinger of what was to come, as ironically another Democratic governor from a southern state would defect from the Democratic Party and wage a similar third-party campaign twenty years later.

Many conservatives saw Truman's foreign policy as his weakness. Communism was becoming an emerging threat overseas with Stalin's repressive government in Russia in 1946 and the fall of Czechoslovakia in 1948. Even more problematic to some conservatives was Truman's containment policy toward communism, otherwise known as the Truman doctrine of 1947. The main objective of this doctrine was to contain

Soviet expansion throughout the world with the collective help from the US' allies. This approach also meant the commitment of American troops and military resources to areas that were vulnerable to communist overthrow. For some conservatives like Senator Robert Taft of Ohio, Truman's containment plan was ill-advised and dangerous. Taft and other conservatives were a part of a wing that wanted much stronger action against Communism. These distinctions in the Republican party later became exacerbated and Senator Taft was considered to belong to a wing known as the mid-western conservatives or isolationists.

Political analysts Chip Berlet and Matthew Lyons describe this cadre of conservatives best as the nationalists, a group of conservatives committed to (1) the United States conducting unilateral attacks over communist states instead of working collectively with its allies; (2) the idea that US-based communists were a dangerous threat to national security and a part of a larger global conspiracy; (3) a "rollback" approach to social and economic issues on the domestic front (they were staunchly hostile toward the labor movement as illustrated by the passage of the 1947 Taft-Hartley act that took away many of the rights laborers had won during the 1930s and made it difficult for many unions to conduct successful labor struggles without breaking the law); and (4) doing away with the welfare state that, according to them, irreparably harmed American business interests and led to a form of socialist governmental control (Berlet and Lyons 2000). Many of the nationalists were opposed to such social movements as the Civil Rights movement. They felt this and other movements were infiltrated and led by communist forces with the purpose of creating internal strife so as to weaken the United States from the "inside out."

Many of these conservatives were also based in the mid-western, southern, and western regions of the United States. This core represented the right-wing segments of both the Republican and Democratic parties who saw themselves as businessmen who were not a part of the silk stocking establishment. Instead, they viewed themselves as regular people who had succeeded by holding true to their traditional values. As Berlet and Lyons also point out, many from this group made their living from old manufacturing sectors like textiles and steel that were labor intensive, which meant that profits were tied to maintaining low wages and benefits. This group of conservatives adamantly adhered to laissez-faire individualism and was hostile to any federal government intervention.

The other prominent cadre of Republicans, known as the interventionists or eastern establishment, can also be labeled best as the multinationalists. This group believed (1) that their and the US' interests were tied to Europe's and they favored a policy aimed at containing the outbreak of communist forces in other regions of the world as encapsulated in the 1947 Truman Doctrine; (2) they favored utilizing Keynesian policies; (3) they favored government involvement in national social and economic matters and accepted the Wagner Act and the passage of the Social Security Act; and (4) this group was more inclined to work with organized labor to reach an accord, again in the necessity of avoiding social discord. The same philosophy applied to their approach to various social movements, especially the civil rights movement.

The multinationalists were mainly composed of white Protestants with some sprinkling of Jewish and Catholic families. Although this group could be found in various parts of the United States, their main concentration was in the Northeastern region, hence the name eastern establishment. This group represented the upper echelons in the most prestigious universities, policy foundations, and media establishments. While the nationalists were in business segments that were labor dependent, the multinationalists could be found in industries that were more capital intensive. Since profits from these firms were not as tied to wages and benefits as those from the labor-intensive sector, the multinationalists had more flexibility in the kinds of relationships they could conduct with organized labor. This wing thus represented the more moderate to liberal segment of the Republican Party.

Conservative optimism would not last when Senator Thomas Dewey, an eastern establishment selection from New York, beat out Taft for the 1948 Republican party presidential nomination. Even though conservatives were disappointed and bitter, they poured their energies behind Dewey only to be upset once again when Truman pulled an election miracle and upset Dewey for the presidency.

As the presidential election of 1952 neared, conservatives became determined not to be undermined again as they had been in 1948. The conservative wing of the Republican Party geared up to get their man Taft elected, but as in 1948, it was not to be. This time they were upset by what they claimed was the hijacking of the Republican presidential nomination by the eastern establishment. In the end, it was not Taft but Dwight Eisenhower who received the GOP nomination and went on to beat Adlai Stevenson to recapture the White House for the Republicans.

Even though the Republican party recaptured the White House with Eisenhower's victory in the 1952 election, during Eisenhower's tenure conservatives within the party and outside of it would not feel Eisenhower was their kind of politician. For example, a supporter for Taft named Robert Welch, a former candy company executive from Belmont Massachusetts, would view Taft's defeat as the work of one-worlders and communists who wanted to have in place their man Eisenhower. On December 8, 1959, in Indianapolis, Welch met with eleven other individuals to go over the perilous state of the world that resulted from the growing power of communism. From that meeting, Welch put forth a proposal to form a national right-wing organization named after John Birch, a 26-year-old fundamentalist missionary who was killed by Chinese communists while on a mission in China during the end of World War II (Hodgson 1997: 59). The organization's main goal was to educate the American people on the dangers of the spread of communism worldwide, particularly the spread of communism at home in the United States. The organization's approach was to use fantastic, conspiratorial claims of a communist plot to take over the world. The conspiracist approach made the John Birch Society an easy target for crit-ics, especially liberals, who marginalized the group as an out of control, extremist, conservative organization. According to Lee Edwards, the for-mation of the John Birch Society was one of many indications signaling the frustrations conservatives had with President Eisenhower:

> Conservative frustration with Eisenhower and his modern brand of Republicanism manifested itself in different ways, including the formation of the John Birch Society in 1958 by Robert Welch...Welch subscribed to the conspiracy theory of history...The conspiracy was everywhere and had ensnared the most unlikely people...Welch persisted in his extremism. Indeed, it was the key to his success; it provided a ready explanation to angry, frustrated conservatives as to why America had lost China, why it had not pursued victory in the Korean War, how Alger Hiss had risen so high in government..., and why government continued to grow and taxes to rise. (Edwards 1999: 84–85)

Another sign that conservatives were disenchanted with Eisenhower came from an upstart conservative Republican Senator, Barry Goldwater from Arizona. Goldwater, who initially provided support to Eisenhower, would eventually become a thorn in Eisenhower's side and in the process help mobilize conservatives inside and outside of the GOP.

DWIGHT EISENHOWER AND THE EMERGENCE
OF THE REPUBLICAN PARTY'S SOUTHERN STRATEGY

For the most part, Eisenhower's main objectives during his stay in the White House were to forge unity between the moderate/liberal and conservative wings of the Republican Party, and to elevate what he thought his leadership represented—modern Republicanism (Rae 1989: 40). As the nation, particularly anti-communist right-wingers, became transfixed on the potential threat that communism posed abroad and at home, another storm was developing—the shake-up of the South. The transformation of the south would take place on many levels—economically, politically, and racially.

From the time of the New Deal to the beginning of the US' entry into the Cold War with the Soviet Union, the federal government had been pouring into the South significant amounts of resources. At the same time, the occurrence of several developments would impact the nation greatly. Technological advances in transportation and communication, the transformation of industrial technology, an increase in economic competition on a regional and international scale, and the expansion of capital into regions like the South, which had a lower wage rate and no significant presence by organized labor, would reconfigure American urban industrial areas all across the nation. Not only were companies looking toward the South but they were also speeding toward fast-growing regions like the West and states like California in particular (Sugrue 1996: 127). As this region known as the Sunbelt was growing and becoming stronger, traditional industrial stronghold areas like the Northeast and Midwest were beginning to wane in power and influence as plants were closing and moving to other areas. This diminution led to the area's labeling as the Rust Belt. As historian Thomas Sugrue attests, the emergence of the southern and western parts of the United States also translated into increasing political power for those regions in Washington:

> The growing power of Sun Belt politicians in Congress further diminished Detroit's share of the massive federal defense budget. By the end of the Korean War, the northeastern and midwestern share of Cold War defense budget had shrunk greatly. Southern members of Congress, many heading influential committees, steered federal military spending towards their home states...Even more impressive was the impact of defense dollars on the West. California was the major beneficiary of defense spending. (Sugrue 1996: 140)

The industrialization, urbanization, and population growth of the South and West had a significant impact on strengthening the burgeoning conservative movement in the United States. According to sociologist Jerome Himmelstein, conservatives reaped benefits from the buildup of the Sunbelt because concomitant with urban development came the creation of a culture that celebrated "unfettered development, free wheeling investment, and individual enterprise—in general unregulated capitalism." The rise of the Sunbelt also had social implications for conservatives:

> The transformation of the Sunbelt also created a class of nouveaux riches, extended affluence more broadly than before, and began to draw the disproportionate number of fundamentalists in the region back into the mainstream of American economic and later political life. In all these ways, it encouraged conservative political trends. (Himmelstein 1990: 75)

The South had always been a Democratic stronghold going back to the Civil War era. Southern whites had never forgotten or forgiven the upstart Republican Party in the North for forcing the South's hand on ending slavery. To many old-time Southerners, the party of Lincoln was an anathema. It was the Democrats who pledged to uphold the legacy of the South, in essence to keep white supremacy intact. In national election after election, the Republicans could not garner any significant support from the South, which functioned as a one-party region. Therefore, when Eisenhower won such Southern states as Texas, Florida, Tennessee, and Virginia in 1952, this raised more than a few eyebrows within the Republican Party, raising their hopes about the possibility of loosening the Democratic Party's viselike grip on the South.

Eisenhower's strong showing in the South led the Republicans to create a program specifically designed to attract more Southerners to the GOP. In 1957, the Republicans formed a Southern division of the Republican National Committee whose sole objective was to redirect Southern voters from the Democratic Party toward the GOP. This plan was named Operation Dixie and represented the first time a version of the "southern strategy" was utilized by a Republican president in the twentieth century. The essence of this "southern strategy" was the cultivation of white Southern support through racist appeals disguised in thinly veiled code language. Over the last forty years, this tactic has continued to bring major results for the Republican Party. President Eisenhower's Vice President Richard Nixon has often been identified as the first presidential candidate to flawlessly use this strategy to gain entry into the White House in 1968 and again in 1972. Others point toward Arizona Senator Barry Goldwater's failed 1964 presidential run as the first time a "southern strategy" was employed. According to historian Kenneth O'Reilly, however, the use of this political ploy can be traced all the way back to the founding of this nation (O'Reilly 1995: 8). When closely examined at its core, the "southern strategy" is a practice that transcends both region and time, or as O'Reilly states, "Southern Strategy though a relatively recent construct can be better understood as a regionless code for 'white over black'" (O'Reilly 1995: 8).

On the surface it appeared as if Eisenhower's Operation Dixie was a plain and simple plan to garner more Southern votes for the Republican party. Increasing support from African American voters for Eisenhower in his 1956 re-election campaign appeared to be a sign that the Republican party had not forgone their attempts at capturing northern and southern black voters (Goldberg 1995: 114).[2] Unfortunately, voting numbers did not reflect reality. When pressed about his feelings toward bringing black voters over toward the Republican party Eisenhower was very resistant, concerned, "that I would be carried away by the hope of capturing the Negro vote in this country, and as a consequence take a stand on the question that would forever defeat any possibility of developing a real Republican or 'Oppositional' Party in the South" (O'Reilly 1995: 169).

A wing of Eisenhower's administration tried to convince the president that aggressively courting African American voters was not only the right thing to do morally, but also, could bring benefits to the Republican party overall. These calls fell on deaf ears as another branch of Eisenhower's administration had a different strategy in mind. The key to reaping success, according to the oppositional wing, was not in bringing blacks into the GOP fold but instead actively ignoring them. It was argued that the only chance the Republicans had of breaking up the New Deal coalition was to direct its energy toward the white South. Eisenhower had to, "prove that 'we are the party of States Rights'" (O'Reilly 1995: 175–176).

Even with the direct objective by some within the White House to attract more of the white South's vote, the GOP's chances of doing this were undermined by developments coming out of Washington. The Supreme Court had sent a major shock wave through the South and the nation by ruling segregation in public schools unconstitutional with its decision in the 1954 Brown v. Topeka Kansas Board of Education case.

Eisenhower's signing of the 1957 Civil Rights Act only increased the boiling animosity white Southerners were already feeling toward the federal government. The white Southern backlash to Washington's direction regarding civil rights was epitomized by Eisenhower's standoff with Arkansas governor Orval Faubus. Faubus's resistance to allowing nine African American students to enter Central High school as mandated by Federal desegregation orders culminated in Eisenhower sending in federal troops to allow the nine black students entry. All hopes President Eisenhower and other Republicans had of building a coalition with white Southerners were dashed with Eisenhower's decision to send in federal troops (O'Reilly 1995: 182).

THE RACIST RIGHT OF THE 1950S

In the 1954 case of Brown v. Topeka Board of Education, the Supreme Court issued its landmark ruling that segregation in public schools was unconstitutional. This ruling overturned the Court's ruling in the 1896 Plessy v. Ferguson case that segregation could be legal as long as there were separate but equal facilities for blacks and whites. The Brown ruling was the first step toward deconstructing the segregated legal and social system of the South. The Brown ruling created optimism in the emerging civil rights movement while it produced fear and outrage not only in a recalcitrant white south, but also, in the radical and racist right. As Godfrey Hodgson states, the emerging fight for freedom waged by blacks sparked an increase in the intensity of backlash from the radical hard right: "One essential element in the shrill tone of the Radical Right in the 1950s was the oncoming locomotive, its smoke clearly visible across Middle America by the middle of the 1950s, of the civil rights revolution" (Hodgson 1997: 63).

As the South experienced burgeoning activism by African Americans mobilized by the nascent civil rights movement, and the continual onslaught of directives coming from Washington that challenged the centuries-old social system of racial segregation, defenders of the Old South and its ways were also mobilizing for a massive battle of resistance. The battle to preserve the Jim Crow South and halt the progress made by the civil rights movement was led by several organizations, prominent among them the White Citizens' Councils. Mississippi circuit court judge Thomas Brady and a Mississippi plantation manager, Robert B. Patterson, were influential in founding the organization (Diamond 1995: 71–72).

The first Citizens' Council chapter was founded in Indianola, Mississippi in July of 1954 by Robert Patterson, after Patterson read a short booklet entitled, *Black Monday*. *Black Monday* was an expanded version of a fiery speech given by Tom Brady to the Sons of the American Revolution denouncing the Supreme Court's ruling in the Brown case. In *Black Monday*, Brady asserted that the Supreme Court's decision forced southerners to either defend segregation or face "amalgamation," and that it was in the nation's best interest if all whites took up the battle against the latter. Brady also claimed that the Brown decision was "socialist" inspired, that action needed to be taken to expose the communist infiltration in America's churches, and America needed to prevent the entry into the country of "Communist-minded immigrants." Brady's most important suggestion was a call for the creation of resistance organizations in every southern state. These organizations would be coordinated by a national affiliate which would spread information and work toward forming a third party (Diamond 1995: 71).

After founding the first chapter, Patterson and others traveled the South giving pro-segregation speeches to various civil organizations and clubs. It was estimated that by 1956 the Councils had a membership pool of around 250,000 in all of the southern states (Diamond 1995: 70). The basic actions taken by the Councilors were in the guise of educating the white public and disseminating their propaganda through appearances on local television and radio, distributing organization literature, and public speaking engagements. The Councils' leadership believed that members' activism would be more productive if instead of focusing on working with sympathetic churches and established political parties, Councilors continued to form more chapters thus creating an independent entity that would have enough name recognition to equal that of the civil rights movement (Diamond 1995: 73).

Since the United States was embroiled in the Cold War with the Soviet Union, and the perception of the threat of a Communist attack was the focus of many in the country, it comes as no surprise that within the Councils' literature, there is a preoccupation with federal government collusion with communist forces. From the federal government's implementation of civil rights initiatives to the buildup of the welfare state, the Councils viewed these developments as the actions of power brokers in Washington to implement a "socialist master plan." Although the Councils took a jaundiced view of the federal government, they were not against working with Southern politicians who expressed pro-segregationist views. This alliance gave Southern politicians the necessary voting support needed to stay in office while on the other hand, the politicians and other Southern elites directed much-needed resources to the organization (Diamond 1995: 75).

The basic objective of the Citizens' Councils' alliance with segregationist politicians was the repression of the civil rights movement. Although in the end, this strategy was unsuccessful, the types of repression ranged from mild forms to strong versions using physical violence. While some Councilors took part in violence against African Americans, much of the physical violence carried out on southern blacks was done by another prominent organization of the segregationist movement—the Ku Klux Klan. During much of the civil rights period, the Councils kept a safe distance from the Klan as their main objective was to appear as a "respectable segregationist" organization. One of the milder forms of repression the Councils used was smear tactics, such as red labeling, against civil rights organizations like the National Association for the Advancement of Colored People (NAACP) (Diamond 1995: 79). Given the political climate of the nation during these times, the Councils' red-baiting tactics had a great impact on their victims, as "numerous reform organizations, from the NAACP to the ACLU to the Mattachine Society (a pioneering gay-rights group) consumed themselves in intense anti-red purges meant to prove their loyalty, much as the CP had purged itself of Japanese Americans members in 1942" (Berlet and Lyons 2000: 160).

Because the Citizens' Councils and the Ku Klux Klan were both southern-based organizations working toward achieving the objective of preserving racial inequality and white supremacy, it is easy to see the two organizations as similar. In fact, many experts of the period lumped these two organizations, along with the John Birch Society, in the same category of the "radical right." While all three organizations did share some similar qualities, Sara Diamond perceptively points out that associating the three groups does more to obfuscate the significant differences between them:

> If one were to apply pluralist scholars' definitions of "radical" and "extremist" tactics…then the Klan would qualify but most Birchers and Councilors would not…. Apart from their tactics, though, Birchists, Councilors, and Klansmen did share a conspiracist worldview which attributed complex social ills to a small, secretive, and powerful clique. This cognitive approach may make a movement unattractive to mainstream

political forces, but it does not necessarily make a movement "extreme" or undemocratic. Furthermore, these three organizations, despite a shared cognitive style, differed in several respects: their social base, their precise tactics, and their significance within broader processes of social change. (Diamond 1995: 80–81)

For example, the White Citizens' Councils drew their membership base from the upper-middle-class strata of business leaders and local politicians. This gave the Councils the benefit of having at their disposal access to a larger resource pool, which enabled the organization to focus more on using large-scale dissemination of rhetoric through media appearances, literature, and public rallies to achieve their objectives. The membership base of the Ku Klux Klan was not as affluent and could not obtain the same access to resources as the Councils' membership. The lack of connections to political elites and the entrenched practice of operating in secrecy and utilizing violence was also connected to the Klan's use of terroristic tactics.

Upon closer examination, neither segregationist organization is comparable with the anti-communist organization, the John Birch Society. While it is true that the Birch society was against the civil rights movement, viewing it as a communist-driven movement, the Birch society had several significant differences from both the Councils and the Klan. While the Councils were able to make alliances with political representatives, the Birch society could not. Because of the strong conspiratorial tone of the organization's message, beginning with founder Robert Welch's claim that President Eisenhower was a dupe of the communists, many elected officials were leery of becoming involved with the John Birch Society. Another important difference between the Birchists and the segregationists was that the Birch organization's objectives were more reformist in tone while the segregationists' objectives were focused on resistance. According to the Birch society, their main problem was with the manner in which elected officials were dealing with the threat of the "red menace." In some instances, the tactics used by the state were seen by Birchists as examples of treason. While the Councils also viewed the government with suspicion, the Councils' feelings of suspicion toward elected officials were not as intense. Instead, the main priority of the White Citizens' Councils was halting the direction the nation was taking in supporting civil rights gains for people of color (Diamond 1995: 81–82).

Another organization that came into existence during this same period was the Liberty Lobby. Although the Liberty Lobby was founded in 1957 by Willis Carto, it would be another four years until the organization started full operations. Interestingly, Carto spent one year, 1959, at the John Birch Society's headquarters in Belmont Massachusetts learning organizational and fund-raising skills. The connection between the two organizations would be long-lasting, as both the Society and the Lobby would share ideas and personnel.

One dominant theme of the Liberty Lobby is racial nationalism and explicit advocacy of white supremacy (Berlet and Lyons 2000: 185–186). Founder Willis Carto was greatly influenced by Francis Parker Yockey's anti-semitic work, *Imperium* (Diamond 1995: 85). Carto established a number of organizational publications such as the Lobby's newspaper, *Spotlight*, and the magazines *Right* and *Western Destiny*. Along with articles written from an ultraconservative perspective, it was not uncommon to find in *Right* advertisements for Ku Klux Klan and Nazi paraphernalia. Nazi Waffen SS, neo-Nazi skinheads, and the oppressive apartheid South African government have at one time or another been heralded in the newspaper (Berlet and Lyons 2000: 186). The magazine *Right* often ran profile pieces on small, obscure, right-wing groups along with approvingly reporting on the actions of the White Citizens' Councils. Carto used this magazine as a forum to blend or synthesize the theme of anti-communism with white supremacist theories. Along with pushing for white supremacy, the magazine also provided a conspiratorial analysis of world events (Diamond 1995: 85–86).

Even though there are some overlaps between the John Birch Society and the Liberty Lobby—for example, the use of conspiratorial themes by both organizations to explain their views of the world events around them—there were major differences between the two. For instance, while both organizations relied heavily on conspiracist themes, they differed over the root causes of those conspiracies. For the Birchists, the problem lay in the control of both American and Soviet governments by a cabal of "internationalists, greedy bankers, and corrupt politicians" (Berlet and Lyons 2000: 177). If this problem was not dealt with, according to the Birchists, then the traitors inside the American government could undermine US sovereignty and allow the United Nations to establish a collectivist new world order, overseen by a one-world socialist government. Collectivism was seen as the major threat to Western civilization and since liberals consciously fostered the process of collectivism, liberals were viewed as secret traitors whose ultimate objective was to replace Western civilization with a unitary world socialist government (Berlet and Lyons 2000: 177–178).

The Liberty Lobby, on the other hand, asserted that the main threat came from a small group of Jewish elites who had as their main goal the deconstruction of America's national unity and popular will. According to the Lobby, this secretive cabal of Jewish elites cleverly manipulated blacks and other groups of color to carry out their actions (Berlet and Lyons 2000: 176). This line of reasoning is similar to other philosophies of other hard right white supremacist organizations. While the Liberty Lobby openly and vigorously expounded theories of white supremacy and anti-semitism, the Birch society discouraged such blatant expressions. While the Birch society disapproved of such displays of racism, the organization also simultaneously promoted policies that also buttressed racial oppression, for instance, its support of states' rights. The racism expressed by the John Birch Society's leaders was no different than the views expressed by leaders of both the Democratic and Republican parties of the time. As Berlet and Lyons point out, however, this does not soften the fact that racism was one thread in the organization's philosophy: "This level of racism should not be dismissed lightly, as it was often crude, treating Black people in particular as second-class citizens, and assuming that most Blacks had limited intelligence and little ambition" (Berlet and Lyons 2000: 177–181).

The John Birch Society organization can be seen as one example of the gradual shift ultraconservative politics was undergoing in the fifties, a shift from using blatant biological racism to a rhetoric that stressed cultural racism, and the advocation of a policy of providing already limited opportunities to those groups who advocated the dominant values of white society. The assimilation of southern and eastern European ethnic groups into US mainstream society and their entry into the classification of whiteness, made the philosophy of biological racism, the ranking of groups by their genetic ancestry, inappropriate as a rallying tool (Berlet and Lyons 2000: 170). The Liberty Lobby along with the Ku Klux Klan were hard-right groups that still operated under the context of other pre-New Deal era conservative organizations where biological racism was the core of the organizational principles.

During the decades of the fifties and early sixties, the racist Right would attempt to form viable third parties to carry out their objectives. These attempts were unsuccessful but, as Sara Diamond notes, the actions of the racist Right had an important impact on the landscape of future US politics: "The lesson of the segregationists' broad though short-lived, campaigns was that racial divisiveness could pay dividends in electoral politics. That message resonated loudly within both political parties and among right-wing movement activists" (Diamond 1995: 66, 87). Diamond's observations would become even more true in the sixties as the presidential campaigns of both Barry Goldwater and George Wallace attracted support from such groups as the John Birch Society, Ku Klux Klan, and Liberty Lobby.

TWIN PILLARS OF WHITE DISCONTENT

Barry Goldwater, and the Use of the Southern Strategy to Create a Subtler Racial Politics

By the 1960s, with the civil rights movement in full swing and urban rioting breaking out in major cities across the United States, many white Americans were not only fearful but also resentful of liberals and liberalism. To many whites, the racial discord, as exemplified through the rioting and looting taking place on the streets in many urban areas, was a sign that liberals did not have the answers to America's most vexing problem—racial inequality. Even as more government money flowed toward programs aimed to alleviate poverty in the nation's ghettos, crime rates were increasing along with the numbers of Americans on the welfare rolls. The crime and welfare rates of African Americans were disproportionately higher than other groups, which gave further evidence to some that liberal solutions were more problematic than helpful. Most importantly, there was a growing sentiment among many white Americans that the price of African American equality came at their expense. In other words, black progress was viewed by many whites not as progress but as encroachment.

Two figures played significant roles in providing an opening for the American conservative movement to pull millions of dissatisfied whites away from their allegiance to the Democratic party. Barry Goldwater, a staunch Republican, and George Wallace, a loyal Democrat, added a one-two punch to the faltering liberal establishment. Both men had a major impact not only on the shift of American conservatism but also the way conservatives utilized race and class as rallying elements to their movement.

In 1960, conservatives watched as then Vice President Richard Nixon lost the presidential election just barely to Massachusetts senator John F. Kennedy. Although conservatives and other Republicans were disappointed in the outcome, it was not clear that if Nixon had won the presidency, he would have had the complete support of the conservative wing of the GOP. In fact, Nixon was viewed by conservatives with some skepticism because of the stances he took on various positions. On the one hand, conservatives could like Nixon because he was not from the eastern establishment elite like Nelson Rockefeller and his strident anti-communism won over many conservatives. However, his stance on civil rights and his support for the expansion of social security and foreign aid raised for many conservatives' questions of where Nixon's political loyalties lay. The various positions Nixon took on these issues raised a number of cautionary flags with those on the Right (Brennan 1995: 28). Their suspicions were raised further when it was disclosed that days before the Republican nomination convention Nixon had struck a deal with Rockefeller, in what was referred to as the "Compact on Fifth Avenue." Upset over the lack of substance in the platform draft, especially around issues like civil rights, Governor Rockefeller began to make overtures about not being able to provide his support to the draft, which would have put Nixon's nomination in jeopardy.[3]

On the evening of July 23rd Nixon, with staff in tow, went to New York and met with Rockefeller in his stately apartment on 810 Fifth Avenue to discuss what platform changes needed to be made. There were a total of fourteen points Rockefeller felt needed to be added to the platform. Several hours later Nixon left, agreeing to adopt in the platform all fourteen of Rockefeller's points. In essence, Nixon had capitulated and the conservative wing of the party was outraged. Not only had Nixon allowed Rockefeller to usurp the formal platform procedure, but also, he had sold out to the liberals. Conservative Republicans called this "me-tooism," arguing that the party looked like it was going to continue to follow the eastern establishment liberal direction. Ready to revolt, conservatives began to seriously mobilize around putting up Goldwater as a possible alternative candidate. Goldwater knew he did not have enough delegate votes to win the nomination and did not want to split the party further, and therefore decided he would decline the nomination. In his speech to the delegates, Goldwater made a point to call on his fellow conservatives to put the priority of party unity over their personal desires. He asserted, "We are conservatives. This great Republican Party is our historical house. This is our home" (Edwards 1999: 94) and continued:

We don't gain anything when you get mad at a candidate because you don't agree with his every philosophy. We don't gain anything when you disagree with the platform and then do not go out and work and vote for your party...We have had our chance and I think the conservatives have made a splendid showing at this Convention...We have fought our battle. Now, let's put our shoulders to the wheel for Dick Nixon and push him across the line...This country is too important for anyone's feelings. This country, in its majesty, is too great for any man, be he conservative or liberal, to stay home and not work just because he doesn't agree. Let's grow up, conservatives. If we want to take back this Party, and I think we can someday, let's get to work. (Perlstein 2001: 94–95)

Some claim that it was this speech that thrust Goldwater into the forefront of the conservative movement (Edwards 1999: 94).

Barry Goldwater's 1964 presidential campaign was important on many levels. First, Goldwater's capturing of the Republican nomination signaled a change in power within the Republican Party. The moderate to liberal eastern establishment wing headed by New York Governor Nelson Rockefeller was being ousted from power by conservative Republicans from the rising sunbelt regions of the United States. Second, many conservative activists who went on to form the New Right in the seventies gained their first experience of conservative activism by working in the Goldwater campaign. Conservatives such as David Stockman, Jesse Helms, George Will, and Phyllis Schlafly either got their start or improved their activist skills in the Goldwater campaign (Goldberg 1995: 236). Third, Goldwater's outspoken support of states' rights, especially in civil rights matters, and his vote against the 1964 Civil Rights Act opened a floodgate of support from southern whites to the Republican Party. Appearing in South Carolina with newly converted Republican Senator Storm Thurmond, Goldwater boldly stated what was fueling his opposition to the 1964 Civil Rights Act: "We are being asked to destroy the rights of some under the false banner of promoting the civil rights of others" (Goldberg 1995: 232). Fourth, Goldwater's candidacy also ended any possibility of the Republican party cultivating a meaningful relationship with African Americans and recapturing their votes from the Democrats. While giving a speech to Georgia Republican activists Goldwater remarked that he, "would bend every muscle to see that the South has a voice in everything that affects the life of the South"; then, he quipped that since the possibility of the Republican Party recapturing the black vote was next to impossible, the GOP, "ought to go hunting where the ducks are" (Perlstein 2001: 190).

Conservatives had recognized Goldwater's potential early on when he was an upstart Senator from Arizona. He had made a favorable impression within hard right circles with his defense of Wisconsin Senator Joseph McCarthy, the various independent stands he took against the Eisenhower administration, and his performance as Senate Republican Campaign Chair.

In 1959, a cadre of conservative operatives, led by Clarence Manion, a Dean at Notre Dame College, began to put into motion a Goldwater for President movement. In June of 1959, Manion had decided that it would be important to have a published document laying out Goldwater's positions to distribute to corporations and supporters. After getting Goldwater to go along with the plan, Manion convinced Brent Bozell, editor of the *National Review* and also William F. Buckley Jr.'s brother in law, to be the ghostwriter of the manuscript. Finally, Manion landed the book with a small obscure publisher, Publishers Printing Company of Shepherdsville, Kentucky. Bozell completed the manuscript toward the end of 1959 and received Goldwater's approval. In the spring of 1960, a slender book, entitled, *Conscience of a Conservative*, of approximately 130 pages, was released. By June, the book had reached the tenth spot on *Time* magazine's best-seller list and had placed number fourteen on the *New York Times's* list (Perlstein 2001: 62–63). The book was capturing the imaginations of Americans all over the nation. Two chapters, in particular, Chapter 4, "States Rights" and Chapter 5, "Civil Rights," sparked an explosion of interest, especially from southern whites who were in the midst of a battle to protect and preserve the Old South from African Americans who were demanding its demise. The following passage was music to the ears of southern whites who felt oppressed by what they viewed as the "tyranny" of federal government intervention:

> The Tenth Amendment recognizes the States' jurisdiction in certain areas. States' Rights means that the States have a right to act or not to act, as they see fit, in the areas reserved to them. The States may have duties corresponding to these rights, but the duties are owed to the people of the States, not to the federal government. Therefore, the recourse lies not with the federal government, which is not sovereign, but with the people who are, and who have full power to take disciplinary action... The Constitution, I repeat, draws a sharp and clear line between federal jurisdiction and state jurisdiction. The federal government's failure to recognize that line has been a crushing blow to the principle of limited government. (Goldwater 1960: 28–29).

Goldwater struck an even deeper connection with segregationists in the south in Chapter 5, "Civil Rights," with his pointed opinions on the Supreme Court's ruling in the Brown v Topeka Kansas Board of Education case:

> It is otherwise let us note, with education. For the federal Constitution does *not* require the States to maintain racially mixed schools. Despite the recent holdings of the Supreme Court, I am firmly convinced—not only that integrated schools are not required—but that the Constitution does not permit any interference whatsoever by the federal government in the field of education. (Goldwater 1960: 33–34)

Goldwater explained that, although he was in disagreement with the Court's ruling, he was in agreement with the objectives of the Court's decision and in principle was in favor of black and white children learning in an integrated setting: "It so happens that I am in agreement with the *objectives* of the Supreme Court as stated in the *Brown* decision. I believe that it *is* both wise and just for whites, and negro children to attend the same schools as whites, and that to deny them this opportunity carries with it strong implications of inferiority" (Goldwater 1960: 37).

But Goldwater overshadowed these sentiments with the rest of the text in the paragraph, where he adds a disclaimer to his view above by rationalizing his opposition to the Brown decision:

> I am not prepared, however, to impose that judgement of mine on the people of Mississippi or South Carolina, or to tell them what methods should be adopted and what pace should be kept in striving toward that goal. That is their business, not mine. I believe that the problem of race relations, like all social and cultural problems, is best handled by the people directly concerned. (Goldwater 1960: 37)

Both Goldwater and his supporters have often argued that he was not a racist and that during his life he treated blacks fairly. They point to his decision as a member of the Phoenix City Council to vote to desegregate the Sky Harbor Airport's restaurant; his fight as a Senator to have the Senate cafeteria open to his black legislative assistant; and his consistent willingness to allow blacks and other minorities to shop at his department store. His supporters also like to point to the fact that Goldwater was a member of the Arizona NAACP and a supporter of the Phoenix Urban League. Goldwater often gave his time and money to these organizations (Edwards 1995: 231). Supporters such as Lee Edwards, who was the public relations director of Goldwater's campaign, claim that the unfair branding of Goldwater as a racist was due to a variety of factors: The use of underhanded political tactics by liberals to achieve victory at any cost, bias from the media, and the lack of black conservative voices to provide support to Goldwater's racial positions.[4] Edwards also claims, in a somewhat patronizing manner, that part of what fueled the perception of Goldwater as a racist, especially among, as he puts it, "older African Americans" is a simplicity in their outlook on the issue:

> But the memory of the Goldwater vote against the Civil Rights Act of 1964 is etched deeply in the minds of most African Americans. For them, the debate was simple: either you wanted to end segregated luncheon counters and restaurants and...motels or you did not...For African Americans, it was literally a black-and-white issue. (Edwards 1999: 125)

Edwards' statements rest on a hidden assumption crucial for my argument throughout, the book, the assumption that racial identity, one's blackness, automatically inhibits black conservatives from adopting racist positions. Only a much less supple understanding of the role of *racialized ideology*, not just racist discourse, in the shaping of American conservatism would view the role of race in the movement as tied simply to blatant racism. It is my contention here that mid-century conservatism was able to articulate a complex discourse of cultural racial conservatism, including the tenet that the laws of the state should not legislate even shared moral opinion concerning civil rights, as an accessible belief system, even for black conservatives. The mere fact that some African Americans might have been in agreement with Goldwater does not mean that the views he expressed automatically became de-racialized and therefore non-problematic.[5]

What Edwards and others who wish to downplay the centrality of race and racialized discourse in American conservatism miss is that "race" and racialism involves much more than simply negative comments and actions against black Americans and other peoples of color. *Inescapability of Race* rests on the argument that "race" is, and is the product of, deeply systemic discourses of white supremacy, shaping economic theories, political rhetorics, and social codes, throughout American history. Hofstadter argued that American conservatism has always rested less on real conservative principles and ideology and more on attitudes and contexts, a critique of conservatism prevalent in the forties and early fifties. For Hofstadter, this fact explains the relative inconsistencies and contradictions of American conservatism over time. It is also my argument here, however, that at least since the fifties, racial interests have been the strongest glue providing the American conservative movement with its internal consistency, and these racial interests resemble less the tenets of blatant and obvious racist discourse, and much more the complex of social, political, moral, and economic discourses that have shaped the constitution of whiteness in the United States.[6]

To really understand the more subtle but nonetheless racialist dimensions of Goldwater's positions, one has to read more closely the social and political realities during this time period and the context in which Goldwater's words were spoken. Goldwater's preference for viewing everything from the perspective of strict constitutionality revealed his blind spots concerning the reality of the situation at hand, blind spots shaped by his own identity location as a white male. His assertion that it should be up to the states and the people of the states to decide their fate did not take into account how entrenched white supremacy was not only among its citizenry but also in the power structures of those states, making any more natural or gradual social progression toward racial equality virtually impossible in states like Mississippi or Alabama. That unwillingness to accept the entrenched nature of racial ideology, as a set of interlinked discourses that went beyond obvious racist statements and acts of discrimination, is precisely where one finds the real blind spot of race in conservatives' own sense of their color-blind discourse. For example, in a meeting in North Carolina, Goldwater argued that federal voting rights laws were only pertinent to national elections. For state elections, the states had the right to evaluate voter qualifications, so long as the measures and evaluation process was not discriminatory. However, as Robert Alan Goldberg so aptly notes, Goldwater's contention completely sidestepped, "the record of southern registrars' systematically denying black voters the franchise" (Goldberg 1995: 197).

To be fair, Goldwater at times did understand how sensitive the issue of race was and wanted to act accordingly. On July 24, 1964, Goldwater met with President Johnson in the Oval Office to discuss how the two men should handle the topic of civil rights between them during the presidential campaign, given the escalating tensions arising in the nation. A couple of weeks earlier a riot had occurred in one of New York's inner city sections, Harlem. At the meeting, Goldwater expressed his desire not to do anything further to escalate the tensions of the situation: "I am scared to death of the [backlash]. I know your big cities in the Northeast and in the Middle West–not only on the West Coast—are tinderboxes, and I'll be darned if I will have my grandchildren accuse their grand-father of setting fire to it [sic]" (Goldberg 1995: 215; Perlstein 2001: 396–397; Edwards 1999: 242; O'Reilly 1995: 251). One could argue that this was less evident of Goldwater's lack of racism than his deep awareness of and sensitivity to the volatile racialized context in which he was operating, a volatility that he would have recognized potentially threatened his own conservative, economic and political interests overall.

To capitalize on the rising backlash sentiment of whites, one of Goldwater's operatives, F. Clifton White, authorized the release of a 30-minute documentary entitled *Choice*, sponsored by an organization called *Mothers for a Moral America*. The clear purpose of this film was to suggest that the continuation of a Johnson-led administration would produce further moral decay in America. It was also apparent that the filmmakers wanted to inflame whites' fear of urban disorder instigated by blacks. In certain segments of the documentary, there were juxtaposed clips of urban rioting by blacks with scenes of white children saluting the flag. Once Goldwater learned of the film, he denounced it as racist and immediately ordered that it be taken off the air (Freedman 1996: 254).

And yet, for every step Goldwater took in the right direction on race issues, at some other juncture during the campaign he would inevitably say or do something that put him two steps behind. For instance, when Mississippi Governor Ross Barnett blatantly defied a federal court order by prohibiting James Meredith from enrolling at the state university, Goldwater stunned even some of his conservative friends by stating that while he believed what the governor was doing was morally wrong, he also felt that the governor was within his constitutional right to block Meredith's entry into the university. One of Goldwater's friends, Dension Kitchel, had to point out to Goldwater that while the Tenth Amendment did provide protection to states' rights, it did not provide a justification for defying a court order (Goldberg 1995: 154). Goldwater's seemingly contradictory position merely reveals the consistency of his conservative belief that despite the presence of *racism* in a society, racial discrimination should not be criminalized through constitutional measures, so much so that, ironically, Goldwater found himself endorsing the perpetuation of another recognized crime—violating a court order—in the effort not to acknowledge segregation as an illegal act.

Even if Goldwater did not want to conduct a campaign that would inflame racial hostilities, that was not fully the case with the people who were running his campaign.[7] Some of Goldwater's campaign advisors and staff were taking in what pollsters and academics had observed four years earlier—that racial animosity and alienation among whites was just as hot and intense in the northern and western parts of the country as it was in the south. As the Democrats were pushing forward more civil rights legislation, not only southern whites but various white ethnic groups, traditional Democratic constituencies, began to voice their displeasure. Some in Goldwater's camp saw the rising backlash as a golden opportunity: The utilization of a much more subtle form of racial politics that has become paradigmatic in mainstream forms of American conservatism at the start of the twenty-first century. A sympathetic, even sincere critique of racism and more blatant forms of white supremacist attitudes and discourses in social practices, did not preclude one's support for conservative policies that upheld and protected the legal, economic, and political institutions of the state from the types of radical reforms and changes that would come with the new civil rights legislation.

Members in Goldwater's camp also recognized the Republicans' potential to cultivate a new group of voters for the GOP—the Goldwater Democrats. In essence, Goldwater could be the candidate that appealed to voters in liberal bastions like the northeastern part of the country just as much as he did in south. Tapping into the opposition northeastern whites had toward federal civil rights legislation like their counterparts in the south while also sending the message that their opposition did not make them racists (Perlstein 2001: 214). Liberal and moderate Republicans, along with prominent African American Republicans like famed baseball player Jackie Robinson, tried to warn Goldwater and his supporters of the damage this approach would do to the relationship between African Americans and the Republican party. Unfortunately, their pleas fell on deaf ears, one conservative's response captured the general feeling among Goldwater's followers: "This isn't South Africa.... The white man outnumbers the Negro 9 to 1 in this country" (Perlstein 2001: 215).

In the end, Goldwater would go on to lose in a landslide to President Johnson, carrying only six states, his home state of Arizona and five deep South states (Alabama, Mississippi, Louisiana, Georgia, and Florida).

Despite his loss, the impact of Goldwater's campaign run in 1964 would have a lasting effect on American politics for decades to come.

Goldwater helped the Republicans to begin to dismantle the Democratic South while also driving away African Americans from the Republican party for good. In 1960, Nixon had garnered close to 32% of the African American vote; four years later, Goldwater received only 6%. From Goldwater on, no other Republican presidential candidate has been able to come close to capturing the percentage of the African American vote that Nixon had in 1960 (Rae 1989: 75).

George Wallace's Impact on the Southernization of American Conservatism

The key to understanding American politics at the end of the century, and the world within American conservatism that black conservative activists, intellectuals, politicians, and religious leaders continue to operate in, lies in the recognition that the dominant group in the party today consists of white southerners. American conservatism today is southern conservatism writ large. The obsessions and themes, the rhetoric and imagery, of today's national right are, with few modifications, those of yesterday's Dixie segregationists and demagogues (Lind 1996: 124). It is without doubt that the South and southern conservatives have become a major influence within the American Right.

Although George Wallace was not a Republican and had liberal views on economic matters, Wallace helped pave the way for both the Republican Party and conservatives to call the South their home. Wallace learned early on in his political career the political value of race, or to be more precise, the success in utilizing race-baiting strategies. In his first attempt at capturing the governorship of Alabama, Wallace lost in the Democratic party primary to state attorney general, John Patterson, who was seen as a formidable foe due to the impressive reputation he garnered as an anti-integrationist (Carter 1995: 92). During the campaign, Patterson courted and received support from Alabama's racist sectors by playing up his association with Ku Klux Klan Grand Dragon, R.M. (Bob) Shelton. Wallace tried to take a higher road by emphasizing in his campaign a program that focused on improving the state's infrastructure (better highways, education, and bringing in more manufacturing plants to the state) and putting forth a more sophisticated argument for the support of segregation. The strategy did not work. On his way in to make his concession speech, Wallace proclaimed, "Well boys, [] no other son-of-a bitch will ever out-nigger me again" (Carter 1995: 95–96).

From that moment on Wallace realized the political power of conducting a campaign centrally focused on race baiting and appeals to whites' racial fears and anxieties. Combined with Wallace's strident anti-communism, nationalist jingoism, anti-intellectualism, and class politics, together all helped foster a conservative populism that would help catapult conservatives to the center of the American political scene. When Wallace decided to take his political act nationwide and began to garner serious attention from whites in cities like Milwaukee, Los Angeles, Baltimore, and Boston his stature grew even more.

By 1963 into early 1964, George Wallace was beginning to receive offers to give speeches up north. Wallace's "Segregation now! Segregation tomorrow! Segregation forever!" line in his inaugural address, his symbolic stand in the doorway at the University of Alabama to protest the admission into the University of two black students, and his charismatic appearance on the national news show *Meet the Press* brought the diminutive southern politician to the nation's attention (Carter 1995: 195).[8] One major coup for Wallace was receiving an invitation to speak at Harvard University, the bastion of eastern establishment liberalism. Wallace was now transcending the narrow box of the South and taking his act nationwide. As Dan Carter noted, moving beyond the South also meant Wallace would have to reconfigure his message to fit the audience he was speaking to:

> Wallace constantly improvised as he abandoned old rhetorical strategies and adopted new ones, but his goal was always the same: to command a more visible political stage. That meant walking a tightrope between defending racial segregation aggressively but with dignity, and catering to powerful impulses of raw racism which the civil rights movement had flushed into the open. (Carter 1995: 160–161)

By going north, Wallace was taking his message beyond his usually associated stereotyped audience of "poor, rural, fundamentalist southern rednecks." Instead, Wallace was now directing his words to urban, working-class, white ethnic neighborhoods. This new direction surprised many political observers as the thought of a southern politician capturing the ear of a northern audience seemed out of hand. Upon closer examination, however, it becomes clear that race, racialized and at times racist discourse, and race-baiting, all played the central role in Wallace's ability to tap into the anxiety of northern white ethnics.

Many observers casually explain Wallace's success outside of the South as due to the presence of racism in the North and the numerous financial contributions Wallace received from various organizations on the hard right like the John Birch Society and the Minutemen (Carter 1996: 9). In Wallace, these and other hard-right organizations saw a kindred spirit for they could associate his attacks on the federal government with their hatred of liberal economic and social legislation. While it is true that Wallace received financial assistance from certain hard-right organizations, these two factors alone cannot completely explain why Wallace was able to capture the attention of many non-southern whites. There were other factors that contributed to his northern appeal. However, looking at even those factors more closely, one begins to find the threads of his race-baiting strategy linking seemingly dissimilar positions and issues.

First, many of the working-class whites in the northern and midwestern urban centers could identify with Wallace, who spoke to their resentment at the hypocrisy of liberal planners bent on subjecting working-class neighborhoods, schools, and jobs to various social reform programs all the while insulating themselves from the same treatment (Carter 1996: 13). For example, Wallace called out the middle and upper-middle-class liberal whites on their hypocrisy, their willingness to subject the children of working-class whites to programs such as busing while they put their own children in private schools. This position leads to the second factor in his success, his use of the racial turmoil of the sixties to draw sharp class lines between various groups of whites. Third, Wallace specifically pointed out by name (the bus driver, policeman, and beautician) the whites he was speaking for, giving recognition to groups of Americans who felt that the system was not speaking for them (Kazin and Isserman 2000: 219). But the most important factor in Wallace's success was his keen ability to know how to couch his views, grounded in racialist attitudes and opinions, in a special language that could make his message more palatable to his non-southern white audiences. Wallace and his people understood that few northern and other non-southern whites would openly embrace racist campaign pitches. Although many non-southern whites could and did harbor intense fear and dislike toward African Americans, the use of overt racial discourse would do more to turn away many whites for fear of being labeled racists. Instead, Wallace cleverly used coded words in his messages to tap into the racial resentments of whites. One fellow politician from Alabama aptly described Wallace's strategy when he stated:

Race was at the bottom of this message. He can use all the other issues–law and order, running your own schools, protecting property rights-and never mention race...But people will know he's telling them, 'A nigger's trying to get your job, trying to move into your neighborhood.' What Wallace is talking to them in a kind of shorthand, a kind of code. (O'Reilly 1995: 280–281)

While Wallace did not come close to capturing the presidency, he was not to be deterred by the fizzle of his presidential aspirations in 1964 and ran again in 1968. The year 1968 was vastly different from 1964, since Goldwater was out of the picture after being soundly trounced by President Johnson in 1964. Ironically, Johnson was also gone from the presidential spotlight as the combination of America's deeper involvement in Vietnam and the rise of domestic unrest from the spread of anti-war protests to rioting in urban ghettos by alienated blacks sent Johnson's approval ratings plummeting, forcing Johnson not to seek a re-election bid. This time Wallace was running as a third-party candidate under the American Independent Party ticket. The Democratic Party put up liberal Minnesota Senator Hubert Humphrey while the Republicans countered with former Vice President Richard Nixon.

The presidency was a long sought-after goal for Nixon; Nixon came close in 1960 but narrowly lost out to a more charismatic John Kennedy. To win this election, Nixon knew it would be vital for him to convince an increasingly conservative majority within the Republican Party that he was conservative enough for the position. To do this, Nixon had to gain the support from the influential southern Republican base. This would be no easy task as many southern GOP leaders had come to power in the party off the wave of Goldwater's run four years earlier. Many of these southern Republicans were like Goldwater in their die-hard support for ultraconservative views. There would be no compromising on principle. In essence, Nixon could not win over this group by being too moderate. One important move that helped Nixon secure the nomination was his cultivation of support from South Carolina senator Strom Thurmond. Thurmond was seen as the key to getting other southern Republicans to support Nixon. Although Thurmond was not overly enthralled with Nixon, he did recognize Nixon's potential in getting the White House back to the GOP.

The setting seemed right for Nixon to fulfill his long-awaited aspiration. The Democratic Party was reeling from the assassination of leading Democratic presidential nominee Attorney General Robert Kennedy.

Liberalism was rapidly falling out of favor with many Americans as it seemed to be impotent in curbing the social disorders engulfing American society. When violent confrontations broke out between anti-war protesters and the police outside of the National Democratic Party convention in Chicago, many interpreted the violence to be one more sign that liberalism was the cause, not the solution to the present chaos in society. Urban area after Urban area to Cities were going up in flames as African Americans who were on the margins in society expressed their outrage at the systemic racial oppression they were toiling under. The economy was sluggish which shook Americans' confidence. Now in plain view was white discontent or as economist Eliot Janeway had described the phenomena five years earlier as "white backlash." Nixon, picking up on the various social changes taking place, honed his message to speak to this white backlash. On the surface, Nixon's chances looked promising except for one nagging element-George Wallace.

To Nixon, Wallace was a real threat as he saw Wallace potentially taking away precious southern votes. Should Wallace capture a majority in the south and take one or two key states in the Midwest, that might leave Nixon with less than a majority to win which would then force the election into the Democratic-controlled House of Representatives, an outcome that would produce certain defeat. This scenario was not lost on Wallace either. In fact, in private moments, Wallace revealed that regardless of the electoral outcome, he wanted to be able to assert enough influence on the election to gain concessions for the South. As Wallace saw it, he would drop out of the race if the other candidates would agree to a number of conditions, which ranged from support of reversion back to state control over local institutions to appointing conservative judges on the Supreme Court who respected the idea of states' rights (Carter 1995: 339).

Eventually, Wallace's 1968 presidential flame would be extinguished by Nixon's shrewdness in playing upon white southern fears of a Humphrey victory by intimating in media advertisements that voting for Wallace would divide the vote and allow the Humphrey Democrats to gain the upper hand. Although Wallace did not win the election, his presence did make the election outcome much tighter than originally anticipated. Wallace took away votes that clearly would have gone toward Nixon, thus making Nixon's margin of victory over Humphrey much closer. The impact Wallace's campaign had on the election and American politics was not lost on others. Wallace's capture of 14% of the popular vote spoke volumes as Wallace, like Goldwater before him, had tapped into the sentiments of an emerging group—the silent majority.

It was clear that George Wallace left an indelible impression on President Nixon. Nixon aide Kevin Phillips recognized the opportunity conservatives and Republicans had to capitalize on the backlash vote brought to the surface of the American political scene by men like Goldwater and Wallace:

> Some of Wallace's support came from aroused conservative Republicans, but most of it represented Democratic voting streams quitting their party…. The Alabaman tapped rather than shaped a protest; his party represents an electorate in motion between the major parties rather than a new, permanent entrant into the national presidential arena. (Phillips 1969: 33)

In his influential book, *The Emerging Republican Majority*, Phillips was eerily prescient in his predictions on the changing direction of the American political landscape. Most significantly, Phillips recognized the opportunities available to Nixon and other conservative Republicans by exploiting the issue of race. In one passage Phillips offered what some would see as Machiavellian advice to Republicans:

> Nothing more than an effective and responsibly conservative Nixon Administration is necessary to bring most of the Southern Wallace electorate into the fold…. Abandonment of civil rights enforcement would be self-defeating. Maintenance of Negro voting rights in Dixie, far from being contrary to GOP interests, is essential if southern conservatives are to be pressured into switching to the Republican Party. (Phillips 1969: 464)

Wallace's presidential campaigns not only showed conservatives such as Phillips the value of stroking white anxieties by using race, but also, the value of conservative populism especially when enhanced by and linked to race-based fears and concerns. As Phillips states, "Equally important was conservatism's adoption of some economic populism to augment its opposition to Negro-oriented social innovation" (Phillips 1969: 206). Even though Wallace's brand of conservative populism met with limited success, the various discourses he propagated were picked up by others on the Right and fine-tuned. Wallace was too rough around the edges to lure in mainstream conservative supporters in conservative bastions like Orange County, California. As Lisa McGirr states,

"Wallace's populism built too much on working-class resentments to sustain an appeal with the mostly middle-class backers of the Right in Orange County" (McGirr 2001: 212). But this did not stop politicians like Nixon and Ronald Reagan from usurping and repackaging Wallace's language to help make the Republican Party appear more and more like the party of the common man, and conservatism the ideology of the average person. To the audiences, Wallace would describe as, "law-abiding, God fearing working Americans," Nixon and others would refer to this group as "middle America." In other words, Nixon and Reagan would go on to put forth a "populism without Wallace's southern blue-collar edge" (McGirr 2001: 215).

In the end, Wallace offered Republicans and conservatives an avenue to recreate themselves.[9] By the end of the 1960s, white backlash had secured a place in the center of the American political landscape. During the next decade, whites who fell into the backlash category would be known by other names such as the "Silent Majority," or as sociologist Donald Warren noted, as "Middle American Radicals." According to Warren, this particular group felt challenged not only by those below them (e.g., blacks) but also from those above them (e.g., white-collar workers), placing themselves squarely in the middle.

In the seventies, it was this wing that would help to establish a modified conservative movement that blended anti-communism, populism, and concern for domestic social issues under the rubric of the "culture wars."

Precisely what we need to understand better about the history of conservatism in American society and politics is how much internal consistency and cohesion race discourse, both subtle and direct, can provide political parties and rhetorics, helping to redraw left/right, radical/conservative boundaries in new ways, especially when a party finds themselves losing ground with constituents.

This book's starting premise is the centrality and inescapability of race to the American conservative movement of the second half of the twentieth century. Race, however, is understood here in much more complex ways than simply as a term for identity and/or individuated psychological attitudes and prejudices. In *this book*, race is also a sociological category that designates the institutions and discourses in a national society that support such social and historical formations as white supremacy, and that can be wielded by both majority and minority groups in furtherance of their particular goals toward achieving power, citizenship, a sense of belonging, and access to resources.

What this introductory chapter has aimed to do thus far is to demonstrate how the American conservative movement, under the auspices of the Republican Party, first attempted to use the southern strategy to reclaim the popularity of the Democrats in the South. Conservatives then learned from and manipulated further the racialized rhetorics of two specific and powerfully influential figures—Barry Goldwater and George Wallace— who despite being on opposite sides of the two-party system, crafted from uniquely American ideological materials a sophisticated and coded discussion of race that is the direct ancestor of our more contemporary discourse of colorblindness in the Republican Party. Chapter 3 will continue to elaborate on this broader context of twentieth-century American conservatism, recounting how content was enhanced by structure, that is, how these ideological underpinnings set in place in the Goldwater and Wallace era have been enhanced by an intellectual infrastructure and new populist strategies that are the backbone of the color-blind conservatism of the present day. The story of African Americans in the American conservative movement depends on this history because it sets the stage for our understanding of both the power and the limits of the tools conservatism has provided black politicians, intellectuals, activists, and religious leaders.

Notes

1. Rossiter, like a number of other individuals who thought of themselves as conservatives, felt the conservatism espoused by individuals like Robert Welch represented the worst in conservative thinking and politics. As Rossiter states, "…the professional haters, have had any real influence on the mind of conservative America, and this they have had by catering to the worst instincts of certain conservative citizens who should have known better" (p. 169). In fact, Barry Goldwater fell within Rossiter's category of ultraconservatives. According to Rossiter, the ultraconservatives' main political program consisted of, "an American version of what France has come to know as poujadisme: an essentially middle-class revolt against the uses to which taxes are increasingly put in the welfare state" (p. 170).

2. According to Goldberg, the 100% increase in African American support (20% of black vote for Eisenhower in 1952, 40% of black vote in 1956) is evidence that the Republican Party did not abandon efforts to entice blacks into the GOP fold. In fact, as Goldberg sees it, the migration of southern blacks to "the electoral-vote-rich states" like California, Pennsylvania, and New York gave the GOP motivation to fight the Democrats for the black vote. Unfortunately, the evidence is not conclusive on what measures the Republican Party used to improve their relationship with black voters.

3. Even though Nixon was the front runner to capture the 1960 presidential nomination, he did not feel secure that the nomination would be his. Lurking in the shadows was Rockefeller as a possible candidate. The last thing Nixon needed was for Rockefeller to start a fight on the convention floor over the scope and direction of his platform. Therefore, if it was necessary to placate Rockefeller to get him to throw his full support behind Nixon's presidential run, then that's what needed to be done. Nixon also needed to make sure that Rockefeller would clearly and openly express that he was not in the running for the nomination. It came down to a choice between accommodating the liberal wing and risking the alienation of the conservatives in the party, or, allowing the original platform drawn up by the platform committee to stand and running the risk of Rockefeller throwing his name into the fray.

4. Edwards would point to the fact that in 1964 there were, "no Thomas Sowell, no Walter Williams, no Clarence Thomas—to articulate the conservative point of view on civil rights" (235). His comments beg the question, who were these black conservative spokespersons supposed to convince that Goldwater's views were not racist? Other white conservatives? White moderates? Or African Americans?

   Edwards' statement also speaks to a larger irony involving conservative politics and racial identity. Conservatives have always derided the Left for conducting a politic that views people not as individuals first but instead by arbitrary categories like race, gender, and sexuality. And yet, what Edwards reveals in his statement is that the main importance of individuals like Sowell, Williams, and Thomas is not just their conservatism but *their* race! In other words, in order to demonstrate the purported non-racist elements of their claims, conservatives have had to utilize race in a different register—in the figure of the black spokesperson—to help buttress the deeply racialized undertones of a discourse that yet purports to be devoid of racial elements.

5. This line of conservative thinking has not been successful with the majority of African Americans precisely because they have a more sophisticated ear for racialized discourse that acts against their political, social, and economic interests even when it is not blatantly racist discourse. The rejection of conservative discourse on the part of many African Americans conservatives has led them to view African American conservatives with suspicion.

6. For insightful examinations on the concept of whiteness in the American social structure, see David Roediger, *Wages of Whiteness* (2007) and *Working Toward Whiteness* (2006), Matthew Frey Jacobson's *Whiteness of a Different Color* (1999), George Lipsitz's *The Possessive Investment in Whiteness* (2006), and Peggy McIntosh's, *White Privilege: Unpacking the Invisible Knapsack* (1989).

7. According to Perlstein, not too long after the rioting broke out in Harlem, reporters began hearing rumors that Goldwater insiders were contemplating how to further exacerbate racial tensions to create more urban outbreaks in order to help Goldwater win the election. Goldwater asserted that if anyone did such a thing on his behalf, he would quit the race in an instant (Perlstein 2001: 396).

8. What made Wallace so effective as a spokesperson for alienated whites was his knowledge that race was his bread butter issue no matter what forum he was about to speak in. According to Wayne Greenhaw, Wallace, trying to anticipate what questions he would be asked by the reporters on *Meet the Press*, became nervous about his lack of a substantive foreign policy. With the help of his advisor, he quickly drew one up before Wallace was to appear on the air. After giving a standout performance, Wallace quipped to his friend, "I don't need a foreign policy. All they wanted to know about was niggers, and I'm the expert" (Greenhaw 1976: 1–3).

9. George Wallace's influence on American politics has produced from experts, within and outside of academia, an array of explanations on the composition of Wallace's constituency and their motivations. Richard Krickus claimed that in addition to racial concerns, Wallace supporters were also individuals who felt alienated by the indifference of the Democratic party to their needs (Krickus 1976: 276). Sociologists Seymour Martin Lipset and Earl Raab attributed status anxiety as a major contributing factor to Wallace's support (1970). The research team of Thomas Pettigrew, Robert Riley, and Reeve Vanneman found in an attitudinal survey that white, northern, urban Wallace supporters overwhelmingly agreed with the sentiment that "the condition of the average man is getting worse." Applying the concept of "relative deprivation" by British sociologist W.G. Runciman to their study ("relative deprivation" captures the sentiment that an individual's feelings of deprivation are derived from the individual's comparing his/her own fortunes with others in the same group or with individuals from other groups, or from both), the Pettigrew research team discovered that Wallace supporters came disproportionately from the "fraternally deprived" category. According to Pettigrew et al., this group felt deprived not as individuals but as a group, hence in this context, their group identification was as white workers. This group expressed feelings of falling behind such groups as blacks but also white-collar professionals (Hixon 1992: 143). For Jody Carlson, it was neither status politics nor relative deprivation that brought many Americans into Wallace's camp, but rather, "their proportionate sense of power," or stated differently, their overwhelming sense of powerlessness. The sense of powerlessness came from the perception that the federal government not only was ignoring the concerns of Wallace's backers but also,

providing preferable treatment to blacks. The Wallace supporters were particularly sensitive to the perception that groups like blacks and student protesters were gaining advantages through the federal government by their threat of the use of force (Carlson 1981). For all of their evidence and erudition, none of these studies make the explicit connection between their results and a broader, linked, racialized discourse upon which many of their factors rest.

REFERENCES

Berlet, Chip, and Matthew N. Lyons. *Right Wing Populism in America: Too Close for Comfort*. New York: Guilford Publisher, 2000.

Bracey, Christopher Alan. *Saviors or Sellouts: The Promise and Peril of Black Conservatism, from Booker T. Washington to Condoleezza Rice*. Boston, MA: Beacon Press, 2008.

Brennan, Mary C. *Turning Right in the Sixties: The Conservative Capture of the GOP*. Chapel Hill: The University of North Carolina Press, 1995.

Buckley, William F., Jr. *Up from Liberalism*. New York: McDowell, Obolensky Publishers, 1959.

Carlson, Jody. *George C. Wallace and the Politics of Powerlessness: The Wallace Campaigns for the Presidency, 1964–1976*. Edison, NJ: Transaction Publishers, 1981.

Carter, Dan T. *The Politics of Rage: George Wallace, the Origins of the New Conservatism, and the Transformation of American Politics*. Baton Rouge: Louisiana State University Press, 1995.

———. *From George Wallace to Newt Gingrich: Race in the Conservative Counterrevolution 1963–1994*. Baton Rouge: Louisiana State University Press, 1996.

Diamond, Sara. *Roads to Dominion: Right-Wing Movements and Political Power in the United States*. New York: The Guilford Press, 1995.

Edwards, Lee. *Goldwater: The Man Who Made a Revolution*. Washington, DC: Regnery, 1995.

———. *The Conservative Revolution: The Movement That Remade America*. New York: The Free Press, 1999.

Freedman, Samuel G. *The Inheritance: How Three Families and America Moved from Roosevelt to Reagan and Beyond*. New York: Simon and Schuster, 1996.

Goldberg, Robert Alan. *Barry Goldwater*. New Haven, CT: Yale University Press, 1995.

Goldwater, Barry. *The Conscience of a Conservative*. Shepherdsville, KY: Victor Publishing Company, 1960.

Greenhaw, Wayne. *Watch Out for George Wallace*. Englewood Cliffs, NJ: Prentice-Hall, 1976.

Himmelstein, Jerome. *To the Right: The Transformation of American Conservatism*. Berkeley: The University of California Press, 1990.

Hixon, William B. *Search for the American Right Wing: An Analysis of the Social Science Record, 1955–1987*. Princeton, NJ: Princeton University Press, 1992.

Hodgson, Godgfrey. *The World Turned Right Side Up: A History of the Conservative Ascendancy in America*. Boston, MA: Mariner Books, 1997.

Hofstader, Richard. *The Paranoid Style in American Politics and Other Essays*. New York: Alfred A. Knopf, 1964.

Hurston, Zora Neale. *Dust Tracks on a Road: An Autobiography*. New York: Harper Perennial Modern Classics, 1942.

Jacobson, Matthew Frye. *Whiteness of a Different Color: European Immigrants and the Alchemy of Race*. Cambridge, MA: Harvard University Press, 1999.

Jones, Rhett. "Black Creole Cultures: The Eighteenth Century Origins of African American Conservatism." In *Dimensions of Black Conservatism in the United States: Made in America*. Eds. Gayle T. Tate and Lewis A. Randolph. New York: Palgrave Press, 2002.

Kazin, Michael, and Maurice Isserman. *America Divided: The Civil War of the 1960s*. New York: Oxford University Press, 2000.

Krickus, Richard. *Pursuing the American Dream: White Ethnics and the New Populism*. Bloomington: Indiana University Press, 1976.

Lind, Michael. *Up from Conservatism: Why the Right Is Wrong for America*. New York: The Free Press, 1996.

Lipset, Seymour Martin, and Earl Raab. *The Politics of Unreason: Right Wing Extremism in America, 1790–1970*. New York, NY: Harper and Row, 1970.

Lipsitz, George. *The Possessive Investment in Whiteness: How White People Profit from Identity Politics*. Philadelphia, PA: Temple University Press, 2006.

McGirr, Lisa. *Suburban Warriors: The Origins of the New American Right*. Princeton, NJ: Princeton University Press, 2001.

McIntosh, Peggy. *White Privilege: Unpacking the Invisible Knapsack*. s.n., 1989.

O'Reilly, Kenneth. *Nixon's Piano: Presidents and Racial Politics from Washington to Clinton*. New York: The Free Press, 1995.

Perlstein, Rick. *Before The Storm: Barry Goldwater and the Unmaking of the American Consensus*. New York: Hill and Wang, 2001.

Phillips, Kevin. *The Emerging Republican Majority*. New Rochelle, NY: Arlington House, 1969.

Rae, Nicole. *The Decline and Fall of the Liberal Republicans: From 1952 to the Present*. New York: Oxford University Press, 1989.

Roediger, David. *Working Toward Whiteness: How America's Immigrants Became White*. New York, NY: Basic Books, 2006.

———. *The Wages of Whiteness: Race and the Making of the American Working Class*. New York, NY: Verso, 2007.

Rossiter, Clinton. *Conservatism in America: The Thankless Persuasion*, 2nd ed. New York: Alfred A. Knopf, 1962.

Sugrue, Thomas. *The Origins of the Urban Crisis: Race and Inequality in Postwar Detroit*. Princeton, NJ: Princeton University Press, 1996, 2005.

Washington, Booker T. *Up from Slavery: An Autobiography*. New York: Doubleday, 1904.

Williams, Oscar. *George S. Schuyler: Portrait of a Black Conservative*. Knoxville: The University of Tennessee Press, 2007.

CHAPTER 3

The New "Color Blind" Conservatism: Creating an Intellectual Infrastructure

This chapter describes the process by which conservative racial ideology has become invisible public opinion and naturalized common sense due to strategies conservatives initiated over the course of the 1970s. I end the chapter with an account of the conservative movement's specific appeal to the religious right, which in turn makes one of the conditions possible for African American conservatives to join the movement. Prior to that, however, and running alongside it, the appeal to the religious right also rested on a history that may at first glance seem to be less connected to the presence of African Americans in the conservative movement. However this history is actually critical for understanding how much African American conservatism relies on and, in turn, supports, an ideological framing of race and American values set in place by both intellectual and populist infrastructural developments in the seventies.

Understanding how conservative viewpoints gain hegemony not just politically but in the sphere of public opinion by the end of the twentieth century, requires first an understanding of the successful convergence of two strands of conservatism in the 1970s, strands whose very different strengths contributed to the creation of a seemingly contradictory formation, populism on the one hand and a new conservative intellectual class on the other. First, conservatives of the New Right used a populist discourse and practical instruments such as direct mailings to reach out to and then claim to speak for a blue-collar, working-class, ordinary American. Ideologically, the New Right's strength lay in its ability to tie disparate and often conflictual issues together under one overriding

© The Author(s) 2018   47
L. G. Prisock, *African Americans in Conservative Movements*,
https://doi.org/10.1007/978-3-319-89351-8_3

message, creating at first the appearance, but soon, the reality, of a coalitional politics. The New Right thus represented the first plank of an ideological war of position in which conservatives sought hegemony by winning the hearts and minds of the people.[1]

A second group, neoconservatives, also used the new social movements and cultural unrest of the sixties and seventies to create journals and publish works leveling explicit critiques of some of the more progressive policies and movements to emerge from those decades, including affirmative action, feminism, and gay rights. Instead of standing back or remaining on the defensive in regards to race and equal rights issues (as may have been more the case in the fifties), neoconservatives countered with an aggressive campaign against contemporary race policies. With a polemical style of rhetoric and an accessible, autobiographical mode of argumentation, neoconservatives went on the offensive in crafting, against affirmative action specifically, an explicit position and set of discourses on the status of African Americans in American society more broadly.

The upshot of the affirmative action debate in the seventies was that it allowed neoconservatives to share space with liberals on popular discussions of racial issues rather than leaving the question of race purely up to left-liberal discussions in the sphere of public opinion. The neoconservative attack gained stridency and visibility with its polemical style and new intellectual resources and research methods provided by the emerging social sciences. Neoconservatives combined these with a greater use of new media outlets and promotional strategies borrowed from the world of business to create, essentially, a counter-class of public intellectuals. Speaking against the group of liberal intellectuals they described by utilizing the term, the New Class, a concept created in 1870 by anarchist Mikhail Bakunin in his book *The Knoto-Germanic Empire and the Social Revolution*, a treatise that critically examined Marx's theory of the formation of a socialist society after capitalism and the social implications of this transition (King 2004: xii–xiii), neoconservatives came to represent a class of conservative "organic" intellectuals who could counter the more liberal and mainstream intellectuals of American society.[2] The neoconservatives thus became the second plank in a broader attempt to make conservative ideology in the United States appear to be common sense.

Color-blind conservatism then, as this chapter will demonstrate, must be historicized within the context of an ideological matrix that developed during the 1970s and provided conservatives with a new and soon, dominant voice in the sphere of public opinion. This matrix was made up of a complex mix of rhetorical styles, arguments against current, progressive policies and movements, new techniques for polling and reaching out to a working-class constituency, and the construction of a new, conservative, and intellectual infrastructure. The combined set of forces that came together under the joined labels of the New Right and the neoconservatives characterized and shaped the conservative discourse of the latter decades of the twentieth century, and was almost impossible to break apart by liberals and Democrats hoping to reclaim the public sphere. This is still true at the beginning of the twenty-first century under the Obama, and now Trump, presidency. While the Republican party itself may be in disarray, the conservative framework of color blindness still holds sway against the opinions of more liberal commentators. Obama himself and the "new black politics" he is described by some as representing, is itself more akin to, and demonstrates the continued pervasiveness of, the narrative of color blindness conservatives began to institutionalize in the seventies. The "new black politics" of men such as Obama, but also former US congressman Harold Ford from Tennessee, Senator Corey Booker from New Jersey, and former governor Deval Patrick from Massachusetts, takes a more cautious or pragmatic approach to black politics in the public sphere, downplaying or eschewing any political investment in a racial identity or community.[3]

Winning Minds and Hearts: The Birth of the New Right

In the 1970s the conservative movement split into two significant factions—neoconservatism and the New Right. Both of these wings resulted from feelings of betrayal (Gottfried 1993: 97). For the neoconservatives to be examined below, the accumulation of alienation from the Democratic party, liberalism, and the New Left forced a number of former liberal-leftists to move rightward politically. For those who made up the New Right, on the other hand, the betrayal came not from those on the Left but from those on the Right. Even with Richard Nixon, a Republican, in the White House, there was the sense among a number of conservatives that the Republican party was not doing enough to further the conservative cause. As Paul Gottfried states, "for the New Right, the villains were moderate Republicans who betrayed the interest and principles of the great majority of ordinary Americans" (Gottfried 1993: 97).

The New Right's motivation to mobilize in the 1970s came not only from feelings of betrayal but also from a sense of purpose that was fueled simultaneously by empowerment, fear, and righteousness. Empowerment came from Goldwater's defeat a decade earlier in 1964, which far from extinguishing the passion of many who worked on his behalf instead provided the fuel to push further toward the goal of political victory. To many in the New Right who worked for Goldwater, the outcome of the election was not viewed as America's definitive rejection of conservatism. Instead, the Goldwater campaign was viewed by many on the New Right to be, "the beginning of the motivation that has never left us" (Weyrich 1982: 51). Along with the emergence of purpose came the feeling of optimism, something particularly lacking among some of the Old Right. According to Gillian Peele, with the arrival of the New Right, "some of the intellectual pessimism associated with the old right has disappeared" (Peele 1984: 55).

The feelings of fear were derived from what many on the New Right saw as the continuing assault on the sanctity of traditional values and beliefs, as illustrated by the various changes in social mores. The rise of various social liberation movements, such as the women's and gay liberation movements, was reason enough for many on the New Right to move into action to change the direction in which American society seemed to be headed.

The New Right's sense of righteousness was fueled by their sense of their movement as speaking and acting in the interest of "regular Americans." To those on the New Right they were not only fighting for their rights and beliefs but they were also doing this for the many millions of Americans whose wishes and desires were either being ignored or dismissed by the liberal establishment (bureaucrats, media, and academia) or overruled in their view by an activist Supreme Court. For the movement to be successful a variety of individuals on the New Right recognized that there needed to be a reconfiguration of the conservative message, and the methods of articulating that message, to make it more amenable to the American public. For this to be achieved, conservatism had to clean up its image and distance itself from elements of the Old Right that were problematic (Berlet 1998: 23). Making connections with "ordinary Americans" was a major priority for the New Right and they saw the defense of traditional morals and values as central to creating those alliances. As Paul Weyrich, one of the main figures within the movement, pointed out, the accentuation of values was one main difference between those of the Old Right and New Rightists like himself:

I said earlier that the Old Right tended to be intellectual and upper class. It is as accurate a generalization that the New Right tends to be middle class, blue- collar and ethnic in its origins.... Though the upper classes had more intellectual expertise, they tended to become deficient in something that was strong in the working middle classes: values. (Weyrich 1982: 52)

Weyrich also asserted, "Another great advantage of the New Right derives, again, from another of the factors which distinguish our general outlook from that of the Old Right [which is that] the New Right does speak the language of the common man" (Weyrich 1982: 57).

In addition to its concentration on populist themes the New Right also opportunistically used such political methods as single-issue politics, direct mail solicitation, and building strong grass roots movements. A figure at the center of the emergence of the New Right was a life-long conservative from Texas, Richard Viguerie, who at one time worked for the Young Americans for Freedom and on the Goldwater campaign. While working at Young Americans For Freedom Viguerie discovered his shyness was preventing him from effectively raising funds for the organization; to alleviate the problem Viguerie switched to writing letters. Here Viguerie discovered a personal and political gold mine–utilizing direct mail as a political tactic (Gottfried 1993: 100). Using the list of Goldwater supporters as his starting point, Viguerie initially copied the names of supporters by hand until, over time, as he accumulated more lists of possible conservative donors, he switched to recording the information in computer files. Coordinating fund-raising efforts with organizations like the Committee for the Survival of a Free Congress headed by Paul Weyrich and the Conservative Caucus led by Howard Phillips, Viguerie went on to amass not only personal wealth but also much needed money for the nascent movement. Viguerie saw direct mail as much more than a method of raising money. Rather, to him direct mail was, "a unique form of advertising. If done properly, it pays for itself which is something almost no other form of advertising can do for conservatives" (Viguerie 1981: 93). Direct mail was a boon to the New Right because it provided them with the ability to, in their view, disseminate their message in its undiluted state while also raising funds. With direct mail conservatives no longer had to worry about the mainstream press, whom they viewed as having a liberal bias, distorting their message. Instead, they could disseminate their message directly to their constituents. Also, the proceeds from fund raisers went straight back to the organization, not political party middleman sources (Peele 1984: 56).

Another important contribution of direct mail to the New Right was its ability to, as Jeffrey Goldfarb states, "have a coalition politics without the difficult process of coalition building" (Goldfarb 1991: 114). For example, a portion of the money received from an ad campaign directed to anti-abortion supporters could be funneled into another campaign calling for the elimination of gun control laws, and a portion of the proceeds from the anti-gun control movement could be diverted toward the start up of a right to work campaign and so on. While the chances of getting a life-long union member to be a supporter of both pro-gun and anti-abortion movements may be good, trying to convince this same laborer about the merits of a right to work movement would be impossible. This process, in essence allowed for the creation of virtual coalitions. The effectiveness of this strategy was not lost on Goldfarb:

> The new right-wing ideology, especially as it has developed during the Reagan years, turns away from the dreams and horrors. Its practice is in a sense a postmodern ideological politics. Sentiment and prejudice connect stances on particular issues.... The connection is made most explicit in the computers of campaign strategists and mailers, not through a highly rationalized program in the older ideological mold. The contributors to the various one-issue campaigns can be perfectly ignorant of the deep ideological script, and it still works. They must simply have a feeling that they are part of social renewal, centered on the issue which concerns them the most. The hard material structure of the synthesis is the computer; the identification of unity by the citizenry is achieved through high-level public relations. (Goldfarb 1991: 114)

In addition to the virtual coalitions the New Right was constructing, they were also building real ones. The pro-family movement brought in a wide diversity of groups. As Richard Viguerie states, "The pro-family movement is made up of people of many faiths – Catholic, Protestant, Jewish, Eastern Orthodox" (Viguerie 1981: 153). Not only was the movement religiously diverse but it also provided an opening for many women to become involved in conservative activism. These women were different in their educational levels, family backgrounds, and experience in grassroots activism but they all had one goal—to stop the rolling tide of social liberalism that was moving through the nation. Concerns over such issues as feminism, sex education in public schools, abortion, and busing would bring a number of women into the New Right movement. For example, Alice Moore, the wife of a fundamentalist minister, sparked a major movement in the small West Virginia town of Kanawha County. The dispute originated over Moore's concern about the new sexual education program the county was planning to implement, but over time Moore and her supporters went from working to block the implementation of the sex education program to banning from the schools what they saw as problematic textbooks (Martin 1996: 117–143).[4] The dispute grew to such prominence that the New Right think tank, the Heritage Foundation, joined in the battle and provided assistance to the protesters (Martin 1996: 135).[5]

The New Right saw other women become involved in the fight. In Boston a former school board member named Louise Day Hicks founded the organization Restore Our Alienated Rights (ROAR). Hicks and her organization were in the forefront in protesting the city's planned busing program. Phyllis Schlafly, long time conservative activist, rose within the movement with her organized drive to block passage of the Equal Rights Amendment, and another woman, Connaught (Connie) Marshner, became noted for her contributions within conservative policy circles. The activism of these women was perceived by some critics as providing the male leadership of the New Right with a convenient shield from criticism: "While the 'pro-family' strategy allowed the New Right to launch an indirect attack against women's rights, they also went for the direct hit-using female intermediates" (Faludi 1991: 239).

In addition to women the New Right also had its sights set on trying to bring into their camp another group that had historically been at odds with the Right—African Americans. In one chapter of his book, *The New Right: We're Ready To Lead*, architect of the New Right Richard Viguerie spoke to his belief that a home could be made for African Americans within the New Right. Viguerie frankly acknowledged the failures of conservatives to attract African Americans, stating, "Undeniably, conservatives have failed to make their case to blacks, nor were blacks particularly listening to it. But this doesn't mean there is no case to be made, that it can't be done, or that it isn't worth trying" (Viguerie 1981: 164). Although Viguerie was candid about the Right's shortcomings he was also quick to point out that the New Right would not make the same mistake as its predecessors, "In the future the New Right will be increasing its efforts to appeal to blacks" (Viguerie 1981: 168).[6]

BUILDING A PUBLIC OPINION VOICE: LIBERALS MUGGED BY NEOCONSERVATIVE INTELLECTUALS

Using such tactics as direct mailing and coalitional engineering, by the 1970s the Republican party and conservatives with the help of the New Right had peeled away most of the constituencies that had comprised FDR's New Deal coalition. However a second faction was also emerging within the conservative movement, one comprised of a set of intellectuals who had been regarded, and regarded themselves, as left-liberals. For this group, the final straw that broke the camel's back came when Senator George McGovern captured the Democratic party's presidential nomination in 1972. To this newly alienated group, McGovern epitomized everything that was wrong with liberalism and the direction in which it was taking the nation and the Democratic Party. McGovern spoke out strongly against the Vietnam War, for example, and allied himself with many of the student movements, feminist movements and New Left ideals of the time. Some of these disgruntled supporters jumped ship and declared their support for President Nixon. Others bit the bullet and switched parties and became Republicans while yet others decided to pass on the election, holding disdain for both McGovern and Nixon. What was notable about this group was that some had histories of being involved in socialist movements, some were former Trotskyites, while some were plain liberals. Many of this cadre came from the New York intellectual community and were Jewish. Socialist Michael Harrington, in trying to comprehend the phenomenon of the rightward shift of some of his former comrades, came up with the label "neoconservatives": "We finally started calling them 'neoconservatives' because we recognized that they represented something new in American politics" (Dorrien 1993: 2).

This group of new conservatives were advocates of modernity, a majority of them were trained in the social sciences not in the humanities or theology as many conservative thinkers were, and they harbored no longing for older forms of capitalism or the preservation of the Old South. Some of these neoconservatives adamantly claimed that they were still socialists or social Democrats (Dorrien 1993: 2). However it was clear that these individuals had given up on much of what the American

Left stood for. In the forefront of this movement was Irving Kristol. Kristol, a New Yorker whose father had been a clothes subcontractor, was a Trotsky follower for quite awhile before finally committing himself to the movement after he graduated from the City College of New York in 1940 (Wald 1987: 350). Kristol honed his polemical skills by writing for and editing a number of impressive journals such as *The Reporter* and *Commentary*. For Kristol and other fellow neoconservatives, the sixties illustrated that liberalism and the Left were spiraling out of control. Many of the neoconservatives placed the blame for societal chaos squarely on the shoulders of a new segment of society—the New Class.

As I mentioned earlier the term New Class was a product of anarchist Mikhail Bakunin originally used to critique the role of intellectuals in society. David Bazelon reactivated the concept in 1966 by positing that one outcome of the rise of corporate capitalism was the creation of a New Class of non-property owning managers, bureaucrats, and intellectuals. This particular group did not have to accumulate property or capital to acquire power or status, instead gaining these things through organizational position. Because American liberalism rested its faith on such practices as the expansion of the welfare state and enlarging bureaucracy, this provided meaningful employment for those who fell within this category (Dorrien 1993: 13–14).[7] Bothered by the manner in which liberal academics, who they viewed as belonging to the New Class, were attempting to solve America's social problems through Lyndon Johnson's Great Society program, Kristol, along with fellow neoconservative Daniel Bell, founded the journal, *The Public Interest*. According to Kristol, it was his feeling that just writing op-eds critiquing Johnson's Great Society agenda was not enough. More needed to be done, and in his mind the answer was the establishment of another magazine (Kristol 1995: 28–29).

The Public Interest was by all accounts a stark contrast to the journals and works produced by liberals and progressives. The articles published in the journal put forth a perspective on social policy that was more cautious, empirical, and weary (Dorrien 1998: 57–58). Although Kristol was perhaps the most conservative of the cadre of people who worked for the journal, he still had difficulties, at the time, aligning himself with the Right:

> I was the most conservative of the lot, my British experience having exposed me to intelligent, thoughtful, and lively conservatives. But conservatism in the States at that moment was represented by the Goldwater

campaign against the New Deal, with which none of us had sympathy, and by *National Review*, which we regarded as too right-wing. (Kristol 1995: 31)

While some identify the founding of the *Public Interest* as being the starting point of neoconservatism, Kristol and others point to the rise of the counterculture and the outbreaks of student protests across campuses nationwide as the influential factors that hastened their rightward shift.[8] Prominent political sociologist Alvin Gouldner explained that the modern university was a contradictory institution:

> For universities both reproduce and subvert the larger society...While the school is designed to teach what is adaptive for society's master institutions, it is also often hospitable to a culture of critical discourse by which authority is unwillingly undermined, deviance fostered, the status quo challenged, and dissent systematically produced. (Gouldner 1979: 45)

Kristol and his peers of the Old Left saw themselves as the products of Gouldner's university where they were trained to think critically, question the status quo, and produce dissent; but the direction they felt America's colleges and universities was going deeply disturbed them. This emerging group of neoconservatives viewed the nation's higher educational institutions as spaces where so-called New Left extremism was building to a rapid boil, and "deviance" definitely was being fostered. According to the neoconservatives, universities were where anti-Americanism, anti-traditional values, and most importantly anti-capitalism beliefs and arguments reigned supreme.

To Kristol and other neoconservatives, the students who were protesting appeared to be nothing more than affluent suburban kids who lacked intellectual seriousness but possessed plenty of immaturity (Gerson 1996: 108). The apparent affluence of the students particularly galled the neoconservatives, who had working-class backgrounds and felt they had to scrap and scratch their way up the mobility ladder. For men like Kristol, their lives were examples of the opportunities that America had to offer. According to the neoconservatives, these "spoiled" students were prime examples of the successes of American society. The relative comfort they were raised in and the opportunities they had at their feet illustrated that America did work. For these young people to reject outright the ideals and values of what made America such a great land was, to the neoconservatives, the equivalent of spitting in the face of America. The unrest on the campuses and in the streets were an indication that liberalism was incapable of fending off the "out of control, nihilistic" radicalism that had taken hold of the nation.

Not one figure in the neoconservative camp felt this sentiment more deeply than Norman Podhoretz. Born and raised in Brooklyn, Podhoretz developed a deep and respectful relationship with public intellectual Lionel Trilling. Trilling's ideas profoundly influenced Podhoretz and shaped his liberal anti-communism. Podhoretz began working for *Commentary* in 1955 and took over the editorial helm in 1960. By the seventies, Podhoretz had transformed the leftist magazine into an organ for neoconservatives. Podhoretz was not shy in expressing in a graphic manner his feelings and thoughts. In *Making It*, the first of his two personal memoirs, Podhoretz bluntly let it be known that acquiring material success and status was the main motivating factor that drove his life. According to Alan Wald, the main points in his life that influenced Podhoretz's turn rightward were the outbreak of the Middle East War in 1967 and the 1968 New York teachers strike that led to an acerbic confrontation between the African American community in the Ocean Hill-Brownsville section of the city and the United Federation of Teachers Union, which had a large Jewish contingent (Wald 1987: 354–355). The war in the Middle East brought out of Podhoretz an ethnic chauvinism toward Israel, while the teachers strike deepened Podhoretz's growing alienation from blacks. What bothered Podhoretz and other neoconservatives about the conflict was the display of black anti-Semitism.[9]

As bitter and intense as the controversy between the African American community in Ocean-Hill Brownsville and the teachers union was, it was not the incident that caused a number of neoconservatives, like Podhoretz, to become apprehensive toward African Americans' quest for racial equality. The tensions and hostility among some of the neoconservatives around race and racial issues had been present much earlier. Four years earlier, in 1963 Podhoretz had published an article in *Commentary* entitled, "My Negro Problem – And Ours." In that article Podhoretz took to task other white liberals for their readiness to "pander" to African Americans and for their hypocrisy in dealing with racism in American society. According to Podhoretz, many white liberals did not know an African American and did not want to establish a meaningful relationship with one. Therefore their commitment to racial equality was superficial:

Thus everywhere we look today in the North, we find the curious phenomenon of white middle-class liberals with no previous personal experience of Negroes...discovering that their abstract commitment to the cause
of Negro rights will not stand the test of direct confrontation. We find
such people fleeing in droves to the suburbs as the Negro population in
the inner city grows.... We find them saying that it will take a very long
time for Negroes to achieve full equality, no matter what anyone does.
(Staub 1999: 10)

White liberals put African Americans on pedestals and did not hold
them up to the same standards that they held themselves and others,
Podhoretz argued, due to the debilitating guilt that white liberals felt
toward African Americans (Dorrien 1993: 152). For Podhoretz, he too
suffered from these feelings but his guilt was not from being a white
person who was complicit in American society's ill treatment of African
Americans. Instead, his guilt came from the fear and *hatred* that he felt
toward African Americans. Reflecting on his youth Podhoretz wrote of
how growing up, he and his friends had a mixture of admiration and
fear for the African Americans in his neighborhood. On the one hand,
they thought the way African Americans carried themselves in public was
cool. On the other hand, they viewed the behavior of blacks as irresponsible and were intimidated by it:

We rarely played hookey, or got into serious trouble in school, for all our
street bravado, *they* were defiant, forever staying out...forever making dis-
turbances in class and in the halls, forever being sent to the principal and
returning uncowed. But most importantly of all, they were *tough*, beauti-
fully, enviably tough. (Dorrien 1993: 152)

Because of his experiences with African Americans as a youth, Podhoretz
felt he was in a better position to chastise his fellow white liberals for
their behavior.

In later parts of the article Podhoretz explained that the feelings
he had for African Americans as a youth had not changed as an adult.
Podhoretz marveled over African Americans' seeming mastery of such
physical activities as basketball and their inherent grace in dancing,
while still harboring an intense distaste for their "paranoid touchiness."
Podhoretz stated that the goal of integration pushed for by the civil
rights movement was mistaken. Instead he felt that African Americans

would be better served by following the strategy Jews had used in surviving centuries of oppression. What had enabled the Jews to continue existing amid the oppression they faced was their memorial reliance on their past glories. Because the Jews had the religious dream of being redeemed, they had no other choice but to continue to fight for their freedom. Upon closer examination, as Podhoretz saw it, "His past is his stigma, his color is a stigma, and his vision of the future is the hope of erasing the stigma by making color irrelevant, by making it disappear as a fact of consciousness." For African Americans, achieving equality and freedom would come from their assimilation into American society. Podhoretz went one step further and declared that the ultimate step for racial equality for African Americans would have to come through miscegenation (Dorrien 1993: 152). When color did not matter in American society African Americans would be free and that meant the disappearance of white and black through the blending of the two races.

The article struck a nerve. For every letter that chastised Podhoretz for his racism, more came into the magazine praising Podhoretz for displaying such courage in expressing his racial feelings. The timing of the article was key in helping Podhoretz to deflect major amounts of criticism. As Michael Staub insightfully observed, the article appeared during a time when, "the shedding of inhibitions...seemed itself cause for celebration" (Staub 1999: 11).[10] In Podhoretz's mind racial liberalism equated guilt.[11] Non-Jewish neoconservative Michael Novak echoed Podhoretz's criticism of the racial double standards by liberals. Novak claimed that when liberals branded someone as racist this had the same effect as an individual being branded a red or pinko during the McCarthy period of the 1950s. According to Novak, the most damaging impact of the liberals' use of the term racism was that it shut down open and honest dialogue about race:

> Certain opinions pass without inspection; others – on plainly ideological grounds – are rejected without inspection...no one dares to think, no one dares to question. The overriding current requirement is that one march in rank. Intellectual muggers stand ready to discipline those who stray. (Gerson 1996: 153)

Other neoconservatives weighed in their opinions on race problems in America. In "A Few Kind Words for Uncle Tom," Irving Kristol argued that the character Uncle Tom from Harriet Beecher Stowe's *Uncle*

Tom's Cabin was an example African Americans could borrow from. In Kristol's mind, the Uncle Tom character represented, "the only true and most perfect Christian in all American literature" who possessed "that inner transcendental freedom which all noble souls possess." For Kristol, pointing to Uncle Tom was his way of suggesting to African Americans the merits of non-rebelliousness and adopting an attitude that, "transcended all daily indignities while achieving a serenity of spirit" (Staub 1999: 11). In other words, African Americans could be the noble victims turning the other cheek while waiting for their redemption not here on earth but in the afterlife. At the National Conference of Jewish Communal Service in 1964, Nathan Glazer put forth the idea that Jews should think about the impact the civil rights movement was having on them as a group. As Glazer stated, Jews had "lived in some comfort for the past ten or fifteen years" but their security, "has now been fatally challenged by the Negro revolution" (Staub 1999: 11). In essence, for Glazer the racial situation looked like a zero sum game. If African Americans achieved their goals of equality and integration then Jews' ability to maintain their own communities would be lost. Another idea proffered by Glazer during the year was the rationalization of exclusionary behaviors practiced by some Jews toward African Americans as "part of the standard Jewish ethnocentrism" or the strong business acumen of Jewish people (Staub 1999: 11).

THE CREATION OF A COLOR-BLIND DISCOURSE

Although I am arguing in this chapter that the seventies was the period where color blindness was elevated into conservative discourse, the concept can be traced back to nation's beginnings. The first example of the concept was in the creation of several amendments of the constitution. While the 13th amendment was created to address enslaved blacks, no where in its language is race mentioned, therefore, technically it is color blind in its meaning and application. The same follows for the 14th amendment, even though this amendment was created with the purpose of addressing the issues of citizenship and equal protection rights to former slaves after the Civil War, the amendment's language makes no explicit mention of race and declares rights and protections shall be applied ro all individuals and American citizens (Mazzocco 2017: 15). As scholar Phillip Mazzocco aptly points out, color-blind supporters often point to Justice John Marshall Harlan's dissent in the Supreme Court's

1896 Plessy v. Ferguson ruling where Harlan uses the word color blind as an illustration of the nation's intention of honoring color blindness:

> ...in the view of the constitution, in the eyes of the law, there is in this country no superior dominant, ruling class of citizens. There is no caste here. Our constitution is *colorblind* (emphasis mine), and neither knows or tolerates classes among citizens. (Mazzocco 2017: 16)

But Mazzocco rightly suggests one needs to look at the previous sentence to the one quoted above to get a clearer sense of Harlan's feelings toward color blindness:

> The white race deems itself to be the dominant race in this country. And so it is, in prestige, in achievements, in education, in wealth, and in power. So, I doubt not, it will continue to be for all time, if it remains true to its great heritage and holds fast to the principles of constitutional liberty. (Mazzocco 2017: 17)

Justice Harlan was not advocating color blindness because he earnestly felt the two races were equal, instead Justice Harlan was providing a foreshadowing of the consequences of adopting a separate but equal practice—the discovery of systematic white privilege. According to Harlan's logic, if the nation were to treat all of its citizens as equals through the prism of individualism then the "natural superiority" of whites would be evident but once society establishes a segregated system by race, it would require the documentation of racial statistical data to see if the philosophy of separate but equal was being carried out properly. This focus would not only shine light to the reality that social and material advantages were being given on the basis for race but also provide the basis for the push for collective action under the guise of group rights (Mazzocco 2017: 17). Throughout the nineteenth and into the twentieth centuries civil rights advocates knew Harlan's concerns to be true and understood that if the nation were to be genuinely committed to racial equality it would have to both acknowledge the realities of race, as in the discrimination and favoritism practiced and provide correctives that specifically address this issue, while progressing forward by moving beyond race. Hence, the discourse of civil rights proponents has always contained what appeared on the surface to be contradictory messages of, in order to disregard race we must first acknowledge it.

For the right there were several factors that played a major role in helping it reinvent how it articulated its racial conservatism with color blindness at the center of its discourse. First, as mentioned in the previous chapter, the utilization of the "southern strategy" a populist discourse that appealed to the alienation and anxieties of whites through the use of a softer more covert style. For example, in this more covert softer style one did not have to defend their opposition to busing by arguing whites should not have to send their children to school with children of a "genetically inferior race." Instead, the disapproval is due to the fact that it is liberal social engineering policies that take away the right of "average Americans" to choose where and who they want their children to go to school with. Second, Dr. Martin Luther King's "I Have a Dream" speech in 1963 where he delivered the famous line, " I have a dream that my four children will one day live in a nation where they will not be judged by the color of their skin but by the content of their character." At the time conservatives did not realize how valuable this line would become in their efforts to reposition racial conservatism. But a decade later appropriation of King's line would be the perfect rhetorical answer to the liberal left's justification for government policies with the objective, in the view of conservatives, on achieving equality of results and supporting group rights over equality of opportunity and individual rights. Whereas historically it was liberals invoking the need for the nation to be color blind so as to eradicate racial inequality by eliminating the structural and legal barriers (Ansell 1997: 107), conservatives redefined color blindness to mean government ignore race as a factor in policy creation (Ansell 1997: 104). Conservatives definition of color blindness allowed them to put the liberal left on the defense by calling them hypocritical racists because they were the ones who preached color should not matter in theory but were doing the exact opposite in practice. Finally, policies such as affirmative action allowed neoconservative intellectuals to craft critiques that were grounded in principle, such as one problem of affirmative action according to the neoconservatives, was it created a special class of people (e.g., blacks) protected by the law who became more equal than others (Ansell 1998: 179). When it came to the topic of affirmative action the neoconservatives' critique and opposition were fierce and intense. Norman Podhoretz was against the policy because it failed his litmus test of advancing the Jewish interest. For Podhoretz, Jews needed to assess always what the impact of any social change would be on them as a group and act accordingly.

Because affirmative action was geared toward assisting racial minorities through preferences and not on merit, as he saw it, Jews would not benefit from the program (Dorrien 1993: 191). Nathan Glazer thought affirmative action was wrong because of the deleterious impact it would have on creating solidarity among Americans. In his book, *Affirmative Discrimination*, Glazer laid out what was wrong about affirmative action:

> Thus the nation is by government action increasingly divided into racial and ethnic categories with different origins. The Orwellian nightmare "All animals are equal, but some animals are more equal than others," comes closer.... New lines of conflict are created by government action. New resentments are created; new turfs are to be protected. (Glazer 1975: 75–76)[12]

The problem with programs like affirmative action according to the neoconservatives, was that they not only fostered resentments from white victims of "reverse discrimination," but also, these programs changed the focus of solving the problem of racial equality. Instead of working to create mechanisms that promoted equal opportunities for all, those in the New Class were now looking for equality of outcomes (Steinfels 1979: 62, 65). In addition, such social engineering produced what the neoconservatives called "unanticipated consequences." In this case the unanticipated consequence was the alleged debilitation beneficiaries like African Americans felt by the program. Affirmative action supposedly made African Americans question whether or not they really had the abilities to achieve in society, especially since it was their race that was the main criterion used by institutions to grant them access.[13]

Neoconservatives Critique of New Left Movements

The neoconservatives not only castigated liberals for their handling of racial issues in America, but also, they showed that they did not have much sympathy or patience for some of the other movements that came out of the sixties and seventies such as feminism and gay liberation. Norman Podhoretz saw feminism as producing, "women driven literally crazy by bitterness and self-pity [and] men emasculated by guilt and female bullying." Irving Kristol blamed the women's movement for putting forth the myth of "modern, liberated women...who can 'handle' sex as easily, as calmly, as confidently, as their male counterparts are presumed to do." It was the falseness of this myth that, "fuels the energy of a radical feminism – i.e., antimale feminism" (Dorrien 1993: 352). Female neoconservatives were just as biting in their criticism of feminism. Midge Decter found it ironic that alongside the loud proclamations from the women's movement calling for society to recognize women's equality and freedom, "women demanding equality should be at such great pains to proclaim themselves unfit for it." According to Decter, the women's movement from its beginning had "intoned a seemingly endless and various litanies of women's incapacities" (Decter 1972: 40). Ruth Wisse and Carol Iannone made sport of feminism and what they saw as the undoing of women who followed this movement. And just like their New Right counterparts, neoconservative women felt that openly gay people of any political persuasion were not welcome. Decter put it best by stating, "one can hope that the country's homosexuals will recover their senses, return to their own private lives, abjure the bathhouses and gay-bar back rooms and faceless couplings that place there" (Decter 2001: 184–185).[14]

THE BUILDING OF THE CONSERVATIVE INTELLECTUAL INFRASTRUCTURE

Not only did the neoconservatives differ from other conservatives around specific political issues (i.e., immigration, welfare, and foreign policy), their style and approach to politics also set them apart from others on the Right. Many conservatives found their neoconservative counterparts abrasive, aggressive, and outright rude at times. Many of the neoconservatives were without a doubt very polemical. A number of them had acquired this skill during their collegial days at City College of New York holding passionate debates, the anti-Stalinist socialists doing battle against the orthodox communists (Hodgson 1997: 131). For the neoconservatives ideology and polemics went hand in hand. In a 1984 September article for *Commentary*, Owen Harries spelled out in detail the strategies neoconservatives needed to gain the upper hand in political debates. Of the twelve steps Harries put forth two in particular highlight the strategy neoconservatives adopted. Rule 2 according to Harries: "Pay great attention to the agenda of the debate. He who defines the issue, and determines their priority, is already well on the way to winning." And rule 12: "Know your enemy" (Harries 1984: 58, 64).

Neoconservatives recognized the importance of these strategies especially when they pertained to the utilization of intellectual institutions like foundations and think tanks; these institutions later became important in the support of African American conservatives. No one figure within the neoconservative camp recognized the importance of having a strong intellectual infrastructure more than Irving Kristol. Although Kristol was not a policy expert he did have a great appreciation for their approach. Peter Steinfels said Kristol was "full of respect for their tough-mindedness, their attention to precisely demonstrable facts, their 'anti-ideological' skepticism about popular generalizations" (Steinfels 1979: 96). During the early seventies Kristol became quite alarmed at the rise of anti-Americanism and anti-capitalism he was witnessing in American society. This was due, in Kristol's opinion, to the New Class of government bureaucrats, intellectuals, journalists, and foundation heads using their newly acquired power in opposition to the interests of American capitalism (Himmelstein 1990: 146). Kristol felt that the corporate leaders did not know how to counter this sentiment effectively and told them so. Their problem was that they had abandoned politics to concentrate more on achieving, "short-range respectability than with long-range survival."

American capitalists were primed to hear from someone like Kristol as they found themselves at crossroads during this period. Jerome Himmelstein reasons that the anxiety American capitalists felt was produced by a number of factors. First, economic growth was declining. Within a short period corporate profits had dropped from the post World War II all time high of 13.7 in 1965 to a yearly average of 8% in the early seventies. Second, American business was facing stiffer competition from industrial countries like Germany and Japan. Third, the capital-labor accord business had with big labor was becoming more difficult to commit to (Himmelstein 1990: 132–133). In addition, the increasing role that government played in the economy also troubled them greatly. The expansion of regulatory agencies was one problem but another problem, viewed as being more grave, was Americans' increasing sense of entitlement. To American capitalists this was inimical to their survival, as Americans felt that what the private sector or market could not provide government was responsible for. The response by the government led to increased spending and regulations, producing higher taxes and less investment in the private sector (Himmelstein 1990: 136). The business community perceived this development as being as a problem of communication. The low support Americans had for business was due to the ineffective way business presented itself to the public. As one businessman stated, "We have been successful in selling products, but not ourselves" (Himmelstein 1990: 136–137). Hence the corporations needed to have a cadre of intellectuals that would not only defend their legitimacy but do battle with the New Class intellectuals.

Kristol also suggested that corporations needed to be wiser and more discriminating in how they doled out their resources. Corporations needed to stop providing funds to intellectuals and institutions that were hostile to their interests and start supporting those who worked on the behalf of business (Smith 1991: 181). Kristol's first effort in achieving this was he and former Treasury secretary William Simon established in 1978 the Institute for Educational Affairs which directed financial resources to pro-capitalist scholars and think tanks. Second Kristol lobbied the corporate sector hard to pour monies toward supportive intellectuals inside and outside of the academy, and also to supportive think tanks. Through his hard work Kristol was rewarded a place at the American Enterprise Institute as a research fellow. James Smith aptly documents the contribution neoconservatives have made to the Right:

> With the arrival of Kristol and other neoconservative reinforcements in the 1970's, the conservative movement gained potential voices that were also highly professional in their approach to philanthropy and able to cast their arguments in the analytical and quantitative language of the social sciences…. Furthermore, the battle would no longer be fought exclusively on the terrain of abstract ideas; it would be extended to the arenas of public opinion, where neoconservatives polemicists – though few – were far more comfortable than were liberal technocrats. (Smith 1991: 182)

Perhaps most enduring for contemporary conservative politics was the intellectual infrastructure neoconservatives took the lead on building up during this period, in direct confrontation with what they identified as a New Class of intellectuals who supported the liberal state. Sociologists have charted, theorized, and debated the rise of this New Class.[15] What is to be emphasized here, however, is the construction of a conservative intellectual counterforce, with an infrastructure to support a new class of conservative writers and speakers whose rise would take the rug out from under the New Class by the eighties, at least in the sphere of public opinion.

Neoconservatives such as Irving Kristol were not the only ones instrumental in the build up of the Right's intellectual infrastructure. New Rightists like Paul Weyrich and Joseph Coors, a member of the Coors brewing family, also played major roles in establishing conservative think tanks, like the Heritage Foundation. In fact, Weyrich attributes his motivation for creating the Heritage Foundation to liberals. In 1969 Weyrich had been mistakenly invited to a meeting of liberal strategists and was impressed by what he heard. From that meeting Weyrich realized that conservatives needed to have a network of institutions similar to the ones liberals had (Paget 1998). The conservative intellectual infrastructure of think tanks, foundations, legal centers, magazines, and journals has become a very influential force in the conservative movement. Through this network conservatives have been very effective at influencing the national discourse on a variety of domestic and foreign policy issues. Conservatives have become very adept at using the media to disseminate their ideas and provide exposure to their thinkers.[16]

Not everyone on the Right quickly and warmly welcomed the new conservatives to the movement with open arms. Clyde Wilcox wrote, "First of all, we have simply been crowded out by overwhelming numbers." Wilcox blamed the presence and discourse of neoconservatives on, "the offenses of radicalism" for pushing "vast herds of liberals across the borders into our territories." Wilcox articulated the distrust many in the Old Right, traditional, conservative camp held toward the neoconservatives when he stated further, "These refugees now speak in our name, but the language they speak is the same one they always spoke" (Gottfried 1993: 91). Paleoconservative Russell Kirk felt the neoconservatives were like the New Class Liberals they derided, and to some degree he was right, in the sense that like their New Class counterparts, the neoconservative were learning how to create and use new institutional resources, rhetorical gambits, and promotional styles to claim the space of public opinion for the long term.

Russell Kirk found the neoconservatives' politics to be utilitarian, self-promoting, and power oriented. For him the neoconservatives had no sense of the importance of the transcendental order. Instead their focus was on acquiring and enacting their power in the everyday world. This Kirk asserted was due to the fact that many of the Old Right thinkers were based in the humanities and theology while the neoconservatives came from the social sciences and the social activism realm (Dorrien 1993: 348). This criticism too could be seen as revealing a shift in intellectual paradigms writ large. If the conservatism of the fifties had been critiqued on humanist grounds, what the neoconservatives provided, both indirectly and intentionally, was access to a new language of the social sciences for conservatives to use to make and bolster their political claims.[17]

The tension between the Old Right sector and the neoconservatives points to a much larger rift within the conservative movement. According to James A. Smith, a number of conservative writers and thinkers like Kirk, "seemed to share one strong conviction: Intellectual error – much of it to be found in the social sciences disciplines – was the root of modern problems" (Smith 1991: 170). To the Old Right the neoconservatives and their liberal counterparts were guilty of the following sins: rationalism and an obsession with scientific and technical solutions. In addition to the differences in political approaches, many conservatives felt uncomfortable at the manner in which neoconservatives were, in their view, "taking over" the think tanks and foundations, as articulated by Paul Gottfried: "The neoconservative ascendancy over policy institutions has occured most demonstrably in Washington. There conservative foundation heads seem always in a hurry to express agreement with fixed neoconservative positions" (Gottfried 1993: 136). By the 1980s, other conservatives felt that the neoconservatives had wormed their way into the good graces of the Reagan adminstration snapping up cabinet positions that should have gone to others in the conservative movement. The fall of communism in Russia and Eastern Europe and the Gulf War have exacerbated tensions between the Old Right and neoconservatives over American foreign policy direction and American support to Israel. Paleoconservatives became exasperated with the neoconservatives' calls for the United States to take the lead in establishing American democracy globally. In addition they felt put off by their perception of neoconservative intolerance of any criticism of American support of Israel and Israel's action in general. Countering, the neoconservatives found the Old Right to be increasingly isolationist and its "disagreements" toward Israel as being fueled by nothing more than pure anti-Semitism. While many observers viewed this feud as the beginning of the break up of the American Right, time proved this assertion to be incorrect. Although both sides viewed the other with suspicion, tension, and animosity, both found a way throughout the eighties and nineties to coolly co-exist within the conservative movement. The continuation of the North America Free Trade Agreement (NAFTA), terrorist attacks on 9-11 and the subsequent invasion of Afghanistan and Iraq would re-open some of these old wounds as America entered into the twenty-first century.

HERE COME GOD'S WARRIORS: REACHING OUT TO THE RELIGIOUS RIGHT

The religious Right mirrors the larger secular conservative movement in many ways. Both movements did not possess the influence fifty years ago that they do today. Each movement was not as polished or sophisticated in its approach to politics back then as they are in this contemporary era. In other words, at an earlier time, overt expressions of anti-Semitism, homophobia, and racism were regular staples within the discourses of the two movements. Just as with the larger conservative movement, changes in the religious right were a crucial part of what made possible the rise of African American conservatives. And like the secular movement, these changes involved both shifting the content of their message, but also and maybe even more importantly, using the media to enter into the realm of politics and public opinion. A consequence of this was the growth of what is now called the "electronic church." If what the New Right and the neoconservatives created over the course of the seventies and eighties was an intellectual infrastructure combined with a populist network and appeal, then what the religious right added was an expansion of this populist network and the build up of an army to do battle in the eighties and nineties in what would be called, the "cultural wars."

The roots of the religious Right can be traced back to the emergence of the fundamentalist movement during the early part of the twentieth century (Wilcox 2000: 25). Entering into the political arena was a major endeavor for the fundamentalist community due to their adherence to the premillennial doctrine. Premillennialism put forth the belief that, during the period known as the Rapture, Christ would return to the earth and call living and dead faithful Christians to heaven. According to this doctrine, for the Rapture to occur the situation on earth would have to degenerate to the point where it would be overtaken by an anti-Christ. Those not "saved" would be left on earth to suffer at the hands of the anti-Christ. Eventually Christ would return to lead his faithful in a battle to overthrow the anti-Christ. For the fundamentalists, engaging in politics was a complicated matter because involvement with politics could lead to compromising with the sin of the outer world, thus making those Christians who compromised "unpure" and not ready to heed the calling of Christ when He came back to retrieve his faithful (Wilcox 2000: 26–27). Therefore, the major impetus within the fundamentalist community was to remain separate from the outside world and to avoid having interaction with "unsaved" Americans.

Yet, even with their separatist ideology fundamentalist leaders found justification for entering into politics. The key for this was the relationship fundamentalists had with the Bible. Fundamentalists interpreted the Bible in a literal sense and felt that knowing God's will came through knowing his words. Therefore, to mobilize a congregation around a specific issue all the pastor needed to do was to splice together different verses and chapters of a biblical segment in his sermon to justify his position. Political action would be justified as acting in God's will (Wilcox 2000: 28, 30).

Anti-evolution was one of the first political causes fundamentalists adopted. As creationists who believed that God created the earth and life as stated in the book of Genesis, fundamentalists saw the teaching of evolution in public schools as sacrilege. The battle between the anti-evolution fundamentalists and evolution's defenders came to a head in the small town of Dayton Tennessee in the 1921 Scopes trial. The Scopes trial pitted William Jennings Bryan, ardent fundamentalist, against Clarence Darrow, defender of John Thomas Scopes, a biology teacher from Tennessee who was accused of violating the law by teaching evolution theory. Even though Scopes was found guilty the trial was a disaster for the fundamentalists as Darrow had his way with Bryan, making Bryan and the anti-evolutionists look ridiculous. After the trial, many in the fundamentalist community felt it was time to pull back from political activism and return to their safe havens. As the twenties came to a close it appeared that the fundamentalist movement was coming to an end, the Scopes trial and other unsuccessful battles leaving the fundamentalist movement grappling for some stability.

The next battle, however, one that took place within the church, would leave the fundamentalist movement in much better condition than before. During the decade of the thirties a bloc of fundamentalists became increasingly uncomfortable with the acceptance of biblical criticism by a number of mainline Protestant churches. In reaction to what the fundamentalists viewed as the mainline churches' validation of modernism, a sect of fundamentalists declared their independence by breaking off from the mainline denominations. In 1941 Pastor Carl McIntire founded the American Council of Christian Churches, a separatist organization for those churches and denominations willing to give up their affiliation with the Federal Council of Churches (Diamond 1995: 95). It was not only the establishment of independent churches that helped the fundamentalists but also the manner in which they disseminated their message to their followers. Along with churches, fundamentalists began to create their own publications that allowed them to get their message out to the people undiluted. More importantly, fundamentalists aptly recognized the potential of using radio as their bully pulpit. The upside of all of these factors was that it strengthened the movement as a whole and gave it a stronger foundation to work from. The negative aspect was that these developments also helped to bring to prominence religious figures like Reverend Gerald L.K. Smith and Father Charles Coughlin, men who often sprewed anti-Semitic and racist invectives against Jews and African Americans (Martin 1996: 17).

Gerald L.K. Smith was an ardent follower and mentoree of Louisiana Senator Huey Long. Smith's publication *The Cross and the Flag*, along with the eloquence and energy he possessed as a speaker, allowed him to build a large following. Smith captivated audiences with his great speaking skills both on the radio and in person at revivals. Smith strongly supported and worked for Long's Share Our Wealth plan that called for radical income redistribution. After Long was assassinated in 1935 Smith became more focused on espousing pro-fascist and anti-Semitic views. Smith went as far as to believe that Long's killing was the result of a Jewish conspiracy and believed that Long's killer was Jewish, when in fact he was actually Catholic (Jeansonne 1988: 105). Smith thought that African Americans were an inferior race, "a child race only 200 years out of cannibalism," who were pawns of the Jewish communists. According to Smith, African Americans also owed their existence entirely to the white race without whom African Americans would have never "gotten past the loin cloth or g-string" (Jeansonne 1988: 122–123). Smith was equally intolerant about the subject of homosexuality. Hating gays and lesbians with an intense passion, Smith thought homosexuality, which he referred to as "this deviance" had infiltrated the media and he also saw a supposed power bloc developing between the "perverts and the marijuana addicts" (Jeansonne 1988: 126).

Catholic priest Charles Coughlin was another example of the demagoguery that came from the fundamentalist movement of that era. Like

Smith, Coughlin originally began his crusade by using the depression as an opening to articulate over the air waves a leftist, populist critique of capitalism. Initially a strong supporter of the New Deal and Franklin Roosevelt, Coughlin over time denounced the New Deal and fell out of favor with Roosevelt. Soon Coughlin began to shift his focus to Jews, placing the blame for the depression in the laps of "international Jewish financiers." Eventually Coughlin's anti-Semitism began to dominate his radio commentaries and stories in his publications. The audience Coughlin built up, however, was quite impressive. Coughlin commanded a listening audience that rivaled any of the audiences of today's right-wing commentators. Coughlin was the first of many on the religious Right to skillfully use the electronic media and soon a number of other influential figures on the religious Right would join Coughlin in exploiting the power of the "electronic church."

The end of the depression and America's victory in World War II brought relief and optimism to the nation. During this period the religious Right went into a lull only to be awakened a decade later with the onset of the Cold War. Anti-communism fueled the fires of the movement. In addition to the Reverend Carl McIntire stumping on the pulpit circuit other individuals got involved. Billy James Hargis created the Christian Crusade and went nationwide to hold fire and brimstone tent revivals speaking out against the evils of the godless communist threat in the United States. In addition to Hargis there was Dr. Fred C. Schwarz and his Christian Anti-Communism Crusade organization, and Edgar Bundy and his Church League of America organization. All of these individuals used their organizations and celebrity to preach against the "red menace" and the infiltration of the "red menace" into the more liberal mainline churches and denominations. It came as no surprise that many on the religious Right viewed the civil rights movement with skepticism and trepidation. One minister who would rise to power twenty years later, Jerry Falwell, preached a sermon in the late fifties where he spoke out against integration, stating that integration was not only morally wrong but would mean the end of the white race (Martin 1996: 57). Other leaders on the religious Right took their cues from the John Birch Society, claiming that the civil rights movement was communist inspired. Gerald L.K. Smith felt that African Americans were the lackeys of the "Jewish led" communist movement. Smith harbored deep resentments against Dr. Martin Luther King whom he felt was "one of the greatest frauds of the century" and "a Communist, a traitor, a revolutionist and an atheist while posing as a Baptist preacher" (Jeansonne 1988: 124). In an ironic twist, at the height of the civil rights movement in 1965, Jerry Falwell preached that the role of ministers should be to know Christ and make him known to others on earth. In his criticism partly directed at Dr. King and the other clergy involved in the movement Falwell said, "Preachers are not called to be politicians, but to be soul winners" (Martin 1996: 69–70). By the end of the seventies Falwell would find himself violating his own principle with his leadership of the organization called the Moral Majority.

Activism among conservative evangelical Christians was very low during the majority of the twentieth century. After the fiasco during the Scopes trial many conservative evangelicals retreated into their homes and lived their lives away from the larger secular society. Over time, tides of change from the secular world inched closer and closer to their own doorsteps, making many rethink their earlier stances on abstaining from getting involved in politics. In the early sixties the Supreme Court passed down two rulings, *Engel v. Vitale* in 1962 *and School District of Abington Township v. Schempp in 1963*. The first ruling stated that it was unconstitutional to have prayers conducted in public schools. The second ruling said it was unconstitutional to have any oral prayers or Biblical readings in public schools. These two rulings, paired with the onslaught of the social disruptions of the latter part of the sixties, added fuel to the fires of many conservative Christians who felt besieged by the rampant "permissiveness" that was occurring around them in American society.

During the seventies the evangelical movement expanded in various ways. There was an increase in the numbers of new fundamentalist and evangelical conservative churches while membership in the more liberal mainline churches declined. These steep increases were especially pronounced in the southern and western parts of the nation. Two factors help explain why this was the case. First, both the south and west regions were experiencing economic growth. As many groups headed to these regions to take advantage of the economic opportunities available, so too did conservative Christians. Companies found the South and West to be more hospitable regions to operate in than the Midwest or Northeast due to the lower taxes these areas offered; and, in the case of the South, the absence of a strong, vibrant labor union presence. A shift in political influence in Washington also paved the way for these regions to benefit economically. For example, during the four years of World War II the federal government had invested close to $40 billion in factories, military bases, and other capital investments out West. During this same period Washington provided close to 90% of the investment capital for the West (White 1991: 496). Richard White aptly summarizes the impact the federal government had on the West:

> The federal government had altered the regional allocation of power within in the United States. The control of capital and industrial production exercised by the Northeast lessened considerably…but by the end of the war the West had secured new sources of federal revenues, an enlarged infrastructure, and a new industrial base. (White 1991: 497)

Second, these regions had built within their cultures a strong conservative ethic. While both the Southern and Western regions celebrated individualism, they valued individualism in a certain context. In their opinion, an individualism that was disconnected from the institutions of family, community, and civic responsibility was to be scorned. Eugene D. Genovese describes southern conservatives' philosophical approach to individualism as being based in an orthodox Christianity, counterposing "an older Christian notion of a God-given dignity of the personality to the bourgeois notion of the individual as the center of the universe. For them, the very dignity of the personality requires roots in the community, and above all, the family" (Genovese 1994: 14).

Both the south and the west were fertile grounds for many on the religious Right because fundamentalism was central to beliefs many southern and westerners had to their relationship with religion. Concomitant with a faith steeped in fundamentalism was the belief that it was better to trust in the will of God on all matters, especially social ones, rather than the abstract reasoning of human thinking. Social change, derived by ideological motivations, which disregarded customs and traditions of the community were rejected as "social engineering" and not viewed as authentic change. In essence, as Eugene Genovese states, this theological approach "insists upon adherence to an Old Testament God of Wrath, whose revealed will remains inscrutable and whose commands must be obeyed, no matter how deeply they may offend ordinary human sensibilities" (Genovese 1994: 26–27). In addition, this belief sternly warned against the destructive outcomes that came from change based on humanist ideology (Genovese 1994: 27). Therefore, feminism, gay rights, and the sexual revolution were examples of the shortcomings of secularism to many Southern and Western conservative Christians.

The economic prosperity occurring in the south and west trickled down to the movement as conservative fundamentalists and evangelicals began building new churches to accommodate their growing congregations. As membership grew so too did the churches, churches that could seat not hundreds but thousands of parishioners. These "super churches" were super in every way, from their flashy architecture and state of the art sound systems to their accompanying institutions: schools, gyms, universities, retirement homes, and summer camps. From Charles Stanley's First Baptist Church in Atlanta and D. James Kennedy's Coral Ridge Presbyterian in Fort Lauderdale to Tim LaHaye's Scott Memorial Baptist Church in San Diego, these "super churches" were not only sprouting like mushrooms but were also bringing attention to the dynamic leaders who headed them, especially by veteran conservative activists.

Also during this period, many within the conservative fundamentalist movement began to take advantage of the access they had to the media, creating the "electric church." Beginning in the 1940s with radio, fundamentalists and evangelicals had been actively lobbying the federal government to gain greater access (Diamond 1995: 95, 97). The opportunities got even better for the religious Right when in the 1960s the Federal Communications Commission (FCC) changed regulations that enabled stations to sell religious organizations more air time. The conservative churches and ministers had the advantage over the more mainline, liberal churches as financial limitations forced the mainline churches to rely on "sustained time" programming, or allotted air time given by the stations. With more money in their coffers conservative churches could, and did, purchase more broadcasting time, eventually dominating the airways with their theological perspectives. The religious Right not only purchased air time on local and national stations, but also, they established their own. Along with radio, television became the next horizon for the religious Right to utilize. Many leaders of the emerging superchurches had their own media outlets. For example, Pat Robertson created his own broadcast network, Christian Broadcast Network (CBN), which aired his show *The 700 Club*, and created a cable channel, the Family Channel.

The wide audiences the ministers of the superchurches and electronic churches spoke to began to attract the interest of several conservative activists. As long time conservative activist Morton Blackwell stated, the key to political victory was in recognizing new untapped political groups and cultivating new relationships with them: "If you can identify some segment of the population which is not active and can be activated, or some segment that is miscast in their current party affiliation and can be switched over to your side, you're going to change things dramatically" (Martin 1996: 191). The timing was right for conservatives, in the mid to late seventies, to build coalitions with the conservative Christian community, as many Christian conservatives were feeling alienated and assaulted by societal changes and, particularly, the ruling powers in government—Democratic President Jimmy Carter and his adminstration and the liberal majority Supreme Court.

Conservative Christians had always felt that it was best to isolate themselves from the sins of the larger society and lead a life where all they wanted was to be left alone. When the actions of government at both the federal and state levels began to seep into what the religious conservative community saw as the private realm, it became apparent that standing on the sidelines would not be an appropriate response. Conservative Christians strongly believed that issues pertaining to the family or how one's child was educated were private matters to be decided by families, not the government. The Supreme Court rulings of the sixties were problematic, to say the least, but what was happening in the seventies made many conservative Christians even more alarmed. In 1972 the Equal Rights Amendment (ERA) was passed by the Senate 84 to 8 calling for a constitutional amendment addressing gender inequality. Its proponents claimed the ERA would revolutionize the economic, political, and social relations between women and men. Its opponents did not see it that way. Instead the ERA was looked upon as a viable threat to the health and survival of the American family. Within a year of its passing thirty states had ratified the ERA, leaving only eight more states needed to make it a part of the constitution. With more than six years left for the remaining states to ratify the amendment, the prospects of the ERA becoming a part of the constitution were strong.

Then veteran conservative activist Phyllis Schlafly became involved. Founding the STOP-ERA organization in October 1972 Schlafly led the charge in preventing the passage of the ERA. As Schlafly put it, "I knew from the start...that I had found enough seriously wrong with ERA to stop it, or at least stall it, for an awfully long time, if only I could get the message out" (Felsenthal 1981: 241).[18] Through the activism of Schlafly and her organization, along with the mobilization of other groups and individuals, the ERA fell short of the thirty-eight states needed for passage.

Conservative Christians received a major judicial jolt when in January 1973 the Supreme Court legalized abortion in its Roe v Wade ruling. The court's ruling brought together for the first time a large-scale coalition of conservative Catholics and Protestants working toward reversing the court's ruling (Luker 1984). Countering the drive by gays and lesbians for gay civil rights was also a focus of the Christian right during the seventies. The battles against gay rights were few and mostly on the local level as anti-gay activism had not yet become as much a mainstay of the Christian Right's agenda as it would in the next two decades (Diamond 1995: 171). One battle that did achieve national status was the 1977 anti-gay campaign led by singer Anita Bryant in Florida. Bryant successfully mobilized supporters to put pressure on the city leaders in Miami-Dade county to overturn the inclusion of gays in the local anti-discrimination law. The following year the Christian Right was mobilized in California to throw support toward a state initiative, Proposition 6, that would ban openly homosexual individuals from teaching in California's public schools. The Briggs initiative, named after sponsor California state representative John Briggs, went down to defeat by the voters but the campaign helped to launch the coming together of a nationwide network of anti-gay activists. In an ironic twist of fate, the Briggs initiative became the catalyst for the formation of the largest gay conservative organization in the country—the Log Cabin Republicans.[19]

The following year after the Briggs initiative was defeated, Beverly LaHaye, wife of Christian Right minister Tim LaHaye, founded the Concerned Women For America organization. According to LaHaye, the motivation for the organization came from her becoming alienated while watching an interview journalist Barbara Walters conducted with Friedan, Betty about the ERA. LaHaye felt that neither woman represented the "true" sentiments of American women (Paige 1987: 26). An initial planning meeting for the organization drew in an estimated 1200 women, a harbinger of the following LaHaye would garner in future years. Concerned Women For America (CWA) in time became the largest conservative women's organization, surpassing Phyllis Schlafly's Eagle Forum.[20] But it wasn't just savvy organizational strategies that catapulted LaHaye into the forefront of the conservative women's movement, it was what LaHaye symbolized for scores of women who identified with her. According to Linda Kintz, when women saw LaHaye they saw familiarity:

Something else engages the women who are LaHaye's audience. First of all, and most obvious to someone, like me, from a small town in the Bible Belt of West Texas, is the familiarity, even the ordinariness, to my eyes of LaHaye's middle class appearance: the respectable, fashionable though not flashy, style of dress; and the soft, gentle tone of voice, her sweetness. (Kintz 1997: 19)

While Beverly LaHaye was building up her battalion of female fundamentalists, other prominent New Right activists were working feverishly to create other organizations to channel and cultivate the support of conservative Christians. In a short-time organizations like the Christian Voice and Religious Roundtable were founded, but the organization, at the time, that was seen as the capstone of the contemporary Religious Right movement was The Moral Majority. The man chosen to head the organization was none other than the Reverend Jerry Falwell. Falwell's decision to head a political organization raised many eyebrows and caused some of his supporters to question his theological principles since nearly twenty years earlier Falwell had stated in one of his fiery sermons that politics was not the place for men of the cloth.[21] In his book, *Listen America* Falwell made clear what he and his organization stood for. Broaching a variety of issues ranging from the threat of communism to the American Family, Falwell concisely laid out what he thought ailed America and what steps were needed to cure the problems afflicting American society.[22] The Moral Majority enjoyed a ten-year existence but by 1989 it was clear that the organization had run out of steam. A number of factors impacted the demise of the organization. A crumbling organizational infrastructure, the drying up of organizational finances, several political missteps by Falwell, and the succession of scandals involving prominent tele-evangelicals all contributed to the Moral Majority's demise.

When Georgia governor Jimmy Carter ran for president in 1976 he received significant support from the fundamentalist and evangelical communities. Carter, a professed born-again Southern Baptist, made a public call for born-again Christians like himself to throw their support to him. Carter asserted that he could provide the leadership that they and all other Americans would feel comfortable with. The marriage between conservative Christians and the Carter adminstration did not last long as religious conservatives became enraged and alienated by a series of events during Carter's reign. For example, many conservative

Christians felt attacked when the Internal Revenue Service in 1978 challenged the charitable status and tax exemptions of independent Christian schools.[23] The 1980 White House conferences on Families further alienated conservative Christians. Finding themselves sharing a platform with feminists and gay and lesbian advocates, Christian conservatives were appalled by the debates over what a family was, abortion, gay rights, and the ERA. Many Religious Righters felt the conferences were an underhanded ploy to help build up support for Carter's reelection bid (Martin 1996: 181). When Republican presidential candidate Ronald Reagan spoke, in August, to the large audience of evangelicals at the National Affairs Briefing in Dallas, he had an eager audience. In his charismatic and elegant manner Reagan reassured the audience that he was the man they needed to support in the upcoming election. At one point during his speech, Reagan stated, "I know this is non-partisan, so you can't endorse me, but I want you to know that I endorse you" (Martin 1996: 216). The evangelicals at Reunion Arena erupted with thunderous applause. To them, they had found their Messiah who would lead America out of its spiritual downfall. On that day Ronald Reagan had cemented his place in American conservative history as the Moses who would lead the Right in November to the promised land.

REAGAN LEADS THE AMERICAN RIGHT TO THE PROMISED LAND: IDENTIFYING BLACK CONSERVATIVE INTELLECTUALS

On the evening of November 4, 1980 Ronald Reagan stood tall and victorious as the majority of Americans spoke loudly with their votes. It was Reagan not Jimmy Carter they wanted as their fortieth president. This was not only a hallmark for Reagan but also for the American Right. After decades of bitter disappointment conservatives finally got their man in office. Richard Nixon, Gerald Ford, and Dwight Eisenhower were never the type of conservatives the Right felt comfortable with nor fully trusted. Although these men may have been Republicans they were not true conservatives and to many on the Right there was a difference between the two. Conservatives trusted Reagan in the same fashion they placed their trust with Barry Goldwater almost twenty years earlier. For those on the Right, however, Reagan's victory came not a moment too soon for they felt that Jimmy Carter had left the nation in shambles. Under Carter inflation was up as was unemployment. Corporate America was being strangled by the bombardment of government regulations and taxes. In foreign affairs America looked weak and indecisive. The Middle East was shaping up to be the US' Achilles heel. The oil embargo of 1977 by OPEC showed how vulnerable the United States was to Middle East oil, as Americans again waited in long lines to purchase gas. The Iran hostage crisis only further diminished America's image, abroad and at home, as the invincible empire. The Soviet Union looked even more menacing when they invaded Afghanistan in 1980.[24]

Domestically, morale was down among many Americans. Poll after poll had shown that Americans were losing faith in their government, and expressing concern over their children's ability to achieve prosperity. Americans were also feeling overburdened by the government. Many felt that the federal government was taking more and more by way of taxes and giving little in return. Middle class and working-class whites were feeling especially burdened by the federal government. From their perspective they saw more of their earnings being eaten away by taxes, going to fund social welfare programs they did not use. In addition, the government was working against them with the implementation of affirmative action and set-aside programs to aid African Americans and other minorities.

One of Reagan's strengths as a politician was his ability to relate to voters and communicate his understanding of their concerns and values. As Stanley Greenberg noted, even though in his personal life Reagan did not personify the quintessential traditional man, his uncanny ability to identify with the "average American" led them to think he was one of them.

> Reagan may not have gotten himself up on Sunday mornings to go to church, but he so closely identified with the traditional family and traditional America that people insisted on associating him with religious faith and sentiment. This association transported him into the lives of important segments of blue collar and rural America, and Reagan understood the partisan opportunity. (Greenberg 1996: 138)

The connection Reagan made with working and middle-class whites illustrated his ability to plug into an oppositional politic adopted by many working and middle-class whites and labeled "plain folk Americanism." Plain folk Americanism was nothing more than the now more common sense form of an oppositional politics descended from the populist traditions of the south and west, a politics the conservative movement had cultivated in reaching out to and supporting the religious right. This brand of politics focused on issues of equality and special status. Hard work was heralded as the equalizing force in society while, also borrowing from producer ideology, the notion that those who did not work were to be castigated. This brand of politic also made a point of elevating and focusing on the specialness of "ordinary folk." Where in different eras the targets of this politic were the business and financial elites, the contemporary enemies were the black poor and radical whites (White 1991: 601).

Reagan understood all too well the anxieties and frustrations average white Americans were feeling, from the seeming encroachment of blacks below them and the intrusion from elite liberals in government above them. During his political tenure in California Reagan repeatedly struck chords with white Californians alienated and fearful of the social upheavals taking place in their state. For example, while campaigning for governor of California Reagan garnered support from suburban whites opposed to the state's Fair Housing Act, when he spoke against the measure, stating that in a free society every individual has the "basic and cherished right to do as they please with their property. If an individual wants to discriminate against Negroes or others in selling or renting his house he has a right to do so" (McGirr 2001: 205). Reagan, like so many other conservatives, felt that open housing laws were problematic in that they trampled over equally important absolute property rights. In Reagan's view the problem of dealing with racism was best left, not to the government, but to individuals (McGirr 2001: 205). Like all of the other conservative politicians of the era, Reagan also capitalized on the urban riots taking place within the inner city. Reagan's calls for "law and order" and "stemming the rising tide of crime" touched a nerve with urban and suburban whites tucked safely away in their enclaves who looked upon inner city blacks with disdain and fear. During Reagan's early tenure as governor, a document circulated within his adminstration addressing the issue of police brutality. At one point the document stated, "For the law abiding, the policeman is a friend. For all our science and sophistication, for all our justified pride in intellectual accomplishment, *the jungle is waiting to take over.* The man with the badge helps to hold it back. Too often the only thanks he gets is a charge of police brutality" (McGirr 2001: 204). To many whites unaware of the life experiences of poor, urban African Americans and their embattled relationship with the police, the inner city seemed to be a "jungle"-like space inhabited by individuals engaging in savage cultural practices.

Racial disorder, generational conflicts, challenges to the moral status quo, and government largesse were Reagan's clear and present dangers; with each issue he scored significant political support. With his pledges to get the tyrannical forces off of the backs of the "average American" Reagan, as Barry Goldwater, George Wallace, and Richard Nixon did in earlier times, gave legitimacy to the sense of victimization many white Americans were feeling. The number one perpetrator of their victimization was the federal government. Part of what has allowed conservatives to mobilize hostility toward an activist government has been their ability to connect governmental intervention broadly with federal action on the behalf of groups of color—especially African Americans. As White describes further:

> Open social conflict had erupted throughout the West, and because of that conflict the attitudes of white westerners toward government intervention had changed. Until 1960 westerners in opinion polls had favored government intervention to provide jobs, health care, and other basic necessities. After 1960 they began to opt for more individualist solutions. Before 1960 federal intervention had largely benefited whites; by 1966 it appeared to many whites to favor minorities and threaten the existing pattern of race relations. Federal efforts had become for them an unjustified interference with local custom and undue favoritism toward minorities. (White 1991: 603)

This strategy helped propel Reagan into the governor's office in 1966 and fourteen years later into the White House, and continued to be an important ingredient toward conservatives gaining a listening audience during the latter half of the twentieth century.

Reagan's winning over of the "average American" voting bloc was significant as he and his Republican party strategists created a new category of voters, Reagan Democrats, who brought together much of the populism first represented in the discourse of the New Right and the "plain folk Americanism" derived from the southern and western regions. Furthermore, by fusing together the issues of race, taxes, and rights Reagan and the Republican Party was able to create a "top-down" coalition. This coalition brought together working and middle class whites, once loyal constituents of the Democratic party, with upper class business and other elites. The common enemy, the federal government, was the magnet that pulled these two historically incompatible voting groups together. As Thomas and Mary Edsall described, this circumstance came about through the ideological marketing by conservatives of a doctrine that preached laize-faire free market principle and cut backs on governmental regulation while also promising to curtail government sponsored civil rights and social programs (Edsall and Edsall 1992: 154). George Wallace used this tactic to accumulate startling support in the 1968 election, and Richard Nixon gained access to the White House in both 1968 and 1972 partly due to this approach. Underneath Reagan's proclamation to reign in "big government" was the underlying meaning, as understood by frustrated working and middle class whites, that Reagan was the one who would keep African Americans in check:

> If Reagan's spoken promise was to get the government off the backs of the American people, his unspoken promise was to get the "niggers" off the backs of the white middle and working classes who had lost control over their schools and neighborhoods while paying taxes to support busing, Medicaid, public housing, assorted welfare programs, and civil rights enforcement lawyers at every level of government. (O'Reilly 1995: 366)

Given the underlying racialism of his message, perhaps Reagan's most intriguing decision, relevant for the increased presence of black conservatives in the movement in the later decades of the twentieth century, involved his employing the similar strategy of creating an intellectual layer that had worked so well in conservatives' ability to gain access to the public sphere over the course of the 1970s. Even though Reagan often took political stances that were perceived as oppositional by many African Americans, he had a difficult time understanding why he came across to many African Americans as a bigot and racist. At a Gridiron dinner during his second term as president, Reagan pleaded his case to African American journalist Carl Rowan that he was not a bigot, but also, he asserted that he had run out of patience in trying to appeal to African American leaders for help. As Reagan put it, "I tried hard to win friendship among blacks [but] I couldn't do it. I talked with black leaders after my election in 1980, and they went out and criticized me in horrible ways...so I said to hell with'em" (O'Reilly 1995: 377). Reagan and his operatives realized that if they were going to make any progress with African Americans it would not be with the cadre of traditional leaders who had come to prominence during the civil rights movement and beyond. Instead, they had to search out and cultivate relationships with a new group of African Americans, "dissidents" who would understand their agenda and not be afraid to challenge the reigning "orthodoxy" of the civil rights leadership within the African American community.

During the beginning of Reagan's second term, this strategy was explicitly spelled out in a series of memos by one of Reagan's political aides emphasizing that it was in the administration's interest to "avoid the 'established' black leadership." The black establishment was "unremittingly hostile" to Reagan and his objectives. The answer was in seeking out "other blacks with whom there is a chance of reaching common ground." As Richard Rahn, chief economist for the U.S. Chamber of Commerce stated, "One thing the White House can do is bestow publicity on people.... If you have credible people, they can be alternative leaders" (Barnes 1985: 9). The Reagan administration was doing more than attempting to make connections with African Americans. They were anointing what they saw as "credible spokespersons" to counter the traditional black leadership that was already in place. This was a very important move. Understanding the importance of public opinion for swaying voters of all races and stripes, conservatives had also come to understand that even without a real black constituency, black spokespeople could play an important role in the war of maneuver the American right has engaged in against the liberal establishment over the course of the twentieth century and on into the twenty-first. This decision to avoid established leaders and cultivate a class of seemingly "organic," conservative, African American intellectuals paralleled the decision on the part of the neoconservatives to counter the rhetoric of members of the New Class back in the seventies.

In the 1980s conservatives recognized the potential opportunities of courting African Americans who were similar ideologically. In early December of 1980, a month after Reagan had been elected, The Institute for Contemporary Studies, a conservative think tank in San Francisco, sponsored a two-day conference at the Fairmont Hotel. Prominent figures on the Right, economist Milton Friedman and incoming Reagan cabinet member Edwin Meese, were in attendance. The opening remarks by Fairmont conference organizer and African American, conservative economist Thomas Sowell spelled out clearly what direction the conference was headed.

We need to accept the responsibility of seeking and devising new approaches for the decade ahead. That is why we are here–to explore alternatives, not create a new orthodoxy with its own messiahs and its own excommunications of those who dare to think for themselves. The people who were invited to be presenters and discussants here are people who are seeking alternatives, people who have challenged the conventional wisdom on one or more issues, people who have thought for themselves instead of marching in step and chanting the familiar refrains. (Sowell 1980: 4–5)

During Reagan's eight-year tenure as president, a number of African American conservatives found their way into the political fold, either as members of his adminstration or as consultants. This included one upstart conservative lawyer who was an aide to Republican Missouri Senator John Danforth and within a decade would be elevated to a seat on the Supreme Court—Clarence Thomas.

The creation of this black conservative cadre, and its relationship to the other complex dimensions of black conservatism to be discussed in the chapters that follow—the social movements on the ground generated in response to such issues as abortion; the political leaders struggling to define an actual constituency; the intellectuals and academics attempting to carve out their own forms of hegemony in race discourse and public opinion; and a home-grown religious right with more access to large black populations in the mega churches of the late twentieth and early twenty-first century—is precisely what much of the remainder of this book is about. Color-blind conservatism has been particularly useful for black politicians and intellectuals seeking a way of going "beyond race." And yet, as the discussions in Chapters 6 and 7 demonstrate, the conservative movement has black conservative politicians and public intellectuals trapped in the irony created by the inescapability of race in conservative politics and ideology. In order to neutralize race as a blind spot covered over by the rhetorics of color blindness, conservatives end up foregrounding black candidates. Their importance to the Republican Party and the broader conservative movement lies precisely in their performance of race and blackness, especially given that they carry along with them no black constituency they can claim to be otherwise representing or serving.

If this irony undergirds the discussion of politicians and intellectuals in Chapters 6 and 7, in Chapters 4 and 5 the focus is more on the subtleties of black conservative race discourse as used in the rhetoric of black social movements, such as the anti-abortion movement, the anti-gay rights and school voucher movements, and in the message of the black religious right that I examine in Chapter 8. Unlike the intellectuals and the politicians, captured and detached from any real constituency in the black community and urgently in search of a sense of belonging in the nation, conservative social movement activists and community church leaders are much more in touch with a black community. This relationship influences their message and practice. In Chapters 4, 5, and 8, I explore the languages both groups inherit from American conservatism, both what those languages enable and what they disallow.

Both the links and the differences between top-down and bottom-up forms of black conservatism must be discussed precisely because otherwise, we not only get a deceptively simplistic picture of black conservatism, but also, we find ourselves unable to read beyond American conservatism's surface contradictions to the deeper consistency and cohesiveness provided by a racialized discourse of the right in this country, from the middle of the twentieth century and on into the twenty-first.

Notes

1. In the 1920s and 1930s, Italian social and political theorist Antonio Gramsci described the strategy of an ideological "war of position" as one in which political struggles shift the terrain of battle to the sphere of civil society and public opinion, engaging in less obviously political debates reframed as issues of general social concern (see Gramsci 1988: 222–224). Race would become for the conservatives an ideal issue for creating this ideological bridge between consolidating the conservative party's strength and spreading the ideals and values of the conservative movement more broadly.
2. In Gramscian terms, an "organic intellectual" is one who arises from the bottom-up out of a social group or movement, and provide[s] the group with an "awareness of its own function" (see Gramsci 1988: 250–251, 301–302, 425).
3. One could even trace this "new" style of black politics back to former Virginia Governor Douglas Wilder's campaign in the late eighties, where he successfully won office to become the first black governor by de-racializing his campaign.
4. Martin provides a riveting account of the battle between the anti-sex education and textbook providers, led by Moore and the town's supporters.

The controversy produced a town-wide boycott of parents keeping their children home from school, a solidarity strike by coal miners and bus drivers, and outbreaks of violence (firebombs, death threats, and the like) from those on both sides of the issue.

5. The raging controversy in the small, tucked away town in West Virginia not only attracted the attention of the Heritage Foundation but also the likes of other organizations such as the John Birch Society, and conservative parental organizations like the Parents of New York United and the New Orleans Hard Core Parental Group. Prominent New Right anti-text book activists Mel and Norma Gabler of Texas were also brought into the fray.

6. While the New Right was bringing more women into its fold and harboring dreams of opening the movement up to African Americans, one group that could not find solace within the New Right were conservative gays and lesbians. No matter how dedicated they were to the cause, the sentiment within the New Right was, no gay conservatives need apply.

7. Neoconservatives would also add to this category social workers, lawyers, academics, and journalists. Ironically, many of the neoconservatives who derided liberals who belonged to this set also fit within this category.

8. Most importantly, many neoconservatives became outraged by what they perceived to be the New Left's stark anti-Americanism and support for communism. In essence, what the neoconservatives were alienated by was the generational gap between themselves and those on the New Left, plus the radical politics of the New Left.

9. According to Herbert Hill, the degree of anti-Semitism by African Americans during the conflict was often overstated. As Hill notes, teachers' union president Albert Shanker was central in using anti-Semitism as a defensive response to the demands made by the African American parents. At one point Shanker circulated an anti-Semitic leaflet that was supposedly produced by an African American community group; after further investigation the community organization was found to be fictitious. While African Americans are certainly not immune from expressing anti-Semitic sentiments, closer examination of the conflict revealed that Shanker's motive for raising the anti-Semitism issue was to exacerbate existing tensions between African Americans and Jews in the city, thereby building support for the union from the Jewish union members and Jewish organizations (Hill 1998: 284–285).

10. Staub points out that the invoking of his pathological youth was used by Podhoretz as a rhetorical tool to deflect criticism that he was degrading the earnest efforts by white liberals in fighting racism. By exposing his life Podhoretz attempted to build sympathy for his hatred by showing, as Staub notes, "that little Norman had been a *nebbish*, bullied, terrorized,

and cursed, forced to wear scratchy clothes and eat spinach soup.... He was not likable, nor was intended to be." Furthermore, the explicitness that Podhoretz revealed in the article effectively obfuscated the explicit anti-left and anti-black ideology of his argument.

11. Other Jewish neoconservatives also expanded on the "racial liberalism equals white guilt" argument. In time, many non-Jewish conservatives also found this idea enticing, and began to deploy this line of argumentation as reasoning for their opposition to racial initiatives put forth by the liberal-left.

12. Ironically, almost twenty years after publishing the book Glazer shifted his position on affirmative action, stating that the intransigence of racism and discrimination in American society made him see the importance of such programs. In the March 27, 1998 issue of *The New Republic* Glazer wrote: "I believe the main reason we have to continue racial preferences for blacks are first, because this country has a special obligation to blacks that has not been fully discharged...and second, because strict application of the principle of qualification would send a message of despair to many blacks, a message that the nation is indifferent to their difficulties and problems." Nathan Glazer, "In Defense of Preference," *The New Republic*, vol. 218, no. 14, pp. 18–25.

13. More recently, African American conservatives have also articulated this line of reasoning. Shelby Steele launched his career with his 1991 book, *The Content of Our Character*, in which this idea was prominently featured. Yale Law professor Stephen Carter also touched upon this idea with his "best black" thesis in his book, *Reflections of an Affirmative Action Baby* (1991).

On the other hand, some have pointed to the neoconservatives' position on affirmative action as being one of the main factors in the elevation of tensions between African Americans and Jews. This tension has even surfaced between some African American conservatives and Jewish neoconservatives. When African American economist Glen Loury announced at the inaugural session of the International Conservative Congress that he was beginning to rethink his position on affirmative action, a heated exchange took place between him and some of the neoconservatives.

At one of the panels Loury stated he believed government action was needed for help in integrating schools and police forces. Decter, Midge expressed her displeasure with his opinion and then her husband, Norman Podhoretz, took his turn by aggressively pointing his finger at Loury and exclaiming, "I much prefer the old Glenn Loury to the new one." When Podhoretz accused Loury of being disingenuous, shouting, "You were one of the most eloquent critics of affirmative action [and] I'm offended by your refusal to see that!" Loury responded in kind by shouting back,

"Those are my people going down the sewer hole with your no-programs" (Heilbrunn 1997: 18). Also, in 1998 when the University of California at Berkeley turned away 800 African American applicants who had 4.0 grade point averages and scores of at least 1200 in the Scholastic Aptitude Test (SAT) Loury responded by exclaiming, "Is the sole measure of merit or worth the performance on these tests? Is there no value at all to racial diversity?" (Holmes 1998: 5).

14. Decter and her husband Podhoretz have both left their marks on the subject of homosexuality. Decter's *Commentary* article, "Boys on the Beach" (1980), raised eyebrows by conjuring up not only every stereotype about gay men but, as Gary Dorrien notes, "presenting gay men as self-loathing, self-obsessed, self-abusing, neurotics bound only by a 'common and mutual loathing of the flesh.'" Podhoretz, upset at what he felt was the undeserved sympathy given to AIDS victims, grumbled that the victims of the disease were "men who bugger and are buggered by dozen or even hundreds of other men every year" (Dorrien 1993: 194).

15. See Alvin Gouldner, *The Future of Intellectuals and The Rise of The New Class* (New York: Macmillan Press, 1979), "Gouldner's Theory of Intellectuals as a Flawed Universal Class" by Ivan Szelenyi in *Theory and Society*, vol. 11, no. 6, November 1982, pp. 779–798, "The Three Waves of New Class Theories" by Ivan Szelenyi and Bill Martin in *Theory and Society*, vol. 17, no. 5, September 1988, pp. 645–667, "Towards a Theory of Intellectuals and Politics" by Jerome Karabel in *Theory and Society*, vol. 25, no. 2, April 1996, pp. 205–233, "The Sociology of Intellectuals" by Charles Kurzman and Lynn Owens in *Annual Review of Sociology*, vol. 28, 2002, pp. 63–90.

16. See Smith (1991) and Lieberman (2000) for excellent accounts of how conservative think tanks have made a major impact in national discourse using the media. Another book worth mentioning is *No Mercy: How Conservative Think Tanks and Foundations Changed America's Social Agenda* (Stefancic and Delgado 1996) in which they examine the role conservative think tanks have played in shifting the social agenda to the right.

17. For works that examine the emergence of social science and the political context in which this emergence took place see Alice O' Conner, *Social Science For What?: Philanthropy and the Social Question in a World Turned Right Side Up* (New York: Russell Sage Publications, 2007), David Paul Haney, *The Americanization of Social Science: Intellectuals and Public Responsibility in the Postwar United States* (Philadelphia: Temple University Press, 2008), "A History of Intellectuals and the Demise of the New Class Academics and the U.S. Government in the 1960s" by Eleanor Townsley in *Theory and Society*, vol. 29, no. 6, December 2000, pp. 739–784.

18. Although it has been assumed that Schlafly single handedly defeated the passage of the ERA, in reality Schlafly teamed with North Carolina Republican Senator Sam Ervin to mobilize the anti-ERA forces.

19. The impact the Briggs initiative had on mobilizing the gay conservative community was not lost on one of the founders of the organization: "Log Cabin Los Angeles can thank State Assemblyman John Briggs for getting our club formed.... His initiative...brought more gay and lesbian Republicans out of the closet than anything to date" (Tafel 1999).

20. Although there is some dispute over the exact number of members of the CWA, the organization is still considered quite large. According to organizational figures, CWA supposedly has over half a million women as members, making it not only the largest conservative women's organization but the largest women's organization of any kind. CWA stands out among the various fundamentalist organizations in that it has expanded its appeal beyond fundamentalists and unlike other fundamentalist groups it specifically shored up its grassroots base by targeting local women's prayer and bible groups (Wilcox 2000: 65).

21. According to William Martin, Falwell had been positioning himself for a leadership position for quite some time. Falwell had made his desires clear to several New Right operatives, so when the opportunity presented itself New Righters Paul Weyrich, Howard Phillips, and Ed McAteer, met with the eager preacher in Lynchburg to hammer out the details. It was Weyrich who inadvertently stumbled across the name Moral Majority for the organization. In his pitch to Falwell, Weyrich stated, "Out there is what one might call a moral majority." Falwell liked the statement so much that he decided on the spot to name the organization the Moral Majority (Martin 1996: 199–205).

22. For example, according to Falwell, at the heart of the feminist movement were women who were "bored with life" and were living in "disobedience to God's laws." As Falwell saw it, not all the women involved with the movement were flaming radicals, instead there were some who were "misinformed" or "lonely." These women were really repressed housewives, helpmates, and mothers whose passion for their "jobs" had been snuffed out by husbands who gave them and their children very little attention at home. To Falwell the Equal Rights Movement was a "definite violation of holy Scripture" because it went against the grain of Ephesians 5:23 that stated husbands were the heads of wives. Falwell felt that there was no need for an ERA movement, instead what was needed was for society to remember women's worth. Although, as Falwell noted, women had been labeled the "weaker vessel" in the scripture, women still possessed plenty of value. Or as Falwell stated, "Because a woman is weaker does not mean that she is less important." On the issue of gay

rights Falwell was just as caustic. In his mind any recognition of gay equality would launch America "under the same hand of judgment as Sodom and Gomorrah" (Falwell 1980: 150–151, 253).

23. The investigation was spurred on by the actions of civil rights and public law organizations that claimed that various independent Christian schools were in violation of racial discrimination. At the time many of the Christian independent schools had very small enrollments of minority children, and previous history had illustrated that one of the main factors behind the emergence of these schools was white parents' desires to avoid sending their children to desegregated schools.

24. To many conservatives, Carter's signing of the Salt Treaty with the Soviet Union was a major mistake. As those on the Right saw it, the United States needed to expand not reduce its military power, especially since the Soviets appeared to be showing no signs of becoming less of a threat to the nation and the world.

REFERENCES

Ansell, Amy Elizabeth. *New Right, New Racism: Race and Reaction in the United States and Britain.* New York: New York University Press, 1997.

———. "The Color of America's Culture Wars." In *Unraveling the Right: The New Conservatism in American Politics.* Ed. Amy E. Ansell. Boulder, CO: Westview Press, 1998.

Barnes, Fred. "InventaNegro, INC." *The New Republic*, April 15, 1985.

Berlet, Chip. "Following the Threads." In *Unraveling the Right.* Ed. Amy Ansell. Boulder, CO: Westview Press, 1998.

Carter, Stephen. *Reflections of an Affirmative Action Baby.* New York, NY: Basic Books, 1991.

Decter, Midge. *The New Chastity and Other Arguments Against Women's Liberation.* New York: Coward, McCann & Geoghegan, 1972.

———. "Boys on the Beach." *Commentary*, 1980.

———. *An Old Wife's Tale: My Seven Decades in Love and War.* New York: Regan Books, 2001.

Diamond, Sara. *Roads to Dominion: Right-Wing Movements and Political Power in the United States.* New York: The Guilford Press, 1995.

Dorrien, Gary. *The Neoconservative Mind: Politics, Culture, and the War of Ideology.* Philadelphia, PA: Temple University Press, 1993.

———. "Inventing an American Conservatism: The Neoconservative Episode." In *Unraveling the Right.* Ed. Amy Ansell. Boulder, CO: Westview Press, 1998.

Edsall, Thomas Byrne, and Mary D. Edsall. *Chain Reaction: The Impact of Race, Rights, and Taxes on American Politics.* New York: W. W. Norton, 1992.

Faludi, Susan. *Backlash: The Undeclared War Against American Women.* New York: Crown Publishers, 1991.

Falwell, Jerry. *Listen, America!* New York: Doubleday, 1980.

Felsenthal, Carol. *The Sweetheart of the Silent Majority: The Biography of Phyllis Schlafly.* New York: Doubleday, 1981.

Genovese, Eugene. *The Southern Tradition: The Achievement and Limitations of an American Conservatism.* Cambridge, MA: Harvard University Press, 1994.

Gerson, Mark. *The Neoconservative Vision: From the Cold War to the Culture Wars.* Lanham, MD: Madison Books, 1996.

Glazer, Nathan. *Affrimative Discrmination: Ethnic Inequality and Public Policy.* Cambridge, MA: Harvard University Press, 1975.

Goldfarb, Jeffrey. *The Cynical Society: The Culture of Politics and the Politics of Culture in American Life.* Chicago, IL: The University of Chicago Press, 1991.

Gottfried, Paul. *The Conservative Movement.* Rev. ed. New York: Twayne Publishers, 1993.

Gouldner, Alvin. *The Future of Intellectuals and the Rise of the New Class.* New York: Macmillan Press, 1979.

Gramsci, Antonio. *An Antonio Gramsci Reader: Selected Writings, 1916–1935.* Ed. David Forgacs. New York: Schocken Books, 1988.

Greenberg, Stanley B. *Middle Class Dreams: The Politics and Power of the New American Majority.* New Haven, CT: Yale University, 1996.

Harries, Owen. "A Primer for Polemicists." *Commentary,* September 1984: 58.

Heilbrunn, Jacob. "Con Games." *The New Republic,* October 20, 1997: 18.

Hill, Herbert. "Black-Jewish Conflict in the Labor Context." In *African Americans and Jews in the Twentieth Century: Studies in Convergence and Conflict.* Eds. V.P. Franklin, et al. Columbia: University of Missouri Press, 1998.

Himmelstein, Jerome. *To the Right: The Transformation of American Conservatism.* Berkeley: The University of California Press, 1990.

Hodgson, Godgfrey. *The World Turned Right Side Up: A History of the Conservative Ascendancy in America.* Boston, MA: Mariner Books, 1997.

Holmes, Steven A. "Re-Rethinking Affirmative Action." *The New York Times,* April 5, 1998: 5.

Jeansonne, Glen. *Gerald L.K. Smith: The Minister of Hate.* New Haven, CT: Yale University Press, 1988.

King, Lawerence Peter. *Theories of the New Class: Intellectuals and Power.* Minneapolis: University of Minnesota Press, 2004.

Kintz, Linda. *Between Jesus and the Market: The Emotions That Matter in Right-Wing America.* Durham, NC: Duke University Press, 1997.

Kristol, Irving. *Neoconservatism: The Autobiography of an Idea.* New York: The Free Press, 1995.

Lieberman, Trudy. *Slanting the Story: The Forces That Shape the News.* New York: The New Press, 2000.

Luker, Kristen. *Abortion & the Politics of Motherhood.* Berkeley: The University of California Press, 1984.

Martin, William. *With God on Our Side: The Rise of the Religious Right in America*. New York: Broadway Books, 1996.

Mazzocco, Philip J. *The Psychology of Racial Colorblindness: A Critical Review*. New York: Palgarve Macmillan, 2017.

McGirr, Lisa. *Suburban Warriors: The Origins of the New American Right*. Princeton, NJ: Princeton University Press, 2001.

O'Reilly, Kenneth. *Nixon's Piano: Presidents and Racial Politics from Washington to Clinton*. New York: The Free Press, 1995.

Paget, Karen M. "Lessons of Right-Wing Philanthropy." *The American Prospect*, September–October 1998.

Paige, Connie. "Watch on the Right: The Amazing Rise of Beverly LaHaye." *Ms Magazine*, February 1987: 26.

Peele, Gillian. *Revival and Reaction: The Right in Contemporary America*. New York: Oxford University Press, 1984.

Smith, James A. *The Idea Brokers: Think Tanks and the Rise of the New Policy Elite*. New York: The Free Press, 1991.

Sowell, Thomas. "Politics and Opportunity: The Background." In *The Fairmont Papers: Black Alternatives Conference December 1980*. San Francisco, CA: Institute for Contemporary Studies, 1980.

Staub, Michael E. "'Negroes Are Not Jews': Race, Holocaust Consciousness, and the Rise of Jewish Neoconservatism." *Radical History Review*, vol. 75, 1999: 3–27.

Steele, Shelby. *The Content of Our Character: A New Vision of Race in America*. New York: Harper Collins, 1991.

Stefancic, Jean, and Richard Delgado. *No Mercy: How Conservative Think Tanks and Foundations Changed America's Social Agenda*. Philadelphia, PA: Temple University Press, 1996.

Steinfels, Peter. *The Neoconservatives: Men Who Are Changing America's Politics*. New York: Simon and Schuster, 1979.

Tafel, Richard. *Party Crasher: A Gay Republican Challenges Politics as Usual*. New York: Simon and Schuster, 1999.

Viguerie, Richard A. *The New Right: We're Ready to Lead*. Falls Church, VA: Caroline House Publishers, 1981.

Wald, Alan M. *The New York Intellectuals: The Rise and Decline of the Anti-Stalinist Left from the 1930s to the 1980s*. Chapel Hill: The University of North Carolina Press, 1987.

Weyrich, Paul. "Blue Collar or Blue Blood?: The New Right Compared with the Old Right." In *The New Right Papers*. Ed. Robert W. Whitaker. New York: St. Martin's Press, 1982.

White, Richard. *"It's Your Misfortune and None of My Own": A History of the American West*. Norman: University of Oklahoma Press, 1991.

Wilcox, Clyde. *Onward Christian Soldiers: The Religious Right in American Politics*. 2nd ed. Boulder, CO: Westview Press, 2000.

CHAPTER 4

Stop the Genocide! Save the Race: The Anti-abortion Movement Within the African American Community

Prominent retired neurosurgeon Benjamin Carson became as one conservative publication called him a "retired neurosurgeon-turned-conservative-rock star" (Chumley 2014). Carson captured the hearts and minds of fellow conservatives with the speech he gave as the keynote speaker at the National Prayer Breakfast. For the twenty seven minutes that Carson spoke he managed to launch an attack on the evils of political correctness, provide a backhand criticism of President Obama's Affordable Care Act with the president in attendance, advocate for placing education as a top priority, making a belief in God the central purpose of one's life, and illustrating that America is the land where Horatio Alger type dreams can come true by invoking his own pull yourself up from your bootstraps life narrative as an example. Carson's star is shining brightly within conservative circles, his books sell very well among conservatives, and he has a regular column in the conservative newspaper *Washington Times*. Among the many subjects he writes about abortion is one of them and as expected Carson is not an advocate for the procedure.

My entire professional life has been devoted to saving and enhancing lives. Thus, the thought of abortion for the sake of convenience does not appeal to me (Carson 2014).

Ben Carson's public denunciation of legalized abortion only represents the tip of the iceberg of anti-abortion sentiments among African Americans.[1] The pro-life or anti-abortion movement among African Americans has been in operation for over a quarter of a century, but

© The Author(s) 2018
L. G. Prisock, *African Americans in Conservative Movements*,
https://doi.org/10.1007/978-3-319-89351-8_4

because this movement's history has fallen under the radar of both the mainstream media and the academy, the anti-abortion activism of African Americans has gone largely unnoticed. Most of the media and academic focus has been on the intellectual and political articulations of black conservatism, and very little attention has been paid to how black conservatism is expressed at the community level through social movements. I argue in this and the following chapter that an examination of African American conservative social movements provides a much clearer picture of the diversity within black conservatism as a whole.[2] In addition, I also argue that within this sector the focus placed on race and racism within the various movements discourses illustrates the inescapability of race.

This chapter begins by unearthing some of the more important figures and organizations in the African American anti-abortion movement. Throughout my discussion, I emphasize how the movement ironically opens up a space for women leaders to emerge as organic spokespeople for a socially conservative agenda on abortion and black women's reproductive rights. As progressive economist Julianne Malveaux pointed out in an article over two decades ago, the most vocal and prominent representatives of black conservatism have tended to be men (Malveaux 1991). The black conservative intellectual and political realms are primarily male domains with only a sprinkle of visible African American women.[3] One of the benefits of examining in much greater depth the conservatism present at the grassroots level is that this is precisely where black female leaders come more clearly into view.

Women such as Milwaukee activist Annette "Polly" Williams, a pivotal figure in the African American school choice movement, who I examine in the next chapter, and Los Angeles resident Ezola Foster, known for her community activism with her organization Black Americans For Family Values, function very much as organic intellectuals articulating a social conservatism on issues related to education, economics, and politics. Foster was even selected by Pat Buchanan to be his running mate in the 2000 presidential elections. The social movements arena is thus the one in which black conservative women can thrive and occupy leadership roles. To emphasize this point, I begin my discussion with an account of three of the more prominent black women leaders who have been able to rise to national prominence, partly due to their work on behalf of the anti-abortion movement. These three women help to demonstrate how a black conservatism from the bottom up has enabled them to carve out successfully a place for themselves in the public sphere—in the popular press and government administrations—spaces usually reserved for the white, male. "traditional intellectuals" of the liberal state.

Founded also by women, some of the more prominent, black, pro-life organizations, such as the African Americans for Life Alliance and Black Americans for Life (BAL), also reflect this point of the centrality of black female leaders and founders to the organizational life of the movement. In my discussion of black anti-abortion organizations, I also emphasize their adoption of organizing practises typically associated with civil rights organizations and the liberal left. African American social movement organizations both inherit and borrow a strategy used often by their white, conservative, grassroots counterparts to blur the line between conservative theory and praxis.[4] While operating in direct opposition to liberal and progressive activists and organizations of the sixties and seventies, various segments in the conservative movement often re-deploy tactics and language used in the sixties and seventies by the liberal left. This co-opting of more liberal, left, and progressive actions and language is also true for African American social movement organizations. For example, Reverend Jimmy Hunter's Life Education and Resources Network (L.E.A.R.N. INC.) has been particularly adept at "borrowing" from the structure of civil rights organizations to create a network with broad branches of outreach. In the discussion that follows, I will illustrate how this blurring is achieved by African American pro-life organizations through the two processes I identify as borrowing and inheriting.

Another goal of this chapter is to use the social movement concept of "framing" to analyze how socially conservative discourses find an audience among black Americans where they stake their claims as natural common sense. By framing I am referring to the manner in which events taking place in our social world are interpreted and presented by an individual or individuals within a social movement to provide meaning and identification to the audience they are communicating with. As sociologist David Snow states, "By rendering events or occurrences meaningful, frames function to organize experience and guide action, whether individual or collective" (Snow et al. 1986: 464).

In the bulk of this chapter, I focus on discourse analysis in order to demonstrate how the black pro-life movement has been successful in linking its conservative social agenda with a sometimes radical, racial critique. It should be noted that the attention African American conservatives have received from other blacks to their cause comes from the inclusion of a radical, racial critique and not from the adherence to a color-blind philosophy, At the grassroots level of the black anti-abortion movement, pro-life activists combine a conservative gender politics with a radical, racialized critique in compelling ways. Without complex theories of intersectionality and multiple jeopardy at their disposal,[5] black pro-lifers layer together inherited gender and race discourses familiar to the black community, to naturalize and rationalize their anti-abortion agenda as essential to the race's survival. Tying the fight against abortion to such issues as slavery, legal cases such as Dred Scott, attempts at population control and examples of the medical abuse of African Americans, black pro-lifers draw on central, inherited themes of racism, victimization, and conspiracy. These give their ideological claims not only the feel of common sense, but also, the emotional charge of historical memory. My primary goal in this analysis of pro-life discourse is to demonstrate how the movement, as a conservative grassroots initiative from within the black community, garners some support and secures a certain amount of hegemony in the black community as a social movement, in ways that contrast with the more atomized and isolated positions of the intellectuals and politicians cultivated by the broader white conservative movement.

At times, the praxis of the African American pro-life movement comes into conflict with both white and black conservative ideals. The manner in which black pro-life activists address racial issues operates in stark contrast to the black conservative intellectuals and politicians who claim that racism in American society has abated. In contrast, as the bulk of my discussion in this chapter shows, racism remains a central tool in the organizing and mobilizing discourse of black pro-life activists. Given this ideological reality, the chapter ends with a discussion of the relationship between African American pro-lifers and their white counterparts, their history showing that this relationship has, at times, been strained, as black conservative activists complain about a lack of racial sensitivity on the part of some white conservatives.

CONSERVATIVE WOMEN AS BLACK ORGANIC INTELLECTUALS

Although African American conservative men like Alan Keyes, Dr. Benjamin Carson, the Reverend Johnny Hunter, and other black male conservative ministers have garnered significant amounts of media coverage for their opposition to abortion, one of the most interesting characteristics of the African American pro-life movement is the active and dominant roles African American women occupy. This is one of a few areas where a number of African American conservative women have a significant profile, especially in leadership positions. Mildred Jefferson has been identified as the matriarch of the African American pro-life movement, significant for both her contributions to the anti-abortion activism of African Americans and her actions within the larger, predominately white, anti-abortion movement. Jefferson is the epitome of a pioneer with her being the first in many arenas. For example, among her accomplishments, she was the first African American woman to graduate from Harvard's Medical School, the first woman to intern at Boston City Hospital, the first female surgeon at the Boston University Medical Center, then went on to become an assistant professor of surgery at Boston University's School of Medicine, and the first woman to be elected to membership of the prestigious Boston Surgical Society (Culture of Life Studies 2016). Jefferson was once the vice president of the Massachusetts Citizens for Life organization and former president of the larger National Right To Life Committee, an organization she helped to found. Jefferson is one of the few African American anti-abortion activists to be recognized also as a leader of the national right to life movement (Paige 1983: 16–17). She gained attention inside and outside of the movement not only for her accomplishments, but also, for the fact that she is an African American Protestant in a movement where whites and Catholics have a strong presence.

Mildred Jefferson's status as a woman and an African American allowed her to deflect charges of anti-feminism and racism from critics of the organization during her tenure at the National Right To Life Committee. She represented herself to the media as proof of the organization's tradition of placing non-Catholics in leadership positions, asserting strongly: "The Catholic Church is not leading the Right To Life Committee, I am" (Paige 1983: 85). Jefferson has also been credited with helping the Right To Life Committee make connections with other individuals and organizations within the larger conservative movement, including connections with figures such as New Right leader Paul Weyrich. In 1994, Jefferson was unsuccessful in her bid to win Senator Ted Kennedy's seat in the US Senate. In spite of this, she positioned herself as a spokesperson for precisely those groups traditionally supportive of the Democrats. Jefferson stated that she ran against Kennedy because, "it is unconscionable that the destiny of minorities and women in this country should be perceived as dependent on the morally bankrupt leadership of this senior Senator of this Commonwealth" (*Association of American Physicians and Surgeons Newsletter* 1994). Jefferson has also linked paths with radical conservative sectors such as the Patriot Movement.[6] In November of 1994, Jefferson spoke at a Patriot meeting in Burlington Massachusetts, where she proceeded to blast the "elite medical profession, liberal feminist group National Organization for Women, and Planned Parenthood for their contributions to the rise in secular humanism" (Berlet and Lyons 2000: 293–294).[7] Jefferson's beliefs in fighting against abortion were driven by the intersectionality of her profession, national, and gender identities:

> I am at once a physician, a citizen, and a woman, and I am not willing to stand aside and allow this concept of expendable human lives to turn this great land of ours into just another exclusive reservation where only the perfect, the privileged, and the planned have the right to live. (Culture of Life Studies 2016)

While Jefferson was one of a few black activists to hold prominence in both the black and white pro-life movements she was not a leader who did not acknowledge the importance of race, in fact the opposite. Jefferson was quite aware of the racial implications of abortion as she stated:

> After 44 million abortions, most people have not noticed that the population descended from the U.S. African slaves, comprising around 12% of the population, make up about 35% of the abortion population. This means that more Americans of African descent have died in the abortion chambers than have died in all the years of slavery and lynchings. (McClarey 2010)

As the above quote illustrates, Mildred Jefferson like other of her conservative black female peers was not colorblind in her activism. Jefferson's beliefs have influenced a diverse range of prominent individuals on the right, from President Ronald Reagan who credited Jefferson as being influential in him becoming an staunch supporter of the anti-abortion movement (Culture of Life Studies 2016), to Kay Cole James, who said she was inspired to become a part of the pro-life movement after hearing Jefferson speak shortly after the Supreme Court ruling in the 1973 Roe v Wade case (Pro-life Action League 2005).

Kay Cole James is another African American woman recognized as an influential figure within the movement. James took up the fight against abortion, among other causes, on behalf of the traditional values movement. James served under President Reagan as a member of the White House Task Force for the Black Family and commissioner of the National Commission on Children. Under President George Bush Sr., James was the Assistant Secretary for Health and Human Services. In addition to serving Presidents Reagan and Bush Sr., James has also served under former Republican governor of Virginia George Allen as Secretary of Health and Human Resources. James has also been the dean of the school of Government at Regent University founded by Christian Right minister Pat Robertson, and a senior fellow at the conservative think tank, Heritage Foundation. James has deep ties with the traditional values movement, serving as a senior vice president of the Family Research Council and on the board of Focus on the Family, an organization founded and headed by influential Christian Right leader James Dobson.[8]

Kay Cole James' approach to organizing on behalf of the fight against abortion came in the form of a moving, personal narrative. She described her introduction to abortion during her time as a volunteer at a crisis pregnancy center in Roanoke, Virginia. As James stated, "that was my first exposure to the issue. I was horrified at what I learned and saw. I knew instinctively that killing an unborn baby was wrong, but I had never studied it as an issue. When I began to read the literature and see the pictures and as I became more educated about the issue, I felt very deeply about it. Something akin to righteous indignation stirred within" (James 1992: 125–126). James worked in President George H. Bush's administration, was the director of the United States Office of Personal and Management from 2001 to 2005 under President George W. Bush, and was the former President of one of the major African American anti-abortion organizations, Black Americans For Life. Currently, James sits on the board of trustees for the influential conservative think tank The Heritage Foundation and is the founder and President of the Gloucester Institute, a think tank and training organization for young African Americans. Like Jefferson, James understands the relationship between race and abortion as she has stated, that "abortion is a form of discrimination" and "its racist too since it causes the death and dismemberment of black boys and girls more than 270,000 times a year (James 2018). James reasoning for why there is such a high number of abortion among black women has a conspiratorial edge to it as she argues "abortion mills most of which are intentionally place in and close to our communities" (James 2018). The theme of conspiracy is commonly used in the discourse of black pro-lifers, a topic I address in the next section of this chapter.

One of the rising stars of the African American anti-abortion movement is Deborah Day Rica Lipford who is widely known as Dr. Day Gardner. Gardner, a former Ms. Delaware contestant in the 1976 Miss America pageant, went on become involved in various media ventures and entrepreneurial and charitable endeavors. Gardner was at one point the director of Blacks Americans for Life and is presently the founder and President of the National Black Pro-Life Union (NBPLU) and public relations director for National Pro-Life Action Center. In 2002, Gardner also attempted to gain a seat in Maryland's state legislature but her efforts came up short. The National Black Pro-Life Union is somewhat similar to L.E.A.R.N in how it functions. NBPLU is an umbrella organization that acts as a clearinghouse institution that coordinates communications among all African American anti-abortion organizations, thereby aiding in the formation of stronger networks among the different African American pro-life organizations and combining resources between them. Gardner also sits on the board of a number of organizations such as the National Pro-Life Religious Council and is an active member of the American Center for Law and Justice (ACLJ).[9] The ACLJ is a non-profit public interest law firm founded in 1990 by the Rev Pat Robertson and serves as the conservative counter to the American Civil Liberties Union. Gardner has been an outspoken critic of President Obama for his stance toward abortion:

> Barak Obama wants all of us to believe that he cares about racial discrimination and the black family, yet the man who wants to be President will not talk about the racism of abortion. He stands by silent—unusually mute—as abortion facilities are stealthily planted in black neighborhoods to kill black children. Mr. Obama has never poured out one eloquent word to shield the body of even one of the 1500 black babies who are violently and gruesomely dismembered and killed by abortion each and every day. (Gardner 2008)[10]

Dr. Gardner passion for being an anti-abortion activist is derived from her recognition of the stigma society has placed on African Americans, especially African American children and women. When an abortion provider in North Carolina was caught on camera saying to pro-life activists that they should "adopt one of those ugly black babies" to Gardner, it was another example of black children "thought of as being worthless right from the very start" and society's desire to "limit the growth of the black population" (McCarthy 2012).

Another African American woman who is leaving her mark within the anti-abortion movement is Dr. Alveda King. King is the niece of Dr. Martin Luther King Jr., and she sees the pro-life movement as the logical continuation of the civil rights movement. Dr. King has had two previous abortions during her lifetime and those experiences have influenced her participation in the Silent No More Awareness campaign, a campaign where King shares her experience of having the abortions and coming to grips with her decision through the spiritual work of seeking forgiveness from God. A former college professor and state representative in the Georgia state House of representatives, King currently serves as the Pastoral Associate and Director of African American outreach for the Priests for Life and Gospels for Life organization.

Dr. King is also the author of two books, one entitled, *How Can the Dream Survive If We Murder The Children?*, and founder of the faith-based organization King for Life (KFL), the main purpose of which is to "enrich the lives of people spiritually, economically, intellectually, and socially."[11] The KFL platform is a hodgepodge of causes, such as working with various pro-life organizations, encouraging and assisting gang members to leave their gangs, helping released convicts become integrated back into society, helping to start a racial reconciliation movement, and conducting seminars that help people build strong families.[12] There is a sense of irony here in the fact that King utilizes her heralded uncle's image and fame as a primary method of bolstering her own visibility, for the individuals and movements Alveda King has aligned herself with are in total contrast with the politics of her famous uncle Dr. Martin Luther Jr. Alveda King spoke out in favor of both California's Proposition 8 and Florida's Proposition 2, which outlawed the legal recognition by those states of gay marriage. During the primaries King initially supported Kansas Senator Sam Brownback for the Republican Party Presidential nomination and eventually endorsed John McCain's candidacy, going so far as to appear in an ad campaign called "Vote MLK Values," produced by a conservative organization that sought to convince African Americans to vote against then candidate Obama. King is also a senior fellow at the conservative Alexis de Tocqueville Institute think tank.[13]

A fifth and highly influential figure is Star Parker, a veteran conservative activist best known for her anti-welfare activism. Parker has been most effective at linking the issue of abortion to her views on welfare. She strongly advocates abolishing the welfare system and is against a woman having an abortion even in cases of rape or incest (Murakami 1995: B1). Parker also has organizational support. She founded and runs the Coalition on Urban Affairs, an African American grassroots organization that advocates for popular conservative causes such as school vouchers, enterprise zones, stressing the use of self-help measures, and bringing moral restoration to society. Parker has worked extensively with other grassroots conservative organizations such as the Traditional Values Coalition headed by Louis Shelton. In fact, Parker credits the Traditional Values Coalition for her involvement in politics, which began around 1991 with her participation in the movement to protest the Los Angeles School Board's decision to allow the distribution of condoms in Los Angeles's public schools (Parker 1997: 7). She has also worked closely with the Christian Coalition to recruit more African Americans into the organization and to promote the organization's mission within the African American community. Parker has a strong following among white conservatives; radio commentator Rush Limbaugh featured her on his radio show after seeing Parker on television speaking at a press conference held for African American conservatives. In addition to the guest appearance on Limbaugh's show, Parker also garnered an invitation to speak at a forum hosted by Pat Buchanan after his sister Bay read a profile of Parker in *The Washington Times* (Parker 1997: 4).

In her autobiography entitled, *Pimps, Whores, and Welfare Brats*, Parker presents herself as the quintessential female version of Horatio Alger, pulling herself up from the culture of poverty and onto the road of righteousness. Parker documents her transformation from being an out of control young woman on welfare, experimenting with drugs and having casual sex that led to 4 abortions, to becoming a woman who, through finding the religious and entrepreneurial spirit, was able to get herself off of welfare.[14] In her confessional, autobiographical style, Parker readily embraces one of the worst stereotypes of African American women, that of the welfare queen. As Rickie Solinger states, for whites, the welfare queen icon symbolized their frustrations and anxieties about race and the social consequences of the civil rights movement.

The iconic Welfare Queen may have been, first of all, an expression of white America's anger about race, about the successes and continuing threats of the civil rights movement. By the early 1970's, many white Americans believed that the government had done enough. New laws, policies, and Supreme Court decisions had acknowledged and ameliorated historical racial prejudice in the United States, many argued. If, after all this accommodation, a growing number of mothers and children were still claiming need, it made sense to assume these people were, one way or another, cheating. (Solinger 2001: 166)

Star Parker's open embrace of the welfare queen icon has garnered her significant attention from various white conservative sectors. When asked the reason for her popularity among white conservatives, Parker responded, "One of the reasons I am so popular with those Republican people is that I validate some of the things they have been thinking for a long time now: Welfare is a waste" (Herrmann 1994: 23).[15]

Reverend Johnny Hunter is one of the few African American males to command prominence and status both inside and outside of the anti-abortion movement.[16] Hunter is the President of Global Life and Family Mission, a ministry that promotes the ideas of traditional values, racial rapport, and speaking in the interest of children worldwide. Hunter is also the founder of the largest African American anti-abortion organization, L.E.A.R.N. A self-proclaimed activist of the civil rights movement Hunter attributed his own fighting against abortion to the catalyst of his wife's arrest outside of an abortion clinic in Buffalo two days before Christmas:

I received a call that day from the Holy Spirit and He just asked one question: 'With whom is God most pleased?' Is God most pleased with ministers like me who could preach a sermon on how the wise men warned Jesus?... Or is He more pleased with those few women from our church who said, 'No child should die two days before Christmas?' (Benson 2001: 3)

Strikingly, in his account, Hunter points to the voices of women in his church from whom he draws moral leadership on the abortion issue.

The realm of reproductive politics has provided conservative black women with a naturalized position from which to speak, as mothers, medical professionals, young women gone astray, on behalf of a socially conservative agenda within the movement. Using both the skills of political organizers and the personal touch provided by autobiographical narratives and confessional accounts, black, conservative female leaders are a key component in the pro-lifers' attempts to present the fight against abortion as a cause consistent with the African American community's central needs and concerns. Women such as Mildred Jefferson, Kay Cole James, and Star Parker personify in a very immediate manner, with their gendered bodies as much as their conservative viewpoints, the potential impact of abortion as a larger social and moral issue for the women and children of the black community.

STRATEGIC BORROWING TO CREATE AN ORGANIZATIONAL FRAMEWORK

There are a number of organizations in operation within the African American anti-abortion movement. They vary by size and scope, with names such as African Americans for Life, Association of Black Catholics Against Abortion, African American Association for the Preservation of Life and Family, and International Black Women's Network. The exact number of African American anti-abortion organizations is still unknown, but there are indications that the numbers are growing as more African Americans are being mobilized to fight against the availability of abortion. The media coverage given to the larger, predominately white, mainstream pro-life organizations, such as Randall Terry's Operation Rescue, often overshadows the contributions African American pro-life organizations make to the pro-life movement.

This section examines several of the more prominent and influential organizations within the African American pro-life movement. The African American Life Alliance is a non-profit organization that was founded in 1991 by Washington, DC native Paulette Roseboro, a single mother of two daughters who quit her job in the federal government to pursue anti-abortion activism full time. The operational base for the organization is Glenn Dale, Maryland, with a specific focus on the Baltimore and Washington, DC areas. The organization states that its mission is to "educate the black community about how sexual promiscuity and illicit moral activities have invaded our communities and are eroding our families, organizations, schools, and churches" (http://www.aala.org). In addition to focusing on abortion, the organization also focuses on other traditional values, preaching abstinence to youth, promoting creationism in schools, and advocating traditional gender roles for men and women. The information disseminated by the organization is heavily couched within the context of fundamentalist readings of the Bible. The organization's main publication is its journal *Life Drum*, which covers a wide range of topics. In the 1998 winter issue, for example, the range of topics included articles on former president Bill Clinton's veto of a bill that would have banned partial-birth abortion, the racist legacy of Planned Parenthood founder Margaret Sanger, and an article speculating on the potential profits abortion providers expected to receive from fetal tissue research.

Besides disseminating information, The African American Life Alliance also performs grassroots activities in the African American community by offering counseling to pregnant women, holding seminars, and providing speakers to churches, community centers, and historically black colleges and universities through its speakers bureau.[17] The hallmark of this organization was its collaboration with Rev. Johnny Hunter's L.E.A.R.N to mobilize supporters to participate in the "Say So" March of October 1999. The name of the march comes from the motto, "If you love Children, say so." One of the first major public actions by the African American anti-abortion movement, the three-day march originated in Newark, New Jersey, winding its way through black neighborhoods in such cities as Philadelphia and Baltimore, and ending at the Supreme Court in Washington, DC where marchers placed 1452 roses on the steps of the Supreme Court. According to representatives of the march, the roses were to represent the alleged average number of African American children aborted everyday. The African American Life Alliance also works closely with another African American organization, Blacks for Life.

The Black Americans For Life (BAL) organization was founded in 1986 with Kay Cole James as its initial president. BAL claims to have a membership of over 3000 members and 40 state and local chapters. Black Americans For Life functions as an outreach organization for the National Right To Life Committee. According to James, the organization was born out of a recognition on the part of African American anti-abortion activists of their lack of a viable organization to attract media attention (*Religious News Services* 1994: 63). In addition to giving speeches to audiences at African American churches and community organizations, Black Americans For Life also aims its message at African American college students by hosting informational sessions and film screenings on the campuses of predominately African American colleges and universities (*Religious News Services* 1994: 66). For James, the organization's strong emphasis on placing abortion in a racialized context is vital to mobilizing African Americans to support the organization's anti-abortion agenda. As she states, "Black Americans for Life produces printed materials that address abortion as it relates to the black community.... We feel that Black Americans for Life can reach the black community in ways the traditional prolife movement cannot" (*Religious News Services* 1994: 66).

Although the organization admits whites, it is clear that its leadership positions must be filled by African Americans. As James also stated, "we felt we needed a specifically black organization in order to make our point with the news media and politicians that the prolife movement is strong in the black community" (*Religious News Services* 1994: 66). The mission statement of Black Americans For Life states the organization "supports education, legislation and political candidates that seek to protect those victimized by abortion, infanticide and euthanasia."[18] The cover story of one of the organization's newsletters featured the voting patterns of members of the Congressional Black Caucus on abortion-related issues during the summer and fall of 1999. All thirty-two members of the caucus were given failing grades with the newsletter stating, "the 32 African American U.S. Representatives who are members of the Congressional Black Caucus have, with rare exception, demonstrated anti life and pro-abortion commitments" (*Black Americans for Life Newsletter* 1999: 1). The only African American representative who escaped the organization's wrath was former Republican Oklahoma congressmen J.C. Watts, an African American conservative who holds anti-abortion views.

The organization that appears to be the largest and possesses the most prominence within the movement is the L.E.A.R.N. INC. founded by Rev. Johnny Hunter, who also serves as the organization's national director. It was while attending the African American pro-life planning conference in Houston, Texas that Hunter got the idea to create L.E.A.R.N. INC. For Hunter, it was important that the organization set out as its main goal establishing meaningful connections with African Americans at the grassroots level:

> In reaching the African American community and the traditional black church...the primary goal of LEARN is to facilitate a strong, viable

grassroots network of African American and minority pro-life and pro family advocates who are motivated by their love for Jesus Christ and their
neighbors, and by the devastating impact abortion has on mothers and
their children.[19]

In addition to educating African Americans about the "racist origins of
Planned Parenthood, its founder Margaret Sanger, and the American
Eugenics Movements," the organization also trains activists, produces a
library of written and visual material for dissemination, provides speakers to other organizations through its Speakers Bureau, and strongly
supports a Right to Life Constitutional amendment.[20] The organization
has two main offices, one in Fayetteville, North Carolina and the other
in Houston Texas. It also claims to have connections with over forty
Christian pro-life organizations run by groups of color.[21]

L.E.A.R.N functions in a unique fashion in that it has an identity
as a separate entity but it also acts as an umbrella organization. It is in
this sense that some aspects of L.E.A.R.N's organizational structure
borrow from and bear a resemblance to the heralded civil rights organization, the Southern Leadership Conference (SCLC). In the same fashion that the SCLC welcomed organizations to become affiliates so too
does L.E.A.R.N, but whereas the SCLC only welcomed organizations,
L.E.A.R.N also allows individuals to become members (Morris 1984:
90). There are other structural similarities between L.E.A.R.N and the
SCLC. According to sociologist Aldon Morris, the SCLC leadership
believed it was in the best interest not to centralize the activities of their
affiliates.

> The SCLC's leaders did not attempt to centralize the activities of its
> affiliates, because it was felt that centralization would stifle local protest.
> Rather, the role of SCLC's affiliates was to organize local movements and
> address grievances salient in local communities. (Morris 1984: 91)

In the same fashion L.E.A.R.N is very careful not to infringe on the
autonomy of its affiliates:

> Each organization or individual that joins the Network remains independ-
> ent. L.E.A.R.N. INC. will help with organizational efforts to facilitate
> incorporation in communities if no similar organization exists. Each organ-
> ization is a voluntary adjunct to the network.[22]

The SCLC also saw itself playing a role in bringing together leaders of different movements to share experiences and resources (Morris 1984: 91). L.E.A.R.N views itself in the same light. At the annual L.E.A.R.N Leadership Conference fellow anti-abortion activists gather to share information, participate in workshops, and "enjoy fellowship with other like-minded Christians who are also fighting the good fight of faith on the front lines of the war against the family."[23] As other conservative organizations have done, L.E.A.R.N's conference also functions as a time when different organizational leaders can gather to evaluate strategies and coordinate new ones. As L.E.A.R.N's founder and president Rev. Johnny Hunter stated, "the conference is a time to share what is working in our different organizations and to learn what pitfalls to avoid."[24]

L.E.A.R.N's mirroring of the SCLC's organizing strategies and organizational structure represents one important instance where the lines between left and right grassroots politics become blurred through the process of borrowing. While L.E.A.R.N's objectives and agenda are conservative in nature, the organizational structure and strategies are patterned after the liberal Southern Christian Leadership Council. Underscoring this as both an instance of, and an effective strategy for, the blurring of right and left, the Erie County chapter of the SCLC in Alabama bestowed Rev. Hunter with the Martin Luther King Award for his anti-abortion activism.[25]

DISCOURSE AND IDEOLOGY: FRAMING THE RATIONALE AGAINST ABORTION

Since much of the focus on black conservatism has been placed on various black conservative thinkers, their ideas influence how black conservatism is perceived by those outside of this movement. Upon examining the discourse within the black anti-abortion movement, however, I discovered some distinctive differences between these African American, conservative, grassroots activists and their intellectual counterparts. I believe these differences illustrate not merely the complexities and fluidity of black conservatism as a sociopolitical and intellectual formation, but furthermore, the fundamental tensions and contradictions of a movement with both top-down and bottom-up genealogies. Between the more traditional intellectuals and party politicians on the one hand, and the organic activists, and ministers working at the level of the community on the other hand, one finds a fundamentally contradictory discourse of race and racism, and contrasting strategies for the promotion and public dissemination of a socially conservative message and agenda. Why the arguments of African American conservatives engaged in social movements may resonate more with some African Americans than those put forth by conservative African American intellectuals? One reason can be attributed to African American social conservative activists are less likely to demonize the African American poor than their intellectual counterparts. African American social activists will not only criticize the behaviors and choices made by poor African Americans but also acknowledge the struggles they face in society.[26]

For many black pro-lifers, racism is central as a point of analysis in how they articulate and justify their opposition toward abortion. In addition to racism, themes of victimization and conspiracy are also mainstays in the discourse of the black pro-life movement, shaping both the content and the style of their political and social rhetoric. When the discourse of this movement is compared with the discourse of black conservative thinkers, it becomes clear that the rhetorical strategies utilized by participants in the black anti-abortion movement are in opposition to what some black conservative thinkers feel is the appropriate approach for African Americans to articulate grievances. For example, black conservative intellectual Shelby Steele strongly disapproves of the rhetorical approach that has as its foundation what he labels as the "memory of oppression":

> I believe that one of the greatest problems black Americans currently face, one of our greatest barriers to our development in society – is that our memory of oppression has such power, magnitude, depth, and nuance that it constantly drains our best resources into more defenses than is strictly necessary. (Steele 1991: 151)

Steele continues, "Not only does the enemy-memory pull us backward, it also indirectly encourages us to remain victims so as to confirm the power of the enemy we remember and believe in" (Steele 1991: 152). Similarly, John McWhorter believes African Americans overemphasize racism, leading to a situation in which blacks fall into the state of victimhood and, as he sees it, "Victimology, in a word, is a disease" (McWhorter 2001: 29).

Emphasis on America's historical mistreatment of African Americans and the ways racism has victimized black Americans is not only the crux of the various arguments used by black pro-lifers; one could say that it is the raison d'etre of the African American anti-abortion movement. As movement participants see it, they are not only speaking out against a medical procedure they view as immoral but as African Americans they are in the forefront of the battle to protect against the "continued violation" of black bodies. In a paternalistic manner, black pro-lifers see their mission as protecting black women's wombs and the unborn black children within them. The discourse within the African American anti-abortion movement ignores the history of black women's agency and activism around their reproductive rights. Instead, as I will illustrate through an examination of their discourse, the foundation of the black pro-life movement's legitimacy is predicated on portraying black people, and black women in particular, as helpless victims not having the consciousness to act in their own reproductive interests.

It is ironic, but also, understandable why women would emerge in this context as important leaders within the movement. As the very individuals the conservative pro-life agenda aims to act upon and improve, the very vessels or conduits for the legitimation of a common sense notion of black degeneracy, women who have stepped forward as leaders in the movement can embody a narrative of self-improvement and a model for an alternative, conservative, black femininity. This then bolsters the ideological message of the pro-lifers that their positions will benefit the black community at large, as a race and as a people.

Abortion Is Slavery

Of the many arguments put forth by African American pro-life activists, two appear in the literature more frequently than others: The "abortion is analogous to slavery" and the "abortion equals racial genocide" arguments. The linking of abortion to slavery, the "peculiar institution" as labeled by slavery advocate John C. Calhoun, is an argument many in the anti-abortion movement articulate. This argument has found favor with both black and white anti- abortionists. It has a deeper resonance for black pro-lifers because the referencing of historical events such as slavery allows blacks to connect America's past history of defiling black bodies with, as these activists see it, abortion as the modern day version of this continuous, historical phenomenon. For black women, the connection of abortion to slavery touches a tender nerve because "this haunting specter of slavery is real and moving" (Ross 1998: 164). The invoking of slavery for black women dredges up a painful history—the abuse of black women's bodies as they were raped at will by white male slave masters; and the degradation of black women as mothers, utilized as breeders to produce children that commanded a price on the open slave market. The use of racial history in this fashion can for some black women raise alternative issues in competition with protecting their reproductive rights.

A thin text entitled, *Abortion and Slavery* by J.C. Willke, M.D. has been a valuable resource for proponents of this argument. Many of the arguments put forth by Willke in his book are often articulated by various African American anti-abortionists. For example, Willke argues that in the same manner proponents of slavery dehumanized enslaved Africans by referring to them as "property," abortion supporters dehumanize the "unborn children" by referring to them in scientific terms:

> Dehumanization was necessary in order to keep others from sympathizing with them. It is always easier to exploit, injure or kill if those in power feel superior and those beneath are called non-human names. The game of semantics is not new to us.... Why the insistence of the pro-abortionists on dehumanizing an unborn child by calling him a "fetus," an "embryo"? (Willke 1984: 21)

Paulette Roseboro, founder of the African American Life Alliance, made this same point in a speech to a Christian student organization at a community college in Maryland:

> What are some of the misinformation abortion supporters use?... Although scientific evidence proves otherwise, abortion supporters camouflage the humanity of pre-born children behind clinical terms: fetus, zygote. However, just as the clinical term homo sapiens does not separate you or I from our personhood; clinical terms for the pre-born homo sapien should not classify them as property to be disposed of if conceived at an inconvenient time. (Roseboro 1999: 2)

African American pro-lifers also like to point to the alleged similarities between the Supreme Court's 1857 ruling in the Dred Scott case and the 1973 ruling in the Roe v Wade case, as another example of the similarities between slavery and abortion.[27] In particular, they focus on or emphasize the lack of recognition by the legal establishment of the humanity of both slaves of African descent and black fetuses. In an article by activist Reginald Jones, Jones makes reference to the Supreme Court's ruling in the Dred Scott case as being similar to the court's decision in the 1973 Roe v Wade case:

> I've often referred to *Roe v Wade* as Dred Scott II. The 1857 *Scott* decision said that Blacks could never be citizens, that they are only three-fifths human and therefore not deserving of legal protection. The *Roe* decision reduced preborn children to a less than fully human status who did not deserve to be protected by law. (Jones 1999: 3)

The main point of the argument that purports that the Dred Scott and Roe v Wade decisions are similar in scope is that the Supreme Court's sanction of the legality of a particular act does not automatically make the act moral, particularly if the Court's ruling does not recognize the humanity of a specific group. In a document produced by the Blacks For Life organization, Jones reiterated this point:

> "One of the more frequently used arguments to defend abortion goes like this: The United States Supreme Court has settled the issue. Because the Court has ruled that abortion is legal, it must, therefore, be a correct and moral act" (Jones 1999: 3). The following line asks rhetorically, "But where would Blacks be today if that reasoning had not been challenged?"

The document then goes on to do a side by side comparison of the Dred Scott and Roe v Wade cases, using excerpts from the rulings of each case to illustrate the supposed similarities in the logic of both decisions. Within the context of this argument, black pro-lifers validate their actions by claiming their cause is similar to the struggles of those involved in the abolitionist movement.

> The abolitionists were hard working people with nothing to gain and everything to lose; but they knew they were right and they were willing to do whatever it took to outlaw the bondage of another human being. Equally the same for abortion…citizens for the abolition of abortion are hard working people; people with a moral steadfastness and conscience. We have nothing to gain financially but all to gain morally. (Roseboro 1999: 3–4)

While many African American pro-lifers see their actions as leading to a noble cause, opponents have a different perspective. Scholar and activist Loretta Ross cogently points to how black women's reproductive agency gets curtailed by the "abortion is slavery" comparison; this argument manipulatively calls for black women's racial loyalty at the expense of their reproductive rights:

> Equating the denial of abortion rights to slavery is convenient intellectual shorthand, but it leaves Black women vulnerable to manipulation by sexists who believe that our role is either to have babies for the long-awaited black revolution or cease reproducing altogether, to comply with racist assumptions about our "overproduction." (Ross 1998: 164)

While Loretta Ross provides an important insight, her critique still does not address why these arguments may have sway with some African Americans. Any analysis seeking a more sophisticated understanding of what is at stake ideologically in the grassroots' influence of pro-lifers among African Americans must be able to answer this question.

I believe the answer can be found in the concept of common sense, as articulated by social and political theorist Antonio Gramsci. According to Gramsci, individuals possess a variety of "conceptions of the world" that are often in contradiction with each other. These conceptions are imposed or absorbed from the outside world or from the past, and are uncritically accepted and lived. There are elements in common sense that influence people's subordination by making situations of inequality or oppression seem natural and unchangeable. The very essence of common sense is its contradictory nature as there are elements of truth present along with misrepresentations (Gramsci 1988: 421).

This is certainly the case with the manner in which the black pro-life movement frames their issues. Black pro-lifers are hard to dismiss off hand because embedded within their arguments are fragments of truth. On the other hand, black pro-lifers also provide a distorted picture of the realities facing African Americans and African American women by selectively omitting other truths (e.g., black women's history of activism for their reproductive rights). The latter is drowned out by the former when the equating of abortion with slavery resonates so powerfully with African Americans because it appears as common sense. In black pro-lifers' comprehension of the world, the Supreme Court's Roe v

Wade decision becomes the contemporary equal of the court's Dred Scott decision because in both decisions black bodies (the unborn black baby and the African slave) are being legally denied their humanity. The power of Gramsci's concept of common sense as a useful analytic for understanding what black Americans may find so compelling about the pro-life message becomes even clearer in the second dominant argument of the African American pro-life movement, "abortion is racial genocide."

Abortion Is Racial Genocide

Labeling abortion as racial or cultural genocide plays a prominent role in the rhetorical battle waged by those in the black anti-abortion movement. Of all of the arguments espoused by pro-life African Americans, no one argument produces more ambivalence among African Americans toward abortion than the linking of abortion with genocide. This has not been lost on this generation of black anti-abortion activists. In fact, as activist Reginald Jones noted, inserting the word genocide into their discourse has been a vital strategy to the success of the movement:

> We must become as adept as our opponents in their use of evocative words and catch phrases…. Two words that really cause a stir in the Black community are 'conspiracy' and 'genocide.' The community will be more eager to listen when the issue of the abortion movement and its true agenda for us are explained in these terms. (Jones 1999: 3)

The argument that abortion is equivalent to or even a form of racial genocide is very compelling for a number of reasons and, consequently, creates quite a bit of uncertainty toward abortion rights from select sectors of the African American community. First, the racial mistreatment of blacks in America has not only led to a lack of trust between some blacks and the American government, but also, has influenced some blacks to view the various social problems impacting African Americans through a conspiratorial lens. For instance, a 1990 *New York Times*/WCBS poll showed that 63% of African Americans polled thought AIDS was a man-made disease created by the American government to target black communities. When the *San Jose Mercury News* published an expose in August 1996 detailing the possible links between the CIA and the sales of crack cocaine in southern California black neighborhoods, the report regenerated fears among some blacks of another government conspiracy to oppress African Americans. As Bob Law, a black radio talk show host stated, "I'm not sure all these things could be happening by chance.... The latest situation with the CIA is just confirmation for what a lot of my audience believes is going on" (*The Philadelphia Tribune* 1996: 8A).

Second, in invoking genocide black pro-lifers are able to touch on and agitate further underlying fears among some African Americans concerning the vulnerability of the race as a whole—becoming extinct or depopulating as a result of the ravages of racial oppression. For example, during the early twentieth century, when racial violence was committed against African Americans segments of the African American community, particularly black nationalists, called for women to reproduce as a response to racial oppression:

> The opposition to fertility control for women in the 1920's came...from Black nationalist leaders like Marcus Garvey, who believed in increasing the African population in response to racial oppression.... As racism, lynchings, and poverty took their heavy toll on African Americans in the early twentieth century, fears of depopulation arose within a rising Black nationalist movement. These fears produced a shift in the views of African Americans. (Ross 1998: 169)

The abortion is genocide argument was also advocated by Black nationalists of the sixties and early seventies. Interestingly, pro-life African Americans today who espouse this view make no acknowledgment of the argument's nationalist history. In fact, some pro-life African Americans view black nationalism as a form of black racism. And yet, even though the nationalist history of this argument is not openly acknowledged by today's black pro-lifers, it is clear that they did not conceive the argument themselves but rather, have become the inheritors of the argument as it has been passed down from generations of African Americans.

While to some the claim that abortion is akin to genocide is hyperbole, this argument still continues to garner attention within the African American community. This argument's ability to, over time, transcend political boundaries within the black community is an indication of how deep the fear of racial violence runs within the black community. The argument's wide appeal not only gives it the appearance of capturing the reality of African Americans in the United States but for several reasons it also lends the argument the veneer of being common sensical.

First, the conspiratorial angle of the argument is a factor in its reception among some African Americans. Ironically, while this aspect of the argument is one that many pro-life blacks highlight frequently, it is also the angle most disdained by other conservative blacks. Here is an important instance in which the praxis of a particular group of black conservatives clashes with a black conservative theoretical principle. In the now defunct black conservative publication *Headway*, one journalist spoke disapprovingly of black Americans' attraction to conspiracy theories, stating, "Conspiracy theories, coupled with the constant rhetoric of victimization, reinforce the view that black Americans, particularly those living in poverty, are little more than impotent bystanders in their own lives. This is simply not true" (Brown 1996: 27). Although the journalist was very critical of the use of conspiracy theories by blacks, he went on to point out that these theories have a continued attraction among some blacks because, "conspiracies against black Americans do have some historical roots." It is the sliver of truth embedded in the rhetoric put forth by pro-life blacks that makes their arguments hard to dismiss.

Second, the abortion is genocide argument of black pro-lifers is layered, comprised of multiple components that tap into important themes and truths drawn from the actual events of slavery, segregation, disenfranchisement, and dehumanization that can be found throughout US history. As such, and like the argument that abortion repeats practises prevalent during slavery, the racial genocide argument can be very persuasive and forceful irrespective of the consequences it may have for black women. The three most prominent components of pro-lifers' racial genocide discourse are: The problematic racial history of the birth control movement, the historical abuse of African Americans by the medical establishment, and the social disarray of contemporary black inner city communities. Integrated throughout each of these components are the three emotionally resonant themes of racism, victimization, and conspiracy.

In the first key component of the discourse on abortion as racial genocide, as it taps into an inherited form of common sense knowledge African Americans glean from their everyday racial experiences, black pro-lifers often point to the history of Planned Parenthood as one example of larger social forces "conspiring" to eliminate African Americans. Akua Furlow, Executive Director of L.E.A.R.N, referred to the connection Planned Parenthood founder Margaret Sanger had with the eugenicist movement and her views about population control and blacks:

Planned Parenthood started back in 1916 to limit the births of minority people.... If people would just study the documentation they would find that Planned Parenthood was rooted in racism and founded by a white supremacist.... Most of Planned Parenthood's clinics are in minority communities. The language has changed, but the original intent is still the same – to limit the births of minority people. (Pack 1995)

Scholar Dorothy Roberts provides a more nuanced analysis of Margaret Sanger and the birth control movement than the one provided by the black anti-abortionists. Roberts points out that Sanger had reasons similar to those of prominent black leaders such as W.E.B. Du Bois who believed in providing education about conception options to poor blacks. Both Sanger and Du Bois felt that better education around birth control would help poor blacks to have an opportunity to live healthier and more successful lives (Roberts 1997: 80). Sanger's sincere desire to improve poor mothers' health by making birth control accessible to them, and her belief that uncontrolled fertility and not genetics or race was the main cause of the problems these women faced, separated Sanger from her eugenicist colleagues (Roberts 1997: 81). Even with these important observations, Roberts also notes that Sanger still had views that were problematic from a racial standpoint:

Sanger nevertheless promoted two of the most perverse tenets of eugenic thinking: that social problems are caused by reproduction of the socially disadvantaged and that their childbearing should therefore be deterred. In a society marked by racial hierarchy, these principles inevitably produced policies designed to reduce Black women's fertility. (Roberts 1997: 81)

Dorothy Roberts and other scholars also provide analysis that shows that the birth control movement of the early twentieth century was not in total opposition to the interests of African Americans, and that African Americans did mobilize to voice their own health interests within that context (Roberts 1997: 82–86; Ross 1994: 146–147, 150–157). It is important that this history of African Americans' activism on behalf of their reproduction rights gets told. As Roberts states, "It would be misleading to paint a picture" of the birth control movement as being "simply thrust upon an unwilling black population" (Roberts 1997: 82). However, this is exactly the outcome the black anti-abortion movement aims for in its use of this history of Planned Parenthood to support the "abortion is racial genocide" argument.

Black pro-lifers omit black people's agency in this matter for at least two reasons. To acknowledge that African Americans debated among themselves the best approach the community should take regarding family planning, and acted together locally to secure family planning clinics in their communities, challenges the black pro-lifers' claim that African American cultural heritage consists of a monolithic embrace of pronatalism, as expressed in one activist's statement: "When you look at African Americans from a historical standpoint, you do not find abortion as an integral part of our culture" (Pack 1995).[28] Also, by omitting black women's activism from the narrative of black women's fertility history, black pro-lifers reinforce the dichotomy between "black woman as victimized" and "family planning institutions as conspiring victimizer." The claim that abortion is racial genocide becomes common sense in the Gramscian sense when black women's oppression by institutions such as Planned Parenthood seems natural and unchangeable, an inevitable aspect of any woman's attempt to get an abortion.

Alongside the problematic racial history of Planned Parenthood and the birth control movement, the second key component in the abortion is racial genocide argument consists of gesturing more broadly to the historical abuse of African Americans by the American medical establishment at large. African American pro-lifers frequently make references in their literature to the Tuskegee syphilis experiments or the 1939 "Negro Project" carried out by the Birth Control Federation of America organization.[29] To African American pro-lifers, these troubling historical events are evidence that African Americans should look warily toward groups, particularly white health organizations, who claim to be looking after their health interests. In a pamphlet distributed by the Family Assistance Center, a pregnancy crisis center founded by African American pro-life activist Juliette Bartlett Pack, activists warned young African American women of Planned Parenthood's intention "to seduce our community into their ideas of 'family planning' by buying influence with our ministers, doctors, other medical professionals and media outlets" (Brooks Hodge 1997: 26).

In another article, activist Michele Jackson invoked the themes of racism and victimization by referencing the historical mistreatment of African Americans by the medical establishment. In this case, Jackson was using the medical abuses committed on African Americans as justification for the support of informed consent and waiting period legislation.

As black people we ought to be cautious of any group that wants to deny people's access to informed consent and waiting periods before life-altering surgical and chemical procedure. We should recall noteworthy times when American health professionals betrayed the trust and privilege society has given them by irreparably harming innocent citizens. (Jackson 1999: 1)

In another section of the article, Jackson refers to the controversy surrounding the contraceptive Norplant as another example of why it is important that African Americans should fight for informed consent legislation. As Jackson stated, the controversy grew because, "it was alleged that health care professionals did not give women information about the risks of Norplant and the range of alternatives" (Jackson 1999: 1). Concerned with articulating her anti-abortion position as clearly and cogently as possible, Jackson oversimplifies the Norplant controversy in the process. The problems pertaining to Norplant went beyond the lack of information health officials provided to poor black women, for example, information about the contraceptive's dangerous side effects.

As progressive scholars and activists have noted, the Norplant controversy was problematic for additional reasons, not the least of which was the manner in which the government utilized this technological advance as a form of population control and not with the purpose of providing poor black women with greater reproductive freedom.[30] Under pressure from conservatives for more stringent measures to curb poverty, at the time of Norplant's availability 13 states had put forth a wide variety of bills that proposed connecting Norplant's use to the receipt of welfare payments or crafting financial incentive programs to get the women to use the contraceptive (Taylor 1999: 246). As scholar activist Marlene Fried correctly points out, these solutions use punitive and coercive measures not only to regulate the lives of poor women, but also, to curb their reproductive capacities. These programs involving Norplant were crafted to operate in the same manner as other conservative social welfare programs like Work fare (requiring welfare recipients to acquire work in order to receive benefits). In essence, these government-endorsed solutions constituted what Fried called a type of "Contraceptive Fare" program (Fried 1998: 217).

In the case of the Tuskegee experiment, African Americans were medically abused due to the lack of their informed consent. Therefore, in the logic of activist Michele Jackson's argument, it is logical to support the implementation of informed consent and waiting periods, these solutions preventing abortion and producing racial empowerment. However, racial empowerment in Jackson's equation is not only derived from African American women having greater control over what happens to their bodies by having more information at their disposal; it also comes from the saved lives that can join the battle against the forces of racial oppression. The emphasis placed on the importance of increasing the black race to join the battle against racial oppression ties neatly into the third component of the abortion is racial genocide argument. This aspect of the argument borrows from another inherited discourse; it is voiced as vigorously by today's anti-abortionist African Americans as it was by black nationalists during the twenties and again in the sixties and seventies.

The combination of cutbacks in governmental aid, deindustrialization, and the continued flight of middle-class families from cities, has had deleterious consequences on a number of metropolitan areas in the United States. With diminished tax bases and reduced federal and state financial support, city governments are forced to address an array of social problems with less resources. Because of the racial inequality produced by institutional racism, African American communities have been disproportionately hurt by these structural shocks. African Americans living in inner city communities on the margins of the urban economy are impacted the hardest. Pro-life blacks use the conditions of this population of African Americans as the basis for arguing that abortion is a form of racial genocide and then extrapolate from that to cover all African Americans.[31] In one article, African American pro-life activist Akua Furlow drove home this point to her readers:

> Recently an anti-violence summit meeting was held in Washington, D.C. in which leading African American elected officials, ministers, community activists and leaders in the entertainment industry participated. The summit was an attempt to find ways to bring order and a sense of value for human life in hope [of stemming] the rising tide of violence.... Pictures of young boys and girls gunned down by other youth are commonplace on the evening news.... Although noble in its efforts, the summit did not address an important aspect of violence – violence in the womb. Abortion has decimated African Americans in genocidal proportions.... The future of African-Americans is surely endangered as never before in history. Violence and other social ills facing our community will continue as long as we do not also seek to protect the lives of our unborn. (Furlow 1993: 1)

According to another activist, the battle to mobilize other African Americans against abortion had greater meaning, "because the policies of abortion on demand threaten our very survival as a people" (Jones 1999: 3).

Why does black women's access to legal abortion get viewed as a threat to the survival of the race? At the core of these articulations of urgency among today's black pro-lifers is their fear of depopulation. Just like their predecessors, today's pro-life activists feel that larger white forces are conspiring to reduce the black population. They see the disproportionate placement of Planned Parenthood clinics in African American neighborhoods as a clear illustration of the "plot" to control the population of African Americans: "The conspiracy is the fact that 78% of abortion mills are located in our neighborhoods. As a result the Black population is 35% smaller than it otherwise should be" (Jones 1999: 3). Combining this observation with the fact that various studies illustrate that a disproportionate number of abortions performed in the United States are done on African American women, movement leaders like Rev. Hunter warn, "Just give us a generation or two and we'll be on the endangered species list" (Hunter).

Expressions of this fear of racial extinction by today's cadre of pro-life African Americans revisits a long-held debate in the black community surrounding the role black women's reproductive choices play in fighting racial oppression. For this very reason, I argue here for a deeper and more serious understanding of the power harnessed by conservative pro-lifers when they borrow from certain, highly resonant, inherited discourses within the black popular mindset. On one side of this inherited historical debate, advocates such as black nationalist Marcus Garvey and the mainly male members of black nationalist organizations such as the Nation of Islam and the Black Panthers felt it was in the best interest of the race for black women to continue to reproduce.[32] At the seventh annual convention of Marcus Garvey's Universal Negro Improvement Association in 1934, the black nationalists passed a resolution that denounced birth control. At the convention, people of African descent were advised not "to accept or practice the theory of birth control... as is being advocated by irresponsible speculators who are attempting to interfere with the course of nature and with the purpose of God in whom we believe" (Weisbord 1975: 43). In the 1960s, associates of the Nation of Islam raided birth control clinics while the Pittsburgh branch of the NAACP released a statement that called the local family planning clinic "an instrument of genocide." At the Black Power conference organized by Amiri Baraka, delegates passed a resolution denouncing birth control (Ross 1998: 180).

On the other side of the debate was noted scholar and progressive activist W.E.B Du Bois who strongly favored birth control use by African Americans, especially poor black women. Du Bois felt the "strength in numbers" argument put forth by the black nationalists was deeply problematic. For Du Bois, it was imperative that blacks understood that "among human races and groups, as among vegetables, quality and not mere quantity really counts" (Weisbord 1975: 43, 51).[33] The black National Medical Association was in the forefront of providing information to the black community about family planning. The National Council of Negro Women, founded by Mary McLeod Bethune in 1935, also led the charge to make birth control more accessible to African Americans. At its 1941 convention, the organization passed a resolution requesting that black organizations with health committees not overlook family planning programs, which in their words set out to "aid each family to have all the children it can afford and support but no more—in order to insure better health, security, and happiness for all" (Weisbord 1975: 47). The prominent black newspaper the *Pittsburgh Courier* ran an editorial in favor of family planning for blacks (Ross 1994: 150). The majority of African American women actively supported family planning. In fact, African American women have consistently provided the best insight on the importance of having control over when they decide to have families. Congresswoman Shirley Chisholm eloquently articulated the importance of family planning to women and the problematic nature of the genocide argument:

> To label family planning and legal abortion programs "genocide" is male rhetoric, for male ears. It falls flat to female listeners and to thoughtful male ones. Women know, and so do many men, that two or three children who are wanted, prepared for, reared amid love and stability, and educated to the limit of their ability will mean more for the future of the black and brown races from which they come than any number of neglected, hungry, ill-housed and ill-clothed youngsters. (Ross 1998: 177)

The abortion is racial genocide argument has been effective for the African American pro-life movement in garnering attention among a segment of the black community. Through various intellectual sleight of hand maneuvers, the argument's proponents weave together bits of information and facts with ideological rhetoric to craft an apocalyptic vision of blacks in America. Because the goal for black pro-lifers is to move as many African Americans as possible away from supporting plans to keep abortions legal and safe, the complexities of African American women's reproductive decisions are often obfuscated. The same is true of any analysis interrogating how the labeling of abortion as genocide can be a way for black men to assert control over black women's reproductive choices. For instance, while it is true that in US history many African American women were sterilized without their consent, black pro-lifers neglect to mention how many poor black women, due to a lack of available family planning options (e.g., contraceptions, abortions), also *chose*, out of desperation, to be sterilized in order to prevent unplanned pregnancies (Ross 1998: 155). By connecting the racism of these historical moments with various examples of the racial oppression many African Americans living on the margins face daily (unemployment, drug addiction, violence, imprisonment, etc.), black pro-lifers are able to make aborting unborn black babies appear to be the underhanded plan of sinister forces aiming to rid the United States of African Americans. This combination of truth and emotional rhetoric produces an argument that is effective in raising feelings of outrage, anger, and fear among some in the African American community. This is despite the fact that the "abortion is racial genocide" argument places African American women in a tough position. Under this rationale, black women who speak out strongly in support of abortion get cast at best as unwilling dupes furthering the "enemy's plan" or at worse as "traitors" to the cause of racial justice. African American women who exercise their reproductive right to an abortion are then constructed as unknowing collaborators in the demise of the race.[34]

Historian Linda Gordon aptly identified the challenges the genocide argument posed to family planning advocates:

> Throughout the 1930's and 1940's the resistance of many blacks to birth control was reflected in the arguments of both black and white birth-control spokesmen. They were continually countering charges that birth control was a policy designed to reduce the size of the black population, thus weakening it politically. That charge – in its extreme form a charge of genocide – must be taken seriously. It has been repeated up to the present

time by many who suspect both the intentions and objective consequences of birth-control programs, and it is hardly odd that representatives of an extremely poor and exploited group might find some security in numbers. (Gordon 1990: 349–350)

For reproductive rights activists, especially white activists, nothing is gained by belittling the extreme claims and historical links that comprise the abortion is racial genocide rationale, as problematic as they are. The counter analyses must be both understanding of the distrust some African Americans have with regard to the American legal, medical, and bureaucratic establishments due to their racism, while also sharp enough to point out the shortcomings in the arguments' seemingly commonsensical logic.

THE RELATIONSHIP BETWEEN AFRICAN AMERICANS, AFRICAN AMERICAN PRO-LIFERS, AND THE WHITE PRO-LIFE MOVEMENT

Since race and racism are central themes within the African American pro-life movement that are voiced forcefully, and due to the volatility of race and the challenges it therefore poses to coalition building, it would be easy to assume that there is little cooperation between the black and white pro-life movements. In fact, there are a variety of instances in which black and white pro-life activists have worked together. The numbers of blacks who become involved with the mainstream pro-life movement, however, is still small. Several factors continue to contribute to African Americans' hesitancy in becoming involved in the pro-life movement, and these factors still serve as a counterbalance limiting the effectivity of pro-lifers' common sense claims.

The first of these is the contentious history between African Americans and the white conservative movement. As one black pro-life leader stated, "In the black community, when you say the word 'conservative' and start talking about states rights and getting the government off of our backs…there's a real bad taste in people's mouth when they hear that." ("Black Baptist pastor speaks at Catholic Interparish Council" www.aala.org.) According to Rev. Johnny Hunter, part of their mission as black pro-lifers is to change the negative image blacks have of conservatism. Black pro-lifers like Hunter see themselves as drawing a more accurate picture of what conservatism means and how blacks can take part in a conservative movement. As Hunter stated, "When we say conservative, we're saying we mean family values" (Hunter).

Second, the negative images and actions by the radical wing of the white anti-abortion movement, limit both black and white pro-lifers' ability to attract more African Americans to the pro-life movement.[35] Both black and white activists accuse the media of providing distorted coverage of the pro-life movement. As one white pro-life leader remarked, "they tended to identify us with stereotypical negative media images, such as 'those people who bomb clinics'" (Lehner 2001: 3). For black pro-lifers their main concern was not with the type of coverage, but with the lack of coverage. A frequent complaint among black pro-lifers was that the media only highlighted the activities of the white pro-life movement, which led African Americans to conclude that abortion was a "white issue." In essence, the media's representations helped "whiten" the movement. According to L.E.A.R.N's cochair, Akua Furlow, "the African American pro-life community has been effectively excluded from the media" (Duin 1997: B7).[36] Some pro-life blacks went as far as to accuse the media of censorship: "Could someone tell me why the liberal socialist media (black and white) has meticulously depicted the pro-life movement as lily-white?... At pro-life demonstrations, the liberal news cameramen have been known to shut off the cameras as they approach a cluster of blacks, and turn them on again to film a white man" (Davis 1996: 1).

The language used by white pro-lifers to mobilize supporters has also been seen as an impediment in attracting more African Americans because of its anti-black female nature. A study conducted by the Dayton Right to Life organization on African Americans' receptiveness to the pro-life movement showed that little of the pro-life literature used by white organizations "held much appeal to the African American women." The perception among the African American women in the study was that the literature was "written by white people, for white people" (Lehner 2001: 4). These opinions reveal the ways in which the views of the white pro-life movement concerning such key issues as female identity, the family, and motherhood are not merely different from those of African American women, but also, potentially alienating.

The conflict around abortion encompasses ethical, legal, and moral issues surrounding women's fertility. As various scholars have pointed out, the struggle over abortion is also a contestation over how womanhood is defined and legitimated in American culture (Dugger 1991: 571). Research examining the views of white pro-lifers has shown that within their perspective, there are clear distinctions in what constitutes womanhood, the family, and mothering. As sociologist Kristin Luker noted, among the pro-life activists she spoke with the view was that the roles of wives and mothers had top priority over other social roles women subscribed to (Luker 1984: 161). Since black women have had a longer history of participation in the labor market than white women, due to the under and unemployment of African American men, black women do not see their roles as mothers, wives, and workers as mutually exclusive (Dugger 1991: 572–573).

Ensconced within the agenda of the larger, predominately white, pro-life movement is the advocacy and defense of the traditional heterosexual, nuclear family (Pollack Petchesky 1984: 263). The employment difficulties of black men have meant not just longer histories of participation in the labor market by black women but also longer and higher frequencies of women heading households. The history of African Americans in the United States also shows that throughout differing eras, various outside forces (slavery, segregation, and racial discrimination) have impacted how black families are structured. As a means of support, black women have relied on what anthropologist Leith Mullings calls, "women-centered networks" (Mullings 1995: 133). These networks of other female relatives or women in the community create supportive families that provide an alternative to the nuclear family. Black women have been more receptive to extended families because of the history of extended family structures within the black community. As Angela Davis notes, the elasticity of the black family structure became a means of survival:

> Our families, of course, have never corresponded in structure and function to the prevailing social ideal. First of all, original African cultural traditions had a much broader definition of the family than that which prevails in this society.... Second, the brutal economic and political pressures connected with slavery and continuing throughout subsequent historical eras have consistently prevented African-American family patterns from conforming to the dominant family models. Finally, Black people...have been compelled to build, creatively and often improvisationally, a family life consistent with the dictates of survival. (Davis 1986: 55)

Without knowledge of and sensitivity to the history of the black family in America, white pro-lifers' message that the only family worth defending is the nuclear family is likely to fall on deaf ears among African Americans, even among those who may harbor anti-abortion feelings.

The actions of the larger pro-life movement also alienate African American women in relation to the subject of motherhood. With respect to abortion, the anti-abortion movement treats all women the same (Chamberlain and Hardisty 2000). Regardless of race or class background, pro-lifers believe no woman should get an abortion. When the issue is expanded to reproductive rights, family and welfare though, a double standard applies and race and class get linked in problematic ways. Middle- and upper-class white women are urged to have children and stay home to rear them while poor women, especially women of color, are told to control the number of children they have and find work to support them (Chamberlain and Hardisty 2000: 14).

White conservatives have often used poor black women as examples of the problems of expanded government domestic spending programs.[37] As Rickie Solinger perceptively points out, Americans have always been uneasy with social programs that provide comfort and dignity to the poor (Solinger 2001: 144). Even with this discomfort, when the recipient in question is a poor white woman, society has looked upon her participation in relief programs more favorably than in the case of poor black women:

> When the typical recipient of public assistance had been the family headed by a poor white mother, likely a widow, choice was a limited category for the recipient, but not a bizarre category.... As soon as childbearing was linked with choice, however, and African-American women became eligible for benefits, "choice" acquired a bad odor in the world of welfare. (Solinger 2001: 148)[38]

The equating of the welfare queen with African American women points to the myriad ways black womanhood and mothering has been degraded and questioned in American society.[39]

If the white pro-lifers' language and messages concerning such issues as femininity and motherhood, and their negative characterizations of poor black women receiving welfare, has done much to alienate African American women, the denigration of black women in American society has also not been lost on black pro-lifers. As activist Michele Jackson describes:

American culture, unfortunately, upholds no popular image of a Black mother tenderly nurturing her child. Instead America has been bombarded with the image of the Black matriarch who...transmits a pathological life-style to her children, perpetuating poverty and antisocial behavior from one generation to the next. (Jackson 1998: 24)

In addition to their mission to move African American women away from having abortions, black pro-lifers also see the consistent maligning of black motherhood as their opportunity to redefine society's image of black mothers. By reducing the frequency of abortions by black women, black pro-lifers see this as the first step in illustrating to all Americans that black women value and cherish their children.

The racialized ways motherhood has been articulated by the larger pro-life movement and other conservatives constrains the effectivity of those white pro-lifers trying to forge connections with African Americans. The common reaction white pro-lifers experience when engaging African Americans is one of skepticism. While conducting their study, the Dayton Right to Life organization discovered that many of the African Americans they spoke with did not believe the information the organization was presenting on the abortion rate in the black community. The President Peggy Lehner attributed this to the distrust blacks had of white organizations like Dayton Right To Life. As she described: "Some accused us of making up the figures to 'make them look bad.' As one woman told me, 'When I first heard you saying these things, my reaction was "Here we go again. White people telling us one more thing we are doing wrong"'" (Lehner 2001: 2). African Americans' suspicion toward representatives of conservative white organizations like Dayton Right To Life stems from decades of negative stereotyping of African Americans by white conservatives.

In spite of these challenges, targeting more African Americans to join the anti-abortion movement has been a common objective of both black and white pro-lifers. Both sides agree that the task of getting more African Americans to participate in the pro-life movement is a difficult one. And yet, white and black pro-life activists also recognize the importance and potential of incorporating more African Americans into the ranks of the movement. As Peggy Lehner stated hopefully:

In conclusion, let me say that our findings reveal that the pro-life message has not fallen on deaf ears in the African American community.... Cultural differences can no longer serve as an excuse for our silence. No one comes to a party without an invitation…start sending out those invitations and believe that if you do so, you will be surprised how many will come! (Lehner 2001: 6)

Addressing what white pro-life activists need to do to attract more African Americans to the movement, black pro-lifer Vincent Watkins stressed that white pro-lifers needed to approach African Americans with an openness and a willingness to address blacks' concerns and apprehensions about the actions of white pro-lifers. Watkins cautioned, "Right to lifers who enter these communities must be prepared to answer questions regarding mistaken impressions about them and in language to which members of the target audience will respond" (Watkins 1998: 4).

There have also been instances where some within the black pro-life movement have been frustrated with working along side white pro-lifers. Some black pro-lifers have gone as far as to argue that black pro-lifers should work only with other African Americans in rallying the black community to its cause. This separatist viewpoint is up for debate, however, opposed by other activists such as Michele Jackson:

> Some have argued that pro-lifers of African descent would best reach the Black community with the pro-life message by forming a Black pro-life movement separate from the National Right to Life Committee (NRLC). However, our civil rights history teaches us that the most successful means to overcome unjust legislation is for people of diverse backgrounds to unite for a common goal…. Black pro-lifers must not separate from the mainstream pro-life movement in our common fight to restore the right to life to all members of the human race. We must work at full participation within the mainstream right to life movement. (Jackson 1997: 14)

In language that, once again, borrows from the lessons of civil rights and earlier calls for integration, Jackson articulates in the context of the female-led, grassroots, anti-abortion social movement a tension that will pose an even greater challenge for the group of primarily male black politicians discussed in Chapter 6. Caught between a broader white movement and its history of racist and alienating rhetoric, and a black mass constituency aware of that history and suspicious of conservatives' attempts to do outreach across color lines, what black politicians lack is the collective organization that defines black conservatism at the social movement level, such as we find in the anti-abortion movement.

The organizational infrastructure of the black pro-life movement has provided opportunities for black, and often female, organizers and activists to take the lead in reshaping more radical forms of racial critique to fit the needs of a socially conservative sexual agenda and gender politics.

CHALLENGES TO THE AFRICAN AMERICAN ANTI-ABORTION MOVEMENT

Even with their criticisms of their white counterparts and acknowledgement of continued racism in society, African American anti-abortionists face various challenges in their goal of building a solid majority of support among African Americans. First, negative images of the anti-abortion movement by the violence committed by radical white anti-abortionists limit their ability to gain more African American supporters. Second, being overshadowed by the media exposure given to white anti-abortionists often gives the impression that abortion is a "white issue." Finally, the backlash from other African Americans produced from some of the tactics used by those in the movement. One prominent example is the erection of billboards in African American neighborhoods. As part of the plan to get more African Americans support for reducing reproductive rights and federal funding for Planned Parenthood, several African American anti-abortionists organizations, set up billboards in major cities such as Atlanta with pro-life messages. In a New York Soho neighborhood, the African American anti-abortion organization Life Always put up a billboard showing an African American girl with the message above her stating "the most dangerous place for an African American is in the womb."[40] In Chicago, a billboard had the message "Every 21 minutes our next possible Leader is Aborted" next to an image of President Obama.[41] The reaction to these billboards produced outrage among some African Americans because their unveiling occurred during the same time as the celebration of Black History Month, but more importantly, the erection of the billboards revealed a schism between genders as more African American women than men were upset with the ads. Many African American women felt the billboards blamed them for exercising their reproductive rights and control over their bodies. Another reason for the difference between African American men and women is the attitudinal gap toward abortion. For example, various studies show that African Americans tend to be less supportive of abortion than their white counterparts[42] but among African Americans, the difference toward abortion is more pronounced between men and women. As one study noted, African American men tend to express more conservative attitudes toward abortion than women:

> The trends for Black males in relation to Black females, on the other hand, appear a bit simpler. Although not always significant across the decades, Black males consistently report more conservative views toward abortion than Black females.[43]

This trend is not surprising as historically African American men have been more conservative toward reproductive rights than African American women. This conservatism toward reproductive rights is borne from living in a patriarchal society where one measure of masculinity is upholding the role of protector. In the context of reproductive rights, this responsibility elevates the need to be protectors of the family (women, children born and unborn) over a woman's right to control her body. This patriarchal need to be protectors gets acerbated when combined with the lack of validation of African American masculinity by American society and the conspiratorial perspective that African Americans are constantly under siege from white society that is looking to exterminate them. While African American anti-abortionists do not shy away from making race and racism the central element of their cause and are willing to criticize their white peers for their racism, which can endear them to African Americans who are opposed to abortion, the various constraints previously mentioned pose a challenge to African American anti-abortionists in mobilizing the majority of the community to actively join their cause.

Notes

1. In the view of some white conservatives, Keyes's presence in the Republican Party's presidential primaries illustrated that there were some African Americans who did not fall "lock stock and barrel" with the supposed "liberal orthodoxy."
2. It is important to note that the African American anti-abortion movement is one of many grassroots movements conducted by a segment of conservative African Americans that advocate traditional values. Deborah Toler has described some of the significant differences between this

segment of conservative African Americans within the community and their conservative intellectual and political counterparts. This grassroots sector is overwhelmingly comprised of African American Christian fundamentalist groups, for whom constituency building is a major priority. Also, the followers of these movements are much more receptive to Afrocentric perspectives and ideologies (Toler 1995).

3. Of course the most prominent African American female Republican is former Secretary of State Condoleezza Rice, but after Rice, there is a large drop off in the stature of black conservative women. Presently there are no African American female Republicans who have the visibility of counterparts such as California Democrat Representative Maxine Waters or Texas Representative Sheila Jackson-Lee. In fact, in the history of the nation no African American woman had ever held office in the Senate or Congress as a Republican until Ludmya, "Mia" Love became the first black female Republican to do so when she was elected on November 4, 2014 to Congress from Utah. In academia, the spotlight shines dimly on conservative African American women scholars. Other than political scientist Carol Swain and sociologist Anne Wortham, at the present time, there does not seem to be others who have as much name recognition.

4. For example, in theory, conservatives are strongly opposed to political mobilization through group-based identity. In reality, it can be argued that the core of the Christian Right's political strategy is an identity-based one and that identity politics is a main strategy of many conservative groups.

5. For excellent analyses on intersectionality and race, see sociologists Deborah K. King's, "Multiple Jeopardy, Multiple Consciousness: The Context of a Black Feminist Ideology," *Signs*, vol. 14, no. 1, 1988, the chapter entitled, "Black Feminist Thought in the Matrix of Domination," in Patricia Hill Collins' *Black Feminist Thought: Knowledge, Consciousness and the Politics of Empowerment* (2000), and legal scholar Kimberlé Crenshaw's "Demarginalizing the Intersection of Race and Sex: A Black Feminist Critique of Antidiscrimination Doctrine, Feminist Theory, and Antiracist Politics," in *The Black Feminist Reader* (2001), and "Mapping the Margins: Intersectionality, Identity Politics, and Violence Against Women of Color," in *The Public Nature of Private Violence* (1994).

6. According to Berlet and Lyons, the Patriot movement emerged during the early 1990s and its core belief was a conspiratorial view that the government was run by a cadre of secret elites whose objective was to impose on Americans various forms of tyranny. The movement's ideological roots can be traced to the conspiracist ideas of the John Birch Society, the insurgency of the Liberty Lobby, and other groups who have historically promoted ideas of White Supremacy and anti-Semitism. For a

more detailed analysis, see chapter 14, "Battling The New World Order: Patriots and Armed Militias" (Berlet and Lyons 2000: 287–304).

7. While Mildred Jefferson dedicated most of her energy toward abolishing abortion, she has also spoken out against welfare and affirmative action, and supports allowing law enforcement to use tougher measures to curtail crime.

8. This information was obtained at the website of the Heritage Foundation, http://www.heritage.org/staff/james.html.

9. http://www.Nationalblackprolifeunion.com/aboutus/.

10. Day Gardner, "Day Gardner National Black Pro-life Union Comments on TD Jakes and Barak Obama," June 11, 2008, at the *Christian Web News* http://www.cwnewz.com.

11. http://www.KingforAmerica.com.

12. Ibid.

13. At the American Enterprise Institute website, http://www.aeispeakers.com.

14. In one chapter, Parker describes her first abortion in a manner that validates the anti-abortionists' dubious claim that women use the procedure as an escape from their obligation to bear children resulting from an unplanned pregnancy. According to Parker, her first abortion was, "pretty easy." The procedure had a minimal effect on her, as she states further, "I was in an up-beat mood. I was scot-free and ready to resume having a good old time. If I was supposed to come away from that experience feeling remorseful and depressed, it was completely lost on me. I didn't learn a thing. I picked up right where I left off and continued to have promiscuous sex with numerous partners" (Parker 1997: 18).

15. Star Parker currently dedicates most of her energy to operating the community-based organization Coalition for Urban Renewal and Education (CURE).

16. In addition to his links with Republican Party insiders, Hunter also has connections with predominately white anti-abortion organizations such as Randall Terry's Operation Rescue, and other social conservative activist groups such as Rev. Donald Wildmon's American Family Association.

17. The information gathered was found at http://www.aala.org in March of 2000, but the organizational website address has since changed to www.lifedrum.org, as of July 14, 2009.

18. Taken from a media release by Black Americans for Life published in an organizational pamphlet.

19. As quoted at http://www.gateway.org/content/learn.htm.

20. As quoted at http://www.learninc.org.

21. Ibid.

22. Information provided at http://www.learninc.org/page/members.php.

23. Ibid.

24. Ibid.
25. Information provided at http://www.afamforlife.org in the library section, "Black Baptist Pastor Speaks at Catholic Interparish Council," p. 1.
26. African American anti-abortionists believe that the disproportionate rates of abortion among African American women are due to a lack of "personal responsibility," "value in marriage," and "assault on the family." See Star Parker, "Stopping Abortion Starts with Focus on African-Americans," LifeNews.com, http://www.lifenews.com/2011/01/18/stopping-abortion-starts-with-focus-on-african-americans/, posted January 18, 2011, accessed June 18, 2011.
27. In the 1857 Dred Scott v Sanford case, a Missouri slave, Dred Scott sued for his right to be free, on the grounds that he and his former slavemaster lived in various states where slavery was not legal. The Supreme Court ruled against Scott stating that the Congress did not have the legal power to outlaw slavery in areas under its jurisdiction (Gorney 1998: 246). In its ruling, the Supreme Court stated that slaves were considered the private property of their slaveowners and thus the Constitution has "provided for the protection of private property against the encroachments of the Government" (as quoted in a pamphlet from Blacks For Life entitled, "Slavery and Abortion: The Parallel"). In essence, slaves were deemed as property not humans and thus, as Chief Justice Roger B. Taney stated, "they had no rights which the white man was bound to respect." Pro-lifers equate the 1973 Roe v Wade ruling to Dred Scott because they perceived the Court's ruling as denying the humanity of the unborn child whose rights are trumped by the mother's. In other words, to anti-abortionists, the unborn child in the Roe case is considered the private property of the mother as slaves were in relation to their slave masters in the Scott case.
28. As quoted by Sharon Weston. It is common to see within the discourse of the black pro-life movement claims like the one made by this activist. Such statements are based more on wishful narration than historical fact. As scholars such as Loretta Ross and Angela Davis have illustrated, the use of abortion has had a long history among black women in Africa and the United States (Ross 1998: 144–146; Davis 1990: 17).
29. According to historian Linda Gordon, the "Negro Project" of 1939 was the cooperative attempt of the Birth Control Federation of America and concerned southern state public health officials to curb the problem of southern poverty through birth control measures. More directly, the core of the problem as seen by officials was in the growth of the black poor in the South. This sentiment was stated as much in the project's proposal: "The mass of Negroes...particularly in the South, still breed carelessly and disastrously, with the result that the increase among Negroes, even more than among whites, is from that portion of the population

least intelligent and fit, and least able to rear children properly" (Gordon 1990: 328). The project hired several Black ministers to travel through the South lobbying Southern Blacks to use birth control. A private letter from Margaret Sanger made clear why black ministers were used in the project: "We do not want word to go out that we want to exterminate the Negro population and the minister is the man who can straighten out that idea if it ever occurs to any of their more rebellious members" (Gordon 1990: 328).

30. Legal Scholar Dorothy Roberts insightfully probes the various problems with the manner in which Norplant was thrust upon poor African American women. One of Roberts's main critiques of the different state-sponsored programs involving the use of Norplant, is that states desired to provide funding for poor women's birth control but not to expand the social welfare net to help these same women meet their basic life needs. For Roberts, this indicates that the government is more interested in solving poor black women's poverty through population control. Roberts and other critics also point out that solutions involving Norplant illustrate the ways black motherhood and poor black women become invalidated and demonized. As Roberts states, "Contemporary welfare rhetoric blames Black single mothers for transmitting a deviant lifestyle to their children, a lifestyle marked not only by persistent welfare dependency but also by moral degeneracy and criminality." See chap. 3, "From Norplant To The Contraceptive Vaccine" (Roberts 1997).

31. The late veteran activist Erma Clardy Craven forcefully made this argument back in the early seventies with her essay, "Abortion, Poverty and Black Genocide: Gifts to the Poor?" This essay has been identified as a classic among movement activists. No wonder: witness Craven's passion and clarity as she puts forth her argument that the conditions of inner city blacks in the seventies were tantamount to organized genocide: "The substandard housing of the poor in this country where heat, water, and plumbing facilities are lacking, and adequate public services such as garbage removal are withheld, is genocide. The poor food found in the ghetto supermarkets, the absence of health services, and the fires which consume the run-down houses and the little kids who live in them is genocide. The fact that Blacks die six years earlier than whites and the infant mortality rate is twice as high for Blacks is genocide. The condition of the ghetto schools and the quality of public education in Black communities is genocide" (quoted in Hilgers and Horan 1972: 147). Unfortunately what Craven's observations demonstrate is that little has been done to eradicate the various structural problems plaguing inner city blacks, since her description appropriately captures much of the realities of urban poverty today as it did three decades ago.

32. There was, however, serious dissension within the Black Panthers around the issue of birth control—the organization was the only black nationalist organization to support free access to abortions and contraceptives (Ross 1998: 181).

33. It must be pointed out, however, that Du Bois and other advocates of the "quality is more important than quantity" argument faced the criticism that implicit in this argument was a class bias against the poor having large families. This criticism is still raised today by pro-life blacks, as illustrated by African American Life Alliance's founder Paulette Roseboro in her commentary in the 1998 winter issue of the publication, *Life Drum*. "We must realize that *elitist bigotry* was not (and is not) reserved for the white Sangers of her day. There were blacks even then who agreed that unfit segments resided in the Negro/Colored population. To some elite Negroes, it was only reasonable to believe elimination of the unfit within the community would clean up the race as a whole. Negroes would then eventually evolve into the *black Aryan* race. Birth control was promoted within the 'Negro' population…as a means to eliminate unwanted pregnancies when, in fact, it was a systematic means to discourage the continued procreation within out poorer, less educated ranks."

34. African American women who have little knowledge of black women's history of reproductive rights activism, lack a strong feminist consciousness, or are not as certain in their conviction of supporting abortion can be vulnerable to such an argument. I am reminded of the story a former student told me about the impact the Five percenters, a splinter group of Nation of Islam followers, on her peer group in New York City. During the eighties, the Five percenters gained popularity among many young inner city black youths like herself with the "abortion is genocide" argument. From the perspective of the Five percenters, these youth were aiding in the combat against white supremacy by reproducing the "next generation" that would continue the struggle. As my student noted, a number of her friends were taken in by the argument. One friend, who went on to have more than 5 children before the age of 33, was firm in her conviction that her decision to bear so many was making a contribution to the "cause."

35. In the eighties, some in the anti-abortion movement felt that more dramatic action was needed, as Berlet and Lyons describe. Not getting the support that they originally expected from the Reagan administration and the Supreme Court, some activists felt it was time to incorporate more violent means into their agenda, including assaults against clinic workers, fire bombings, death threats, and vandalism. By the 1990s, the attacks intensified as several abortion providers were murdered and others targeted (Berlet and Lyons 2000: 234).

36. As an example, Furlow pointed to a Buffalo demonstration that was organized by Rev. Hunter but credited to Operation Rescue's Randall Terry by the media.

37. For example, during his first term in office, President Reagan often told the story of a woman from Chicago who had been caught cheating the government on welfare payments. The tale became known as the "Chicago welfare queen story." The fact that Linda Taylor, the woman in the center of the controversy, was black was not lost on observers. Historian Kenneth O'Reilly notes that Reagan embellished the tale each time he told the story. At one point, Taylor was "using eighty names, thirty addresses, and twelve Social Security cards." According to Reagan, Taylor was collecting tax-free benefits equaling close to $150,000. In reality, Taylor had been convicted in 1977 for fraud and perjury of $8000 in benefit checks (O'Reilly 1995: 360).

38. The American public's impression of who falls under the category of "deserving" and "undeserving" poor is often racially influenced. In the eyes of many white Americans, poor black women are seen not only as incompetent mothers but also as making bad choices that are the main cause of their poverty. After the introduction of the pill in the sixties and the legalization of abortion in 1973, Americans began to view both pregnancy and having families in terms of individual choice. When expanding welfare benefits combined with Americans' assumptions about motherhood as shaped in the context of choice, together they intensified the racialized ways Americans thought about women and welfare (Solinger 2001: 148–149).

39. Conservative activists often malign all poor women with stereotypes of them as "dependent, irresponsible, prone to addictions, and inadequate mothers" (Chamberlain and Hardisty 2000: 14). However, race subtly shapes the differential impact of the denigration of poor mothers on white and black women. As sociologist Patricia Hill Collins explains:

> Whereas working-class white women's fitness for motherhood is measured against the assumed norms of middle-class white women, African-American women experience a reversal of this process. Specifically, working-class African American experiences are stereotyped and labeled as deviant from those of middle-class white women and are simultaneously considered normative for African American women as a collectivity. (Hill Collins 2000: 276)

40. John Del Signore, "Anti-abortion Billboard in SoHo Targets Blacks, Sparks Outrage," http://gothamist.com/2011/04/27/anti-abortion_billboard_sparks_laws.php, posted April 27, 2011, accessed June 20, 2011.

41. Michelle Goldberg, "The Antiabortion Crowd's Latest Target: African Americans," http://www.thedailybeast.com/articles/2011/03/31/obama-billboard-shows-anti-abortion-focus-on-african-americans.html, posted on March 27, 2011, accessed June 20, 2011.
42. See M. Combs and Susan Welch, "Blacks, Whites, and Attitudes Towards Abortion: A Research Note," *Public Opinion Quarterly*, vol. 46, 1982, pp. 510–520, Elaine J. Hall, and Myra Marx Ferree, "Race Differences in Abortion Attitudes," *Public Opinion Quarterly*, vol. 50, 1986, pp. 193–207, Philip E. Secret, "The Impact of Region on Racial Differences in Attitudes Towards Legal Abortion," *Journal Of Black Studies*, March 1987, pp. 347–69, Clyde Wilcox, "Race Differences in Abortion Attitudes: Some Additional Evidence," *Public Opinion Quarterly*, vol. 54: 248–255, 1990, Clyde Wilcox, "Race, Religion, Region, and Abortion Attitudes," *Sociological Analysis*, vol. 53, no. 1, 1992, pp. 97–105.
43. J. Scott Carter et al., "Trends in Abortion Attitudes by Race and Gender: A Reassessment Over a Four-Decade Period," *Journal of Sociological Research*, vol. 1, no. 1, 2009, p. 14.

References

American Life League, Culture of Life Studies Program, Mildred Fay Jefferson, uploaded February 6, 2016, http://cultureoflifestudies.com/newsletter/drmildred-fay-jefferson/, accessed February 23, 2018.
Association of American Physicians and Surgeons Newsletter, vol. 50, no. 5, May 1994.
Benson, Rusty. "Black Community Waking to Most Basic Civil Right: African American Pastors Are New Abolitionists." *American Family Association Journal*, January 2001.
Berlet, Chip, and Matthew N. Lyons. *Right Wing Populism in America: Too Close for Comfort*. New York: Guilford Publisher, 2000.
Black Americans for Life Newsletter. 1999: 1.
Brooks Hodge, Sharon. "Pregnant Women Seek Help from Pro-life Groups." *Headway*, August 31, 1997: 26.
Brown, Joseph. "Conspiracy Theories Blind Us to Real Problems, Solutions." *Headway*, June 30, 1996: 27.
Carson, Ben. "CARSON: A Physician's View on the Sanctity of Life." *Washington Times*, January 21, 2014, https://www.washingtontimes.com/news/2014/jan/21/a-physicians-view-on-the-sanctity-of-life/.
Chamberlain, Pam, and Jean Hardisty. "Reproducing Patriarchy: Reproductive Rights Under Siege." *The Public Eye*, Spring 2000: 14.
Chumley, Cheryl K. "Ben Carson Likens Abortion in America to 'Human Sacrifice' of Paganists," uploaded July 2, 2014, https://www.washingtontimes.com/news/2014/jul/2/ben-carson-likens-abortion-america-human-sacrifice/, accessed June 15, 2016.

"CIA-Drug Accusations Revive Fears of Conspiracy." *The Philadelphia Tribune*, October, 8 1996: 8A.

Crenshaw, Kimberlé. "Mapping the Margins: Intersectionality, Identity Politics, and Violence Against Women of Color." In *The Public Nature of Private Violence: The Discovery of Domestic Abuse.* Eds. Martha Albertson Fineman and Roxanne Mykitiuk. New York, NY: Routledge, 1994.

———. "Demarginalizing the Intersection of Race and Sex: A Black Feminist Critique of Antidiscrimination Doctrine, Feminist Theory and Antiracist Politics." In *The Black Feminist Reader.* Eds. Joy James and T. Denean Sharpley-Whiting. Malden, MA: Blackwell, 2001, pp. 208–238.

Davis, Angela. "Slaying the Dream: The Black Family and the Crisis of Capitalism." *Black Scholar*, September/October 1986: 3.

———. "Racism, Birth Control, and Reproductive Rights." In *From Abortion to Reproductive Rights: Transforming a Movement.* Ed. Marlene Fried. Boston: South End Press, 1990, p. 3.

Davis, R.D. "Could Someone Please Tell Me Why?" *New Visions Commentary*, The National Center for Public Policy Research, July 1996: 1.

Dugger, Karen. "Race Differences in the Determinants of Support for Legalized Abortion." *Social Science Quarterly*, September 1991.

Duin, Julia. "Pastor's Crusade Aims to Halt Wave of Black Abortions, 'It's Killed More Than Ku Klux Klan.'" *The Washington Times*, January 10, 1997: B7.

Fried, Marlene. "Abortion in the United States-Legal But Inaccessible." In *Abortion Wars: A Half Century of Struggle, 1950–2000.* Ed. Rickie Solinger. Berkeley: University of California Press, 1998.

Furlow, Akua. "African-Americans and Induced Abortion." *Newsletter of the Association for Interdisciplinary Research in Values and Social Change*, vol. 6, no. 1, November/December 1993.

Gardner, Day. "*Day Gardner National Black Pro-Life Union Comments on TD Jakes and Barak Obama*," June 11, 2008, at the Christian Web News http://www.cwnewz.com.

Gordon, Linda. *Woman's Body, Woman's Right: Birth Control in America.* New York: Penguin Book, 1990.

Gorney, Cynthia. *Article of Faith: A Frontline History of the Abortion Wars.* New York: Simon and Schuster, 1998.

Gramsci, Antonio. *An Antonio Gramsci Reader: Selected Writings, 1916–1935.* Ed. David Forgacs. New York: Schocken Books, 1988.

Herrmann, Andrew. "Anti-welfare Stance Makes Her Star of Right." *Chicago Sun-Times*, December 17, 1994: 23.

Hilgers, T.W., and D.J. Horan eds. *Abortion and Social Justice.* New York: Sheed & Ward, 1972.

Hill Collins, Patricia. *Black Feminist Thought: Knowledge, Consciousness and the Politics of Empowerment.* New York, NY: Routledge, 2000.

Jackson, Michele. "Should We Allow Denial of Our Right to Informed Consent About Abortion?" *Black Americans for Life Newsletter*, Spring 1999: 1.
———. "End the Ignorance Now!" *National Right to Life News*, vol. 24, no. 3, August 12, 1998.
———. "Should Pro-life Black Americans Work Separately or Join NRLC?" *National Right to Life News*, vol. 14, no. 3, April 22, 1997.
James, Kay Cole. *Never Forget: The Riveting Story of One's Woman's Journey from Public Housing to the Corridors of Power.* Grand Rapids, MI: Zondervan, 1992.
———. "Abortion Is a Form of Discrimination," uploaded January 18, 2018, https://twitter.com/KayColesJames/status/954430209176100866, accessed February 23, 2018.
Jones, Reginald. *Black Americans for Life Newsletter*, Spring 1999: 3.
King, Deborah K. "Multiple Jeopardy, Multiple Consciousness: The Context of a Black Feminist Ideology." *Signs*, vol. 14, no. 1, 1988: 42–72.
Lehner, Peggy. "Abortion and the African-American Community." *Newsletter. Crisis Pregnancy Ministry—Focus on the Family*, November 2001.
Luker, Kristen. *Abortion & the Politics of Motherhood.* Berkeley: The University of California Press, 1984.
Malveaux, Julianne. "Why Are the Black Conservatives All Men?" *Ms. Magazine*, March/April 1991.
McCarthy, Jean. "Dr. Day Gardner on Abortionist's 'Ugly Black Babies' Remark: She's Heard Before." *LifeSite*, uploaded August 7, 2012, https://www.life-sitenews.com/news/dr.-day-gardner-on-abortionists-ugly-black-babies-re-mark-shes-heard-it-befo, accessed February 23, 2018.
McClarey, Donald R. "Mildred Fay Jefferson, Requiescat in Pace." *The American Catholic*, uploaded October 18, 2010, https://www.issues4life.org/blast/2011080.html, accessed February 23, 2018.
McWhorter, John. *Losing The Race: Self-Sabotage in Black America.* New York: Perennial, 2001.
Morris, Aldon. *The Origins of the Civil Rights Movement: Black Communities Organizing for Change.* New York: The Free Press, 1984.
Mullings, Leith. "Households Headed by Women: The Politics of Race, Class, and Gender." In *Conceiving the New World Order: The Global Politics of Reproduction.* Eds. Faye D. Ginsburg and Rayna Rapp. Berkeley: University of California Press, 1995.
Murakami, Keri. "Christian Coalition Trying to Reach Out—African Americans, Rabbi Are Speakers." *The Seattle Times*, June 25, 1995: B1.
O'Reilly, Kenneth. *Nixon's Piano: Presidents and Racial Politics from Washington to Clinton.* New York: The Free Press, 1995.
Pack, Juluette Bartlett. "Abortion: The Black Woman's Voice." Pamphlet. Texas Black Americans for Life, 1995.

Paige, Connie. *The Right to Lifers: Who They Are, How They Operate, Where Do They Get Their Money.* New York: Summit Books, 1983.

Parker, Star. *Pimps, Whores and Welfare Brats: The Stunning Conservative Transformation of a Former Welfare Queen.* New York: Pocket Books, 1997.

Pollack Petchesky, Rosalind. *Abortion and Woman's Choice: The State, Sexuality, and Reproductive Freedom.* New York: Longman, 1984.

Pro-life Action League. "Scheidlers Cheer Black Americans for Life Honorees," uploaded August 14, 2005, https://prolifeaction.org/2005/2005v24n-2bafl/, accessed February 23, 2018.

Religious News Services. "Enlisting Blacks in the Battle Against Abortion." *Christianity Today,* October 1994.

Roberts, Dorothy. *Killing the Black Body: Race, Reproduction, and the Meaning of Liberty.* New York: Pantheon, 1997.

Roseboro, Paulette. "The Rape of Black America." Speech. Charles County Community College, March 1999.

Ross, Loretta. "African American Women and Abortion." In *Abortion Wars: A Half Century of Struggle, 1950–2000.* Ed. Rickie Solinger. Berkeley: University of California Press, 1998.

———. "African-American Women and Abortion: 1800–1970." In *Theorizing Black Feminisms: The Visionary Pragmatism of Black Women.* Eds. Stanlie M. James and Abena P.A. Busia. New York: Routledge, 1994.

Snow, David, E. Burke Rockford, Jr., Steven K. Worden, and Robert D. Benford. "Frame Alignment Processes, Micromoblization, and Movement Participation." *American Sociological Review,* August 1986.

Solinger, Rickie. *Beggars and Choosers: How The Politics of Choice Shapes Adoption, Abortion, and Welfare in the United States.* New York: Hill and Wang, 2001.

Steele, Shelby. *The Content of Our Character: A New Vision of Race in America.* New York: Harper Collins, 1991.

Taylor, April J. "High-Tech, Pop-A-Pill Culture: New Forms of Social Control for Black Women." In *Dangerous Intersections: Feminist Perspectives on Population, Environment, and Development.* Eds. Jael Silliman and Ynestra King. Cambridge, MA: South End Press, 1999.

Toler, Deborah. "Black Conservatives." In *Eyes Right!: Challenging the Right Wing Backlash.* Ed. Chip Berlet. Boston, MA: South End Press, 1995.

Watkins, Vincent B. "Black or White, the Issue Must Be Life." *National Right to Life News,* August 12, 1998.

Weisbord, Robert G. *Genocide?: Birth Control and the Black American.* New York: Greenwood Press, 1975.

Willke, J.C. *Abortion and Slavery: History Repeats.* Cincinnati, OH: Hayes Publishing, 1984.

CHAPTER 5

Fight Against the "Special Rights" Movement and End the Mis-education of Black Children: Support School Vouchers!

THE ANTI-GAY RIGHTS MOVEMENT

One area that the right has used to tap into the social conservatism of African Americans and attempt to establish connections within the African American community revolves around the issue of sexuality. The push for the expansion of gay rights and the continuation of legalizing gay marriage has produced a firestorm of reaction from social conservatives. The frequent invoking of the heralded Civil Rights movement by white gay rights advocates and organizations to support their claims for equality and freedom has allowed those on the right to tap into the discomfort present among some African Americans. I will address this issue later in the chapter. To mobilize African Americans who hold conservative viewpoints on social issues, the conservative branch of the black church has been recognized by some white conservatives as a perfect conduit to the black community. Conservative organizations such as the Traditional Values Coalition have sent materials to various African American ministers that provide them with a language and a rationale for framing gay rights and civil rights as inherently different kinds of struggles. For example, while also holding workshops in black churches on how to mobilize the community around anti-gay rights, this literature encourages anti-gay proponents to emphasize that gay rights are "special rights" and not the same as "legitimate" civil rights, with its more "universalist" push for racial equality.[1]

© The Author(s) 2018   145
L. G. Prisock, *African Americans in Conservative Movements*,
https://doi.org/10.1007/978-3-319-89351-8_5

Using the momentum of President George W. Bush's re-election the religious right reached out to conservative African American ministers, building their support in the fight against the budding movement to legalize gay marriage. In February 2005, over one hundred African American ministers met with white conservative religious leaders at the Crenshaw Christian Center in Los Angeles, headed by Pastor Fred Price, an African American televangelist and influential member of the black Christian Right.[2] The rally included a screening of the inflammatory documentary, "Gay rights, special rights," made by Reverend Lou Sheldon, the founder of the Traditional Values Coalition. The documentary portrayed gays and lesbians offensively as "sex fiends, invoking Martin Luther King's name" (Griffin 2006: 85). The propaganda video also featured several African Americans arguing that the passage of gay rights laws would jeopardize the civil rights of African Americans and other groups of color.[3]

Of the many conservative African American ministers who have spoken out against gay rights and legalization of gay marriage, none have been as upfront and outspoken in his disagreement with the legalization of gay marriage as Bishop Harry R. Jackson of the Hope Christian Church in College Park Maryland. Jackson actively engaged in promoting what he calls a "Black Contract With America," a play on the socially conservative agenda emphasizing opposition to gay marriage and abortion that was put forth by Newt Gingrich and the other Republicans who came into power during the 1994 mid-term electoral victories. Jackson's "Black Contract" was the main agenda of his newly launched High Impact Leadership Coalition organization. For Bishop Jackson, the steps toward legalizing and validating gay marriage was an illustration of deeper a social crisis:

> When societies have gone off kilter, there has been rampant same-sex marriage.... What tends to happen is that people tend to devalue the institution of marriage as a whole. People start rearing kids without two parents, and the black community already has this incredibly alarming and, I may say, this shameful number of babies being born without fathers. (Banerjee 2005: 15)

While Jackson's association of gay marriage with societal collapse may come across as alarmist homophobic hyperbole it is an argument that can resonate with some African Americans particularly when one of Jackson's rationale for his anti-gay stance is working to strengthen the black family.

Given the widespread concern among African Americans about the state of the black family which gets articulated regularly in common discourse as "the epidemic of absentee black fathers" or "babies having babies," pointing the expansion of gay rights as illustrated by the legalization of gay marriage as a possible cause can come across as "common sense." To Jackson and other African Americans who are deeply disturbed over the perceived trouble of African Americans to form and sustain the gender traditional nuclear family anything that challenges the view that this family structure is the only valid family formation is seen as a viable threat.

> The fact that one of the key arguments against homosexuality by black clergy is its effect on the black family does not bode well for the struggle for equality by LGBT's in black culture. It is, after all, a spiritual leader's duty to shepherd his or her congregation to a morally right lifestyle. (Stanford 2013: 36)

Jackson is well connected with leaders of the white religious right movement such as James Dobson and Tony Perkins, and Jackson has also been welcomed into the inner sanctum of the clandestine Arlington Group, an organization founded by Reverend Donald Wildmon, founder of the American Family Association with strong ties to the Bush administration.[4] As senior fellow Peter Montgomery of the People for the American Way points out, Jackson has made a name for himself with his staunch social conservatism, from leading anti-gay rallies and mobilizing support for the anti-gay marriage Propositions 8 and 2 in California and Florida respectively, to supporting former President George W. Bush's election. Ultimately, this emerging coalition of the white and black religious right against gay rights is only comprehensible in light of the following factor. One has to take note of and reckon with the increasing *racialization* of the gay rights movement by the right, and this is very much the case even though gay people of color, especially African Americans, are not in visible leadership roles in the gay rights movement. In addition, at a much more discursive, ideological, and "common sense" level, comparisons of gay equality with racial equality (i.e., the passage of the Supreme Court case Loving v. Virginia as a rationalization for the legalization of gay marriages[5]) allows those on the right to find a niche, which in this instance is race, which they can then use to enter into a dialogue with those in the African American community. In the next section, I explain how this racialized discourse operates.

The Racialized Discourse of the Anti-gay Rights Movement

On February 7, 2012, the US 9th Circuit Court of Appeals ruled that California's Proposition 8, the ballot measure that restricted the definition of marriage to be one man and one woman, unconstitutional. The following year, on June 26, 2013, the Supreme Court ruled that the proponents of Proposition 8 did not have legal standing to defend the law in federal court and thus dismissed their appeal and ordered that the stay on the ninth district's ruling be lifted. Four years earlier when Proposition 8 passed in California one of the side stories to this development was the overwhelming support African Americans voters gave to the proposition. Many in the media asserted that Proposition 8 passed mainly due to the support given to it by African Americans and this was a clear indication that African Americans were staunchly against gay rights. There is no denying that African Americans have been mixed on the passage of gay rights, particularly legalized gay marriage. Various conservative African American ministers have been outspoken in their opposition to gay rights and have mobilized other African Americans in several urban areas to oppose the passage of gay rights legislation.[6] But the key question that needs to be asked is, how effective are social conservatives in cultivating the homophobia of a segment of the African American community into solid support for a conservative agenda? There are no simple answers to this question. The main factor that helps explain how both white and African American social conservatives have been able to tap into the anti-gay rights sentiment present within the African American community is the racialization of the movement. This has been an established strategy practiced by those on the right for over two decades. In the nineties, various social conservative organizations such as the Traditional Values Coalition went into African American churches and provided documentation and training on how best to mobilize others to their anti-gay agenda. They even created Today it is organizations such as the National Organization for Marriage, an organization created to spearhead the push for the passage of California's Proposition 8, making the creation of a riff between African Americans and gay rights movement a central strategy in their fight against gay rights.[7] The gay rights is not civil rights dialogue gets framed as if it is in the interest of African Americans to become involved in the fight against gay rights *in order to protect a civil rights legacy*—given the problematic "co-opting" and "tarnishing" of the legacy of a valid and worthy movement (civil rights) by one that is invalid on its own merits (gay rights) as articulated by the Reverend Patrick Wooden of The Upper Room Church of God in Christ in Raleigh, North Carolina:

> African-Americans are appalled that their Civil Rights Movement has been co-opted by the so-called Civil Rights movement of the homosexuals...It is an insult; it is angering when LGBT groups say there is no difference between being black and being homosexual. (Kaufman 2012)

For the racialization strategy to be successful social conservatives must rely on two others: historical amnesia and the invisibility of African American gays and lesbians. Historical amnesia occurs when both sides—white conservatives and black religious conservatives—either overlook or downplay the antagonism that the white right had toward the civil rights movement, equally labeling the proponents of racial equality as asking for "special rights" in the heyday of the civil rights struggle. This selective forgetting of history lessens the possibility of tensions arising between the black religious right and white conservatives. In addition, the invisibility of black gays and lesbians is in some ways the glue that keeps the coalition together. The white right can then portray the gay rights movement as comprised of whites who already have privileges, such as material wealth, and thus do not need the so-called added "special privilege" of being recognized by the state as deserving equal treatment under the law. The construction of the gay movement as a white movement that has no legitimacy enables African Americans to express their homophobia much more easily, and what is disregarded is how these attacks on gay rights impact blacks that are also gay. As activist and scholar Barbara Smith states: "Because we are rendered invisible in both Black and gay contexts, it is that much easier for the Black community to oppose gay rights and to express homophobia without recognizing that these attacks and the lack of legal protections affects its own members" (Smith 1995: 273).

For African Americans, the impression that the gay rights movement is a movement of whites who are already privileged produces resentment, especially when paired with the view that what white gays have suffered is less than the centuries of oppression created by racism in American society. Even conservatives who favor gay marriage can adopt this viewpoint as one young conservative expressed on a conservative website.

There have been instances during the gay-rights movement that arguably could be compared to the black civil rights struggle, like the Stonewall riots of the 1960s or Matthew Shepard murder in 1998...Still, with the possible exception of the mistreatment of Native Americans, there has been nothing quite like the systematic exploitation and institutional degradation experienced by earlier black Americans...My purpose here is not to belittle the fight for gay marriage, only to note that those who keep attempting to draw a reasonable comparison to the struggle of African Americans are in many ways belittling the black experience in the United States. (Hunter 2013)

This line of reasoning is enticing for a number of reasons. First, the acknowledgement of the "systematic exploitation and institutional degradation" experienced by African Americans not only sends the message to African Americans of the recognition to the true extent of the oppression they have experienced in the United States but also puts forth a reverence for the struggle encountered by those involved in the civil rights movement. Second, the same invoking of the "systematic exploitation and institutional degradation" suffered by African Americans privileges the victimization of African Americans in comparison to the victimization of white gays and lesbians,[8] therefore, rhetorically, those who attempt to compare the struggle for gay marriage with the struggle for racial equality is in the words of the author "belittling the black experience in the United States." Third, the favoring of the mistreatment of African Americans over that toward gays and lesbians in essence elevates or gives a higher standing or importance to, racial victimization over sexual victimization. Finally, this line of reasoning further reinforces the false perception that the gay rights movement is a movement that is only focused on garnering benefits to white gays and lesbians. Therefore, it is vital that African American gays and lesbians are elided in this argument because the recognition of African American gays and lesbians causes the argument to fall apart. In addition to cultivating homophobia as motivation to oppose gay rights formulating resentment to white privilege (e.g., white gays and lesbians are successful and affluent because of the advantages their whiteness brings them) is also used as an agent to curry opposition. Because of their blackness, African American gay and lesbians cannot benefit from white privilege, which nullifies the logic of the argument. What is also necessary for this argument to be convincing is the simultaneous essentializing of race and the social construction of sexuality. For example, when Shirley Phelps-Roper, member of the Phelps' Westboro Baptist

Church and daughter of notorious anti-gay activist the late Reverend Fred Phelps, was asked if she sees the hypocrisy in her father's anti-gay activism and his history as a civil rights lawyer, fighting for the legal rights of African Americans, she said the two are perfectly compatible because one does not have the ability to choose their race as they can with their sexuality and thus act in a manner that is sinful to God.

> You're born black. It's something you can't change even if you're Michael Jackson... God never said it was an abomination to be black. (Blake 2010)[9]

The logic behind this sentiment is race is an immutable characteristic that is biologically based which an individual has no agency in changing while sexuality is a socially constructed entity individuals have agency over. Ironically, what conservative proponents may or may not realize is, in the attempt to delegitimize gay rights this argument's logic subtly acknowledges that American society was premised on the belief of white supremacy. The rationale goes something like this: because African Americans are individuals born with a characteristic (blackness) that society deemed to be inferior to those that have a more appealing and alleged superior characteristic (whiteness) and thus qualifying the marginalization and oppression exacted upon them, therefore, the civil rights movement, in a land that professes equality for all, was justified. On the other hand, since sexuality is something we supposedly have the ability "to choose or be influenced to practice," individuals who "elect" to act in a manner that is "not normal" and goes against "God's desires" are electing to bring about their own victimization. Therefore, there is no need for a gay rights movement because what they are asking for can be received if, and only if, they would begin to act "normal" (heterosexuality) as society sees fit.

Anti-gay rights activists are not solely responsible for the invisibility of black gays and lesbians in the mainstream gay rights movement. Gay rights advocates also contribute to this by not recognizing the importance of adopting an analysis that is nuanced in recognizing how individuals' multiple identities intersect, and therefore can produce similarities, but also, important differences in their societal experiences. The comparison of gay rights with civil rights would provide an even more powerful analysis if they were seen less in an additive sense, as simply layering a parallel and new oppression on top of an old one, and more in a multiplicative and intersectional sense, where race and sexuality are seen to have mutually reciprocal and intensifying effects on each other

(King 1988; Crenshaw 1994, 2001). Barbara Smith recounts the struggles she and other gay activists of color have had in getting the mainstream movement to expand the scope of its agenda to include an anti-racist component: "Lesbians and gay men of color have been trying to push the gay movement to grasp the necessity of anti-racist practice for near 20 years. Except in the context of organizing within the women's movement with progressive white lesbians feminists, we haven't made much progress" (Smith 1995: 274).

The cavalier manner in which some white gays and lesbians connect the struggle for gay rights to the movement for racial equality is a factor that produces hostility among African Americans toward gay right advocates. For example, in the early nineties the New York-based white lesbian organization *Lesbian Avengers* called their mobilization journey in several northeastern states "freedom ride," in reference to the famed freedom rides of the civil rights movement. This move did not go over well with some African Americans. As Smith points out, what was bothersome about the title was, "the appropriation of this term was offensive because the organization had not demonstrated involvement in anti-racist organizing and has made no links with people of color, including non-lesbians and gays in the communities they planned to visit" (Smith 1995: 275). In addition to the cavalier manner in which some white gays and lesbians connect the struggle for gay rights to the movement for racial equality, opposition by some African Americans to the gay rights movement is also borne through the racism present within the gay rights movement that anti-gay rights opponents exploit to their benefit. For example, an African American lesbian activist recounted the racial epithets directed at her and her friends from white gay rights advocates when they attended a protest rally the night Proposition 8 passed.

> It didn't take them long to go there,..And I'll tell you something: it can't be all 'Kumbaya' on Nov. 3, and 'we hate all black people' on Nov. 5. That's just unacceptable. (Grisby Gates 2008)

The exploitation by white and black conservative opponents of the racism among some white gay rights proponents enables the opponents to gay rights to easily construct the gay movement as a white movement that has no legitimacy which allows African Americans to express their homophobia much more easily. In the process what gets disregarded is how these attacks on gay rights impact African Americans who are also gay.

African American gay and lesbians are placed in a difficult position as they feel the pressure coming from both communities to choose which side they are on.

But this begs the question, are African Americans more homophobic and outspoken against gay rights than other groups? While various surveys have illustrated higher levels of African American opposition to homosexuality than whites, when it pertains to issues of sodomy laws, gay civil liberties, and employment discrimination African American and whites hold similar opinions on these matters. In fact, African Americans are more likely to support laws that prohibit anti-gay discrimination (Lewis 2003: 75–76).

Referring back to the question I posed earlier, can the tapping into African Americans' homophobia be an effective tool in mobilizing African Americans to a larger conservative agenda? There are a couple of reasons that indicate the gains conservatives could possibly receive from this strategy may be limited. First, let us take a closer look at the political behavior of African Americans during the 2008 Proposition 8 vote. While a record number of African Americans came out to vote in California, this was not because of Proposition 8 but attributed to Barack Obama running for the presidency. The media latched on to this development and attributed the high turnout of African American voters as the cause of the anti-gay marriage legislation passing but a closer look at the data shows that if African American voting participation stayed at the level it was during the 2004 presidential election Proposition 8 would have passed anyway (Abrajano 2010: 929). Therefore, it is not correct to assume that the large turnout of African American voters in California was the main reason for the success of Proposition 8. One vital lesson learned from this outcome was gay rights activists needed to do a better job in mobilizing support within communities of color (ibid.: 930).[10] Second, African Americans who hold anti-gay views do not necessarily use those views as a litmus test for politicians. In other words, African Americans will not vote against a political candidate because she or he expresses support for gay rights. One example of this is when the Obama administration announced earlier in 2011 they would continue to enforce the Defense of Marriage Act as it was still in existence but would no longer defend the law in court that outlawed same-sex marriages.[11] After this announcement, there were no significant signs of reduction of support among African Americans toward President Obama because of his stance. For instance, according to University of Connecticut's Roper

Public Opinion center's demographic breakdown of voting patterns in the 2012 presidential election, President Obama received 93% of the African American vote to Governor Romney's 6% (Roper 2012).[12] What comes to light with this development is the fact that African Americans, like other voting blocs, are more likely to place priority to a variety of issues such as economic concerns, jobs, health care, education, and social justice than be focused on just one single issue, like gay rights. The continued support of President Obama can also be understood as African Americans being more willing to cast their vote for candidates who they perceive to have progressive stances on the aforementioned issues even though they may differ with them regarding their position on LGBT matters (Kaufman 2011). In the end it appears, thankfully, that all of the effort put forth by the anti-gay rights movement will go for naught as the steady overturning by the courts of previously passed anti-gay marriage measures increase the possibility that one day gay marriage will be the law of the land.

SCHOOL CHOICE AND VOUCHERS PROGRAMS

It has been over sixty years since the Supreme Court made their landmark ruling in the Brown versus Board of Education of Topeka case, which ruled that state laws enabling segregation in public education was unconstitutional. The Brown decision overturned the court's previous ruling in Plessey v. Ferguson that allowed for state-sanctioned segregation. For African Americans, the Brown ruling gave hope and optimism that the Court's clearing the path to educational integration would be their opportunity in achieving educational equality. At the beginning of the twenty-first century, the levels of racial segregation and class inequality within the nation's public schools are on the rise, leaving many African Americans parents frustrated and eager to look for solutions.[13] The frustration African American parents have with the public school systems and eagerness to find quality education for their children has provided African American social conservatives with their best opportunity to win support from a majority of African Americans.[14] As David Bositis points out, "...African Americans have been the center of the school vouchers debate...largely because black children disproportionately attend poor schools-and parents know when their children's schools are not working. Because of this dissatisfaction much of black public opinion will favor any alternative to the status quo (Bositis 2004: 177-178)."

African Americans consistently convey support for school voucher and charter programs as educational options for their children. Surveys conducted by the Joint Center for Political and Educational Studies, a think tank that examines issues pertaining to African Americans consistently show African Americans strong support for school voucher programs. In 1999 (60% favor to 33% opposed school vouchers) and 2002 (57–43%), and in 2008 the support for school vouchers reached an all time high of 63–29% opposed (Bositis 2009: 15). A strong urban tax base and a neighborhood's wealth are key components in determining a public school district's ability to gain access to various resources needed in providing a quality education to its children. Given substantial numbers of African Americans still live in post-industrial urban areas (particularly in the Midwest and Northeast) that have weakened tax bases and racially segregated communities where black neighborhoods do not possess the same levels of wealth as white neighborhoods it is not surprising that support for school voucher and charter programs are high among African Americans.[15]

The white right has been searching for ways to penetrate the African American community and cultivate support for their agenda. In pursuit of building alliances with African Americans, white conservatives have been more than willing to provide both exposure and institutional support to African Americans who are in support of school choice (*Journal of Blacks in Higher Education* 2002: 79). For instance, The Black Alliance for Educational Options (BAEO) is an organization founded by former Milwaukee school superintendent Howard Fuller in 1999 and has on its board of directors and advisory board notable figures such as former mayor of Newark, New Jersey and now Senator Cory Booker and former Ohio gubernatorial GOP candidate Kenneth Blackwell. While BAEO meetings are closed off to whites the organization is not shy in taking money from white conservative organizations. The BAEO has been the recipient of generous funding by such conservative institutions as the Bradley, Walton, and Milton and Rose Friedman foundations (Themba 2001). Another important figure that has had involvement with the school voucher program is Reverend Floyd Flake of New York, a strident defender of school vouchers for poor African American children. Like a number of conservative African American ministers, Flake has built up plenty of political, social, and financial capital through his various connections and projects. I provide a more detail analysis of Flake in Chapter 8 that examines the African American religious right. African American school voucher advocates are similar to their African

American peers in the anti-abortion movement in a number of ways. First, they do not demonize the African American poor in the manner in which they pitch their cause to other African Americans. Whereas most of the blame, particularly by conservatives, on African Americans educational problems has been on the stereotypical "incorrigible black student" or defects in African Americans culture,[16] organizations such as the BAEO instead put the focus on faulty schools and crafts television and radio advertisements that have everyday African American parents eloquently expressing their desires for their children to receive a quality education. These commercials aim to achieve two main objectives. One, to provide a corrective to the dominant stereotype of the lackadaisical or misguided African American parent present in common discourse about the academic achievement gap between black and white students. For instance, African American parents are often charged with a variety of shortcomings such as accepting mediocre academic performances from their children, not becoming involved in school matters, like attending parent-teacher meetings, or not instilling the importance of educational success in their children. Two, to illustrate that not only are African American parents just as concerned in the quality of education their children receive like parents of other races but are willing to move beyond relying on the government to provide solutions to the chronic problem of unequal education and put faith in such market-based policies like school vouchers. The second commonality, African American school choice supporters have with their anti-abortion counterparts is their acknowledgement of the role race and racism plays in the educational inequality African Americans experience. Third, some are outspoken in their criticism of the racism they sometimes encounter from their white counterparts. One individual who comes to mind is Annette "Polly" Williams, a former Wisconsin Democrat state representative from Milwaukee who has been in the forefront of the school voucher movement and central in getting the voucher program established in the Milwaukee school district.

Matriarch of the African American School Voucher Movement Annette "Polly" Williams

Annette "Polly" Williams has been a passionate educational advocate for poor African Americans who live in her district and until recently a popular figure among conservatives for quite some time. Williams was born in Belzoni, Mississippi but raised in Milwaukee, Wisconsin when her parents, like so many other African Americans during the post-World War II era, migrated northward in search for better opportunities. After three unsuccessful attempts at occupying political office, Williams was finally successful in 1980 by first winning the Democratic nomination and then the general election to represent the 17th district[17] in Wisconsin's state assembly. Williams spent thirty years in office before retiring in 2010, during that time Williams' voting record and actions provides a picture of a woman whose politics are quite fluid, meaning on some issues she was conservative and others not. For example, Williams' conservatism was illustrated when she voted in favor of a proposed amendment to the state's constitution defining marriage as being between one man and one woman, voted against the state's plan to implement regulations on the payday lending industry, and voted against a bill that called for a change in the state's sex education curriculum to include as part of the discussion the benefits, side effects, and proper use of contraceptives, approved by the Federal Drug Administration (FDA), used to prevent pregnancy and sexually transmitted diseases. On the other hand, Williams took more liberal positions on other issues. For instance, she sponsored a bill that restricted health insurance companies the ability to exclude individuals for coverage, voted against another bill that would allow school boards to use student test scores in evaluating teachers, and co-sponsored a bill calling for the increase in the state's minimum wage.[18] But no one issue defined Williams' political career more than her advocacy of school voucher or choice programs. This is an issue that makes Williams, as an African American Democrat, different than most of her African American Democratic peers.

Frustrated and weary of the lack of improvement of public schools in her district Williams decided there had to be another solution in providing quality education to impoverished African American children. Working with then Governor Tommy Thompson and several Republican lawmakers, in 1990 Williams helped usher in Milwaukee's school choice program the nation's first publicly funded program for low-income students. Williams was first given exposure to the larger conservative movement by speaking in front of enthusiastic audiences at various conservative think tanks and then national acclaim when the news program 60 Minutes did a feature on her back in the eighties.

Williams Ruffles Feathers

For all the accolades and institutional assistance Williams has received by her white counterparts[19] she has never shied away from pointing out, what she believes are, the racial and class motives behind her white allies actions. For as much that whites in the school choice movement speak of the importance of school vouchers for African Americans and how excited they are to be finding common ground with them on this issue Williams is quick to point out that these same whites do not work with existing African American leaders but instead choose to select those that they feel are amenable to their agenda (Morken and Formicola 1999: 203). Williams is also skeptical about her white counterparts genuine care for the educational needs of the African American poor; instead, she claims they see vouchers as a way to insulate their children from encroaching African American students (ibid.: 204). There is some merit to Williams' point as history has shown that when southern whites were faced with integration after the Brown decision school voucher plans were created as one of the ways to avoid the desegregated schools. As legal scholar, Wendy Parker states, "Choice may be as American as 'apple pie,' but so is racism and separatism, and choice has a history of unlawfully segregating students" (Parker 2001: 568).[20] Williams points out that when religious schools were included in Milwaukee's school voucher plan the number of students increased 5 times its original number with white students being the majority and African American students losing out. For example, Williams points to the transportation costs constraints many poor African American parents in her district faced when the schools available were far away from their neighborhoods. In essence, as Williams sees it, when Milwaukee's voucher program mainly addressed the needs of whites it was an instance of "white people throwing their baggage on our train" (Morken and Formicola 1999: 206). What concerns Williams about the proposal by current governor Scott Walker and his Republican peers to do away with the income requirement and make the program available to school districts that have a minimum of four thousand students and at least two schools that are not meeting the state's educational standards is that the needs of the group the program was initially targeted to low-income African American children will get lost in the shuffle. As the program currently stands a married couple that has two children and a household income of close to $77,000 is eligible to participate. But as Williams sees it, a couple at that income level is in a better position to seek other options for their children like paying for private school education or moving to other areas with better public schools, something the constituents she use to represent did not have (Murphy 2014). In reality, as the cost of living steadily increases while wages remain stagnate or decline it is not a certainty that a family with a household income of $77,000 can easily enact those options Williams mentions. The umbrage Williams takes with the present direction of the program is one where she feels now that the fight to get the voucher program in existence has been won, the proposed changes allow the middle-class and other classes to reap the rewards of that struggle. A struggle Williams feels many in those classes were not as invested in before she and others were successful.

> "As soon as the doors open for the low-income children, they're trampled by the high income," she said. "It's as if the struggle we went through 20-some years ago—now the upper crust have taken over. (Murphy 2014)"

Interestingly, what Williams is describing is a similar process that takes place with gentrification. The families of the lower-income children are metaphorically the older residents who get shunted aside as they watch their once downtrodden community go through a structural makeover and become a desirable area to the newer more affluent incoming inhabitants. Also what Williams is articulating here is her concern of low-income African American children and their families being impacted by the process known as state racism, a concept created by social theorist Michel Foucault. According to Foucault, state racism involves the deployment of death or the elimination of a racialized subpopulation with the intent of improving the life and health of the general population (Foucault et al. 2003: 254–257). State racism can take place in a direct or indirect manner. An example of a direct manner of state racism is illustrated by the genocide of Native Americans by European settlers to the United States. An indirect form of state racism involves "exposing someone to death, increasing the risk of death for some people, or quite simply political death, expulsion, rejection, and so on" (ibid.: 256). Gentrification is an example of the enactment of state racism in a spatial or geopolitical manner, as in most cases it is the older poorer residents of color who eventually get shifted out of the rejuvenated area to make room for groups of newer residents, mainly white, who possess higher levels of human, social, and financial capitals.

In this instance, the expansion of the school voucher program to middle-class and more affluent classes poses the potential of further marginalizing lower-income children as the vouchers, in essence, become subsidies to families that can afford, or are in need of small amounts of financial assistance, to pay the tuitions charged by the private schools in the programs. Also, children from higher income brackets have a leg up on their poorer counterparts when it comes to preparedness, desirability, and eligibility for acceptance to private schools that participate in the choice programs. Therefore, as the program becomes more universal in scope the interests of lower-income children, who as Williams asserts are the ones who need the program the most, are overshadowed by those of the middle-class.

Another problem that has curtailed attempts at providing educational equality in public schools has been the ability of suburban areas to insulate themselves from any program that links them with their urban counterparts. From a racial standpoint, this means that white suburbanites often act to protect the financial and other advantages they have over their urbanities of color counterparts. While school vouchers may provide parents in poor school districts the ability to move their children to other schools, this choice is somewhat limited as typically most suburban schools districts fight to exclude themselves from any plan that calls for their involvement. Which means that most school voucher and other school choice plans tend to be structurally intra-district and not inter-district. As legal scholars, James Ryan and Michael Heise point out unless this situation is changed what benefits that school choice programs have to offer will be limited.

> The political economy of school choice, which we have tried to explicate, suggests that the biggest obstacle to expanding choice in meaningful ways stems from suburban opposition to any changes to the status quo that might upset the suburbs' advantaged position. This opposition has been a constant in the area of school reform, and it has worked to shape reforms in ways that leave the financial and physical independence of suburban schools intact. Existing school choice programs conform to this historical pattern, as most leave suburban schools untouched... If this pattern remains unaltered, we should not expect school choice to reach its theoretical potential in terms of racial or socioeconomic integration, academic achievement, or beneficial competition among public schools. (Heise and Ryan 2002: 2135)

But even if more suburban schools were involved in the voucher programs the memories of the indifference or outright hostility African American children and parents received from some white teachers and school administrators in white school districts that were mandated to participate in busing programs are still fresh in the minds of African Americans in Williams' generation. It is this concern that causes Williams to adamantly believe African Americans should have complete control over schools in their neighborhoods, from curriculum design to teachers and administrators being African American. As Williams forcefully states, "We run our own schools." While Williams' call for African Americans to control their neighborhood schools comes across to some as racist hyperbole, in the same fashion as the calls for local control of schools by African Americans, in major cities such as New York, during the Sixties, what Williams is touching upon is the importance of looking out for African American interests. There is research that shows Williams may have a better understanding of the pulse of the African American community than we think. For example, scholars Wayne Lewis and Arnold Danzig discovered in their study that race was an important criterion for African American parents in their selection of a charter school they wanted to send their children to. The small class sizes, respectful treatment received from both the faculty and administration were also important factors that determined the choice of school they made for their children. But the chances that a school had a predominately African American faculty or administration made the school more appealing to the parents in Lewis and Danzig's study, even if the school's academic performance was not as high as the academic performances in other racially mixed schools. For example, having teachers that looked like their children was important because to the parents it meant the teachers could serve multiple roles to their children as both educators and role models (Lewis and Danzig 2010: 205–223). On the surface, it is easy to interpret the findings from Lewis and Danzig's study as an instance where the desire for racial homogeneity on the part of the African American parents is an example of an illogical desire for racial separatism. But the authors aptly summarize what fuels the parents use of race in their decision on which charter school to send their children.

These parents' beliefs and preferences should be contextualized with the understanding that African Americans have and continue to be victims of racial prejudice and hatred in the United States. Study participants' preferences to have their children in the charge of other African Americans, their own higher degree of comfort in the presence of other African Americans, and their beliefs that White teachers are less capable of truly understanding African American students may come as a result of racism and racist interactions in predominately White schools as well as broader American society. (Lewis and Danzig: 218)

While not all African American parents share the same sentiments as the ones in Lewis and Danzig's study it does not negate the reality that America is not a color-blind society and historically African Americans have had uneven experiences with white educators and schools, both of these things Williams clearly understands.

Williams's stridency in articulating African American interests in school voucher programs and assertiveness in calling out what she perceives as racism within the movement has brought strong criticism from other voucher advocates. For example, educational and public policy consultant George Mitchell, who is white and an active crusader in the school voucher program in Wisconsin, has not taken too kindly to Williams's criticism of Governor Scott's changes and in various conservative blogs charged Williams of racism and claimed she was "irrelevant" to the current movement.

Polly was useful to the school choice movement because of her race and her party affiliation,.. But she was and remains a racist... When you connect with Polly, I would doubt that she would dispute my assessment of her racial (and religious) bigotry... She wore this dislike of whites on her sleeve. (Brice 2013)

This is a telling accusation, not only because of Mitchell's willingness to "play the race card" as conservatives often accuse those who raise the issue of race but also in his attempt to substantiate Williams' "irrelevancy" by claiming that her value to the voucher movement was in essence, as a token or racial mascot. Ironically Mitchell would vehemently refute this claim if someone on the liberal left made this charge. Yet, Mitchell goes further by responding to the question of who exactly used Williams with the answer "who didn't use her (Brice 2013)?" This begs the question, why would a white conservative like Mitchell, who probably believes in the validity of color blindness, think Williams derived her significance to the voucher movement from her race?

Could it be that historically one of the motivating elements fueling the voucher movement was racism and that Williams is an African American espousing support for a policy whose origins came about as a counter to the integration of African American children in predominately white public schools? Or that conservatives have been on the "wrong side of history" when it pertains to African Americans and racial equality? Williams refutes Mitchell's claim that white conservatives anointed her as a spokesperson for the voucher movement.

> I was used? I don't understand that..Nobody came to me and said..We want you to lead on this. (Brice 2013)

While it is safe to say that Williams rightfully earned her recognition from the determination and tireless effort she put forth in mobilizing supporters and creating alliances to the cause there is no denying that her race definitely helped in bringing some of the attention toward her. When Williams was on the conservative circuit making her appeal to conservative audiences, who were mainly white, it is hard to believe that Williams' race was something that went unnoticed. And although Williams adamantly disputes the notion she was anointed the spokesperson for the school choice movement because of her blackness, in a comment about Howard Fuller, an individual Williams has had history with, she seems to contradict herself by stating, "Howard ... is the person that the white people have selected to lead the choice movement now because I don't cooperate (Murphy 2001)," indicating that she was once the right's golden girl until she stopped walking lock stock and barrel with their agenda. In any case, a movement, such as the conservative one, desiring to see itself as one that can attract Americans from all walks of life, particularly African Americans, to think that race does not matter or is invisible in American society is surely misguided at best and folly at worst. Conservatives are impacted like other Americans of different ideological persuasions by the inescapability of race.

What also distinguishes Williams from some of her other school voucher advocates is her strong belief that the goal of voucher programs should not be to destroy public schools. Instead according to Williams, underperforming public schools should also receive assistance in reaching their full potential and not be subjected to state receivership (Morken and Formicola 1999: 207). This view differs sharply with many school advocates who see the educational crisis in stark black and white terms or where school reform is a sum zero gain where for vouchers to win the concept of public schools must lose. In addition to the recognition of importance in sustaining a societal common good like public education, there is another vital reason in acknowledging Williams is correct in her sentiment. As anthropologist Amanda Walker Johnson insightfully points out, the impact of the closure of an underperforming school is more substantial than how it is usually reported in the media or understood in the context of a school reform built on the philosophy of "starting anew" or with a "clean slate."

> One aspect ignored by the idealistic views of "clean slate" and "fresh start" is that reconstitution deconstructs the working infrastructure and complex social networks of a school, and in the context of constant media scrutiny and stigma in addition to lack of proper resources, such deconstruction can produce a "strained and demoralized workforce" and student body. (Walker Johnson 2013: 240)

In addition to demoralization, the loss of a school can produce in neighborhood residents a sense that a death has occurred. Schools, homes, stores, and other entities present in neighborhoods are not only buildings that occupy land spaces but embedded within them are collective memories, experiences, and complex social ties. These various entities are not only useful in a functional manner but also from a psychological standpoint they help in our identity formation and emotional connection to an area or space. For example, it is not uncommon to see some individuals silently weep when an old sports stadium or arena is taken down, even though the team is relocating to a more modern and fancier building the sense of loss is not dissipated by this fact. When a neighborhood loses such an important entity like schools they are vulnerable to experiencing what psychiatrist Mindy Fullilove calls root shock. According to Fullilove, root shock is "the traumatic stress reaction to the destruction of all or part of one's emotional ecosystem." As Fullilove states, our bodies have a built-in system to maintain its internal balance in the same manner we also have a system to sustain the external balance between the larger social world (Fullilove 2005: 11). At the individual level root shock brings about intense "emotional upheaval that destroys the working model of the world that had existed in the individual's head" while at the community level, root shock deracinates the existing social bonds that were formed over time in the area. Williams understands all too well, through the experiences of serving her constituents in her district, what the impact of losing important community entities such as public schools has on a community. While Williams's call to save public schools and advocating for school choice may seem contradictory, if not, hypocritical, it is not. From Williams's perspective, the two principles can co-exist and help low-income African American parents achieve their goal of providing a quality education to their children. It is this sort of nuanced position that could appeal to African Americans, as David Bositis understands the support of vouchers among African Americans to represent their "rejection of the status quo – that is, poorly performing schools and students – rather than an endorsement of this particular reform" (Bositis 2001).

In addition to individuals like Polly Williams another agent that plays a role in mobilizing a segment of African Americans to social conservative views is the conservative wing of the African American church, a subject that I examine in Chapter 8. The African American Christian right has been actively involved in all three social causes mentioned in this and the previous chapter with some ministers having at their disposal finances and large congregations to make an impact within the community. The fact that various African American conservative activists openly speak of the impact race and racism has played in conflicts that arise between them and their white counterparts, and the assertive manner in which they integrate these subjects into their discourse as a means to garner support among their peers are examples of the inescapability of race in play. Another example of the inescapability of race, is the Republican Party's adversarial relationship it has with African Americans and the challenge it poses, to African American conservatives and other conservatives, in transforming the social conservatism among some African Americans into support for a larger political conservative agenda, this and other issues I address in the next chapter.

NOTES

1. The ironic aspect of this situation is precisely how the lack of historical memory enables this ideologically anti-gay bond to develop between white religious and social conservatives and conservative black ministers. For it was the same white conservatives who, several decades earlier, were making identical accusations about the civil rights movement's

call for racial equality as involving "special" interests and representing non-universal values.

2. Frederick Price is a disciple of Reverend Kenneth Hagin who was a devout proponent of the prosperity gospel. Rev. Price heads the mega church Crenshaw Christian Center in Los Angeles with a membership of eighteen thousand. Price has been known to actively distance himself from anything deemed racial, as illustrated by his hostility to local black community organizations during the 1980s. Price prohibited them from using his facilities, eschewing any connection to racial advocacy organizations such as the NAACP, and refusing to take stands on racial issues (Asadullah 1998: A7).

3. Sean Cahill, "The Disproportionate Impact of Antigay Family Policies Black and Latino Same-sex Couple Households," *Journal of African American Studies*, September 2009, p. 224.

4. According to Doug Ireland, the Arlington Group is, "so secretive it doesn't even have a website—was formed in 2003 by a key White House Christian Right ally, the Rev. Donald Wildmon. Wildmon is head of the Tupelo, Mississippi-based American Family Association, which—through its broadcasting arm, American Family Radio—runs a network of more than 200 Christian radio stations and affiliate groups. The Arlington Group was formed in response to the Supreme Court's ruling striking down the sodomy laws, and in expectation that the Massachusetts Supreme Judicial Court would hold gay marriage to be a civil right (as indeed it did in 2003)" (Ireland 2006: 6).

5. In the Loving v. Virginia case, the court struck down Virginia's anti-miscegenation statute stating the law prohibiting interracial marriages was unconstitutional.

6. One such individual is Bishop Harry Jackson of the Hope Christian Church in Beltsville, MD is in the forefront of fighting against gay rights, particularly legalized gay marriage. Jackson is the founder and leader of the High Impact Leadership Coalition (HILC). The HILC is an organization that focuses on moral issues such as gay rights and abortion. In 2009, Jackson filed a lawsuit against the District of Columbia after the D.C. Board of Elections rejected a ballot initiative on the issue of same-sex marriage that Jackson had mobilized support for. The Board of Elections rejected the initiative because they felt it would violate D.C.'s Human Rights Act. Jackson appealed the decision all the way to the Supreme Court but the Court declined to hear the case. This setback has not deterred Jackson from his ultimate goal, which is to restore a sense of moral and cultural normalcy in American society.

7. According to National Organization For marriage's internal documents, one of the organization's projects was called "Not A Civil Right." The

project's main goal was "driving a wedge between Gays and Blacks" with a strategy that aimed to "Find, Equip, and connect African American spokespeople for marriage; develop a media campaign around their objection to gay marriage as a civil right; provoke the gay marriage base into responding by denouncing these spokesmen and women as bigots." *National Marriage Board Update 2008–2009*, courtesy of http://s3. documentcloud.org/documents/328445/national-organization-for-marriage-memo.pdf, accessed August 6, 2014.

8. I specifically make the distinction that gays and lesbians are white because for this line of argumentation to work African American gays and lesbians must not exist. The argument's strength rests on the implied notion that being black and gay is mutually exclusive. To include black gays and lesbians into the picture inserts the interconnectivity of race and sexuality oppression, which complicates this simplistic reasoning.

9. John Blake, "'Most-Hated,' Anti-gay Preacher Once Fought for Civil Rights," http://www.cnn.com/2010/US/05/05/hate.preacher/, accessed August 6, 2014. According to a number of African Americans who knew and worked alongside with Phelps, Phelps had the reputation in Kansas of not only being a talented lawyer but also a jurist with a steely courageousness to take on cases other African American and white attorneys would shy away from. There is some debate about who Phelps really was and his motivation for becoming a civil rights activist. According to his estranged son Nate Phelps, his father was an undercover racist who spoke about blacks in a disparaging manner behind their backs and saw the opportunity to accumulate wealth in becoming a civil rights attorney. Others such as Phelps' daughter refutes her brother's claim that Phelps was a racist while scholar Matthew Rozsa, acknowledging that Phelps did make a tidy sum of money from taking on discrimination cases in Topeka, points out that there was no guarantee that Phelps would be victorious in those cases. Rozsa also points out that a close examination of Phelps' overall career shows that greed was not what motivated Phelps. See Napp Nazworth, "Before Fred Phelps Preached Hate, He Was a Civil Rights Hero," March 20, 2014, http://www.christianpost.com/news/before-fred-phelps-preached-hate-he-was-a-civil-rights-hero-116492/, accessed August 6, 2014.

10. As Marisa Abrajano states, "It may be the case that with greater mobilization efforts to inform ethnic/racial minorities about this issue, particularly in the form of personal contact attitudes toward same-sex marriage could potentially shift over time." Ibid., p. 930.

11. The Obama administration's decision in 2011 to discontinue defending the law in court was derived from the belief that the third section in the act, which defined a legally recognized marriage as only one between a man and woman, was unconstitutional. Two years later the Supreme

Court would validate this belief by ruling section three of the act was indeed unconstitutional.

12. Roper Public Opinion Center, US Elections: How Groups Voted in 2012, http://www.ropercenter.uconn.edu/elections/how_groups_voted/voted_12.html, accessed July 17, 2014.

13. For an excellent analysis of this phenomenon see chap. 3, "The Growth of Segregation: African Americans, Latinos, and Unequal Education" by Gary Orfield in *Dismantling Desegregation: The Quiet Reversal of Brown v. Board*, eds. Gary Orfield, Susan E. Eaton, et al. (New York: The New Press, 1996), pp. 53–73.

14. In surveys taken by the Joint Center for Political and Educational Studies, African Americans have stated higher levels of dissatisfaction with the public schools than their white counterparts. See David A. Bositis, "1999 National Opinion Poll: Education" (Washington, DC: Joint Center for Political and Educational Studies Publications, 1999), pp. 4 and 5, "2002 National Opinion Poll: Education," p. 4.

15. For more on the racial wealth divide see Melvin Oliver and Thomas Shapiro, *Black Wealth White Wealth: A New Perspective on Racial Inequality* (New York: Routledge, 2005), Thomas Shapiro, *The Hidden Cost of Being African American: How Wealth Perpetuates Inequality* (New York: Oxford University Press, 2004). Chap. 3, "Forged in Blood: Black Wealth Injustice in the United States." In *The Color of Wealth: The Story Behind The U.S. Racial Wealth Divide*, eds. Meizhu Lui, et al. (New York: The New Press, 2006), pp. 73–130.

16. In John McWhorter's Losing The Race, the book that helped launch him as a public intellectual, the unmotivated student and defective culture explanations, such as his use of the late anthropologist John Ogbu's oppositional culture theory, are the bedrock for McWhorter's argument for what ails African American students.

17. The 17th district eventually became known as the 10th district.

18. All information was collected from a database on Williams' voting history by the political watchdog organization *Project Vote Smart*, http://votesmart.org/bill/961/2790/3556/constitutional-amendment-defining-marriage-between-one-man-and-one-woman#.U81WAFYs5tf, http://votesmart.org/bill/10846/29009/3556/payday-lending-regulations#.U81WeFYs5tc, http://votesmart.org/bill/10749/28670/3556/sex-education-curriculum-requirements#.U81Wv1Ys5tc, http://votesmart.org/bill/9317/25379/3556/restricting-health-insurance-companies-ability-to-exclude-individuals#.U81XWVYs5tc, http://votesmart.org/bill/10571/28195/3556/teacher-evaluation-amendments#.U81XeFYs5tc, http://votesmart.org/bill/8779/23705/3556/minimum-wage-increase#.U81XnlYs5tc, accessed July 21, 2014.

19. According to journalist Bruce Murphy, between 1990 and 1997 Williams earned around $163,000 from speaking engagements on the conservative talk circuit. *Bruce Murphy*, "The Rise and Fall of Polly Williams," June 27, 2001, http://urbanmilwaukee.com/2001/06/27/murphys-law-the-rise-and-fall-of-polly-williams/, accessed July 30, 2014.

20. Wendy Parker, "The Color of Choice: Race and Charter Schools," *Tulane Law Review*, vol. 75, no. 3, February 2001, p. 568. *See also* Molly Townes O'Brien, "Private School Tuition Vouchers and the Realities of Racial Politics," *University of Tennessee Law Review*, 1997.

References

Abrajano, Marisa. "Are Blacks and Latinos Responsible for the Passage of Proposition 8? Analyzing Voter Attitudes on California's Proposal to Ban Same-Sex Marriage in 2008." In *Political Research Quarterly*, vol. 63, no. 4, 2010: 922–932.

Asadullah, Samad A. "Between the Lines: Racism in the Church; The Price Is Right." *Los Angeles Sentinel*, April 8, 1998: A7.

Banerjee, Neela. "Black Churches Struggle Over Their Role in Politics." *The New York Times*, March 6, 2005: 15.

Brice, Daniel. "School choice advocate George Mitchell blasts ex-lawmaker Annette Polly Williams." In *Milwaukee-Wisconsin Journal Sentinel*, May 29, 2013, http://archive.jsonline.com/watchdog/noquarter/school-choice-advocate-george-mitchell-blastsex-lawmakerannette-polly-williams-b9922201z1-209452781.html.

Blake, John. "'Most-hated,' Anti-Gay Preacher Once Fought for Civil Rights," May 14, 2010, http://www.cnn.com/2010/US/05/05/hate.preacher/index.html.

Bositis, David. "The Politics of School Choice: African-Americans and Vouchers" In *Educational Freedom in Urban America: Brown V. Board After Half a Century*. Eds. David Salisbury and Casey Lartigue Jr. Washington DC: Cato Institute Publications, 2004: 177–204.

Bositis, David A. "2008 Center National Survey of African American Families' Views on Education." Washington DC: Joint Center for Political and Educational Studies Publications, 2009.

———. *Diverging Generations: The Transformation of African American Views*. Washington, DC: The Joint Center for Political and Economic Studies, 2001.

Crenshaw, Kimberlé. "Demarginalizing the Intersection of Race and Sex: A Black Feminist Critique of Antidiscrimination Doctrine, Feminist Theory and Antiracist Politics." In *The Black Feminist Reader*. Eds. Joy James and T. Denean Sharpley-Whiting. Malden, MA: Blackwell, 2001, 208–238.

———. "Mapping the Margins: Intersectionality, Identity Politics, and Violence Against Women of Color." In *The Public Nature of Private Violence: The*

Discovery of Domestic Abuse. Eds. Martha Albertson Fineman and Roxanne Mykitiuk. New York, NY: Routledge, 1994.

Foucault, Michel, Mauro Bertani, Alessandro Fontana, Arnold I. Davidson, and David Macey. "*Society Must Be Defended*": *Lectures at the College de France, 1975–76.* New York: Picador Books, 2003.

Fullilove, Mindy. *Root Shock; How Tearing Up City Neighborhoods Hurts America, & What We Can Do About It.* New York: One World/Ballantine, 2005.

Gates Karen Grisby. "Racial Divisions Challenge Gay Rights Movement," December 4, 2008, https://www.npr.org/templates/story/story.php?storyId=97826119.

Griffin, Horace L. *Their Own Receive Them Not: African American Lesbians & Gays in Black Churches.* Cleveland, OH: The Pilgrim Press, 2006.

Heise, Michael, and James E. Ryan. "The Political Economy of School Choice." In *Yale Law Journal*, vol. 111, no. 8, June 2002.

Hunter, Jack. "*Why Gay Marriage Isn't the '60s Civil Rights Fight What black Americans suffered is without parallel in our history—a fact all sides of the SSM debate should recognize*," April 1, 2013, http://www.theamericanconservative.com/articles/why-gay-marriage-isnt-like-the-civil-rights-struggle/.

Ireland, Doug. "Back to the Future GOP Revives Anti-gay Marriage Campaign for '06." *Public Eye*, Summer 2006: 6.

Journal of Blacks in Higher Education. "News and Views: School Vouchers: An Educational Conundrum for Black America." In *Journal of Blacks in Higher Education*, vol. 35, no. 2, 2002: 79–80.

Kaufman, David, "The Root: The Misjudged Black Vote On Gay Marriage," March 4, 2011, https://www.npr.org/2011/03/04/134257733/the-root-the-misjudged-black-vote-on-gay-marriage.

Kaufman, David. "Tensions Between Black and Gay Groups Rise Anew in Advance of Anti-Gay Marriage Vote in N.C: Groups are fanning the flames of conflict–by accident and by design," May 4, 2012, https://www.theatlanticcompoliticsarchive/2012/05tensionsbetweenblack-andgaygroups-rise-anew-inadvance-of-anti-gaymarriage-vote-in-nc/256695/.

King, Deborah K. "Multiple Jeopardy, Multiple Consciousness: The Context of a Black Feminist Ideology." *Signs*, vol. 14, no. 1, 1988: 42–72.

Lewis, Gregory B. "Black-White Differences in Attitudes toward Homosexuality and Gay Rights." In *The Public Opinion Quarterly*, vol. 67, no. 1, 2003: 59–78.

Lewis, Wayne D., and Arnold Danzig. "Seeing Color in School Choice." *Journal of School Public Relations*, vol. 31, no. 3, Sum 2010: 205–223.

Morken, Hubert, and Jo Renee Formicola. *The Politics of School Choice.* Lanham, MD: Rowman and Littlefield, 1999.

Murphy, Bruce. "The Rise and Fall of Polly Williams." *Urban Milwaukee*, June 27, 2001, https://urbanmilwaukee.com/2001/06/27/murphys-law-the-rise-and-fall-of-polly-williams/.

Murphy, Bruce. "The Legacy of Annette Polly Williams." In *Urban Milwaukee*, November 11, 2014, https://urbanmilwaukee.com/2014/11/11/murphys-law-the-legacy-of-annette-polly-williams/.

Parker, Star. "GOP Can't Get It Right with Black Outreach." *The Philadelphia Tribune*, May 4, 2001: 7A.

Roper Public Opinion Center. *US Elections: How Groups Voted in 2012*, December 2012, http://www.ropercenter.uconn.edu/elections/how_groups_voted/voted_12.html.

Smith, Barbara. "Blacks & Gays: Healing the Great Divide." In *Eyes Right: Challenging the Right Wing Backlash*. Ed. Chip Berlet. Boston, MA: South End Press, 1995.

Stanford, Anthony. *Homophobia in the Black Church: How Faith, Politics, and Fear Divide the Black Community*. Santa Barbara, CA: Praeger Publishers, 2013.

Themba, M. N. "Choice" and other White lies. *Rethinking Schools*, vol. 16, 2001: Fall.

Walker Johnson, Amanda. "'Turnaround' as Shock Therapy: Race, Neoliberalism, and School Reform." In *Urban Education*, vol. 48, no. 2, March 2013: 232–256.

CHAPTER 6

Chasing Fools Gold: African Americans and the Party of Lincoln

A still-sluggish economy and more Americans feeling and expressing dissatisfaction with the lack of political progress in Washington, things looked promising that the Republicans might recapture the White House. Adding to Republicans optimism was the outcome of the 2010 mid-term elections where Republicans picked up five seats in the Senate closing the deficit between them and the Democrats. In House elections, Republicans did quite well adding 63 new members expanding their already sizable lead over Democrats. Yet, on November 6, 2012, sometime after 9 p.m., President Obama had made history again by being the first African American to repeat as President of the United States. Like four years earlier, the Republicans failed in their attempt to capture the White House and increase their support among African Americans. After the election Republicans drew up a mission statement document laying out what needed to be done to turn the tide and ensure victories in future elections. One area that this document addressed was diversity and what steps the party needed to take to bring more groups such as African Americans into the fold:

> The African American community has a lot in common with the Republican Party, and it is important to share this rich history. More importantly, the Republican Party must be committed to building a lasting relationship within the African American community year-round, based on mutual respect and with a spirit of caring. (Republican National Committee 2013: 18)[1]

© The Author(s) 2018
L. G. Prisock, *African Americans in Conservative Movements*,
https://doi.org/10.1007/978-3-319-89351-8_6

173

Even with the recognized commonalities the GOP has not been able to cultivate a meaningful relationship with African American voters going on fifty years, in fact many African Americans feel the party does not respect their needs and concerns or demonstrate a "spirit of caring." It is beyond the scope of this chapter to provide a comprehensive analysis on why the Republicans lost the 2008 and 2012 presidential elections. Instead, I will examine the feeble relationship the Republican party has with African Americans, the ineffectiveness of conservative African American Republicans in mobilizing African Americans to the GOP, the experiences of both Michael Steele and Herman Cain to illustrate the challenges African American conservative Republicans face within their party and outside of it. In this chapter I also analyze the relationship the Tea Party has to race in general and African Americans in particular. There is a debate raging over whether various expressions of racism by Tea Party members accurately portrays a movement based on and centered around racism. This chapter looks at the role African American participants play within it and how they view the movement. Lastly I discuss what I call the "Obama conundrum" among some African American conservatives.

A Party Devoid of Black Support and Votes

On the surface, one would expect that conservative African Americans as a group would elect to make today's conservative-dominated Republican Party their political home. Analyses of the past decade and a half show, however, that this has not been the case. A national opinion poll conducted by the Joint Center for Political and Economic Studies illustrated that the Republican Party was not the party of choice for most self-identified African American conservatives during the nineties, a situation continuing into the twenty-first century. For instance, when asked the question, "Suppose the 2000 Presidential election were being held today. Among the four major candidates (Gore, Bush, Nader, and Buchanan) who would you like to see win?", among secular African American conservatives an overwhelming 72% said they would support Democratic Vice President Al Gore as opposed to the 10% who favored then Texas Governor George W. Bush. The majority of self-identified African American Christian conservatives also favored Gore over Bush 69–11% (Bositis 2000: 21).

When asked their opinion on the direction of the country, 60% of African American secular conservatives thought the country was going in the right direction to 33% who felt the nation had gotten off on the wrong track. The gap was much closer for African American Christian conservatives—a slight majority (46%) felt the country was going in the right direction compared to (43%) who felt otherwise. This outcome among African American Christian conservatives is noteworthy because, at the time of this poll, the scandal around President Clinton's adulterous relationship with intern Monica Lewinsky had just come to a close. Given the moral outrage expressed by the Republican Party and the social and religious segments of the white conservative population, one would assume that African American Christian conservatives would overwhelmingly perceive President Clinton's indiscretion as evidence that the country was headed in the wrong direction. The results, however, showed a different response (Bositis 2000: 17).

Another interesting outcome from the poll showed that large majorities, 81 and 76%, respectively, of both secular and Christian African American conservatives polled gave President Clinton favorable ratings (Bositis 2000: 14). When conservative African Americans went to the polls during the nineties, the results show that the trend of African American conservatives favoring Democrats over Republicans continued.[2] For example, voting data from the 1992 presidential election illustrated that among African Americans who identified themselves as conservative—a subgroup which comprised close to 20% (18%) of the total voting black population for both the 1988 and 1992 elections—only 26% of the self-identified African American conservatives voted for President George Bush Sr. On the other hand, more than two-thirds (69%) of conservative African Americans supported Democrat Bill Clinton (Bolce 1993: 258–259). According to Bolce et al., Bush could not even hold on to the African American base that supported him in the 1988 election, for almost half (49%) of Bush's black base voted for Clinton (Bolce 1993: 259).

One group of African Americans thought to be a natural constituency for the Republican Party was African Americans of higher socioeconomic status. African American conservative activist Star Parker suggested that the GOP direct their energies toward pulling in this group of African Americans, stating:

> While it is true that at least half of Black voters won't even consider pulling the GOP lever anytime soon, there are two constituencies Republicans should court: young Black professionals and evangelicals. The former

group is attracted to economic empowerment in the form of tax cuts and reduced red tape for small business. The latter finds appeals in welfare reform, pro-life policies, and policies with a strong moral fiber. (Parker 2001: 7A)

Unfortunately for the Republicans, African Americans of higher socioeconomic status were also not hearing the calls from the GOP to join the party in significant numbers. Again examining voting data from the 1992 presidential election, the percentage of African Americans with incomes between fifty and seventy-five thousand dollars, and those earning over seventy-five thousand dollars, who cast their votes for Democratic Bill Clinton was 81 and 67%, respectively. Interestingly, the data also showed that African American conservatives who fell in the fifty to seventy-five thousand earnings bracket threw more of their support behind Clinton than Bush (Bolce 1993: 259–260). As the nation entered the twenty-first century the relationship between African Americans and the GOP did not significantly change. According to the Joint Center for Political and Economic Studies, African American identification with the Republican Party continued to fluctuate while also steadily remaining under 20%. For example, in 2000 only 6.6% of African Americans surveyed identified themselves as Republicans, in 2002 the number increased to almost 13% (12.6) including those who classify themselves as independent but lean more toward Republicans, without the leaners the level of identification decreased to 10% (9.5). In 2004 the levels of identification reached their highest level with 15% (14.9) of African Americans including leaning independents and 10% (10.4) without the leaners expressing identification with the GOP, yet this increase in affiliation with Republicans did not positively change the support African Americans gave toward the Republicans as the percentage of votes President George W. Bush received from African Americans in 2004 was only 11%. (Bositis 2008: 2, 10).[3] By 2008, with Barack Obama as the Democratic candidate African American identification with the Republican Party dropped down to 7% (7.3%) and so to did the percentage of votes as Senator John McCain only received a paltry 4% of the African American vote (Bositis 2012: 2–3).[4] In 2012 Republicans did no better in garnering African American support as Mitt Romney picked up a minimal 6% of the African American vote (Roper Center 2012).[5] These results indicate that it will be quite awhile before a Republican presidential candidate will capture a substantial amount of support from African Americans.

The GOP's Lack of Connection with the Post-civil Rights Generation of African Americans

According to a recent study by the Joint Center for Political and Economic Studies, when it comes to views on various policy issues differences among African Americans fall along generational lines. For example, when asked whether many of the government's functions should be transferred to the state level, African Americans in the two youngest categories, 18–25 and 26–35, solidly supported the idea (56 and 63%, respectively) in contrast to the oldest grouping of African Americans of 65+ who overwhelmingly disagreed with the idea of transferral (25–56%) (Bositis 2001: 58). On the issue of school voucher programs there was also significant difference in opinion between the generations. While only 49 and 42% of African Americans in the 51–64 and 65+ categories expressed support for a voucher plan, in contrast, 71 and 76% of African Americans in the 18–25 and 26–35 categories registered their support (Bositis 2001: 65). This difference in policy views was also demonstrated in party identification differences as younger generations of African Americans (18–25 years of age) showed higher levels of identifying with the Republican Party than their older counterparts. Since 1984 when the Joint Center began conducting surveys Republican Party identification had always been higher among younger African Americans, reaching an all time high of 17% (17.2) in 2002, but by 2002 the level of identification among younger African Americans has been steadily on the decline beginning in 2004 where the level of identification with the GOP among older African Americans outpaced their younger counterparts 15% (14.9) to 10% (10.3) (Bositis 2008: 3) and by 2008 identification with the GOP by younger African Americans reached an all time low of 5% (Bositis 2012: 3). Although younger African Americans tended to be more supportive of policies typically advocated by the Republican Party their support was not leading to a stampede toward the GOP.

Why can't the Republican Party and black conservative Republicans cultivate these examples of conservatism among some of the younger members of the African American community, and convert them into increased numbers of African American Republicans? Are there fundamental differences between the party and the beliefs held by these members of the post-civil rights generation? Or rather, does this gap begin to reveal some of the problems in the Republican approach to recruiting African Americans into the party in general? African American

Republican activist Stuart DeVeaux attributes this disconnect to several factors: lack of effective outreach by the Republican Party, misunderstanding of the Republican and Democratic parties' character, and peer pressure others put on young African Americans encouraging them not to align with the Republicans (DeVeaux 1997: 26).

Providing evidence for the latter, in her insightful study of the political identities and attitudes of African Americans of the post-civil rights generation, political scientist Andrea Simpson documents the challenges young African American conservatives face in trying to negotiate their racial and political identities. Many African Americans are leery of the affiliation some of the young have made with a political party that has a very poor track record when dealing with African Americans. One young African American college student who is both conservative and Republican described how he and his cohort are perceived by other African Americans:

> I think a lot of times when people hear that African-Americans are conservative Republicans they automatically think the worst – Jessie Helms....
> I get the feeling when you say 'I am a conservative' black people say 'Oh, anti-affirmative action, oh, you sleep with Clarence Thomas.'... I had the hardest time coming to accept that I was conservative. Because there's such a stigma once you label yourself like that. (Simpson 1998: 38–39)

However, one could also make the argument that the stigmatization this young African American feels for being a Republican results from the numerous political campaigns in which the Republican Party has used racially divisive tactics for political gains.[6]

In addition, African Americans are not the only group whose suspicions become obstacles for a younger generation of African American conservatives. Young African American Republicans must also deal with white Republican counterparts who sometimes view them condescendingly as pleasant surprises instead of equal partners within the party. One young African American Republican relayed his frustration at the treatment he received from his white counterparts by stating, "Same thing you run into every day when you're around white people. It didn't matter that we had some of the same political ideology. We were still seen as -- we were an anomaly. People would come up to us, want to touch, want to talk to you" (Simpson 1998: 38).

Some young African Americans, who pair their conservative beliefs with a strong racial identity, face the other problem of balancing their form of conservatism—race focused with elements of black nationalism—with their alignment with a political party that operates under the cloak of adherence to individualism and a "color-blind" ideology. When one young African American conservative was asked how he reconciled being a fan of Nation of Islam leader, Louis Farrakhan, with being a conservative Republican, the young man's reply was, "I don't see any conflict because my conservatism, my Republicanism, is for black people" (Simpson 1998: 42). However, the way in which the Republican Party and the right has used the discourse of color blindness to reposition itself in relation to race makes that young man's comment inherently problematic and contradictory with respect to imagining a rapprochement between conservative black nationalism and the Republican Party's conservative ideologies of color blindness.

As I recount in Chapters 2 and 3, and as sociologist Amy Elizabeth Ansell has further documented, with the emergence of the New Right came a readjustment in how conservatives approach race and racial issues. Conservatives' revised discourse partly involves the utilization of language and ideas co-opted from progressives and liberals, now reconfigured in a conservative context. The term color blind, for example, was originally used by liberals, particularly before the passage of the 1964 Civil Rights Act, to argue for the treatment of individuals not on the basis of race. The argument was intended to encourage the elimination of both institutional and legal barriers that prevented the achievement of both racial inclusion and progress (Ansell 1997: 107). In the context of a New Right discourse, the logic of color blindness is that any emphasis on race is viewed as illegitimate. Therefore, any governmental actions aimed at addressing inequality that specifically focuses on race, such as the case with affirmative action, violates the New Right's principle of color blindness. Color blindness then connects with the New Right's focus on individualism, where the emphasis on group relations and group power dynamics are particularly delegitimized in the context of race. Little in the "color-blindness" framework leaves room for the more nationalist understanding of racial identity held by some young black conservatives. And yet, the difficulties these young Black Republicans of the post-civil rights era face are just the tip of the iceberg in the continued, troubled relationship between the Republican Party and contemporary generations of African Americans.

BLACK REPUBLICANS: A CAPTURED GROUP

The relationship between Republicans and African Americans has been fractured for quite some time. For reasons I describe in Chapters 2 and 3, a plausible argument can be made that a significant portion of the political success the Republican Party enjoyed in the latter decades of the twentieth century came at the expense of African Americans. Given the ways in which the Republican Party has used race in its campaign strategies and policy decisions, African Americans who openly proclaim their preference or loyalty to the Republican party are viewed by whites as a curiosity, while they are looked upon by other African Americans with a mixture of suspicion and contempt. There was a time when the Republican Party garnered a significant portion of the African American vote, but the last time a Republican presidential candidate received more than 15% of the African American vote was fifty years ago in the 1960 election between Richard Nixon and John F. Kennedy. Four years later Republican presidential candidate Arizona Senator Barry Goldwater was declaring at a campaign rally in Georgia that the GOP should "go hunting where the ducks are," in essence suggesting that the Republican Party view cultivating African American voters as a lost cause (Perlstein 2001: 190).[7]

Barry Goldwater was also one of a minority of senators who voted against the passage of the 1964 Civil Rights Act. It comes as no surprise that after Goldwater's presidential run in 1964, no Republican presidential candidate has come close to collecting 20% of the African American vote. In the years following Goldwater's "go hunting where the ducks are" declaration, African Americans witnessed Republican Richard Nixon masterfully utilizing the southern strategy to win two terms in the White House.[8] Ironically it was the same Richard Nixon who two years before being elected president warned Republicans to avoid getting into a competition with southern Democrats to win over what he called, "the fool's gold of racist votes" (Kabaservice 2012: 192).[9] Another Republican, Ronald Reagan, began his presidential campaign in the southern town where three civil rights activists were murdered, proclaiming to the all-white audience the political legitimacy of "states rights." The final straw was the 1988 release of a racially inflammatory political commercial put out by supporters of Republican George Bush, Sr.[10]

These developments lead one to ask the following questions: Why would any African American back a political party that sees the support of African Americans as inconsequential to their electoral success? And even though conservatives dominate within the Republican Party, why have conservative African American Republicans then been unable to translate their ideological alignment with the party into significant political gains for African Americans, or get the GOP leadership to meaningfully address African American political interests? The short answer to both questions is essentially the same—African Americans have limited options and little choice in shaping the directions of either party, given African Americans' particular positioning within the US two-party electoral system. In this chapter I argue that the various struggles faced by African American Republicans, particularly the problem of attracting more African Americans to the party, is indicative of a broader contradiction in America's democratic electoral system that shapes whether it works, or does not work, for the everyday African American voter.

The marginalization of African American Republicans within their own party reflects the overall marginalization African Americans experience within the American political system. Borrowing a concept developed by political scientist Paul Frymer, in this chapter I illustrate how African American Republicans are an "electorally captured group" within the Republican Party.[11] Frymer uses the phrase "electorally captured group" to describe a group such as African Americans where their concerns and interests are overlooked or minimally addressed as both political parties in the zeal to woo the white swing vote distance themselves from African Americans. Thus leaving a group such as African Americans with few meaningful political options. In my analysis, the term is analytically appropriate for African American Republicans also to the degree that they share some of the very constraints Frymer describes of African American Democrats. For example, one major constraint Republican African Americans face like their Democratic counterparts is the inability to get their party to give serious focus on such topics like urban issues.

The deeper implication of seeing African American Republicans as an equally captured or trapped electoral group is the following. Our assumption is that being a black Republican is an oxymoron and against African Americans' self-interest. However, if the landscape of real political representation does not look much better on the other side of the party lines, then political scientists, sociologists, and historians need to address more honestly the obstacles in African Americans' participation in the two-party system, and demystify some of the supposed distinctions between Democrats' and Republicans' political stands on race.[12] The fact of the matter is that, entering into the twenty-first century and following the various racial campaigns of the last forty years, conservatives have achieved such hegemony with the notion of color blindness that for both parties it has become a liability for any candidate to appear to represent the interests of African Americans as a group.

Unfortunately, until there are significant structural changes in the American political system, the impact African American Republicans make within their party will continue to be limited. Many African American Republicans claim that for African Americans to have a stronger voice within American politics, African Americans need to be active members of both major political parties. In theory this claim is valid, as the political interests of African Americans could be better served if there was a genuine competition between both the Democratic and Republican parties for African American votes. However, the reality is that the continued success of the Republican Party hinges on the party maintaining a "safe" distance from African Americans. In the upcoming section I illustrate further how the Republicans' slow and cautious approach to incorporating more African Americans into the party reveals the degree to which they believe, in the American political context, that African Americans are a political liability that must be manipulated or handled, rather than a political asset that must be nurtured.

Since the Republican Party's political success has partly come from its deployment of race-baiting strategies, not surprisingly, when the Republican Party actively reaches out to African Americans the party's motives are often viewed suspiciously as having more cosmetic than substantive goals. African Americans' fears are grounded given an inescapable reality in the political and social discourse of American conservatism—the centrality of conservatives' use of race to garner popular support for the Republican Party specifically and the broader conservative movement as a whole. Democratic electoral principles cover a very different terrain than the realms of social mindset and civil society in which conservative Republicans have sought to secure power. As Gramsci described, in the developed capitalist state the realm of politics in the stricter electoral sense expands "with the formation of a new ideological 'terrain'," in which parties work to secure "political, cultural and moral leadership" through the winning of "consent" (Gramsci 1988: 423). To the degree that African Americans as an electoral group bring with them into either party a social and political identity the GOP has been at great pains to organize the *consent* of a white electorate *against*, then conservative African American Republicans will continue to remain trapped within the tensions and contradictions of a racialist, rather than universalist, conservative discourse of color blindness.

Evasion and Avoidance: The Struggles of African American Republicans with the Party's Efforts to Organize African Americans

The reason that there has been no significant upsurge in support among African Americans toward Republicans appears very simple at first—the poor image the Republican Party has among African Americans. As former Secretary of State Colin Powell stated in a television interview about the GOP, "It is certainly not seen as the Black guy's party" (Tyler 2000: 7E). However, as we explore further the impact of the lack of a black constituency on those black conservative Republicans who have remained loyal to the party, we find that more so than any "natural" antipathy blacks may have to Republican principles, the party's unpopular image rests on active strategies of disregard, evasion, and avoidance on the part of the party in the recruiting of more African American members.

Many African American Republicans speak of the dual battles they have to wage because of their political choice. They have to fight both with their white peers to gain a hearing and opportunity to win over African Americans, and with their communities of origin to receive validation. African American Republicans find that they must address pointed questions from other African Americans about their perceived lack of status and power among Republicans. Often these questions concerning Black Republicans' power and status within the GOP are related to the general sentiment among African Americans that African American Republicans are aesthetic figures, racial mascots, or "tokens" for the party.

On the other side, however, when Black Republicans speak of their experiences within the Republican Party they express a gamut of emotions ranging from hopefulness to frustration, to outrage. At the core of these experiences is the feeling many black Republicans have of not being seen and treated as equal members within the party. Black Republicans cite several reasons for feeling this way but among the most prominent are: first, the Republicans' handling of racial issues within and outside of the party; second, the ineffectiveness of the GOP's outreach programs aimed at African Americans and the lack of meaningful institutional support given to African American Republican candidates and activists; and finally, African American Republicans' resentments concerning the myopia of the party, the shortsightedness reflected in the kinds of contributions their white peers call upon them to make for the party.

African American Republicans' complaints are repeated here less as an account of their naïvete about the obstacles to full membership they should have anticipated facing within the Republican Party (although that may be an easy conclusion to draw from my discussion). Rather, their comments are of more significance to my argument because they underscore one of the central arguments of this chapter. Republican Party strategy, for all of its rhetoric in regards to diversity, has been to actively avoid and evade the recruitment of African Americans, whose "trapped" votes can never secure the type of social and political hegemony the party has been able to achieve among white voters by combining a more problematic discourse of race with a seemingly race-neutral discourse of color blindness.

Over twenty-five years ago, an African American Republican activist complained about then-President Nixon and his administration's handling of the controversial issue of busing. Feeling like Nixon's administration was pandering to anti-black sentiment, Jackson Champion declared, "by attempting to appease those opposed to busing, the Administration is playing into the hands of the racists and at the same time inciting blacks" (Champion 1976: 31). At the beginning of the twenty-first century another African American Republican activist leveled a similar charge at the Republican Party. During the middle of 2000, long time former Republican activist, Faye Anderson, called on the GOP to address a series of racial missteps.

First, there was the refusal by the Republican-dominated Congress to provide support for a resolution castigating the white nationalist organization, Council of Conservative Citizens (CCC).[13] It had been revealed that the CCC had significant connections to some inside the party, most notably Senator Trent Lott of Mississippi, who was discovered to be a member of the organization.[14] Second, while giving a speech at Bob Jones University during his campaign, candidate George W. Bush elided any criticism of the university's policy of banning interracial dating. Third, during the Republican presidential primaries in 2000, both George W. Bush and his opponent, Arizona Senator John McCain, refused to condemn South Carolina for flying the confederate flag over the state house. Appalled and frustrated by the racial insensitivity evident in these events, Anderson threw in the towel and left both her position as the national vice chairman of the Republican National Committee (RNC)'s New Majority Council, a newly created outreach organization, and the Republican Party altogether.

In explaining further the motive behind her decision to leave the GOP, Anderson cited her feeling that the above-mentioned developments were not random racial oversights by the party. "While it's accurate to say I've switched from a registered Republican to an independent, truth be told, the Republican Party left me sometime ago. My switch comes in the wake of a pattern of racial blunders that I cannot dismiss as mere 'mistakes'" (Anderson 2000c: 2). Anderson's assertion gains some credibility from the fact that each of the three cases mentioned above involves the south. Capturing the white southern vote was one factor that helped the Republican Party to occupy the White House for most of the past four decades. It is no secret that one factor that drew many southern whites into the GOP fold were racial appeals that, at best, can be described as racially conservative and, at their worst, as pure race-baiting.[15] Today the south is the bastion of the GOP and the white south one of its loyal voting bases.

The response by conservative columnist Ann Coulter to an op-ed piece Faye Anderson penned for the *New York Times*, in which Anderson criticized the Republican Party's parade of different Republican groups of color at its 2000 presidential convention, typifies the type of white conservative response that leads to some African Americans' feelings of invisibility and lack of respect inside the Republican Party. In her article Coulter referred to Anderson as an "alleged former Republican," "Republican Party little wig," and megalomaniac: "I hate to accuse anyone of megalomania, but Ms. Anderson's belief that her departure was 'noisy' may be somewhat overstated, inasmuch as no one has ever heard of her" (Coulter 2000). While Coulter's intent was probably to espouse her opinion in that caustic, polemical manner that has made her one of the most recognizable, conservative, political pundits today, ironically, her remarks represent in an inverted form the severe exclusion of African American Republicans that they feel from within the party. As Coulter's virulent response to Anderson's comment reflect, many African American conservatives are right to worry that if they protest too loudly about race or racism within the party, their concerns may make other white Republicans suspicious of their party loyalty. Borrowing another of Coulter's terms, the overall manner in which the Republican Party approaches bringing in more African Americans also produces the feeling among some African American GOP activists that they are "Republican little-wigs," undervalued, and overlooked.

Many African American Republicans feel that the problems with the Republican Party's actions regarding the recruitment of African Americans can be boiled down to—confusion, disregard, and avoidance. First, the Republican Party appears to be confused regarding their objectives toward African Americans. As one African American Republican noted, "It just doesn't seem that this whole strategy of outreach has been -- has anyone thought this through? What's the goal? Is it to get more black elected officials? Is it to bring in more rank and file blacks into the party or to have more blanket voting?" ("GOP Outreach" 1998: 14). The Republican Party's actions tend to support this activist's observation. During a roundtable discussion about the GOP's efforts to diversify one white Republican operative declared, "There is a big push, right now, at the state party level – from the top down and the bottom up – to recruit minority candidates. You're going to see more minority candidates at every level recruited this year, we believe" ("GOP Outreach" 1998: 13–14). And yet, in spite of the party's claim that African American recruitment is a top area of focus, the party also underutilizes one of its greatest assets in that endeavor. African American conservatives complain of a blind spot within the Republican party when it comes to providing meaningful exposure of minority candidates to the communities from which the party claims to want to draw potential members. Copublisher of the now defunct African American conservative publication *Headway*, Gwen Richardson, noted that in 1996 when there were several African American Republicans running for Congress, it was she and her husband who, through their magazine, put together a symposium that aired on C-Span about African American Republican Congressional candidates. Richardson raised the point that the symposium she helped put together was something "the RNC should have actually done." Since there was no effort on the part of the GOP to actively build exposure for their African American candidates Robertson and her husband saw the need to take charge so "that people could even know that these people exist" ("GOP Outreach" 1998: 12).

Black Republicans also describe an inability or unwillingness by the Republican Party to do the grassroots work within African American communities. Several activists such as Star Parker have pointed out that part of the problem with the Republican Party's approach to reaching out to African Americans is Republicans' lack of visibility in community institutions like black churches (Parker 2001: 7A). Some point to the growth of the Latino and Latina population in the United States as one possible reason why the Republican Party's actions toward African Americans have been less than satisfactory. As various demographic studies illustrate, the Latino population is growing at a higher rate than African Africans. Latinos are now the largest minority population in the United States surpassing African Americans. Although many Latinos have a strong history of alliance with the Democratic Party, the Republicans believe there is a window for the GOP to build up stronger support for their party within the Latino community. Republicans have taken note of the fact that while the party gets less than 10% of the African American vote, it receives more than three times that of the Latino vote. Also important to note, in key political states such as California and Texas the Latino population is growing while the African American population is not. All of this has had an impact on how much investment the Republicans decide to put toward recruiting African American voters. For example, during the 1998 mid-term elections, the Republican party overlooked black inner cities in the state of California and allocated no money for voter drives or any other recruitment strategy in those areas. For conservative African American Republicans like Parker these realities are frustrating. During a summit between African American Republicans and state Republican leaders Parker exclaimed, "Don't invite me back to these meetings. I'm not going to prance on your stage anymore. These people are out there with their Dan Lungren signs and their millions of dollars in their pocket and we're still talking strategy" ("GOP Woos Minorities" 1998: 2).[16]

The Republican Party's confused and evasive maneuvers in recruiting African Americans also reflect the fact that for some white Republicans, a strong association with African Americans may very well appear to be a political risk. Elaine Brown Jenkins notes the various ways some Republicans avoid connecting with African Americans:

> We still have some elected white Republicans who do not respond to appeals for financial support of causes espoused by their black constituents. Nor do they respond to appeals from their fellow black Republican officials…. If they respond at all to appeals from black voters or black fellow Republicans, they want the lowest profile possible. You will not see recognizable, white elected Republicans sponsoring scholarships for black artists

or athletes. In fact, some white Republicans may donate money to a black cause and say, "don't mention my name".... Unfortunately, this is a persistent pattern in the Republican Party, requiring urgent attention. (Brown Jenkins 1996: 37)

The reluctance on the part of some white Republicans to make outward overtures toward African Americans could reflect their fear of falling victim to what one might call, "the Jack Kemp syndrome." The late former Republican Senator from Buffalo was recognizable not only for his conservative views on the economy, but also, for his earnestness in regards to making the Republican Party and conservatism more hospitable to African Americans. Kemp had consistently argued that the Republican Party missed countless opportunities to broaden its voting base. The party both overlooks African Americans, and continues to represent itself in images and with messages that are exclusive instead of inclusive, mired in the dregs of racism and intolerance. In 1996, Senator Bob Dole and Kemp ran as the Republican Presidential and Vice Presidential candidates and did poorly against incumbent President Bill Clinton. Some of the mumbling from Republicans and conservatives about the GOP loss in 1996 was that the Dole-Kemp ticket represented a watered down version of conservative Republicanism. Kemp's racial advocacy in particular was pointed to as one factor. Viewed as being too liberal, many speculated that Kemp's racial politics turned off one of the Republican Party's core bases—white southerners. As one reporter noted during one of Kemp's campaign speeches to a mainly white audience in Augusta Georgia, "as Kemp kept reaching out to the...black audience...he began to lose his white audience. Listening to Kemp in gape-jawed wonder, the crowd lapsed into a puzzled silence" (Shapiro 1996: 52). Kemp also aroused suspicion among hard right conservatives for what they perceived to be his overly eager effort to connect with African Americans (Frum 1994: 88). The possibility of incurring disapproval from peers within the party, from their constituents, or from conservatives outside of the party could be reason enough for some white Republicans to be hesitant in associating themselves with African Americans.

Faye Anderson has called the outreach efforts by Republicans "bargain basement" and for good reason (Anderson 2000b: 1). In his study examining political parties' mobilization of African Americans, political scientist Peter Welhouwer noted the low attention to African Americans given by the Republican party:

The Republicans' canvassing of blacks is substantially lower than the party's contact of whites, and is substantially lower than the black presence in the VAP (voting age population). In fact, the Republican contact rate is almost low enough to be accidental.... If the GOP is serious about making inroads into this last holdout of the New Deal coalition, perhaps a more serious effort at a personal contact mobilization strategy that targets blacks is one place to start. (Welhouwer 2000: 620)

Even the manner in which African American Republicans are called upon to further the goals and objectives of the Republican Party could be called "bargain basement." Many African American Republicans working inside the party are not content with being handed limited assignments or offered circumscribed roles. African American Republicans feel their value to the party is recognized by their white peers only when the issue at hand pertains to race:

Our phones/fax machines/computers virtually hum with entreaties to participate in photo-ops whenever the issue is affirmative action, school choice or welfare reform. However, when it comes to the party's bread and butter issues – tax cuts, small businesses, strengthening families, preserving Social Security – well, we become invisible. (Anderson 1998: A5)

In April of 1998 a cadre of African American female Republican activists held a press conference to castigate the Republican Party for the way in which they and other African American Republican women activists felt they were being treated by the party. Their press gathering was reported in a wide array of newspapers across the country. As Faye Anderson stated, "The reason why the story had 'legs' was because, let's face it, the GOP is perceived to be hostile to Blacks and condescending to its Black activists" (Anderson 1998: A5). For Gwen Richardson, most of the experience her publication *Headway* has had with Republican organizations has been based on race:

We've worked with a lot of different Republican groups from coast to coast.... For the most part, I've seen window dressing. If people are having an event and they need a black face, they call. Okay? But as far as having you involved in any kind of policy or decision making, you're not at any of those meetings. They just want a black face so they can say they have a black face. ("GOP Outreach" 1998: 13)

The racial ghettoization some African American Republicans experience is a chronic problem. In another instance, the racialized role of African American Republicans was raised by African American conservative pundit Armstrong Williams, at a January 2003 press conference held in response to Senator Trent Lott's controversial remarks at Senator Strom Thurmond's centennial birthday party. During the conference Williams rattled off a list of requests that ranged from calling on Republicans to broaden the scope of opportunities for their African American members to challenging the party to develop policies that were more sensitive to people of color. According to Williams, "the party can no longer be lily white" (Walters 2003: 9; "Black Republicans Say 'Party can no Longer Be Lily White'" 2003: 4). The response this group received from then-RNC Chairman Marc Racicot was telling—he told the group of African American Republicans to not expect too much too soon. According to Recicot, the Republican party was "not going to turn around 40 years of years of history in two years. We've got some miles to go before we sleep" ("Black Republicans Say 'Party can no Longer Be Lily White'" 2003: 5). In essence Recicot was telling these and other African American Republicans with similar concerns that they would have to be patient and go slowly. Unfortunately for African American Republicans the struggle to get meaningful support and recognition by the Republican party continues. According to Cynthia Wright, an African American Republican Party activist, the tepid recruitment effort toward African American voters made by Mitt Romney's campaign was "…nothing more than cosmetic wall paper" while also giving lip service on wanting to support various outreach projects Wright suggested like holding town hall meetings at historically black colleges and universities but as Wright states the "RNC refused to fund any black outreach activities" (Wright 2012).[17]

The GOP has had to maintain a delicate balancing act so as not to disturb the mixture of constituency bases that delivered electoral victories for the Republicans in the latter decades of the twentieth century.[18] These victories have come about partly through the Republican Party's ability to take control of the south and garner significant support from urban, lower-middle and working-class white ethnics. The Republican Party's infamous "southern strategy" not only relayed an implicit anti-black message, but also, a pro-white message as well. In the process of courting southern whites to the party, southern politicians received greater prominence and influence within the party and so too did the ideas and values that comprised southern conservatism. And yet, while the influence of the south on the Republican party has led many to claim that the GOP has become southernized, on the other hand, the Republicans have also been successful in attracting more moderate, solid middle-class and upper-middle-class suburban whites.[19] The support and promotion of African American Republicans by the GOP has a positive impact with these affluent suburbanites who express a strong desire to be affiliated with a party that proclaims and practices tolerance over divisiveness.

The challenge for white Republicans will be to discover how to promote and foster a stronger relationship with the party's African American members while at the same time not going so far as to cross that invisible tipping point where the cultivation of African American Republicans, and African Americans in general, sparks a chain reaction of hostility from their southern and urban white, ethnic bases. Finding African American Republicans who espouse conservative rhetoric that is as harsh and divisive as articulated by some white Republicans may keep in line those whites who find a politics based on divisiveness attractive, but will only further alienate the moderate voting bloc of Republicans. On the other hand if the Republican Party's efforts at cultivating a more stable relationship with African American Republicans come across as the GOP acting in a "politically correct" manner, or the African American Republicans that are promoted are viewed as too moderate in their politics, the GOP risks alienating its southern and urban white ethnic bases and the party will be perceived as watering down its core conservative ideas for the purpose of tolerance.

BLACK REPUBLICANS AS AN ELECTORALLY TRAPPED GROUP

The core of the political problem that all African Americans faced throughout the nineties—be they Republicans or Democrats—was the dominant belief among the two major parties that a strong association with African Americans is not politically advantageous. Even throughout President Barack Obama's first campaign, his being black was often placed in direct contrast with his *not* being seen to represent African Americans in the ways some of the black politicians from the civil rights establishment have in the past, such as Jesse Jackson. Paul Frymer argues that because our political system is one in which winner takes all, and leaders of both parties operate in a context in which they function without having complete information on what strategies will lead to electoral victory, they avoid crafting messages or enacting strategies that appear risky. This strategy especially applies to issues of race, as he argues: "The successes and failures of previous electoral strategies are used to legitimate certain types of party behavior and condemn others. For American party politics, this has meant that party leaders continually focus on primarily white swing voters who party leaders believe are hostile to black interests" (Frymer 1999: 41). African Americans are recognized as having value as a voting constituency, but because of the racialized stigma they possess as a group, the perception is also that a political relationship with African Americans must be developed carefully.

The party that is courting the support of African Americans must walk a fine line between demonstrating enough interest in the issues and concerns of African Americans to garner their support, while not appearing to the larger white swing voting base to be "capitulating" wholesale to the demands or agendas of African Americans. Democrats have learned the hard way what happens when white voters perceive the party as crossing beyond an acceptable threshold in building a relationship with African American voters. From the latter part of the sixties and continuing through the eighties, the Democratic party did poorly in presidential elections because of a drop off of support from various white voting blocs. Racial reaction by white voters to the Democratic Party's "overemphasis" on civil rights, paired with the Republican Party's opportunistic manipulation of white resentment toward the Democratic Party, have together been identified as the major factors in the Democratic Party's decline (Edsall and Edsall 1992; Rieder 1985; Freedman 1996; Sleeper 1997).[20] Unfortunately, in the counterstrategy the Democrats implemented they constructed African Americans as the problem.

As political scientists Philip Klinkner and Rogers Smith note, the Democrats began distancing themselves in symbolic and substantive ways from African Americans, even though this approach did not yield electoral success early on:

> Beginning in the mid-1970's, many Democratic leaders tried to appear less threatening to white Americans by distancing themselves from a vigorous promotion of civil rights. But compared to Republican candidates, they could not so easily repudiate the policies their party had sponsored in the 1960's, with which many Democratic voters still identified.... Democrats lost every presidential election from 1968 to 1988 and also saw their hold on Congress weaken. (Klinkner and Smith 1999: 290)

In essence, the Democratic Party was forced to find ways to reinvent itself to make itself more attractive to the white majority, by not appearing to be "held hostage" to "special interest groups" such as African Americans. One facet of this strategy called for the avoidance of "sensitive" issues such as civil rights and a refocusing on more universal issues such as economic concerns, the "bread-and butter" issues.

African Americans' political leverage has, therefore, narrowed with the Democrats adopting a more pragmatic and less aggressive approach to civil rights, and the Republican Party continuing its opposition to broad-based federal actions toward achieving racial equality. The result is that African Americans continue to support the Democratic Party even though the Democratic Party's response to their support has been less than satisfactory in turn. Operating within the two-party American political system, the options for African Americans have lessened. The political system becomes more like a steel cage than an avenue for participating in a democracy.

It is in this context that African Americans suffer from what Paul Frymer refers to as electoral capture. According to Frymer, a political group becomes electorally captured when developments arise that narrow the scope of political choices available to that group. As a result, even though the quality of the treatment by one party toward the electorally captured group has diminished, the electorally captured group continues to direct their support toward that party, especially if the opposing party shows little to no interest in competing for the electorally captured group's support. The electorally captured group's treatment by the party with which they are aligned does not substantially or radically change, because party leaders recognize that the electorally captured group has no other viable option to exert pressure or influence party policies, other than withdrawing from the political process or aligning with an outside party (Frymer 1999: 8). Frymer is referring to the relationship African Americans have with the Democratic Party. My argument is that that African Americans as a group find themselves in this situation regardless of party affiliation, and thus Republicans, particularly conservative African Americans, are also a group "captured," in Frymer's sense, by the Republican party. The deeper implication here, of course, is that the question of African American conservatives' motivations in allying themselves with the Republicans looks a little more nuanced and complex when African Americans have also been increasingly less well served by the Democrats over the course of the same political era.

The political relationship between captured African American Republicans and the Republican Party is asymmetrical. For there to be a more equal relationship, there needs to be both elements of mutual reward for both parties, and each having the ability to punish when necessary—the two "bargaining chips of political exchange" (Robinson 1982: 228). Unfortunately for African American Republicans, at the present time they do not have much to offer the Republican Party to initiate a feeling of mutual advantage. The Republican Party has seen it can be electorally successful without substantial support from African Americans. For Republican Party leaders to feel it is in the party's interest to make a major investment in creating a stronger and more meaningful relationship with its African American membership, expanding the leadership roles within the party to include more African Americans or throwing significant support behind an African American running for a major office such as governor, senator, or president, there must be something for the party to receive for their efforts. And while the presence of African American Republicans allows the GOP to appear to be a party open to all and sensitive to the importance of diversity, since the act of illustrating an acceptance for diversity does not guarantee political victory and may even hinder it, the political value of the African American presence will remain small in terms of votes, even when it appears larger in party rhetoric.

Furthermore, in terms of their contribution to a relationship of mutual reward with Republicans, African American Republicans are, and will continue to be, at a serious disadvantage. First, African Americans as a group do not possess similar amounts of resources (e.g., money or votes) as other groups (big business, upper-middle and upper-class Americans) who are also competing for the attention of Republican party leaders:

> In the U.S. political system, where public policy is formulated in an environment of competing groups and interests, those who are resource-poor are at a serious disadvantage... Since asymmetrical power relationships are derivatives of the differential allocation of resources in the socioeconomic order, blacks are bound to have a difficult time convincing the GOP to embrace their policy views, influencing elected Republican officials, getting adequate rewards for their support, and exercising power within the party's councils. (Robinson 1982: 228)

African American Republicans recognize this problem to some degree. Elaine Brown Jenkins describes how African American Republicans often miss opportunities to gain entry into channels of influence within the party due to their resource deficiencies:

> The RNC routinely sends out letters to all members of the party soliciting money. This request is, of course, essential to meet party financial obligations incurred in regular operational and electoral activities. There is a rumor that if you become an Eagle (by giving the party at least $15,000 annually) your needs and concerns will be listened to and acted upon.... Sometimes being an Eagle means you will be invited to high-level Republican meetings where you will meet other Eagles who may be truly wealthy and willing to work with you because you are an Eagle.... Certainly, the rewards for being an Eagle are great, but for many Republicans, especially black Republicans, Eagle status is not even an option. (Brown Jenkins 1996: 35)

While a variety of independent, African American Republican organizations have emerged over the years (such as the National Black Republican Council (NBRC), the Council of 100 Black Republicans (that ceased operations in 2000), Black America's Political Action Committee (Bampac), and the African American Republican Leadership Council), all working toward increasing the Republican voting base among African Americans and African American influence within the party, still "black involvement in internal party affairs has been very limited" (Bositis 1996: 3). Of the 153 members on the RNC only one was African American (Bositis 1996: 3). Notwithstanding the election of African American Michael Steele as leader RNC, a subject I address later in this chapter, there is still a paucity of African Americans in the RNC. To date there are only two black members in the RNC—Ms. Lilliana Belardo De O'Neal of the US Virgin Islands and a National committeeman-elect from the state of South Carolina (Bositis 2008: 7).

In addition, while African American Republicans can take a stab at convincing their white colleagues of mutual rewards, they are currently in no position to enact the second component of the political exchange model—the ability to punish. Since the Republican party knows that it can win without African Americans, African Americans in the GOP cannot use the threat of withholding their support from the party as a political weapon. In terms of calling for African Americans to withhold their votes unless the party takes seriously their concerns, African American Republicans have yet to demonstrate their ability to mobilize a significant percentage of the African American voting population. Even if they could, given the conservative take over of the Republican Party, they would face the impossible task of convincing their African American constituencies to stay loyal to a party that not only advocates reducing the size and scope of the federal government, but also, diminishing the federal government's aggressiveness in addressing such social problems as racial inequality.

Due to significant interventions by the federal government between the 1960s and 1970s, African Americans were able to gain access to occupations and lifestyles previously closed off to them, and their social mobility led to an unprecedented growth of the African American middle class (Collins 1997: 18).[21] From the New Deal to the present, African Americans have mainly worked in the public sector and thus, as sociologist Sharon Collins notes, the federal government has been vital to the employment opportunities available for African Americans. Not surprisingly, then, the majority of African Americans hold a view toward the government that differs from that of the Republican Party.[22] As long as these differences persist, the Republican Party will not appear to be a viable alternative for many African Americans and conservative African American Republicans will continue to face an almost insurmountable barrier within the African American community. As Pearl Robinson notes, "to be a credible alternative for blacks, however, the Republican party must provide policy options that are congruent with the gains of the civil rights movement -- policies that reinforce the new patterns of black economic and social mobility and sustain government-backed anti-discrimination and employment activities" (Robinson 1982: 218).

The tone in which some conservative African American Republicans speak about race-related issues further hinders their success in persuading African Americans to join the party, simultaneously bolstering my argument that, at least for cynical, hard right Republicans, the African American presence in the party works to draw white votes at the expense of, and in ways sure to alienate African Americans. Some African American Republicans leave little room for constructive dialogue between themselves and other African Americans. Winston-Salem

City Councilman Vernon Robinson, an African American Republican running for the 5th Congressional District seat in 2000, spoke out in defense of conservative commentator Rush Limbaugh, who sparked a controversy with his comments on the media's preferential treatment of Philadelphia's African American quarterback Donavan McNabb. Robinson stated:

> The syndrome Rush has reference to is very much alive and well.... Every time an NFL owner hires a white coach, here comes Johnnie Cochran threatening to sue, claiming white racism.... The people bringing these specious allegations and demanding that Rush be fired are the same whiners and malcontents who demand reparations for slavery, and who try to excuse every failure of black Americans as a CIA plot. (Moore 2003: 3)

Conservative African American Republicans such as Robinson like to think of themselves as what legal scholar Ronald Suresh Roberts refers to as the "Tough Love crowd," presenting themselves as, "harsh truth tellers, motivated by *concern* for those they criticize" (Roberts 1995: xii). The harshness of Robinson's criticisms raises questions, however, concerning which audience he aims to address. Robinson's characterizations of African Americans as "whiners" and "malcontents" mirror the language used by conservative African American radio host Ken Hamblin who, speaking to a mainly white audience, regularly refers to inner-city African Americans as "black trash":

> At the heart of the black welfare culture today is a black underclass, which I say should be called out for what it is – black trash.... Their ever-growing dependence on welfare and their isolation from traditional American values and rewards have worked together to make this underclass society within the black urban ghetto not just poor folks but socially and morally deviant black trash. (Hamblin 1997: 52–53)

The harsh critique and caustic tone of both Robinson's and Hamblin's comments are clearly addressed to white conservatives, exposing the thinness of each's efforts to appeal to a mass African American constituency. Their comments also reflect the fact that, unlike the strategic populist appeals of their white cohorts to the white poor and working classes, the core of African American conservatism is located in the ideology of the African American bourgeoisie (Toler 1995: 302).[23]

While African American Republicans such as Robinson accumulate legitimacy among white conservatives for taking "courageous" positions on racially sensitive issues such as welfare, they also serve another important function—deflecting charges of racism from the liberal left. Robinson admitted, "As a black Republican, I will be especially reviled by the left.... That's because I will able to say the kinds of things many conservatives are afraid to say out of fear that the liberal media will brand them racist" (Moore 2003). These conservative African American Republicans may provide the GOP some racial cover against the liberal left's criticism of racism but they also risk appearing to the larger African American community as racial mascots of the Republican Party's racial conservatism and being ineffective in mobilizing support among their fellow African Americans. This criticism is not off base since, as political scientist Hanes Walton explains, during the height of conservative rule in the GOP during Ronald Reagan's presidency, ideological allegiance became more important than experience as the main criterion for demonstrating support of, and gaining support from, the party leadership. This was especially true for African Americans in their adherence to the correct stance on race as defined by the party under Reagan's administration:

> Moveover, the aspirants' espousal of the Reagan brand of political correctness took precedence over all other qualifications and achievements. Experience, talent, mentorship, or length of party affiliation were not as important as this political correctness. Traditional African American Republicans who failed to join the new bandwagon were swept aside or quickly removed from office and eliminated from the list of potential appointments. (Walton 1997: 24)

Long time African American Republican J. Clay Smith tried to warn of the dangers of this development within the GOP over thirty years ago when he stated, "Black Republicans...cannot be the point persons for policies which are reasonably calculated to cause a political ambush" (Smith Jr. 1983: 223). Unfortunately for Smith, with the conservatives' displacement of the moderate and liberal wings of power within the Republican Party his warnings went unheeded.[24]

On the surface then, one of the primary challenges African American Republican politicians seem to face in securing electoral support and the hegemony of conservative values and ideals within the black constituency, is African Americans' perceptions of their lack of legitimacy within the Republican Party. In turn, African American Republicans do not have recourse to strategies rewarding enough, such as delivering a large number of black votes, or threatening enough, such as withdrawing from the party, to pressure party leaders into changing their discourse or strategies to become more appealing to African Americans. What a closer examination of this relationship between black conservatives and the party also reveals, however, is that the lack of broader African American allegiance to the Republican Party is not simply a matter of irreconcilable ideological differences and some kind of natural repulsive force alienating and keeping African Americans away.

In answer to the questions I posed at the start—Why don't conservative African Americans join the Republican party in larger numbers?—and—Why have conservative African American Republicans been unable to translate their ideological alignment with the party into significant political gains for African Americans?—I suggest that in the face of the party's deliberate tactics of avoidance and evasion in recruiting African Americans, and African Americans' status as an electorally trapped group with few options and places to turn within the US two-party system, both African American Democrats and Republicans may have to find new strategies for raising their profiles and being effective, *on behalf of African Americans*, in both parties.

THE POLITICAL CHALLENGES OF AFRICAN AMERICAN REPUBLICAN OFFICE HOLDERS AND ASPIRANTS

On January 30, 2009 former Maryland lieutenant Governor Michael Steele became the 64th head of the RNC and the first African American to be elected for the position. Many Republicans black and white alike were hopeful and optimistic that Steele's tenure would be a benefit to both the Republican Party and Black Republicans. Unfortunately two years later due to a variety of missteps and controversies Steele was ousted by current RNC chair Reince Priebus, one gaffe that got Steele in hot water was his desire to make the GOP message more inclusive to underrepresented constituencies like young voters and communities of color:

> We need messengers to really capture that region - young, Hispanic, black, a cross section ... We want to convey that the modern-day GOP looks like the conservative party that stands on principles. But we want to apply them to urban-suburban hip-hop settings. (Hallow 2009)[25]

On the surface Steele's comment seems harmless and is something one would expect the GOP to want to do but what brought on such strong pushback from party members had to come from the mistaken and stereotypical connatations of hip-hop as an inner-city, black, criminal, and morally adrift art form. Because the GOP has effectively utilized these stereotypes of urban inner cities for political gains it becomes unthinkable to see them turn around and embrace "urban-suburban hip-hop settings" that allegedly produce individuals of this kind. The organization's financial state also contributed to questions surrounding Steele's leadership abilities, under Steele's realm the RNC was spending as much money as it was raising, to the point where the organization's budget was running a deficit. But what was very telling about Steele's tenure as RNC Chairman was the strong pushback he received among conservatives in and outside of the GOP whenever he provided his opinion about the Republican party and race. Two examples come to mind. The first, a dispute between Steele and popular conservative radio commentator Rush Limbaugh. The second, Steele's assertion that the margin of error for an African American politician like himself was much thinner than for his white counterparts. The first came when appearing on a CNN television program host D.L. Hughley made the statement that Rush Limbaugh was in essence the "de facto leader of the GOP." In which Steele replied, "no he's not I'm the de facto leader of the Republican Party." This exchange was started when Hughley stated that no one in the Republican party criticizes Limbaugh for some of the statements he has made during his program and because of that Limbaugh takes on the "de facto" leadership status of the GOP. Hughley then went on to contradict himself by stating that on one hand he understood when Limbaugh expressed his desires to see President Obama fail Limbaugh was talking about "liberalism to fail… not about the man" but then in the next sentence seem to decry the fact that Limbaugh would "rather have an idea fail so his idea would move to the forefront and have it succeed" which Hughley thought was "destructive." Steele naturally responded by asking, "how's that any different than what was said during George Bush's presidency?" Steele then went on to assert that what Limbaugh said was in the context of an "entertainer…who's whole thing is an entertainer and yes it's incendiary and yes its ugly."[26] In his next radio show Limbaugh chastised Steele for betraying him especially when he (Limbaugh) defended Steele during his run for the senate, from distorted political ads by Steele's political opponents and in addition gave Steele airtime to defend himself. In essence Steele according to Limbaugh, was a tool used by the liberal media to distort the truth:

> Michael Steele has been around long enough to know that the liberal media will use him by twisting what I say or what others say. He took the bait, he bit down hard on the bait, he launched an attack on me even though the premise of what was said to him was false. He took the bait and he went for it.[27]

But upon closer examination Limbaugh has often said things, particularly around the issue of race, that have been in the words of Steele "incendiary" and "ugly." For example, Limbaugh has run a segment on his show called "Barack The Magic Negro" that parodies President Obama to the tune of Puff the Magic Dragon. Or on another program discussing the reality show *Survivor*, that one season placed contestants into teams based on their racial background, speculated which team had the best chance of winning the contest. Limbaugh felt the Hispanics would win because "these people have shown a remarkable ability, ladies and gentlemen, to cross borders, boundaries – they get anywhere they want to go. They can do it without water for a long time. They don't get apprehended, and they will do things other people won't do. So, our money, early money, is on the Hispanics." The African American tribe "it's tough to handicap on this one. You know, there are many characteristics here that you would think would give them the lead and the heads up in terms of skill and athleticism and so forth." The Asian American tribe wouldn't do so well because in Limbaugh's words "would probably outsmart everybody," but their intelligence would not be as useful especially when what was needed was a "raw native understanding of the land" which according to Limbaugh, the Native Americans have which is why the show excluded them because this would give that group an unfair advantage.[28] Steele eventually backed away from his earlier statements by claiming he had misspoken. As Limbaugh's comments illustrate Steele was correct in his description of Limbaugh and had solid ground to stand on to defend what he said. Steele missed an important opportunity by not continuing to support his comments, for if he had it would have illustrated to Americans, particularly African Americans, that he actually represents change in the GOP.

But because Limbaugh has an audience of around 25 million daily listeners that comprise the demographic profile Republicans count on for support, for Steele to stand by his comments and continue to anger Limbaugh and his legions of fans Steele ran the risk of alienating the base Republicans need to win elections and this was too high a price to pay. By backtracking on his criticism Steele in essence validated the charge that Limbaugh was the "de facto" leader of the Republican Party particularly when it comes to expressing views pertaining to race.

While on ABC's Good Morning America Steele, addressing a series of controversies: a fund-raising letter that mistakenly directed donors to call a phone sex number, the revelation that an RNC employee authorized a $2000 excursion to a Hollywood strip club, and charges that Steele was spending too much money on flights on private jets and fancy catered affairs, was asked by host George Stephanopoulos if he thought there is a slimmer margin of error for him because he is African American. Steele replied, "ah the honest answer is yes." When asked by Stephanopoulos to explain Steele responded, "It just is, Barack Obama has a slimmer margin, we all, a lot folks do, it's a different role for me you know to play and for others to play and that is just the reality of it, I take that as part of the nature of it."[29] Steele was articulating what a number of African Americans have felt and studies have demonstrated. For example, one factor that contributes to the perception by Steele, and other forerunners like him, that their margin of error is slimmer is what I call pioneer pressure. Pioneer pressure refers to an individual from an underrepresented group (Black, female, gay) who occupies a position that has been the domain of a particular group (e.g., white males) and with this occupation comes a sense by the pioneer of heighten expectations and evaluations placed on their performance and competency. One element that contributes to the pioneer pressure is fighting against negative stereotypes attributed to the group the individual belongs to. In her study examining the experiences of African American male professionals, scholar Cornelius, Tonya found that a number of black male professionals felt stereotypes of African American men (e.g., aggressive, belligerent, lacking acumen) were a factor that impacted their career growth. Fighting against stereotypes is one form of what Cornileus calls a repressive structure. According to Cornileus, repressive structures are "recursive social rules and practices that constrain the career development of African American men"

(Cornileus 2013: 452).[30] In addition to repressive structures such as fighting against stereotypes another element that produces pioneer pressure is what scholar and psychotherapist Frank Lowe identifies as the connection between a group's status characteristics and society's expectation of that group's leadership abilities. According to Lowe, society places higher levels of worthiness and competence to individuals from certain social categories than others which in turn impacts how the individual is perceived as a leader. As Lowe states, people choose leaders from unconscious and conscious definitions of what a leader is or should be, in essence there is a prototype individuals have in mind of who should occupy a leadership role (Lowe 2013).[31] As Lowe rightfully points out, these definitions are culturally and socially determined so Steele is correct when he states "it's a different role for me to play," it is different not only for him but for society as well because he does not fit the norm or prototype of who should occupy the leadership of an organization like the RNC. Therefore, when an individual fits the prototype they are more likely to be placed on the path of leadership and most importantly perceived as a capable leader (Hogg 2001).[32] Unfortunately for Steele there was little support for his comments as then-White House press secretary quickly rebuked his comment by stating that "it was a fairly silly statement to make" and Steele's problem "isn't the race card; it's the credit card" (Lee 2010),[33] referencing the spending scandal that plagued Steele and the RNC. For those on the left Steele's comment demonstrated the hypocrisy of a conservative, particularly one of color, raising the issue of race when in many instances criticizing those who cry racism when it is not warranted. For example, Steele strongly chastised former President Jimmy Carter for his speculation that some of the criticism President Obama receiving during his first term in office was racially motivated. According to Steele, "playing the race card shows that Democrats are willing to deal from the bottom of the deck" (Smith 2009).[34] A year later it was Steele who appeared to be "dealing from the bottom of the deck." On the right Steele's comment illustrated to some how overwhelmed he was with the position, so much so that he had to resort to blaming, as one conservative journalist stated, "the soft bigotry of low expectations...by Republicans" (Cline 2010).[35] Fellow African American conservative Larry Elder saw Steele's comment as an opportunity missed to point out the double standards applied to Republicans, particularly Black Republicans:

"Yes, there is a slimmer margin of error- but not because of racism. It comes from the double standard applied to Republicans...when Republicans preach hard work, accountability and strong family values, they call us scolds. When we let our hair down and show that we're receptive to alternative lifestyles, they call us hypocrites. Can't win...He could have said: 'Black Republicans pose a special threat because black Republicans disarm the left wing's weapons of racial grievance and victicrat mentality. Black Republicans are a scary bunch. They don't follow the script by blaming everything on race, as if nothing's changed...Steele faces Republican trouble from Republican unhappiness about his Republican leadership. This has nothing to do with race. By raising it, he diminishes himself, his party, and his country." (Elder 2010)[36]

What Elder's comment suggest is, when a Black Republican, like Steele, mentions the continuing impact of race they can expect to be castigated from those on the right because borrowing Elder's phrase they "don't follow the script" of arguing the diminishing significance of race. Even though the Republicans did well in the 2010 mid-term elections it was not enough for Steele to hold on to his position. Because Steele's election was coming off the heels of Barack Obama's historical victory, Steele's victory was looked upon cynically by some as a political ploy by the Republicans to demonstrate that they too could be a party open to having a person of color be its leader. In other words, this perspective sees Steele's election as having more symbolic value to the GOP than about the GOP electing Steele on the merits of his ability to be a good leader for the party. For example, Lola Adesioye, a columnist for the English publication the *Guardian* stated: "Call me a cynic, but I can't help but wonder if this isn't just another blatant attempt at tokenism" (Adesioye 2009).[37] The various verbal and tactical missteps Steele made further concretized the argument that Steele's election was a form of tokenism. It was no surprise that Steele could not garner another term as chairman of the RNC. Within his own party Steele's leadership produced very little confidence and in the end made him appear like the alleged unqualified affirmative action hire that conservatives so revile. The continued perception among African Americans that little has changed in the GOP's racial rhetoric and ideology diminishes Steele's and other Black Republicans political victories as instances of tokenism.

Businessman and former CEO of Godfather's Pizza chain Herman Cain had the 2012 Republican presidential primaries buzzing for a brief moment as he unexpectedly became the frontrunner for the nomination. Unfortunately for Cain, the combination of poor debate performances, muddled articulation of policy ideas (e.g., 9-9-9 flat tax rate plan), and sexual harassment charges by a number of women put an end to him realistically winning the president nomination. Cain was appealing to some conservatives, not only for his racial conservatism, but growing up in the south (Georgia) during the civil rights movement and coming from a family where his parents, particularly his father, instilled in him the virtues of hard work, perseverance, and belief in God which allowed Cain to speak to what it was like growing up in the Old South with its brand of racism but succeeding in spite of that due to his strong faith and traditional family ties. All of which allows Cain to construct himself as the epitome of the American Achievement Ideology (Prisock 2015). He is also appealing because he sees himself as a conservative of color who has profound love toward his country as illustrated in his response to reporter's question to whether he should be angry toward America on how it has treated him. In relaying this story in front of the predominately white audience at the conservative Values Voters Summit Cain stated, "I said: 'Sir, you don't get it. I have achieved all of my American dreams and then some because of the great nation United States of America. What's there to be angry about? Angry?'" (Weiner 2011).[38] Cain of course received an enthusiastic response from the mostly white audience, but what is important to note in Cain's response is his implicit signaling to whites that he does not think of himself as a victim of racism and does not go through lie as one of those perpetually angry black men with a chip on his shoulder toward America and whites. Cain is not shy in chided African Americans in their alleged "blind faith" toward liberalism and the Democratic party as he stated to CNN reporter Wolf Blitzer: "Many African-Americans have been brainwashed into not being open-minded, not even considering a conservative point of view...I have received some of that same vitriol simply because I am running for the Republican nomination as a conservative" (Martin 2011).[39] There is nothing in either of these examples of Cain's conservatism that should raise any question of his authenticity or loyalty. Yet, like his counterpart Steele, when Cain raised the issue of race or more specifically racism on the right there was pushback from white conservatives. For instance, during the Republican presidential primaries the Washington Post ran a story on a campground that then-Texas Governor Rick Perry and his father leased time at a for family hunting vacations, on the campground was a rock painted with the slur "niggerhead." During an appearance on a news program Cain brought this fact up and stated: "There isn't a more vile, negative word than the N-word, and for him to leave it there as long as he did, until before, I hear, they finally painted over it, it is just plain insensitive to a lot of black people in this country" (Fox news 2011).[40] Even though Cain has repeatedly proclaimed his pride of being a conservative and his disdain for liberals and African Americans who loosely hurl the term racist and construct blacks as a hapless group continually victimized by racism, these were not enough to immune him from the castigation of white conservatives who disapproved of Cain raising the issue. Some felt Cain was cynically exploiting the controversy to further his standing in the primary. Journalist Matt Lewis of the conservative website *The Daily Caller* accused Cain of "playing the race card against a fellow Republican when it benefits him" (Lewis 2011) and Erick Erickson of *Red State* charged Cain with "picking up and running with" the alleged slanderous accusation "as a way to get into second place" (Erickson 2011).[41] In the same fashion Steele was accused of helping the liberal left when he spoke out against Rush Limbaugh so too was Cain accused of aiding the left as Lewis went on to say that Cain's so-called knee-jerk reaction to the "thinly-sourced article published by an outlet many conservatives believe to have a liberal bias" was an indicator of Cain lacking "political judgment." In Lewis's opinion Cain's criticism is close to being a sign of treason, according to Lewis, not only does Cain's criticism demonstrate a lack of political acumen but is also an indicator that Cain has "aided and abetted those who wish to portray southern conservatives as racists" (Lewis 2011) furthermore Cain's blackness "provides cover for anyone wishing to cast Perry as such" (Lewis 2011). It is ironic that a white conservative like Lewis makes the charge that Cain's blackness provides "cover" or legitimacy to those who cry racism when the Right has been critical of this charge coming from the Left because, as they state, this line of thinking demeans black conservatives by reducing them to their race and not individuals who hold conservative values. Yet, Lewis seems to be doing the same thing with his accusation. The criticism of Cain was just as sharp on the social media forum Twitter as one white former Cain backer said: "Now an EX Herman Cain supporter after his racial remarks about Governor Perry *It is all about the race card with those People*" (emphasis mine) Perry 2012 (Amira 2011).[42] Although Cain was correct that the racial slur painted on the rock is vile and for the Perry family to have continued to use the campgrounds, once they were aware of the slur on the rock, was insensitive to all African Americans. Yet, like Steele, Cain eventually moved away from his criticism due to the backlash he encountered and the realization that to continue with his position only further weakened his chances of winning the nomination. On ABC's Sunday news program Cain had been confident in his criticism yet the next day Cain was more defensive and backtracking from his earlier comment: "all I said was the mere fact that word was there is insensitive... that is not playing the race card, I am not attacking Governor Perry... I really don't care about that word. They painted over it. End of story" (Lewison 2011).[43] The accusation that one is "playing the race card" is often used to nullify critiques that point out the presence of racism. But what exactly is meant by the race card? According to communication scholars Ronald Lee and Aysel Morin, playing the "race card" is a "contemporary phenomenon of the post-civil rights era, where racism has become a taboo and the accusation of racism is harmful to the accused" (Lee and Morin 2009: 378).[44] But upon further examination there is no singular definitive meaning of the metaphoric phrase, instead its definition is contextual. For example, according to film scholar Linda Williams, the power of the race card comes from a "melodramatic presentation of racial suffering" which relies on a "historical memory of racial abuse" (Williams 2002: 252) and is operating when "whenever racial abuse is invoked to cast one racially constituted group as a victim (p. 5)."[45] But as political scientist Tali Mendelberg sees it, playing the race card is comprised of four elements: (1) a conservative strategy used to curry support among whites, (2) within the context of the post-civil rights era the use of the race card is viewed as a form of racial backlash, (3) the assumption behind the use of the race card is the social context in which it is evoked is one where there is an egalitarian social norm where whites "want to avoid not only the public perception that they are racists but also thinking of themselves as racist," and (4) to be effective the appeals must be implicit in nature, through the use of implied statements that have racial connotations or code words and symbols (Mendelberg 2001: 7). Cain's assertion that he was not playing the race card is dependent of its context and meaning. Using Mendelberg's meaning of the concept, Cain's assertion is correct because his criticism of Governor Perry is at odds with the first element of Mendelberg's definition. It is difficult to see how, in Cain's case, pointing out an inconvenient racial fact about Governor Perry could have bolstered his appeal among white conservatives, particularly when a portion of Cain's support from them was due to his racial conservatism that strongly opposed race-based solutions to racial inequality, asserts racism's impacts are minimal to African American abilities to achieve

success, and dislike of any form of racial particularism (e.g., Cain's opposition to the label African American). On the other hand, Williams' definition of playing the race card seems to be more applicable to Cain's
criticism. For instance, when Cain exclaims "There isn't a more vile, negative word than the N-word" Cain is invoking both the memory of racial
suffering and historical memory of racial abuse of African Americans by
referencing the dehumanization of African Americans embedded within
the slur. And when Cain chides Governor Perry "for him to leave it there
as long as he did, until before, I hear, they finally painted over it, it is just
plain insensitive to a lot of black people in this country" he is casting
African Americans as victims of Perry's lack of awareness or insensitivity
to the inimical power of the word nigger. Critics, conservatives in particular, of "playing the race card" assert that this tactic is a rhetorical and
strategic ploy to interject race in a situation where it may not have been
present so as to garner opportunities or advantages by exploiting racial
tensions. So if applying Williams' definition to the situation leads to the
conclusion that Cain was indeed playing the race card we then need to
ask what did Cain hope to gain from this approach? The most obvious
answer to the above question would be to increase his standing among
African Americans but because Cain has been so vociferous in expressing
his racial conservatism, particularly the charge that African Americans
unequal racial status is mainly due to their own actions, has led many
African Americans to feel Cain is out of touch with their daily experiences. Therefore, a moment of racial criticism does not seem to be an
effective move to increase the support of African Americans. So is Cain
really playing the race card if it appears he does not gain any substantive
advantage from it? One factor that can provide a better understanding of
the response Cain received from his comments is the increasing feeling
and expression of white victimization. According to a 2008 Gallup poll,
conducted before the presidential election, that measured Americans perceptions about the level of anti-racism against blacks showed that while
the majority surveyed thought anti-black racism was widespread 40% felt
anti-white racism was on the rise (Jones 2008).[46] This begs the question,
what is causing whites to feel victimized when it has been demonstrated
empirically as a group whites outperform African Americans and other
groups of color in the areas of income earned, wealth accumulation, life
expectancy, and homeownership rates? There are several elements that
can explain this phenomenon. First, the creation and utilization of race-
based policies like affirmative action that help to construct a sum zero

perspective that socioeconomic gains by groups of color, such as African Americans, come at the cost of white advancement. According to psychologists, Michael Norton and Samuel Sommers, policies like affirmative action whose purpose is to increase minority access and representation in America's institutions "may focus Whites' attention on the impact of quota-like procedures on their own access to education and employment, in effect threatening their resources" (Norton and Sommers 2011: 217).[47] For example, African American conservative Thomas Sowell states:

> Those people of good will who will want to replace the racism of the past with a post-racial society have too often overlooked the fact that there are others who instead want to put racism under new management to have reverse discrimination as racial payback for past injustices. (Sowell 2011)[48]

Although Sowell's statement was in reference to the Justice Department's decision to not pursue further investigation into the charge that members of the New Black Panthers party were intimidating white voters at polling places in Philadelphia during the presidential election of 2008, it is just as applicable to the way conservatives view affirmative action programs as nothing more than a reparations policy that produces reverse discrimination. Second, the emergence of a discourse, put forth by conservatives that argues white Americans way of life is under attack through the elevation of minority culture and values in society (Norton and Sommers 2011: 217) or the threat posed to western civilization from the rise of multiculturalism as illustrated by the question asked by Phil Kent board member of the white nationalist ProEnglish organization: "will that mean rejecting the values of the founding fathers and, say, the Eurocentric legal system?" (Kent 2009)[49]. Third, the various social, cultural, and demographic changes taking place in American society produces psychological responses from some whites that they are indeed the "new oppressed minority." For example, legal scholar Russell Robinson argues that what plays a role in the different perceptions blacks and whites have toward the level of societal discrimination directed at their groups is a by-product of what he calls perceptional segregation. According to Robinson, perceptional segregation states that on average blacks and whites will use different perceptual processes in interpreting the claims of racial discrimination and from these perceptual processes will reach different conclusions (Robinson 2008). The two frameworks that shape the perceptional processes are color-blind perspective and the pervasive prejudice perspective. The color-blind perspective framework, typically used by whites, is a perspective that sees "discrimination as aberration from a colorblind norm and regards most forms of race-consciousness as socially disruptive." The pervasive prejudice perspective, mainly used by blacks, "views discrimination as a commonplace event, rooted in daily social dynamics" (Robinson 2008: 1117). For the purposes of my analysis I will focus only on the color-blind perspective framework. According to Robinson, whites with the color-blind perspective framework tend to think of themselves as such and view the harshness of racism lessening in society. Therefore, when discrimination takes place, for whites who hold this framework, it is seen as an aberration, an aberration that is explicit in nature such as slurs or other clear expressions of racism (Robinson 2008: 1126), for instance, the burning of a cross. Because of the racial slur that was painted on the campground's rock white conservatives holding the color-blind perspective, according to Robinson, should have understood the reasoning behind Cain's criticism and supported him but instead they chastised him. Does this mean Robinson's theory is nullified or non-applicable to Cain's situation? I posit that Robinson's theory still holds. For instance, as Robinson points out, whites who hold the color-blind perception framework need "overt, indisputable proof" that discrimination has taken place, in addition they may also "focus on the intent of the white person, while blacks may be concerned with the effect of the white person's conduct given their belief in the interactional and implicit nature of much discrimination" (Robinson 2008: 1127). This is exactly what happened with white conservatives defense of Perry and their criticism of Cain. Cain's critics focused more on what was Perry's intent and not on the meaning Perry's continued attendance at the campground had toward African Americans. Rush Limbaugh exemplifies this instance with his criticism of Cain:

> They're trying to say that Perry's a racist, and Herman Cain has jumped in and basically joined that chorus – and it is absurd. It's painted over and they tried to cover it up and then they eventually turned it over so people wouldn't see it. (Limbaugh 2011)[50]

Upon closer examination of what Cain said, Cain did not accuse Perry of being a racist instead he charged that the rock demonstrated insensitivity toward African Americans on the part of Perry and his family for hunting there in the first place or not showing signs of disapproval sooner. The fact that Cain would receive such pushback from his comments should not come as a surprise. Cain and other African American conservatives like him have garnered attention and support from their white peers for espousing opinions that have contributed to solidifying the color-blind perception framework. Some of Cain's beliefs illustrate this point. From arguing that racism does not have the same impact on African American lives as it did decades ago: "I don't believe racism in this country today holds anybody back in a big way,..." "Many of them do have a level playing field,..I absolutely believe that (Liptak 2011)." to castigating African Americans from being too focused on racism and cultivating a victim mentality: "They weren't held back because of racism...People sometimes hold themselves back because they want to use racism as an excuse for them not being able to achieve what they want to achieve" (Liptak 2011)[51] to eschewing forms of racial particularism: ""I don't use African-American, because I'm American... African-American is socially acceptable for some people, but I am not some people... And I'm sure my ancestors go all the way back to Africa, but I feel more of an affinity for America than I do for Africa" (Goldberg 2011).[52] It is interesting to note that while Cain's racial beliefs have buttressed the color-blind philosophy he has never downplayed the fact that he is Black: "I'm black and I'm conservative" (Goldberg 2011). Therefore, to Cain's white counterparts and supporters Cain's criticism of Perry came across as betrayal because he violated a sensibility they had around race and the opposition to any form of race-consciousness. As conservative blogger Glenn Reynolds illustrated with his statement: "I think that Herman Cain hurts himself by joining in on these attacks. His big appeal is that he's not just another black race card-playing politician. Climbing on board with the *Post*'s hit piece suggests that actually, he is" (Reynolds 2011).[53] So how has Cain avoided the accusation of "playing the race card" for so long even when he has raised the issue of racism or brought up the subject of race? There are two reasons for why this may be the case. First, as Robinson states, "while many whites view race-consciousness as an evil that must be strenuously avoided blacks tend to see race-consciousness as critical to their survival in white-dominated realm" (Robinson 2008). Cain's race-consciousness was tolerable when he was linking his pride of being both black and conservative, with extra emphasis placed on being conservative, or speaking to the "reverse racism" practiced by those on the left, or when he was chiding liberal left African

Americans and whites for incessantly focusing on racism and race. But it quickly became unacceptable, or as Robinson puts it "an evil," when Cain's race-consciousness lens turned rightward. Second, the response to Cain's criticism highlights the complex manner in which conservatives relate to race. The stances conservatives take on race are at times contradictory at best and hypocritical at worst. For example, there was little if any umbrage coming from white conservatives when Cain and other African American conservatives accused African Americans of being "brainwashed" for their strong allegiance to the Democratic Party or would describe their support for Democrats as "still on the plantation." Yet, when African American conservatives are called an "Uncle Tom" or "Oreos" by those on the left for their conservative politics or support for the Republican Party objections from black and white conservatives are swift. When Cain put forth the charge that he is more authentically black than President Obama: "He's never been part of the black experience in America...I can talk about that. I can talk about what it really meant to be 'po' before I was poor" (Travis 2011)[54] not only did he receive little contestation from fellow conservatives but some conservatives provided support for Cain's claim! For instance, conservative pundit Laura Ingraham stated: "Herman Cain, if he became president, he would be the first black president, when you measure it by — because he doesn't — does he have a white mother, white father, grandparents, no, right?" (Somanader 2011)[55]. Rush Limbaugh went on to speculate the implications of Cain becoming elected to the White House:

> Congratulations to Herman Cain and the 9-9-9 plan. Herman Cain, the big surprise winner of the Florida straw poll on Saturday. Folks, do you realize, I mean Herman Cain won big, and think about this. We could be on the brink of an historic election. Think about this. Let's say that Herman Cain goes all the way, wins the Republican presidential nomination...Herman Cain could be our first authentically black president. Stop and think about that. (Limbaugh 2011)[56]

Even some African American conservatives fall into the trap of playing the "black authenticity" game as Thomas Sowell addressing the issue of Herman Cain's blackness versus President Obama's on Neil Navato's Fox Business show said: "My gosh, he is certainly one of us far more so than Barack Obama. Raised in Hawaii and going to a private school, an expensive private school" (Town Hall staff 2011).[57] This is notable because black conservatives like Sowell have reprimanded African Americans who have questioned their racial authenticity because of their political views; furthermore to suggest that President Obama cannot be seen as a "real" African American because he was "raised in Hawaii" and went "to a private school, an expensive private school" sends the message that to be black is synonymous with growing up in the south or urban centers of the Northeast and Midwest; or being poor and attending inadequate public schools. It is this type of thinking that some African American conservatives, like John McWhorter, point out is problematic:

> Because it is unhealthy to turn a blind eye to one's progress, we must resist enshrining stories of misery and discrimination as "the way it is" while dismissing stories of success or normality as unrepresentative "anecdotes." Too often, the black person with a beautiful house, nice cars, and children in private school is processed as "an exception..."Quite simply, there are now far too many millions and millions of black people living comfortable lives to be processed as "lucky". (McWhorter 2000: 217)

If McWhorter's criticism of racial authenticity follows the logic of the saying "what's good for the goose" when he is arguing against those on the left who use this rhetoric it must then be "good for the gander" when his peers on the right make the same charges. It seems that for African Americans Republicans if they should question their party's or peers racial beliefs or actions they run the risk of "playing the race card."

The recent elections of African American conservative Republican Senator Tim Scott of South Carolina and black Republican Congresswoman Mia Love from Utah, illustrates that African Americans and non-African American blacks can achieve political success running as Republicans, as both Scott's and Love's elections were historic. Scott, running for a full term after being appointed by Governor Nikki Haley, a path maker herself being a woman of Indian descent, appointed him to take over the seat held by his predecessor Jim DeMint, who resigned under scandalous circumstances. By winning Scott became the first African American from South Carolina elected to senate and the first African American to be elected to statewide office since Reconstruction. Love, was notable for not only her Mormonism and being the first black politician elected from Utah, but also becoming the very first black female Republican ever elected to Congress. According to NBC's exit poll, voting patterns were true to form as Scott received an overwhelming 82% of the white vote while only capturing 10% of the black vote. When broken down by gender there was a similar split as Scott received the majority of votes from both white men and women (85 and 78%, respectively) while his challenger African American female Democrat Joyce Dickerson received the majority of votes from African American men and women (83 and 91%, respectively) (NBC News 2014).[58] According to Brigham Young University's exit poll, Mia Love garnered support from the expected groups: winning the majority of votes from women, Mormons, and whites which is not surprising given her district (District 4) is overwhelming white (whites are 92% of the voting population). One factor that aided Love was the fact she was not running against incumbent Democrat Jim Matheson who retired. When Love ran against him in the previous election Matheson received more support from all the above-mentioned groups plus pulled in 22% of the Republican vote whereas in the 2014 election her opponent Doug Owens only received 17% of the Republican vote (Brigham Young University 2014).[59] Both Scott and Love come from hardscrabble backgrounds, Scott grew up poor in North Charleston raised by a single mother (Scott 2013),[60] whereas Love the child of working-class Haitian immigrants was born in Brooklyn but raised in Connecticut. Scott points to his mother and an owner of local Chick Fil-A franchise as helping to instill in him conservative principles and values. Scott chiefly singles out his mentor for helping him get on the right track as he was close to failing out of high school his freshman year (Scott 2013). Love points to her hardworking parents as laying the foundation of her conservatism, particularly her father who expressed pride for being a supporter of Ronald Reagan, and told her at her college orientation: "Mia, your mother and I never took a handout. You will not be a burden to society. You will give back" (Love 2013).[61] Scott and Love are attractive to conservatives because both epitomize the Horatio Alger's narratives but in different ways. For conservatives Scott is the perfect example of the American achievement ideology at play. The American Achievement Ideology argues success in America is predicated more on an individual's strengths (perseverance, work ethic, intelligence, and weakness (lack of confidence, inability to delay gratification, laziness) than various societal barriers (racism, sexism, classism, etc.). In short as Macleod puts it, "Individuals do not inherit their social status-they attain it on their own" (1987, p. 1).[62] In Scott's case he succeeded in spite of facing various barriers: growing up poor with a single parent (poverty) in the deep South (racism) while Love is an example of the model minority syndrome at play coming from an immigrant household where success and progress can be attributed to the supposed superior cultural ideas and practices. Scott's and Love's strong belief in individualism, personal responsibility, limited government, and racism is no excuse for failure, will allow them to be favorites among conservatives for quite awhile, particularly those in the Tea Party of which both identify with. While black conservatives like Scott and Love have no problem calling themselves Tea Partiers the same can't be said for their peers as few African Americans have gravitated toward the Tea Party and often view the movement as being hostile to the interests of African Americans. In the next section I address what role African Americans play as participants in the Tea Party and the debate over whether racism is a core element of the movement.

Blacks and the Tea Party

"The Tea Party is not a racist movement, period!" (Goldberg 2011) according to Herman Cain. Cain and other African Americans who have aligned themselves with the Tea Party are certain of this fact, meanwhile academics, journalists, and activists from both the right and left debate the accuracy of this claim. For example, scholars in one study challenged the notion that racial resentment is a fueling element of the Tea Party by examining political races for governor and lieutenant governor in Virginia. According to the study's authors, if racial resentment is a major motivating element for white support of the Tea Party as critics claim then the voting patterns by white Tea Partiers should demonstrate this by their support for white gubernatorial candidate Ken Cuccinelli and lack of support for conservative African American minister Earl Jackson Sr. running for lieutenant governor. Although Jackson failed in his bid to become lieutenant governor according to the authors of the study, votes showed that there was no prominent gap in the support between the two candidates, as party supporters were as likely to cast a vote for both candidates (Hood et al. 2015).[63] Political Scientist Zachary Courser sees the Tea Party not as a conservative movement that is predicated on illiberalism, intolerance, and radicalism but a movement who's agenda fit "within the mainstream of American politics" and is motivated by "an inchoate demand for representation among a significant portion of the American electorate that feels frustrated and marginalized by what is perceived as an unrepresentative political system" (Courser 2011: 43).[64]

Yuri Maltsev and Roman Skaskiw believe charges of the Tea Party movement as racist come from the Left's habit of labeling those they disagree
with as racist and the supposed liberal bias in the media as one cause of
the perception that the Tea Party is racist (Maltsev and Skaskiw 2013:
78–80).[65] On the other hand, Eric D. Knowles et al. found in their
longitudinal study that "the Tea Party is–for some white supporters, at
least–a racially motivated movement. Anti-Black sentiment was associated
with Tea Party identification across time points" (Knowles et al. 2013:
8).[66] Justin T. Pickett et al. argue one of the motivations of white Tea
Partiers is fueled through their perception of racial threat to their status in the American racial hierarchy and is illustrated through white Tea
Party members support of punitive crime policies that disproportionally
impact blacks (Pickett et al. 2014).[67] In their interviews Theda Skocpol
and Vanessa Williamson picked up among white Tea party members a
clear demarcation between themselves and others:

> A sense of 'us versus them' along racial and ethnic fault lines clearly marks
> the worldview of many people active in the Tea Party. (Skocpol and
> Williamson 2013: 69)[68]

So do race and or racism play a role in the attraction to the Tea Party for
some whites or is it the movement's calls for a more fiscally responsible
and smaller government and declaration to defend liberty and freedom
by fighting against the ever-increasing intrusion of government into the
lives of Americans? I believe the answer is both. There is no denying the
Tea Party movement's agenda is centered around the ideas of fiscal conservatism and limited government, but there is also no denying that race
and racism are elements of the movement as well. For instance, the
posters and placards at various rallies that depicted President Obama
in a racially insensitive manner or when various members of the
Congressional Black Caucus on their way to participate in the historical
signing of the affordable health care act into law were bombarded with
racial epithets and spat at by Tea Party members protesting the passage
of the health care reform act are examples of the presence of
racism within the movement (Zeskind 2011: 501).[69] As scholar Leonard
Zeskind points out, as a counter against the charge that racism is present
in the Tea Party movement leaders are quick to point to a handful of
African Americans participants and give them prominence at rallies and
other gatherings (Zeskind 2011: 501). On the surface it would appear

here is another instance where African American conservatives are functioning as "racial mascots" but I assert that the blacks who take part in the Tea Party have more meaning to their white counterparts than acting as shields to opponent's charges of racism or examples of the movement's acceptance of tolerance and diversity. First, the presence of blacks in the Tea Party, and particularly their outspoken opposition to social programs like welfare, helps solidify the movement as, what political scientist Lisa Disch calls, a "white citizenship" movement. According to Disch, the Tea Party functions more as a "white citizenship" movement than one that is based on white supremacy. The major distinction between the two concepts according to Disch, a white citizenship movement is the "collective political action in defense of material benefits that (while seeming neutral) have perpetuated racial inequality" (Disch 2012: 142).[70] Whereas a movement based on white supremacy, mobilizes around the concept that individuals classified as white are imbued with a natural superiority and this superiority is materialized through the overt advocacy and protection of white only schools, neighborhoods, occupations, and so forth (Disch 2012: 140). Disch's definition of white citizenship movement is instructive in helping explain why Tea Party members can on one hand advocate for limited government and reduced federal spending while on the other hand maintain their support for programs such as social security and Medicare. The defense of the latter was borne from the establishment of the New Deal where embedded within the various policies were distinctions that helped solidify the concept of whiteness. For example, the Social Security act of 1935 had multi-tiers where there was an universal provision that called for workers to be provided some financial security in old age and a need-based measure that gave relief to the non-elderly poor who met certain criteria (such as aged widows or widows with children). Within the universal tier important exceptions were made such as the exclusion of domestic and agricultural workers, which at the time were predominately black, and as Disch states, gave "material, institutional, expression to discourses that worked to gloss over class differences and mark race differences" (Disch 2012: 139). The emphasis of making the distinction between "independent" and "dependent" by Roosevelt and others in the promotion of the Social Security Act played a role in influencing workers to identify as white because first, they were receiving benefits from the various New Deal programs while their black counterparts were not, even though the New Deal programs were in theory race neutral and not explicit in supporting racial separation or advocating black biological inferiority. Second, contrasting dependency with wage labor further solidified the connection between wage labor and independence, even wages that were low enough to fall in the category of "wage slavery" (Disch 2012: 139). Therefore, work of any kind is seen as independence while reliance on the state, like social programs as welfare, is seen as problematic dependence. In addition, the manner in which the Federal Housing Authority instituted racial differences in its lending criteria that favored white borrowers over black and kept suburban housing markets closed off to generations of black homeowners, while the federal government provided necessary resources to establish the infrastructure of suburbia at the cost of urban centers where most blacks resided made it easy for white workers and home owning aspirants to view their social advancement/independence as the natural outcome of hard work and merit instead of an independence that made race privilege invisible and was "publically subsidized" (Disch 2012: 140). This view is further reinforced by the personal narratives of some of the black Tea Party members and their reasoning for joining the movement. For example, Lloyd Marcus, Chairman of the Conservative Campaign Committee in telling his life narrative speaks of the time when his family lived in a Baltimore housing project when he was a little boy. According to Marcus, it was brand new and vibrant with earnest hardworking families until the arrival of those who were on government assistance then the quality of life declined, as Marcus claims, because this group of newcomers consisted of drug users, criminals and the like, but most importantly, Marcus asserts, they brought with them the sloth and lack of desire to be self-sufficient. As Marcus states, "Within one year, it was ruined,..It taught me a lot about liberalism. If you don't work for something, you don't care about it. People blame the white man. It wasn't the white man in the halls raping people" (Marcus 2006).[71] Here Marcus is reinforcing the simplistic notion that being poor and reliance on the state, particularly by black people, must always translate into decline and destruction of property and or individual character. Not only is Marcus reinforcing a conventional notion about poor people and behavior, he is also solidifying racial and class stereotypes that get associated with affordable housing which helps produce opposition to such policies (Tighe 2012).[72] So what allowed Marcus to escape the pitfalls of ghetto life while a number of his relatives, he laments, did not? Marcus points to his father passing the civil service exam and receiving a position with the Baltimore Fire department as the catalyst that enabled him and his family to move out of the housing project to a nearby suburban community. As means of motivation Marcus describes the times his father would drive him around to affluent neighborhoods with large homes on spacious lots and tell him, "if you get a good education and work hard, this could be yours" (Marcus 2006). This is an uplifting portrayal Marcus provides but unfortunately it is one that leaves out other important elements that provide a more complex picture of social advancement and race. For example, while the personal qualities and beliefs that Marcus' father held played a role in his acquiring one of the few spots open to African Americans in the fire department at that time, the activism of local civil rights groups were as equally responsible for making that opportunity possible for Marcus's father. The purpose in raising this point is to illustrate that success and or failure is result of the interaction of a number of factors yet as sociologist William Julius Wilson points out, in the United States when it comes to the issue of poverty and welfare the overriding belief system is one that "frames economic and social outcomes in individual terms" (Wilson 1996: 158) which ultimately holds those in poverty as responsible for their situation. The contrast Marcus presents of what the housing project was like before and after the arrival of residents on government assistance furthers the dichotomy of the deserving mannerly and undeserving recalcitrant recipients of governmental assistance. In addition, Marcus' contrast cements the common stereotype of the black poor while also elevating his father and the rest of his family as "the more noble" independent-minded blacks that white Tea Partiers can identify with. But Wilson provides a different dichotomy that is more appropriate. Wilson makes a distinction between what he calls ghetto-related and ghetto-specific behavior. According to Wilson, the combination of social constraints with restricted opportunities in larger society can have an influence on behaviors and attitudes or what Wilson refers to as ghetto-related behaviors (inability to delay self gratification, substance abuse, apathy, low tolerance to failure and struggle, depression, lack of desire to work, unplanned pregnancies, etc.). According to Wilson, ghetto-related behaviors, while not unique to the inner city occur more frequently in the ghettos, are attitudes and behaviors embedded in the unique circumstances of the poor areas (high rates of unemployment, weak community infrastructure. poor quality schools, and high level of poverty) "that reinforce the economic marginality," the fact that these same behaviors and attitudes can be found in larger society, is what does not make them ghetto-specific (Wilson 1996: 52). In fact, the so-called culture of poverty that conservatives like Marcus point to as the main reason why poor people are in poverty can also be found in some of America's toniest communities. For example, according to psychologist Madeline Levine, when researchers examine children across the socioeconomic scale the most troubled frequently come from affluent backgrounds (Levine 2006: 17).[73] Affluent boys have been identified as having problems with substance abuse using drugs or alcohol to self medicate their anxiety and depression (Levine 2006: 18) In addition, the peers of this group of adolescent boys are more likely to support this behavior along with those who demonstrate defiance to authority and rule breaking, therefore, showing no difference between themselves and their poorer counterparts.

> This peer admiration of rule-breaking behaviors is *equally* prevalent among urban kids in poverty and affluent suburban kids, challenging the stereotype that it is "tough" inner-city boys who are the most likely to endorse delinquent behavior. (Levine 2006: 19)

Psychologist Jessie H. O'Neill knows first hand, growing up in an affluent family, what the dysfunctions of an affluent life can produce. In describing the struggles of one her affluent friends O'Neill provides similar characteristics that have been identified as elements of the culture of poverty:

> Many children of affluence have little patience or ability to stay on task in the face of frustration and less-than-immediate gratification. Without the self-esteem that encouraging parents help generate, Robin and many like her struggle to sustain motivation. In careers as well as intimate relationships, when the going gets rough, people with affluenza tend to move on to a different career or another person. (O'Neill 1997: 102)[74]

O'Neill also provides valuable insight to why the dysfunctional behavior of the affluent stay under society's radar. When O'Neill was sixteen she became pregnant with the boy she was dating, as O'Neill confesses neither her parents nor her boyfriend's parents had taught them the "facts of life." Working up the courage O'Neill revealed this development to her parents in which her father responded by arranging what O'Neill called a "very illegal and very expensive abortion" (O'Neill 1997: 124).

Whisked off to New York City where O'Neill and her family stayed in their "usual corner suite at the Plaza" she was "drugged" and taken to Newark by limousine where the procedure was done and came to "safely tucked back in my bed at the hotel." In short as O'Neill states, "our money had allowed my parents to buy their way out of my 'mistake'" (O'Neill 1997: 124). It is the material wealth and supportive infrastructure that allows the bad behavior of the white affluent to go unnoticed but the absence of the wealth and infrastructure is what puts poor inner-city blacks, that Marcus castigates, into the cross hairs of the debates about the moral breakdown of America.

It is interesting to note Black Tea Partiers, like Marcus, that have gained media attention have an interesting commonality: they tend to provide a narrative that consists of the following elements: growing up poor, being on some form of governmental assistance, seeing or experiencing the alleged harmful effects of the governmental safety net, overcoming their plight, and becoming, somewhat similar to born-again Christians, testifying witnesses to their salvation. These narratives not only serve the purpose of providing ideological reinforcement against liberalism and liberal social programs but as historian Clarence Walker states, the telling of these stories by black Tea Partiers is an attempt by them as Black people to "normalize their history and escape the stigma of being thought of as outsiders" (Walker 2011: 126). According to Walker, this normalizing is done through the disassociation of the "history of black welfare dependency, crime, and racial militancy" (Walker 2011: 127). So as Marcus chides some Blacks who want to blame societal racism, colloquially referred to as "the white man," on the plight of poor African Americans the presence of black Tea Partiers like Marcus also provides their white counterparts with, borrowing the concept from scholar Laurie Balfour, a "racial innocence." According to Balfour, innocence is "a kind of disconnection. Embodied in the dream of clean hands and clean breaks, innocence impedes engagement with the difficulties of living" (Balfour 2001: 88).[75] When African American Tea Party members like Kevin Jackson state that the real problem of racism lays not within the Tea party itself but within the black community he is providing his white counterparts with what Balfour calls "clean hands." According to Jackson, the treatment by the black community toward African American conservatives, like himself, who vote Republican, dislike President Obama, and support the Tea Party are forms of "racism:"

There is a lot more racism and destruction within the Black community. We shouldn't even be talking about racism at a Tea Party until we deal with racism in our own culture. Go to a Black community and say 'I didn't vote for Obama' and watch the racism that you get. Go to a Black community and say 'you know what, I'm a conservative.' Go to a Black community and say, 'I voted republican.' 'You what!?' Go to a Black community and tell them you attended a Tea Pa...' You won't even get party out of your mouth before someone wants to slap you.' That's the racism that's occurring. (Koconis 2010: 8)[76]

In actuality what Jackson is describing is intolerance not racism. But more importantly the effect of this statement is by equating racism to political intolerance; the ostracism blacks have shown to other blacks is comparable to the systematic mistreatment blacks have endured from whites as a group. Therefore, whites are relieved from feeling any sense of guilt or ownership for the racial inequality that has been produced. This is important to note because as Balfour points out, with the concept of guilt "systemic patterns of subordination disappear" (Balfour 2001: 94) due to the fact that it is a concept, as she states, "best suited for individual crimes (Balfour 2001: 94)" and the lack of an individual perpetrator leads to the impression that "no harm has been done." It is interesting that Jackson elected to illustrate how blacks mistreat other blacks and not how blacks can mistreat whites to make his point. Logically it would make more sense for Jackson to show that blacks can demonstrate forms of "racism" toward whites making them as "guilty" as their white counterparts but by Jackson emphasizing "black on black" intolerance he does several things. First, Jackson perpetuates the common stereotype of the African American community as being reflexively liberal in their mindset, which furthers the thinking among some conservatives that the reason why more African Americans do not advocate for conservative positions is due to some misguided loyalty to liberalism and the Democratic Party or as Herman Cain claims "brainwashing," instead of the possibility African Americans are leery of providing full fledge support to conservatism due to conservatives record on the issues of race and its treatment of African Americans during political campaigns. Second, Jackson's highlighting the opposition fellow African American conservatives, like himself, face among their peers allows him and other African American conservatives to adopt the role of victimized individuals constantly suffering from some form of political persecution. This is a position that conservatives have taken at times, for instance, their claim that the alleged liberal bias in the media, universities, and Hollywood prevents their ideas from getting a fair hearing. When in actuality conservatives have built an infrastructure of radio and television networks, think tanks, publishing outlets, and strong connections to the mainstream media that is very effective in disseminating their ideas and messages to the larger public. Finally, with his statement Jackson is pointing out that blacks are not the perpetual "noble victims" of discrimination but can also be the discriminators as well thus leveling the morality field in race relations to where both racial groups are culpable of misbehaving which diminishes any guilt whites may feel.

When it comes to race it appears African American conservatives are in the proverbial between a rock and hard place. By denying the significance of racism and placing the majority of blame on African Americans for their unequal status in America they are accused by the left as being "racial mascots" that provide cover for the right to express racist arguments and ideas. In addition, black conservatives are also viewed with disdain by segments of the African American population who question their racial "authenticity" and feel they are out of touch with the realities of African Americans experiences in the United States. On the other hand, when African American conservatives point out racism on the right they can be quickly downgraded from an important ally to being a traitor who "aides and abets" the enemy and be reduced to, as one outraged twitter user exclaimed: "*It is all about the race card with those People*" (emphasis mine). Finding the right racial consciousness balance that can increase support among their black peers while maintaining the trust of their white counterparts is the challenge African American conservatives constantly face.

The cynicism by African Americans to the recent promotion and election of black Republicans is reflective of the inescapability of race. Although the election of black conservatives Steele, West, Scott, or Love sends the message that Republicans are in the process of change and open to inclusion and looking beyond color (color blindness) the fact remains a sizeable segment of African Americans are still suspicious about the motives of both the GOP and conservatives due to their racial histories with African Americans. It seems for African Americans to believe that the GOP and conservatives are sincere in their desire to cultivate a new and vibrant relationship with them, the elections of fellow African Americans is not enough. Forward change must be more substantial and by substantial it must come from not only a change in tone on issues relating to African Americans (e.g., black poverty due to behavioral and cultural deficiencies) but as well as shifts on some policy positions (e.g., affirmative action and anti-discrimination laws to name a few).

The Obama Presidency and the Crisis of a Conservative, Color-Blind, Black Politics

The capture of the Democratic Party's presidential nomination by Illinois Senator Barack Obama in 2008 was historic in that it was the first time an African American from either party had been accorded the honor. Obama went on to win in the general election and become the first African American president of the United States. Needless to say, Obama's candidacy and election sparked excitement and intense discussions among many African Americans about both his policies and his racial identity.[77] In terms of his politics, since Obama did not emerge from a traditional civil rights trajectory as previous generations of African American political leaders have, his ascendancy raised questions about the usefulness and vitality of the traditional manner of black politics. In terms of both his political and racial identity, for many Obama's victory posed interesting questions about what it means to be black in the United States today, and also, what now constitutes contemporary black politics.

My concern here, however, is with the ways in which Barack Obama's victory posed, and continues to pose some interesting dilemmas for African American conservatives, bringing many to a political crossroads they have never faced before. Obama's historical run at the White House produced a mixture of feelings of pride, admiration, and opposition among some African American conservatives. In the first and perhaps most telling irony, while African American conservatives have constantly called for blacks to focus less on their racial identity and more on their national identity as Americans, the pride that some African American conservatives felt upon witnessing Obama's historical success was, without a doubt, based on Obama's race. For many of these conservatives, Obama's triumph demonstrated that America's Achilles heel had been overcome, offering firm proof that race, in the end, does not matter in the success or failure of (African) Americans.

And yet, as much as some of these black conservatives reveled in seeing an African American at the top of the US political hierarchy, they also remained ambivalent and at odds with Obama on ideological grounds. As black conservative Joseph Phillips, an actor and author, states:

I am wondering if this is the time where we get over the hump, where an Obama victory will finally, at long last, move us beyond some of the old conversations about race.... That possibly, just possibly, this great country can finally be forgiven for its original sin, or find some absolution.... We have to not judge him based on his race, but on his desirability as a political candidate.... And based on that, I have a lot of disagreements with him on a lot of issues. I go back and forth. (Frommer 2008: 1)

Conservative scholar John McWhorter saw the Obama candidacy as a "watershed moment" even though "Obama is probably more to the left than I would prefer on a lot of issues.... But this issue of getting past race for real is such a wedge issue for me. And he is so intelligent, and I think he would be a perfectly competent president, that I'm for him" (Frommer 2008: 1).

The support Obama has among a large swath of the African American community also produced some twinges of envy among black conservatives. This was particularly the case since upon close examination of Obama's positions, there are key areas in which he overlaps with some of the beliefs that black conservatives have espoused. For example, in his platform Obama addressed the importance of the role fathers must play in strengthening the family and proposed to enact the Responsible Fatherhood and Healthy Families act, which calls for some of the following: the removal of penalties on married families (this "penalty" is in reference to taxes since many conservatives claim that the tax structure poses an unfair penalty on Americans who are married vs. those who are not); a crackdown on men avoiding child support payments; and a guarantee that payments would go to families instead of state bureaucracies.[78]

In a speech he gave on Father's Day in 2008 before a black church congregation, Obama called on black men to show more responsibility for their children. While acknowledging the role racism has played in the disruption of black families he also urged the black community not to use racism as an excuse for the delinquency of absent black fathers:

They have abandoned their responsibilities, acting like boys instead of men. And the foundations of our families are weaker because of it.... Any fool can have a child. That doesn't make you a father.... It's the courage to raise a child that makes you a father....

We can't simply write these problems off to past injustices.... Those injustices are real. There's a reason our families are in disrepair, and some of it has to do with a tragic history, but we can't keep using that as an excuse. (Wills 2008: 1)[79]

In this same speech Obama urged black parents to demand more from their children. In response to meeting black parents on the campaign trail who reported with great excitement that their children were bringing home all B grades on their report cards, Obama stated: "All B's? Is that the highest grade?..." It's great that you can get a B, but you can get a better grade. It's great that you've got a job, but you can get a better job (Wills 2008: 1).

Obama shares with black conservatives a belief in the merits of American capitalism and the advocacy of greater participation by people of color and women in the economy as entrepreneurs. One of his campaign promises was to increase minorities and women's access to venture capital and business loans. Part of this solution would come from strengthening the Small Business Administration programs, which some conservatives criticize as a problematic expansion of government.[80] And yet, Obama's plan is somewhat reminiscent of Richard Nixon's plan to create black power through the development of black capitalism. As such, it underscores the reality that Obama's economic plans and policies place him nowhere near the category of a socialist. In fact, black conservatives have also argued that the development of a strong, black, capitalist infrastructure is the key to the societal elevation of African Americans as a whole (Brown 1995).

Throughout both his campaign and his presidency thus far, Barack Obama has spoken out in favor of the importance of religious faith and its role in helping address various social problems, in fact President Obama has elected to continue the use of faith-based programs. This is one of the key areas in which he draws black conservative attention and support. Black conservatives often claim that because liberals are hostile to people of faith, African Americans' supposed uncritical allegiance to liberals requires that they deny an important aspect of who they are— their strong belief in religion. As Angela McGlowan states:

> The dramatic schism between those in so-called leadership positions within communities of color and those they represent raises fair and legitimate questions. There comes a moment in every young black person's life, sometimes in college, when he or she asks a silent but powerful question: *Why do we all vote for a party that's against almost everything that's integral to our faith? The faith that is reflected in the powerful Negro hymnals, which*

sustained us through slavery, Jim Crow, and the civil rights movement? Are
we to believe that it is no longer relevant today? Why are we so loyal to those
hostile to our faith? (McGlowan 2007: 119)

In his book *Audacity of Hope*, Obama speaks to the need for progressives
to cultivate a stronger relationship with those in communities of faith.
Obama states, "Our fear of getting preachy may also lead us to discount
the role that values and culture play in addressing some of our urgent
social problems" (Obama 2006: 214–215).

When he announced his intention to seek the presidency, Obama also
stated that government was not the answer to all of the social problems
facing the nation. Instead, everyone bore the responsibility of helping to
find solutions:

> And although government will play a crucial role in bringing about the
> changes we need, more money and programs alone will not get us where
> we need to go. Each of us, in our own lives, will have to accept responsibil-
> ity – for instilling an ethic of achievement in our children, for adapting to a
> more competitive economy, for strengthening our communities, and shar-
> ing some measure of sacrifice. So let us begin. Let us begin this hard work
> together. Let us transform this nation.[81]

While Obama was not suggesting eliminating the role of government,
his emphasis on the role of individual responsibility pleased black conservatives who often charge that an alleged weakness of the left is their
discounting of values and culture, their antipathy toward religion, and
their downplaying of the importance of personal responsibility for the
choices individuals make. In this instance, Obama did not sound like the
"typical" black politician who, according to black conservatives, over-
emphasizes racism and structural determinism when speaking about the
challenges within the black community. Overall, the racial pride of some
black conservatives in Obama's accomplishments, their ability to see
commonalities in some of his positions and their own, and a more insid-
ious feeling that some of the pressing issues facing African Americans get
a better hearing within the Democratic party, are all factors which began
to tip some black Republicans and black conservatives into feeling torn
over where their political allegiances should lie for the 2008 election.

Former congressman and staunch black conservative Republican, J.C.
Watts, considered casting his vote for Obama, but not solely for racial

reasons. As he put it, "I wouldn't just vote for a Republican candidate just because they are Republican, no more than I would vote for a black candidate just because they're black." Instead, Watts referenced the religious factor, stating further, "African-American Republicans in the faith community are the most forgotten demographic in the Republican Party and Obama highlights that even more" (Frommer 2008: 2). Watts also felt that issues such as poverty and urban policy would get better attention from a president such as Obama than in his own party. As he stated, "Republicans often seem indifferent to those things" (Frommer 2008: 1). Even though Watts professed to be color blind in being drawn to Barack Obama, one does wonder how secure his color blindness was in the face of the unprecedented fact that an African American man achieved the highest political position in the nation.

Even more disturbingly, given everything I have argued thus far it should have been clear to J.C. Watts that a Barack Obama could not have come from his own party. For some Black Republicans it was this political fact that most influenced their decision to support Obama and even switch parties. As one former black Republican stated, "Really early in his presidential campaign, when I got the opportunity to listen intently to his ideas and his platforms, I immediately said, 'This is beyond belief.... I joined the effort and it became clear to me that I was better able to work in my community in a broad way and support this outstanding candidate as a Democrat'" (Farrington 2008: 1). This speaker's sense that he would be better able to work in his community in a "broad way" as a Democrat reflects the historical fact that the Republican Party has had very little traction among African Americans at the local and grassroots level (even when other forms of conservatism, such as the anti-abortion social movement, has had some influence).

The irony of the dilemma Barack Obama posed for black conservatives was precisely the ways he epitomized and espoused many of the dictates and central values of a color-blind ideology, while yet speaking from the other side.

CONCLUSION

Referring to the well-known statistic that roughly 90% of African American voters pull the lever for the Democratic Party, conservative scholar John McWhorter has argued that African American political participation is more about enacting, as he terms it, "the black way" of voting. By voting for the Democrats African Americans are engaging in a stubborn and habitual resistance to the other side, "showing the finger to the Republicans regardless of the potential impact of [the Democrats] proposals" (McWhorter 2006: 365). McWhorter points out further that African Americans' skewed voting pattern—reflecting a mindset that fixes and determines how "blackness" is supposed to operate in the political context—is detrimental to black interests especially when compared to other groups of color: "In 2004, Latinos went 53 percent for Kerry and 44 percent for Bush; Asians were 56 percent for Kerry and 44 percent for Bush. They look like they think for themselves as individuals. We look like sheep." Since one of the core elements of conservatism is the elevation of individualism and discouragement of collectivism, black conservatives like McWhorter often feel conflicted about the way African Americans act politically and the emphasis the group places on their collective, "linked fate."[82] Hence the call from black conservatives for African Americans to spread their votes more evenly between the two major parties, allowing African Americans to get both parties to meaningfully address the various needs of the African American community.

The use of racially coded words and phrases continues, however, to be a way for Republicans to cultivate the support of their racially conservative, white base while not alienating more moderate whites. As political scientist Tali Mendelberg describes:

> The power of racial appeals today is due to the coexistence of two contradictory elements in American politics: powerful egalitarian norms about race, and a party system based on the cleavage of race. Politicians convey racial messages implicitly when two contradictory conditions hold: (1) they wish to avoid violating the norm of racial equality, and (2) they face incentives to mobilize racially resentful white voters. White voters respond to implicitly racial messages when two contradictory conditions hold: (1) they wish to adhere to the norms of racial equality, and (2) they resent blacks' claims for public resources and hold negative stereotypes regarding work, violence, and sexuality. Today, these conditions hold for most Republican politicians and for many – arguably most – white voters. (Mendelberg 2001: 6–7)

Through the use of implicit racial messages, African Americans still get constructed as the "other," the group that is outside the mainstream of American culture, the embodiment of everything that is not American.

During her acceptance speech for the Republican vice presidential nomination, Alaska Governor Sarah Palin spoke of her small-town background and the many contributions small-town citizens make to American society. Palin stated, "They are the ones who do some of the hardest work in America who grow our food, run our factories and fight our wars. They love their country, in good times and bad, and they're always proud of America."[83]

On the surface, Governor Palin's description of her background and the patriotism of small-town Americans appeared to be innocent. However, Palin also made her remarks in clear reference to a statement made by Michelle Obama, then-Senator Barack Obama's wife, at a Milwaukee rally for her husband. Michelle Obama had stated: "For the first time in my adult life I am proud of my country because it feels like hope is finally making a comeback." When a firestorm erupted immediately in relation to her comment, Mrs. Obama gave a revised version at her next stop, saying: "For the first time in my adult life, I am really proud of my country. Not just because Barack is doing well, but I think people are hungry for change."[84] Even with Michelle Obama's attempt to clarify her comment, the outrage among many conservatives was red hot. To many on the right, Michelle Obama's remarks illustrated that even a woman of her stature, with all of her of accomplishments and success, was still at the core that universal "angry African American" who will always have a chip on her shoulder toward America.

Governor Palin did not explicitly reference Mrs. Obama's comment when she described herself as "always proud of America." However, there was an underlying message that played off certain tensions Palin highlighted with her coded statement about small-town America. "Real Americans" like herself, who are white and live in middle America, are the ones that comprise the core of American greatness while "others" such as Michelle Obama, a black native of Chicago, represent the opposite of American exceptionalism. As the logic continues, everything that is wrong with America ferments within urban boundaries, permeating outward to infect the innocent American homeland. Political scientist Tali Mendelberg terms the rhetorical sleight of hand Governor Palin was performing with her remarks a form of racial priming. According to Mendelberg, racial priming uses "racial stereotypes, fears, and resentments, leading to increased opposition to racial policies (such as government aid to blacks)" to secure "greater support for the candidate who relays the message" (Mendelberg 2001: 13). Hovering over then

Governor Palin's speech was the stereotype of the perpetually angry, African American from the dysfunctional city who harbors strong anti-American sentiments.[85]

Black conservatives both inside and outside of the Republican Party raised very little opposition to Palin's speech, even though there were grounds for pointing out the importance of hearing Michelle Obama's comments in context. As Michael Fauntroy points outs, "when conservatives criticize blacks...without acknowledging the context in which blacks live...they make a mistake which costs them possible support and contributes to their unpopularity" (Fauntroy 2007: 25). Black Republicans' silence only heightens the impression among many African Americans that they are merely window dressing and not real players within the GOP. But some black Republicans do not see the problematic relationship between Republicans and African Americans as strictly racial. On the topic, "How do Black Republicans Deal with white racism in the GOP" on the blog site hiphoprepublican.com, aimed at young, urban, African American Republicans, one individual wrote:

> There's a good reason that GOP candidates ignore the black vote and it is that based on the time and resources they have at their disposal, they are going to be more likely to get elected by focusing elsewhere.
> The party itself is what needs to build the bridges but they are also doing that arithmetic whereby the instant gratification is absent, jobs and prestige are on the line in the short term therefore there's not a lot of long term creative, committed effort taking place.[86]

When others took issue with this statement the individual explained further that he was merely utilizing market principles: "Its more like free market analysis on why Republicans don't attempt to penetrate the black vote. It's not cost efficient. That's the 'why.' Its not an apology on behalf of the party, its a market analysis. Getting past that reality would be my next commentary!"

Alongside this dose of healthy realism, there are some who still feel that the Republican Party is a viable possibility for African Americans to get their political needs addressed. Matthew Rees states confidently, "The window of opportunity for blacks to participate in the Republican party is wide open, and is beckoning blacks to pass through based on individual initiative" (Rees 1991: 412; Williams 2004). However, until Republicans begin to directly address the Republican Party's problematic relationship to African Americans and tackle the problem with dedication and sincerity, the creation of endless "outreach" organizations, and the prominence given to a few African American Republicans at national conventions or in elected offices, will do little to increase African Americans' trust in the GOP. Nor will they refute former Republican Faye Anderson's charge that the Republican Party is more interested in practicing the "illusion of inclusion" than the real thing.[87] Unless there is a real change in the GOP's approach to race, the African Americans dedicated to making the Republican party more amenable and empowering to African Americans will continue to find their road to political success an uphill one. African American conservative Republicans in particular will continue to be seen by their peers as mere tokens who are the articulators of white supremacy in blackface.

NOTES

1. See Republican National Committee, "Growth & Opportunity Project," 2013.
2. A decade later these trends appear to have stayed the same. In a survey of African Americans by David A. Bositis of the Joint Center for Political and Economics Studies think tank, a number of self-identified African American conservatives showed a preference for the Democratic candidate in the past two presidential campaigns. According to Bositis, among African Americans who identified themselves as Christian Conservatives their stated preference for Massachusetts Democratic Senator John Kerry over President George W. Bush was by a 13% margin (49–36%). For self-identified African American secular conservatives the margin was even larger at 34% (63–23%). Four years later in the recent presidential Campaign the margins for both sets of African American conservatives grew larger as African American Christian conservatives expressed a preference for then-Democratic Illinois Senator Barack Obama by an almost 5:1 ratio (73–15%) over Arizona Republican Senator John McCain. Among secular African American conservatives their preference for Obama was almost 9:1 (69–8%) (see Bositis, *National Opinion Poll: October 21, 2008*, http://www.jointcenter.org).
3. See David Bositis, *Blacks & The 2008 Republican National Convention* (Washington, DC: Joint Political and Economic Studies, 2008).
4. See David Bositis, *Blacks & the 2012 Republican National Convention* (Washington, DC: Joint Political and Economic Studies, 2012).

5. See Roper Center, "How Groups Voted in 2012," http://www.roper-center.uconn.edu/polls/us-elections/how-groups-voted/how-groups-voted-2012/, accessed April 14, 2015.
6. It appears that even in the era of President George W. Bush's "compassionate conservatism" there were still some conservatives who were not heeding the message. Another instance of this took place more recently in the Mississippi 2003 gubernatorial race when former chairman of the Republican National Committee, Haley Barbour, was accused of running a campaign that was filled with racial overtones. According to Derrick Z. Jackson, Barbour stirred up controversy by refusing to demand that the Council of Conservative Citizens, a white supremacist organization, remove his picture from their website. Although Barbour stated that some of the CCC's opinions were "indefensible," his criticism seemed to have very little merit given that Barbour had yet to apologize for a racially insensitive remark he made during his run for the Senate back in 1982. When an aide referred to African Americans as "coons" Barbour replied that the aide should watch his comments or he would be "reincarnated as a watermelon and placed at the mercy of blacks" (Jackson 2003: 27).
7. In fact, Goldwater was somewhat prescient in seeing how the political winds would change over time as he stated in an entry in his personal journal that at some point Southern Democrats would be a natural ally with their Pacific and Rocky Mountain Democratic and Republican peers in providing the Republican Party the coalition needed in obtaining political hegemony. Goldwater was clear that race would be a wedge issue that could transform the American political landscape and boost the political power of conservatives as he alludes to the liberal forces of the Democratic Party being under the thumb of the agenda of what he called "stronger minority groups," which leads no doubt that Goldwater was referring to African Americans. As Goldwater stated, "I sense here a realignment of Southern conservative Democrats with Democrats and Republicans of the West and Middle West. The New Deal and the Fair Deal folks are coming from the eastern seaboard, and it is alarming to me to see how far they have gone. They are controlled by dictates of the labor unions {;} the dictates of the stronger minority groups are felt in almost every decision they make, in almost every debate they enter. This is a far cry from that of the Western senator and the Southern senator who believe in the free enterprise system, who believe in the freedom of the individual and the freedom of states" (Critchlow and MacLean 2009: 182).
8. In Chapter 2, I describe the Southern strategy as one in which the Republican party made their appeals to white southern and white working and middle-class ethnic voters in the Northeast, Midwest, and West

by using racially charged code words such as "law and order" and "welfare dependency." This coded, racial language mobilized certain prejudices as a way of attracting white working-class voters.

9. See Geoffrey Kabaservice, *Rule and Ruin: The Downfall of Moderation and the Destruction of the Republican Party, from Eisenhower to the Tea Party* (New York: Oxford University Press, 2012).

10. For most of the 1988 presidential campaign Vice President George Bush was trailing liberal Democratic presidential nominee Michael Dukakis in the polls. In an attempt to discredit Dukakis' liberalism, an unaffiliated organization supporting Bush put out a commercial that questioned Dukakis' stance on crime. With ominous music playing in the background and a menacing photo of Willie Horton, an African American, superimposed in the center of the screen, the narrator pointed out that Horton participated in a prison furlough program in operation while Dukakis was Governor of Massachusetts. During one of the furloughs Horton escaped and raped a Maryland woman and murdered both the woman and her husband. The commercial ends by suggesting that electing Dukakis could have devastating social consequences because of his "soft on crime" liberalism. Although the race of the victims was not revealed in the commercial, it was somehow "discovered" that they were white. The commercial's racial implications were quite apparent, and after it aired, Bush caught up with and then passed Dukakis in the polls, eventually going on to win the election by a wide margin.

11. In, *Uneasy Alliances* Frymer examines the status of African Americans' political power in a macro context by examining how African American political interests have been dealt with in national elections. I, on the other hand, intend to apply Frymer's theory in a micro context by looking at how the electoral process also places conservative African Americans within the Republican party in a similar captured status that Frymer describes as the condition of the group as a whole.

12. Some scholars who address this issue in their scholarship are political scientists Adolph Reed, Rogers Smith and Philip Klinkner, Hanes Walton, and historian Kenneth O'Reilly.

13. The Council of Conservative Citizens claims to be an organization that represents the interests of the white race and is focused on the objective of preserving Western civilization. A southern-based organization with a predominately southern membership, the CCC is often referred to as the contemporary version of the White Citizens Council of the 1950s and 1960s. One belief espoused by members of the organization is that whites are the "creators" of complex civilizations and cultures while Asians are "copiers" and groups such as African Americans are "destroyers."

14. Right after the revelation that Trent Lott was a member of the CCC Lott's troubles continued. At a party celebrating the 100th birthday of South Carolina Senator Strom Thurmond, during his tribute speech to Thurmond, Lott proceeded to make a statement that was interpreted as favoring racial segregation. The uproar over Lott's remark eventually led to his resigning from his post as the Senate Majority Leader. After the Lott incident, a group of African American Republicans led by media figure Armstrong Williams, met with Republican leaders to discuss the ways the GOP needed to clean up its racial image and be more supportive of African Americans in the party.

15. As political scientists Earl and Merle Black document, it was Barry Goldwater's presidential run in 1964 and his opposition to the Civil Rights Act that started the massive shift in support to Republican presidential candidates amongst southern whites. As they also note, Ronald Reagan continued this shift twenty years later by further influencing the *partisan identification* of southern whites. Reagan's charisma and ability to connect with whites without the blatant and ugly racial fanfare of a George Wallace helped draw many southern whites to him and the Republican party. In essence Reagan was a "master in applying 'racism-free conservative principles to each case at hand,'" which "reinforced the reputation of the southern Republican party as a respectable version of the newest 'white people's party' for many conservatives and some moderate whites" (Black and Black 2002: 217). For more on Reagan's racial history in politics see Mayer, *Running on Race* (2002), pp. 152–155, 157–158, 164–168, and 192–195.

16. Star Parker's critique that Republicans have overlooked black churches is more puzzling, however, given the developing history between white conservatives and conservative segments of the African American religious community, which I discuss further in Chapter 7. One example I can provide here is the targeting of African American churches by social conservative organizations, such as the Traditional Values Coalition during their fight against gay rights. The 2004 presidential election provided one test of whether President George W. Bush's faith-based initiative program could help the Republicans to make inroads with African Americans. While the answer then was no, the faith-based government programs have been viewed as one way for Republicans to bring more conservative African American clergy into the fold, and by 2009 this strategy has proved quite successful, as I describe at length in Chapter 7.

17. See Crystal Wright, "Mitt Romney's Neglect of Black Americans Failed Him at the Polls," uploaded July 11, 2012, http://www.washingtonpost.com/blogs/therootdc/post/mitt-romneys-neglect-of-black-americans-failed-him-at-the-polls/2012/11/07/05331e2e-28f1-11e2-96b6-8e6a7524553f_blog.html, accessed April 14, 2015.

18. Today the GOP is facing the challenge of maintaining its ability to keep hold of the different constituencies that have brought them electoral success in past elections. The more moderate secularized conservative base of the Republican party feels that the party is off track due to the takeover of a strident social and religious conservative sector. The same religious and social conservatives feel that the GOP does not do enough to address their concerns in such areas as immigration. The seemingly disarray of the Republican Party has produced a dissatisfaction among the electorate culminating in presently less than 30% of Americans identifying as Republicans.

19. In chapter five of *Up from Conservatism* (1996), Micheal Lind provides a comprehensive analysis of the rise and influence of the south and its regional values in both the Republican party and the conservative movement.

20. For counterarguments to this thesis see Reed and Bond (1991); Grossman (1993); Wypijewski (1996).

21. African Americans have always recognized the centrality of the federal government in providing Americans with the ability to live quality lives. For many whites during the post-World War II era, various forms of federal assistance allowed them to achieve middle-class status, with access to higher educational institutions, white collar jobs, and homes in suburban communities. For the most part these opportunities were closed off to African Americans. One of the major objectives of the Civil Rights movement was to insure that the government provides the same support to African Americans as it had to other groups of Americans. African Americans achieved middle-class status through what sociologist Sharon Collins identifies as a politically mediated opportunity structure (Collins 1997). Political pressure on the government by civil rights and Black Power activism led to government-created federal offices such as the Office of Federal Contract Compliance and the Equal Employment Opportunity Commission, along with affirmative action and federal set aside programs that helped create a demand in various labor markets for African American labor. As Collins argues further:

> It seems evident that government directly contributed to blacks' enhanced economic opportunities, particularly in the higher-paying white-collar occupations. Between 1960 and 1982 the proportion of black men who were public employees rose to about twice the proportion of white men in managerial and administrative occupations. (1997: 25)

22. In 1996 a majority of African Americans expressed opposition to the Republicans' proposal to reduce Medicare spending. Also in the same year, close to 87% (86.9%) of African Americans polled articulated a preference for smaller tax cuts and increased social spending over larger tax

cuts and a reduction in social spending. On the racially sensitive issue of affirmative action a majority of African Americans surveyed (59.9%) conveyed continued support for the program (Bositis 1996: 5).

23. Two dominant themes in African American bourgeois thought are the belief that values and behavior determine economic success, and that the African American middle-class is distinct in character from other African Americans. One African American, moderate Republican speaking some twenty years ago at a conference held to showcase African American conservatives expressed some concern at the need to make this distinction between the "uncivilized ordinary masses" and the "cultured":

> It seems to me that a very dangerous undercurrent surrounds some of the *Fairmont Papers* analysis, that is that somehow Black Americans caught up in poverty are going to embarrass the middle class causing it to be damaged by their actions. (Smith, Jr. 1983: 213)

24. Of note, African American Republicans tend to be more involved in auxiliary Republican organizations that are ideologically moderate (Bositis 1996).

25. See Ralph Z. Hallow, "Steele: GOP Needs 'Hip-Hop' Makeover" uploaded February 19, 2009, http://www.washingtontimes.com/news/2009/feb/19/steele-gop-needs-hip-hop-makeover/?page=all, accessed April 17, 2015.

26. See youtube, "D.L. Hughley with Michael Steele and Chuck D," uploaded March 2, 2009 by SST, https://www.youtube.com/watch?v=kP7Ceh4h0KA, accessed May 4, 2015.

27. See transcript from Rush Limbaugh show "A Few Words for Michael Steele," uploaded March 9, 2009, http://www.rushlimbaugh.com/daily/2009/03/02/a_few_words_for_michael_steele, accessed May 4, 2015.

28. See transcript from Rush Limbaugh show "New Survivor Season: A War of the Races," uploaded August 23, 2006, http://www.rushlimbaugh.com/daily/2006/08/23/new_survivor_season_a_war_of_the_race, accessed May 4, 2015.

29. See youtube, "Good Morning America (4-5-10)—Steele Implies GOP is Racist," uploaded April 5, 2010 by Nathanielc2, https://www.youtube.com/watch?v=CYy4oVDCG0s, accessed May 6, 2015.

30. See Tonya Cornileus, "'I'm a Black Man and I'm Doing This Job Very Well': How African American Professional Men Negotiate the Impact of Racism on Their Career Development," *Journal of African American Studies*, vol. 17, no. 4, December 2013, pp. 444–460.

31. See Frank Lowe, "Keeping Leadership White: Invisible Blocks to Black Leadership and Its Denial in White Organizations," *Journal of Social Work Practice*, vol. 27, no. 2, 2013, pp. 149–162.

32. See Michael Hogg, "A Social Identity Theory of Leadership," *Personality and Social Psychology Review*, vol. 5, no. 3, 2001, pp. 184–200.
33. See Carol E. Lee, "Gibbs: No 'Race Card' Mocking RNC 'Credit Card' problem," uploaded April 5, 2010, http://www.politico.com/politico44/perm/0410/gibbs_no_race_card_d8b78a62-53f6-499c-9170-1a7b937bb9fb.html, accessed May 11, 2015.
34. See Ben Smith, "Steele Denounces 'Race Card,'" uploaded September 16, 2009, http://www.politico.com/blogs/bensmith/0909/Steele_denounces_race_card.html, accessed May 11, 2015.
35. See Andrew Cline, "Michael Steele's House of Race Cards: A Pattern of Pathetic Excuses by the RNC Chairman." *The American Spector*, uploaded April 9, 2010, http://spectator.org/articles/39771/michael-steeles-house-race-cards, accessed May 11, 2015.
36. See Larry Elder, "Michael Steele Plays the Race Card," uploaded April 9, 2010, http://www.frontpagemag.com/2010/larry-elder/michael-steele-plays-the-race-card/, accessed May 11, 2015.
37. See Lola Adesioye, "Lipstick on a Pig." *The Guardian*, uploaded February 2, 2009, http://www.theguardian.com/commentisfree/cifamerica/2009/feb/02/michael-steele-republicans-race, accessed March 30, 2015.
38. See Rachel Weiner, "Herman Cain and the 'Race Card.'" *The Washington Post*, http://www.washingtonpost.com/blogs/the-fix/post/herman-cain-and-the-race-card/2011/10/10/gIQAVJsRaL_blog.html, accessed May 12, 2015.
39. See Roland Martin, "Herman Cain Denies GOP's Horrible History with Blacks," uploaded October 3, 2011, http://www.cnn.com/2011/10/01/opinion/martin-cain-brainwashed/, accessed May 12, 2015.
40. See Fox news.com, "Cain: Name of Perry's Hunting Camp 'Insulting' to Blacks," uploaded October 2, 2011, http://www.foxnews.com/politics/2011/10/02/cain-tea-party-movement-pushed-black-candidate-to-top-gop-pack/, accessed May 15, 2015.
41. See Erick Errickson, "Maybe Stephanie McCrummen Just Likes Using the N Word," uploaded October 2, 2011, http://www.redstate.com/diary/Erick/2011/10/02/maybe-stephanie-mccrummen-just-likes-using-the-n-word/, accessed May 15, 2015.
42. See Dan Amira, "N-WordheadGate: Conservatives Are Outraged ... at Herman Cain," *The New Yorker*, uploaded October 3, 2011, http://nymag.com/daily/intelligencer/2011/10/niggerhead_herman_cain_rick_perry.html?utm_source=feedburner&utm_medium=feed&utm_campaign=Feed%253A+nymag%252Fintel+%2528Daily+Intelligencer+-+New+York+Magazine%2529&utm_content=Google+Reader, accessed May 15, 2015.

43. See Jed Lewison, "Cain Flip-Flops on Perry Hunting Grounds Criticism After Conservative Backlash," uploaded October 4, 2011, http://www.dailykos.com/story/2011/10/04/1022657/-Cain-flip-flops-on-Perry-hunting-grounds-criticism-after-conservative-backlash#, accessed May 15, 2015.

44. See Ronald Lee and Aysel Morin, "Using the 2008 Presidential Election to Think about 'Playing the Race Card,'" *Communication Studies*, vol. 60, no. 4, September–October 2009, pp. 376–391.

45. See Linda Williams, *Playing the Race Card: Melodramas of Black and White from Uncle Tom to O. J. Simpson* (Princeton, NJ: Princeton University Press).

46. See Jeffrey M. Jones, "Majority of Americans Say Racism Against Blacks Widespread," uploaded August 4, 2008, http://www.gallup.com/poll/109258/majority-americans-say-racism-against-blacks-widespread.aspx, accessed May 24, 2015.

47. See Michael I. Norton and Samuel R. Sommers, "Whites See Racism as a Zero-Sum Game That They Are Now Losing," *Perspectives on Psychological Science* vol. 6, no. 3, 2011, pp. 215–218.

48. See Thomas Sowell, "Reverse Racism," uploaded October 11, 2011, http://townhall.com/columnists/thomassowell/2011/10/11/reverse_racism, accessed on May 25, 2015.

49. See Phil Kent, "A Demographic 'Tipping Point' for the U.S.," http://www.philkent.com/columns_popup.php?columns_id=68, accessed May 24, 2015.

50. See Rush Limbaugh, "Herman Cain Piggybacks on WaPo's Perry Smear and Obama's Debate Lie," uploaded October 3, 2011, http://www.rushlimbaugh.com/daily/2011/10/03/herman_cain_piggybacks_on_wapo_s_perry_smear_and_obama_s_debate_lie, accessed May 25, 2015.

51. See Kevin Liptak, "Cain: Racism Not Holding Anyone Back," uploaded October 9, 2011, http://politicalticker.blogs.cnn.com/2011/10/09/cain-racism-not-holding-anyone-back, accessed May 21, 2015.

52. See Jeffrey Goldberg, "Herman Cain on Why 'The Black Guy Is Winning'," uploaded June 13, 2011, http://www.bloomberg.com/news/articles/2011-06-13/herman-cain-on-why-the-black-guy-is-winning-jeffrey-goldberg, accessed May 21, 2015.

53. See Glenn Reynolds, uploaded October 2, 2011, http://pjmedia.com/instapundit/128979/, accessed May 21, 2015.

54. See Shannon Travis, "Cain's Race Not as Big an Issue with Conservatives as Obama's Was Three Years Ago," uploaded October 13, 2011, http://politicalticker.blogs.cnn.com/2011/10/13/cains-race-not-as-big-an-issue-with-conservatives-as-obamas-was-three-years-ago/, accessed May 25, 2015.

55. See Tanya Somanader, "Ingraham Suggests Cain Would Be The Real First Black President Because Obama Has White Relatives," uploaded October 6, 2011, http://thinkprogress.org/media/2011/10/06/338107/ingraham-suggests-cain-would-be-the-real-first-black-president-because-obama-has-white-relatives/, accessed May 25, 2015.

56. See Rush Limbaugh, "Herman Cain Could Be Our First Authentically Black President," uploaded September 26, 2011, http://www.rush-limbaugh.com/daily/2011/09/26/herman_cain_could_be_our_first_authentically_black_president, accessed May 25, 2015.

57. See Town Hall Staff, "Thomas Sowell: Herman Cain More Black Than Barack Obama," uploaded October 20, 2011, http://townhall.com/tipsheet/townhallcomstaff/2011/10/20/thomas_sowell_herman_cain_more_black_than_barack_obama, accessed May 25, 2011.

58. See NBC News, "Decision 2014," http://www.nbcnews.com/politics/elections/2014/SC/S2/exitpoll, accessed May 25, 2015.

59. See Brigham Young University Exit Poll, "Love Wins by Getting More GOP Votes the Second Time Around," http://exitpoll.byu.edu/Documents/2014%20UCEP-%20Love%20wins%20by%20getting%20more%20GOP%20votes%20the%20second%20time%20around.pdf, accessed May 25, 2015.

60. See Tim Scott, "Tim Scott for Senate," http://votetimscott.com/about-tim/, accessed May 25, 2015.

61. See Mia Love, "About Mia Love," http://love4utah.com/about/, accessed May 25, 2015.

62. See Jay Mcloud, *Ain't No Making It: Leveled Aspirations in a Low-Income Neighborhood* (Boulder, CO: Westview Press, 1987).

63. M.V. Hood III, Quentin Kidd, and Irwin L. Morris, "Race and the Tea Party in the Old Dominion: Split-Ticket Voting in the 2013 Virginia Elections," *PS: Political Science & Politics*, vol. 48, no. 1, January 2015, pp. 107–114.

64. Zachary Courser, "The Tea 'Party' as a Conservative Social Movement," *Society*, vol. 49, 2012, pp. 43–53.

65. See Yuri Maltsev and Roman Skasiw, *The Tea Party Explained: From Crisis to Crusade* (Chicago, IL: Open Court Publishers, 2013).

66. Eric D. Knowles, Brian S. Lowery, Elizabeth P. Shulman, and Rebecca L. Schaumberg, "Race, Ideology, and the Tea Party: A Longitudinal Study," *Plos One*, vol. 8, no. 6, June 2013, pp. 1–11.

67. See Justin T. Pickett, Daniel Tope, and Rose Bellandi, "'Taking Back Our Country': Tea Party Membership and Support for Punitive Crime Control Policies," *Sociological Inquiry*, vol. 84, no. 2, May 2014, pp. 167–190.

68. See Theda Skocpol and Vanessa Wiliamson, *The Tea Party and the Remaking of Republican Conservatism* (New York: Oxford University Press, 2013).
69. Leonard Zeskind, "A Nation Dispossessed: The Tea Party Movement and Race," *Critical Sociology*, vol. 38, no. 4, pp. 495–509.
70. See Lisa Disch, "A White Citizenship Movement," in *Steep: The Precipitous Rise of the Tea Party*, eds. Lawrence Rosenthal and Christine Trost (Berkeley, CA: University of California Press, 2012).
71. See Lloyd Marcus, "Biography," http://www.lloydmarcus.com/biography/.
72. See J. Rosie Tighe, "How Race and Class Stereotyping Shapes Attitudes Toward Affordable Housing," *Housing Studies*, vol. 27, no. 7, October 2012, pp. 962–983.
73. See Madeline Levine, *The Price of Privilege: How Parental Pressure and Material Advantage Are Creating a Generation of Disconnected and Unhappy Kids* (New York: HarperCollins, 2006).
74. See Jessie H. O'Neill, *The Golden Ghetto: The Psychology of Affluence* (Milwaukee, WI: Affluenza Project Publishers, 1997).
75. See Laurie Balfour, *The Evidence of Things Not Said: James Baldwin and the Promise of American Democracy* (Ithaca, NY: Cornell University Press, 2001).
76. Ben Koconis, "Black Conservatives Insist Tea Party Misunderstood by Many," *The Washington Informer*, vol. 46, no. 45, August 26–September 1, 2010.
77. Although Obama is of mixed race heritage (a white American mother and an African father) he calls himself African American.
78. Barack Obama at http://www.barackobama.com/issues/family.
79. Christopher Wills, "ObamaTells Black Fathers to Engage Their Children," *Associated Press*, June 17, 2008, p. 1.
80. See http://www.barackobama.com/pdf/SmallBusiness for more extensive details on his economic plan for the development of small businesses.
81. http://www.barackobama.com/pdf/ObamaonFaith.
82. Public policy scholar Michael Fauntroy borrows the term "linked fate" from political scientist Michael Dawson to offer a different way of thinking about what McWhorter, and other conservatives, can see only as a form oppressive "groupthink." African Americans share a legacy of racial oppression manifested through forms of violence, segregation, and blocked economic and political opportunities. This has led to the sense among a substantial number of African Americans that they share a "linked fate," which represents the belief that what happens to African Americans collectively in society will also have an effect on how they are seen as individuals (Fauntroy 2007: 21). Black criminality is one prime

example; when the media presents an endless string of black criminals on the news who are wanted or captured for committing criminal acts, the concern for other African Americans is how the media representation will impact society's perception of them. Historian Thomas Sugrue also identifies this perspective, in which white society at large makes no distinction between African Americans who are poor and those who are more affluent, as, "the ghetto as an ideological construct" (Sugrue 2005: 229). According to Sugrue, because segregation in Detroit, as in other American cities, kept many whites from having meaningful contact with African Americans on a regular basis, the grim situation of African American inner-city life offered the only cues on how African Americans were to be understood as a group overall (216).

83. Transcript of Sarah Palin's acceptance speech at the Republican Party National Convention, September 3, 2008.

84. Jennifer Parker, Bret Hovell, and Sunien Miller, "McCain vs Obama... Cindy and Michelle, That is," February 19, 2008, http://www.abcnews-blogs.abcnews.com/politicalradar/.../mccain-vs-obama.html.

85. For more on this stereotypical image see chapters 2 and 3 in Steve Macek's, *Urban Nightmares* (2006). Conservatives have a history of fomenting antipathy toward cities, an antipathy that can also have a strong racial element. Within conservative discourse, the image of cities is that they are havens for "cosmopolitan" liberals, who, in their elitism, look down on the average American and their values while elevating "dangerous," non-traditional ideas (such as feminism, non-married heterosexual families, same-sex couples) and anti-American sentiments (communism, socialism). In his study on rural America, journalist Brian Mann documents a solid, anti-urban sentiment within pockets of rural America. Mann calls these conservatives, "homelanders," a collection of rural, exurban mainly white, anti-urban conservatives, "scattered in small towns and exurbs across the country, from farm counties of California to the old mining towns of Pennsylvania," whose sense of the idyllic country life is more imaginative than actual (Mann 2006: 11). As Mann continues, "They view the nation's cities as fallen places, Sodom's of secular indulgence, Gomorrah's of vice" and "reject the larger framework of urban life...They despise the liberal modernism that shaped metro culture in the twentieth century and see it as an ideology that is every bit as foreign and threatening as communism" (6, 18).

86. As quoted on thread, "How Do Black Republicans Deal with white racism in the GOP," http://hiphoprepublican.com.

87. In an op-ed article for the *New York Times* Faye Anderson lambasted the Republican party's attempt to appear more diversified by showcasing at its 2000 National convention prominent Republicans of color.

Anderson was not convinced by the tactic, as she stated, "At the convention, Mr.Powell and a parade of African American and Hispanic speakers have taken center stage, a made for television illusion of inclusion. Fans of reality TV, meantime, may want to check their local listings" (Anderson 2000a).

REFERENCES

Adesioye, Lola. "Lipstick on a Pig." *The Guardian*, uploaded February 2, 2009, http://www.theguardian.com/commentisfree/cifamerica/2009/feb/02/michael-steele-republicans-race, accessed March 30, 2015.

Amira, Dan. "N-WordheadGate: Conservatives Are Outraged ... at Herman Cain," *The New Yorker*, uploaded October 3, 2011, http://nymag.com/daily/intelligencer/2011/10/niggerhead_herman_cain_rick_perry.htmlutm_source=feedburner&utm_medium=feed&utm_campaign=Feed%253A+nymag%252Fintel+%2528Daily+Intelligencer++New+York+Magazine%2529&utm_content=Google+Reader, accessed May 15, 2015.

Anderson, Faye M. "The Value of Black GOP Activists." *Washington Afro-American*, vol. 106, June 12, 1998: A5.

———. "'The Republicans' Illusion of Inclusion." *The New York Times*, August 1, 2000a.

———. "Why I Left." *The Capital Report*, July 8, 2000b: 1, http://www.politicallyblack.com.

———. "Do Some Serious Spring-Cleaning in Your Big Tent...The Stench Has Become Intolerable—Letter of Resignation from the Republican Party." *The Capital Report*, July 8, 2000c: 2, http://www.politicallyblack.com.

Ansell, Amy Elizabeth. *New Right, New Racism: Race and Reaction in the United States and Britain*. New York: New York University Press, 1997.

Balfour, Laurie. *The Evidence of Things Not Said: James Baldwin and the Promise of American Democracy*. Ithaca, NY: Cornell University Press, 2001.

"Black Republicans Say 'Party Can No Longer Be Lily White.'" *The Atlanta Inquirer*, February 8, 2003.

Black, Earl, and Merle Black. *The Rise of Southern Republicanism*. Cambridge, MA: Harvard University Press, 2002.

Bolce, Louis, et al. "The 1992 Republican 'Tent': No Blacks Walked In." *Political Science Quarterly*, vol. 108, no. 2, 1993: 255–270.

Bositis, David A. *African Americans and the Republican Party*. Washington, DC: The Joint Center for Political and Economic Studies, 1996.

———. *2000 Joint Center for Political and Economic Studies National Opinion Poll*. Washington, DC: Joint Center for Political and Economic Studies, 2000.

———. *Diverging Generations: The Transformation of African American Views*. Washington, DC: The Joint Center for Political and Economic Studies, 2001.

————. *Blacks and the 2008 Republican National Convention.* Washington, DC: The Joint Center for Political and Economic Studies, 2008.

————. *Blacks and the 2012 Republican National Convention.* Washington, DC: Joint Political and Economic Studies Publication, 2012.

Brigham Young University. Exit Poll, "Love Wins by Getting More GOP Votes the Second Time Around," 2014, http://exitpoll.byu.edu/Documents/2014%20 UCEP-%20Love%20wins%20by%20getting%20more%20GOP%20votes%20 the%20second%20time%20around.pdf, accessed May 25, 2015.

Brown, Tony. *Black Lies, White Lies: The Truth According to Tony Brown.* New York: William Morrow, 1995.

Brown Jenkins, Elaine. *Jumping Double Dutch: A New Agenda for Blacks and the Republican Party.* Silver Spring, MD: Beckham Publishers, 1996.

Champion, Jackson R. *Blacks in the Republican Party? The Story of a Revolutionary Conservative Black Republican.* Washington, DC: LenChamps Publishers, 1976.

Cline, Andrew. "Michael Steele's House of Race Cards: A Pattern of Pathetic Excuses by the RNC Chairman." *The American Spector,* uploaded April 9, 2010, http://spectator.org/articles/39771/michael-steeles-house-racecards, accessed May 11, 2015.

Collins, Sharon. *Black Corporate Executives: The Making and Breaking of a Black Middle Class.* Philadelphia, PA: Temple University Press, 1997.

Coulter, Ann. "Another Damascus Road Conversion." August 18, 2000, www. townhall.com/columnists/anncoulter.

Courser, Zachary. "The Tea 'Party' as a Conservative Social Movement," *Society,* vol. 49, 2012: 43–53.

Cornileus, Tonya. "'I'm a Black Man and I'm Doing This Job Very Well': How African American Professional Men Negotiate the Impact of Racism on Their Career Development," *Journal of African American Studies,* vol. 17, no. 4, December 2013: 444–460.

Critchlow, Donald T., and Nancy MacLean. *Debating the American Conservative Movement: 1945 to the Present.* Lanham, MD: Rowman and Littlefield, 2009.

DeVeaux, Stuart. "Young, Black, and Republican." In *Black and Right: The Bold New Voice of Black Conservatives in America.* Eds. Stan Faryna, Brad Stetson, and Joseph G. Conti. Westport, CT: Praeger, 1997.

Disch, Lisa. "A White Citizenship Movement." In *Steep: The Precipitous Rise of the Tea Party.* eds. Lawrence Rosenthal, and Christine Trost. Berkeley, CA: University of California Press, 2012: 133–151.

Edsall, Thomas Byrne, and Mary D. Edsall. *Chain Reaction: The Impact of Race, Rights, and Taxes on American Politics.* New York: W. W. Norton, 1992.

Elder, Larry. "Michael Steele Plays the Race Card," uploaded April 9, 2010, http://www.frontpagemag.com/2010/larry-elder/michael-steele-plays-the-race-card/, accessed May 11, 2015.

Erickson, Erick. "Maybe Stephanie McCrummen Just Likes Using the N Word," uploaded October 2, 2011, http://www.redstate.com/diary/Erick/2011/10/02/maybe-stephanie-mccrummen-just-likes-using-the-n-word/, accessed May 15, 2015.

Farrington, Brendan. "Obama Inspires Black Republicans to Switch Parties." *Associated Press*, August 21, 2008.

Fauntroy, Michael K. *Republicans and the Black Vote*. Boulder, CO: Lynne Rienner, 2007.

Fox News.com, "Cain: Name of Perry's Hunting Camp 'Insulting' to Blacks," uploaded October 2, 2011, http://www.foxnews.com/politics/2011/10/02/cain-tea-party-movement-pushed-black-candidate-to-top-gop-pack/, accessed May 15, 2015.

Freedman, Samuel G. *The Inheritance: How Three Families and America Moved from Roosevelt to Reagan and Beyond*. New York: Simon and Schuster, 1996.

Frommer, Frederick J. "Black Conservatives Conflicted on Obama Campaign." *Associated Press*, June 14, 2008: 1.

Frum, David. *Dead Right: "A New Republican Era Has Dawned...Or Has It? Will the Right Do What It Must to Shrink Government and Strengthen Family Values?"* New York: Basic Books, 1994.

Frymer, Paul. *Uneasy Alliances: Race and Party Competition in America*. Princeton, NJ: Princeton University Press, 1999.

Goldberg, Jeffrey. "Herman Cain on Why 'The Black Guy Is Winning'," uploaded June 13, 2011, http://www.bloomberg.com/news/articles/2011-06-13/herman-cain-on-why-the-black-guy-is-winning-jeffreygoldberg, accessed May 21, 2015.

"GOP Outreach: Fact or Fiction? A Roundtable Discussion." *Headway*, March 31, 1998.

"GOP Woos Minorities." *Oakland Post*, March 4, 1998: 2.

Gramsci, Antonio. *An Antonio Gramsci Reader: Selected Writings, 1916–1935*. Ed. David Forgacs. New York: Schocken Books, 1988.

Grossman, James R. "Traditional Politics or the Politics of Tradition." *Reviews in American History*, vol. 21, 1993: 533–538.

Hallow, Ralph Z. "Steele: GOP Needs 'Hip-Hop' Makeover" uploaded February 19, 2009, http://www.washingtontimes.com/news/2009/feb/19/steele-gop-needs-hip-hop-makeover/?page=all, accessed April 17, 2015.

Hamblin, Ken. *Pick a Better Country: An Unassuming Colored Guy Speaks His Mind About America*. New York: Touchtone Books, 1997.

Hogg, Michael. "A Social Identity Theory of Leadership," *Personality and Social Psychology Review*, vol. 5, no. 3, 2001: 184–200.

Hood III, M.V., Quentin Kidd, and Irwin L. Morris. "Race and the Tea Party in the Old Dominion: Split-Ticket Voting in the 2013 Virginia Elections," *PS: Political Science and Politics*, vol. 48, no. 1, January 2015: 107–114.

Jackson, Derrick Z. "Barbour Campaign Shows GOP's Racist Side." *The Boston Globe*, October 29, 2003: 27.

Jones, Jeffrey M. "Majority of Americans Say Racism Against Blacks Widespread," uploaded August 4, 2008, http://www.gallup.com/poll/109258/majority-americans-say-racism-against-blacks-widespread.aspx, accessed May 24, 2015.

Kabaservice, Geoffrey. *Rule and Ruin: The Downfall of Moderation and the Destruction of the Republican Party, from Eisenhower to the Tea Party*. New York: Oxford University Press, 2012.

Kent, Phil. "A Demographic 'Tipping Point' for the U.S.," 2009, http://www.philkent.com/columns_popup.php?columns_id=68, accessed May 24, 2015.

Klinkner, Philip A., and Rogers M. Smith. *The Unsteady March: The Rise and Decline of Racial Equality*. Chicago, IL: The University of Chicago Press, 1999.

Knowles, Eric D., Brian S. Lowery, Elizabeth P. Shulman, and Rebecca L. Schaumberg. "Race, Ideology, and the Tea Party: A Longitudinal Study," *Plos One*, vol. 8, no. 6, June 2013: 1–11.

Koconis, Ben. "Black Conservatives Insist Tea Party Misunderstood by Many," *The Washington Informer*, vol. 46, no. 45, August 26–September 1, 2010.

Lee, Carol E. "Gibbs: No 'Race Card' Mocking RNC 'Credit Card' problem," uploaded April 5, 2010, http://www.politico.com/politico44/perm/0410/gibbs_no_race_card_d8b78a62-53f6-499c-9170-1a7b937bb9fb.html, accessed May 11, 2015.

Lee, Ronald, and Aysel Morin, "Using the 2008 Presidential Election to Think about 'Playing the Race Card,'" *Communication Studies*, vol. 60, no. 4, September–October 2009: 376–391.

Levine, Madeline. *The Price of Privilege: How Parental Pressure and Material Advantage Are Creating a Generation of Disconnected and Unhappy Kids*. New York: HarperCollins, 2006.

Lewis, Matt K. "Herman Cain's Attack on Rick Perry was a Mistake," uploaded March 10, 2011, http://dailycaller.com/2011/10/03/herman-cains-attack-on-rick-perry-was-a-rookie-mistake/, accessed June 16, 2017.

Lewison, Jed. "Cain Flip-Flops on Perry Hunting Grounds Criticism After Conservative Backlash," uploaded October 4, 2011, http://www.dailykos.com/story/2011/10/04/1022657/-Cain-flip-flops-on-Perry-hunting-groundscriticism-after-conservative-backlash#, accessed May 15, 2015.

Limbaugh, Rush. "Herman Cain Piggybacks on WaPo's Perry Smear and Obama's Debate Lie," uploaded October 3, 2011, http://www.rushlimbaugh.com/daily/2011/10/03/herman_cain_piggybacks_on_wapo_s_perry_smear_and_obama_s_debate_lie, accessed May 25, 2015.

Lind, Michael. *Up from Conservatism: Why the Right Is Wrong for America*. New York: The Free Press, 1996.

Liptak, Kevin. "Cain: Racism Not Holding Anyone Back," uploaded October 9, 2011, http://politicalticker.blogs.cnn.com/2011/10/09/cain-racism-not-holding-anyone-back, accessed May 21, 2015.

Love, Mia. "About Mia Love," 2013, http://love4utah.com/about/, accessed May 25, 2015.

Lowe, Frank. "Keeping Leadership White: Invisible Blocks to Black Leadership and Its Denial in White Organizations," *Journal of Social Work Practice*, vol. 27, no. 2, 2013: 149–162.

Macek, Steve. *Urban Nightmares: The Media, the Right, and the Moral Panic over the City*. Minneapolis: University of Minnesota Press, 2006.

Macleod, Jay. *Ain't No Making It: Leveled Aspirations in a Low-Income Neighborhood*. Boulder, CO: Westview Press, 1987.

Maltsev, Yuri, and Roman Skasiw. The Tea Party Explained: From Crisis to Crusade. Chicago, IL: Open Court Publishers, 2013.

Mann, Brian. *Welcome to the Homeland: A Journey to the Rural Heart of America's Conservative Revolution*. Hanover, NH: Steerforth Press, 2006.

Marcus, Lloyd. "Biography," 2006, http://www.lloydmarcus.com/biography/.

Martin, Roland. "Herman Cain Denies GOP's Horrible History with Blacks," uploaded October 3, 2011, http://www.cnn.com/2011/10/01/opinion/martin-cain-brainwashed/, accessed May 12, 2015.

Mayer, Jeremy D. *Running on Race: Racial Politics in Presidential Campaigns, 1960–2000*. New York: Random House, 2002.

McGlowan, Angela. *Bamboozled: How Americans Are Being Exploited by the Lies of the Liberal Agenda*. Nashville, TN: Thomas Nelson, 2007.

McWhorter, John. *Losing the Race Self-Sabotage in Black America*. New York: The Free Press, 2000.

McWhorter, John. *Winning the Race: Beyond the Crisis in Black America*. New York: Gotham Books, 2006.

Mendelberg, Tali. *The Race Card: Campaign Strategy, Implicit Messages, and the Norm of Equality*. Princeton, NJ: Princeton University, 2001.

Moore, Jimmy. "Fiery Black Conservative Running for Congress in North Carolina." *Talon News*, October 10, 2003: 3, http://www.gopusa.com.

NBC News. "Decision 2014," http://www.nbcnews.com/politics/elections/2014/SC/S2/exitpoll, accessed May 25, 2015.

Norton, Michael I., and Samuel R. Sommers. "Whites See Racism as a Zero-Sum Game that they are Now Losing," *Perspectives on Psychological Science*, vol. 6, no. 3, 2011: 215–218.

Obama, Barack. *The Audacity of Hope: Thoughts on Reclaiming the American Dream*. New York, NY: Crown Publishers, 2006.

O'Neill, Jessie H. *The Golden Ghetto: The Psychology of Affluence*. Milwaukee, WI: Affluenza Project Publishers, 1997.

Parker, Star. "GOP Can't Get It Right with Black Outreach." *The Philadelphia Tribune*, May 4, 2001: 7A.

Perlstein, Rick. *Before the Storm: Barry Goldwater and the Unmaking of the American Consensus*. New York: Hill and Wang, 2001.

Pickett, Justin T., Daniel Tope, and Rose Bellandi, "'Taking Back Our Country': Tea Party Membership and Support for Punitive Crime Control Policies," *Sociological Inquiry*, vol. 84, no. 2, May 2014: 167–190.

Prisock, Louis. "The CEO of Self: Herman Cain, Black Conservatism and the Achievement Ideology," *Journal of African American Studies*, vol. 19, no. 2, June 2015: 178–191.

Reed, Adolph, and Julian Bond. "Equality: Why We Can't Wait." *The Nation*, December 9, 1991.

Rees, Matthew. *From the Deck to the Sea: Blacks and the Republican Party*. Wakefield, NH: Longwood Academic, 1991.

Republican National Committee. RNC Growth Opportunity Book, https://gop.com/growth-and-opportunity-project, 2013.

Reynolds, Glenn. uploaded October 2, 2011, http://pjmedia.com/instapundit/128979/, accessed May 21, 2015.

Rieder, Jonathan. *Carnarsie: The Jews and Italians of Brooklyn Against Liberalism*. Cambridge, MA: Harvard University Press, 1985.

Roberts, Ronald Suresh. *Clarence Thomas and the Tough Love Crowd: Counterfeit Heroes and Unhappy Truths*. New York: New York University Press, 1995.

Robinson, Pearl. "Whither the Future of Blacks in the Republican Party?" *Political Science Quarterly*, vol. 97, Summer 1982: 207–231.

Robinson, Russell K. "Perceptual Segregation," *Columbia Law Review*, vol. 108, no. 5, June 2008: 1093–1180.

Roper Center. "How Groups Voted in 2012," http://www.ropercenter.uconn.edu/polls/us-elections/how-groupsvoted/how-groups-voted-2012/.

Scott, Tim. "Tim Scott for Senate," 2013, http://votetimscott.com/about-tim/, accessed May 25, 2015.

Shapiro, Walter. "Jack Kemp's Race Card." *Esquire*, November 1996.

Simpson, Andrea Y. *The Tie That Binds: Identity and Political Attitudes in the Post-civil Rights Generation*. New York: New York University Press, 1998.

Sleeper, Jim. *Closest of Strangers*. New York: W. W. Norton, 1997.

Skocpol, Theda, and Vanessa Wiliamson. *The Tea Party and the Remaking of Republican Conservatism*. New York: Oxford University Press, 2013.

Smith, Ben. "Steele Denounces 'Race Card,'" uploaded September 16, 2009, http://www.politico.com/blogs/bensmith/0909/Steele_denounces_race_card.html, accessed May 11, 2015.

Smith Jr., J. Clay. "A Black Lawyer's Response to the Fairmont Papers." *Howard Law Journal*, vol. 23, 1983: 195–225.

Somanader, Tanya. "Ingraham Suggests Cain Would Be The Real First Black President Because Obama Has White Relatives," uploaded October 6, 2011, http://thinkprogress.org/media/2011/10/06/338107/

ingrahamsuggests-cain-would-be-the-real-first-black-president-because-obama-has-white-relatives/, accessed May 25, 2015.

Sowell, Thomas. "Reverse Racism," uploaded October 11, 2011, http://townhall.com/columnists/thomassowell/2011/10/11/reverse_racism, accessed on May 25, 2015.

Sugrue, Thomas. *The Origins of the Urban Crisis: Race and Inequality in Postwar Detroit.* Princeton, NJ: Princeton University Press, 1996, 2005.

Tighe, J. Rosie. "How Race and Class Stereotyping Shapes Attitudes Toward Affordable Housing," *Housing Studies,* vol. 27, no. 7, October 2012: 962–983.

Toler, Deborah. "Black Conservatives." In *Eyes Right!: Challenging the Right Wing Backlash.* Ed. Chip Berlet. Boston, MA: South End Press, 1995.

Town Hall Staff. "Thomas Sowell: Herman Cain More Black Than Barack Obama," uploaded October 20, 2011, http://townhall.com/tipsheet/townhallcomstaff/2011/10/20/thomas_sowell_herman_cain_more_black_than_barack_obama, accessed May 25, 2011.

Travis, Shannon. "Cain's Race Not as Big an Issue with Conservatives as Obama's Was Three Years Ago," uploaded October 13, 2011, http://politicalticker.blogs.cnn.com/2011/10/13/cains-race-not-as-big-an-issue-with-conservatives-as-obamas-was-three-years-ago/, accessed May 25, 2015.

Tyler, Raven. "Rising Stars in the Party of Lincoln." *The Philadelphia Tribune,* August 1, 2000: 7E.

Walker, Clarence E., "We're losing our country: Barack Obama, Race and the Tea Party". *Daedalus,* vol. 140, no. 1, Winter 2011: 125–130.

Walters, Ronald. "Black Conservatives Failed a Leadership Test." *The New York Beacon,* January 29, 2003: 9.

Walton Jr., Hanes, ed. *African American Power and Politics: The Political Context Variable.* New York: Columbia University Press, 1997.

Weiner, Rachel. "Herman Cain and the 'Race Card.'" *The Washington Post,* http://www.washingtonpost.com/blogs/the-fix/post/herman-cain-and-the-racecard/2011/10/10/gIQAVJsRaL_blog.html, accessed May 12, 2015.

Welhouwer, Peter W. "Releasing the Fetters: Parties and the Mobilization of the African-American Electorate." *The Journal of Politics,* vol. 62, February 2000: 206–222.

Williams, Juan. "Bush Shouldn't Write Off the Black Vote." *New York Times,* June 16, 2004.

Williams, Linda. *Playing the Race Card: Melodramas of Black and White from Uncle Tom to O. J. Simpson.* Princeton, NJ: Princeton University Press, 2002.

Wills, Christopher. "Obama Tells Black Fathers to Engage Their Children." *Associated Press,* June 17, 2008: 1.

Wilson, William J. *When Work Disappears: The World of the New Urban Poor.* New York: Vintage, 1996.

Wright, Crystal. "Mitt Romney's Neglect of Black Americans Failed Him at the Polls," uploaded July 11, 2012, http://www.washingtonpost.com/blogs/therootdc/post/mitt-romneys-neglect-ofblack-americans-failed-him-at-the-polls/2012/11/07/05331e2e-28f1-11e2-96b6-8e6a7524553f_blog.html, accessed April 14, 2015.

Wypijewski, JoAnn. "The De-alignment of America." *The Nation*, October 28, 1996.

Zeskind, Leonard. "A Nation Dispossessed: The Tea Party Movement and Race," *Critical Sociology*, vol. 38, no. 4, 2011: 495–509.

CHAPTER 7

The Creation of the Black Conservative Intelligentsia and Its Impact on Black America

Black conservative intellectuals often assert that because they are black thinkers who observe African American life in the United States from a conservative point of view, their positions and arguments are misconstrued, maligned, or not given a fair hearing. The villains these intellectuals point to are the white liberal elite and the old guard African American civil rights "orthodoxy." The black conservative intelligentsia's raison d'etre is two fold. First, they claim they are the only ones who will say the hard truths about the plight of African Americans in the United States. The civil rights "orthodoxy" will not because they have a vested interest in maintaining a reality where African Americans are perpetually victimized. Black conservative intellectuals argue that because of white liberals' racial guilt over the plight of African Americans, they (white liberals) are inclined to allow African Americans to see themselves as victims and not hold them accountable for their own fates. It is this state of victimization, black conservative intellectuals posit, that also provides white liberals with a sense of power as they argue for programs and policies, such as affirmative action, that have good intentions but bad consequences for African Americans.

Black conservative intellectuals also claim that while their ideas may be unpleasant and disliked by some they speak for the unheard "black silent majority." As John McWhorter states boldly in his 2003 work, *Authentically Black*:

© The Author(s) 2018
L. G. Prisock, *African Americans in Conservative Movements*,
https://doi.org/10.1007/978-3-319-89351-8_7

> I dedicate this book to the over one thousand African-Americans who have given me their support for my public writings and statements on race since the publication of *Losing The Race* in the fall of 2000. In letters, e-mails, phone calls, reviews, and public encounters from black businesspeople, teachers...police officers...seniors, and even prisoners, I have been confirmed in my opinion that there is a Black Silent Majority in America, committed to real progress but too seldom heard from. (McWhorter 2003a: ix)

Black conservative thinkers are disdainful when their leftist counterparts, in their view, project a marginal status on African Americans that absolves African Americans from having responsibility and agency for their own lives.

When talking of themselves and their ideas, black conservative intellectuals will often switch back and forth between a sense of conviction and feelings of marginality. One of the goals of this chapter is to examine this movement back and forth more closely, on the one hand examining to what extent it is actually true in terms of the amount of space black conservative intellectuals are accorded in the public sphere in comparison with their more liberal or even left colleagues. On the other hand, I am also interested in examining more closely the deep sense of insecurity and yearning for belonging that underlies black conservative intellectuals' relation to the nation as a whole. It was a radical intellectual from the Caribbean who first noted one of the central contradictions in mainstream African Americans' political and social relationship to the nation as a whole. Speaking to the most radical of groups about the potential of organizing African American workers and intellectuals into the Communist party in the 1930s, C.L.R. James asserted: "*Whereas in Europe the national movements have usually aimed at a separation from the oppressing power, in the U.S. the race consciousness and chauvinism of the Negro represents fundamentally a consolidation of his forces for the purposes of integration into American society*" (McLemee 1996: 87). Ironically, despite their extreme divergence from radical views, I argue in this chapter that underlying the rhetoric of the black conservative intellectual is a deep desire to acquire a true sense of belonging in the American nation, a desire that in effect shapes a movement toward integration that they share with the more liberal of their colleagues in the black intelligentsia. What differs, again, is the question of how they frame their relationship to a larger black community in their efforts to justify their right to belong.

Another prominent black intellectual, Shelby Steele states, "The black conservative...may console himself with the idea that he is on the side of truth, but even truth is cold comfort against group authority (which often has no special regard for truth)" (Steele 1998: 6). How marginal are black conservative thinkers? Upon closer examination it becomes apparent that black conservative thinkers are not as marginal as they claim to be. In using the term marginal I borrow specifically from Susan Herbst's definition of marginality when she argues, "social groups are considered marginal when conventional institutions (or individuals associated with those institutions) attempt to *silence* them" (Herbst 1994: 10). Herbst makes the very important point that feelings of marginality do not necessarily make a group marginal. The legitimacy of any complaint of marginalization rests on some form of significant evidence that a group's ideas or language have been systematically excluded from the mainstream because of that group's beliefs or some other arbitrary characteristic. The evidence illustrates that black conservative thinkers are not being systematically excluded from America's mainstream discourse outlets. A number of black conservative thinkers publish books with some of the most impressive academic and trade publishing houses in the industry. Their works often get reviewed in many notable review outlets, they write op-ed articles for major market metropolitan newspapers, and are invited to promulgate their viewpoints on network news channels that have a sizable viewership, such as Fox News. The conservative black intelligentsia are like many of their counterparts in this respect, for conservatives of all stripes have adopted this rhetorical approach of claiming a marginality that may have been accurate in the first half of the twentieth century, but is not the case today. Although black conservative thinkers may feel marginal because they are not readily embraced by African Americans, as they would like to be, this does not mean that they are marginal in the larger intellectual infrastructure of American society as a whole.

In contrast to black conservative intellectuals' sense of their own marginalization, this chapter rests on my strong belief that black conservative thinkers are actually quite influential when it comes to shaping the national discourse on race. In other words, while black conservative intellectuals vigorously argue the diminished power of race in American society, I argue that precisely where they are positioned as part of the intellectual infrastructure of the conservative right is to frame current policies and debates on almost all matters relating to African Americans specifically and race more broadly. Thus the very topics they speak on and discursive niche they fit in within the conservative movement provides the greatest evidence for the very inescapability of race as a fundamental aspect of conservative discourse on what it means to be an American and to belong in American society. It is for this reason that in the bulk of this chapter I focus on demonstrating first the "nuts and bolts" of black conservative intellectuals' arguments on such hot-button issues as the racial achievement gap between African American students and others in education, with the major figure in this debate being John McWhorter. I also examine arguments made by other African American intellectuals Shelby Steele and Kevin Williamson on such topics as the supposed lack of appreciation among African Americans, the poor in particular, of traditional values like hard work, self-sufficiency, and delayed self-gratification; and the alleged harm labor unions and increase in the minimum wage do to low-income African Americans employment opportunities.

Indeed, black conservative thinkers are actually one of the groups of conservative intellectuals to be the beneficiaries of the right's focus on the importance of intellectual activism during the seventies and onward. Conservative black intellectuals are literally and figuratively, that is, both in terms of their ideas and their institutional and think-tank support, the products of the intellectual war of position the neo-conservatives and the New Right initiated in the seventies, and the concerted effort from the top to find black conservative spokesmen during Ronald Reagan's presidency.

Some may question why I do not include Thomas Sowell, thought of as the pioneer of contemporary black conservative intellectualism, or Walter Williams, another economist and intellectual of Sowell's generation. While both of these men made significant contributions in establishing the foundation of contemporary black conservative intellectualism in the United States, as we are now in the twenty-first century I feel it is important to look both forward at the next generation of black conservative intellectuals and also back at the experience of another path breaking intellectual—Glenn Loury for his experience is instructive in understanding how race is just as much a fault line within the conservative community as it is in American society. I conclude this chapter by examining the dissolution of the relationship between former conservative economist Glenn Loury and his white counterparts over the publishing of both Charles Murray's *The Bell Curve* and Dinesh D'Souza's *The End of Racism*. Loury's disgruntlement with his former conservative peers not only illustrates the fallacy of "colorblindness ideology" propagated by both black and white conservatives but also the Faustian bargain some African American conservatives, like Loury, discover they have made by aligning with a movement that achieved its success partly due to the scapegoating and maligning of African Americans.

I also make a point here of counterpoising against a black conservative style of intellectual discourse short on evidence but long on common sense, actual academic studies with real empirical evidence that refute, particularly from the disciplines of the social sciences, some of these intellectuals' most virulent claims. Overall my point is to demonstrate how many black conservative intellectuals arguments have become shaping forces in defining the terms of these debates even when scholars see them as making spurious claims.

Conservative think tanks and foundations have played a key role in helping to expand the Right's ability to have their ideas and policies penetrate the mainstream media. Some of today's most prominent African American conservative intellectuals, Thomas Sowell, Walter Williams, Glenn Loury, John McWhorter, Shelby Steele, are all housed in or have received support from one of the four major conservative think tanks: American Enterprise Institute, Hoover Institute, Manhattan Institute, and Heritage Foundation. These and other African American conservative intellectuals partly owe their prominence to the above-mentioned think tanks. The marketing ability of conservative think tanks has not been missed by today's black conservative public intellectuals, as illustrated by John McWhorter who attests to the perks of being a fellow at the Manhattan Institute: "They're also very good at getting all of we fellows at the Manhattan Institute media exposure, which is important if you want to get your message out there. And I decided that I wanted to do something like that for a year" (McWhorter 2003b).

THE NUTS AND BOLTS OF BECOMING A PUBLIC INTELLECTUAL

During the mid-nineties, a cadre of well-known and left-wing African American academics received attention in various mainstream publications ranging from the *Atlantic Monthly* to the *New Yorker* magazine. Most of the articles were celebratory in tone with the exception of a few articles thought by some to be more caustic and critical in nature.[1] The initial media coverage of this specific group of African American celebrity academics working at elite institutions revived a long-held debate concerning the role of the black public intellectual. Since most, if not all, of the mainstream print media's attention was focused on a small number of left-liberal African American scholars, African American conservative public intellectuals were either left out of the discussions or mentioned as a side thought.

It was actually quite unfortunate that the role that African American conservative public intellectuals have played in shaping the national discourse on race and African American life in the United States was not addressed then, and continues to take a back seat, in the many debates and discussions on the meaning and role of African American public intellectuals. Their marginalization in the world of academic celebrity is almost the exact opposite of their prominence as pundits and experts on matters of race outside of the rarefied air of black studies in the academy and in the more mainstream realms of the public sphere. To gain a fuller and more complete understanding of why African American conservative intellectuals have been successful in garnering attention both to themselves and their ideas, one has to examine more closely how their prominence in national debates around race emerges from the interactions of a variety factors: their talents as thinkers, their connections with powerful patrons, and the coalescence of socio-political forces in the United States that has elevated American conservatism to the center of American political and social life.

The rise of black, conservative, public intellectuals such as Shelby Steele and others is not merely illustrative, but moreover, the logical outcome, of how dominant the right's intellectual hegemony has been in the United States for the past four decades. James Q. Wilson makes an important insight on a key element in an intellectual's ability to become influential. According to Wilson, an intellectual gains stature from his or her ability to craft ideas that give, "a persuasive simplification" of policy issues that is aligned with the beliefs and values of the present political leadership. In this particular ideological and discursive context, public intellectuals' ideas and arguments do not need strong empirical data and evidence to be influential or compelling:

> Clarifying and making persuasive those ideas is largely a matter of argument and the careful use of analogies; rarely...does this process involve matters of proof and evidence of the sort that is, in their scholarly as opposed to their public lives, supposed to be the particular skill and obligation of the intellectual in the university. (Wilson 1981: 36)

Therefore it is not surprising that when an intellectual publishes a text that locates the cause of the African American educational performance gap within African Americans themselves, it not only raises eyebrows but also garners plenty of attention. Given the common sense perception that when it comes to race African Americans always adopt a "blame white racism first" perspective, then any analysis that differs from the assumed orthodoxy is viewed as "provocative," "controversial," or "brave." In the next section I make a closer examination of John McWhorter's works on the question of the educational performance gap in order to show how McWhorter's arguments fit the mode of the public intellectual mode that James Wilson speaks of above.

The Golden Boy: John McWhorter on the Racial Educational Achievement Gap

John McWhorter is the most recent African American conservative intellectual to emerge on the national scene as a race commentator, espousing the familiar arguments that African American conservatives have been making for decades: the decline of racism in the United States and the concomitant increase in opportunities available to African Americans; criticizing African Americans for holding onto their "victim status"; and decrying the harmful effects of public policies such as welfare and affirmative action. A former professor of linguistics at University of California, Berkeley, and senior fellow at the Manhattan Institute, McWhorter has written numerous articles and several books within his field. McWhorter began to garner major media coverage in 1996 during the controversy surrounding the Oakland school board's resolution that Ebonics, a particular African American dialect, should be considered black students' native tongue and bilingual programs should be established to assist black students in the classroom. McWhorter is clear that what brought him to the attention of various media outlets was not only his opposition to the resolution but also the fact that he was African American:

> Many linguists were asked their opinions on the Ebonics issue during these weeks, but almost none of them were besieged as I was. Why was I, an unknown linguistics professor, consulted so relentlessly ... For the sole and simple reason that every single other African American linguist or education specialist supported Oakland's resolution. The media, predictably, tended to cast the issue in terms of "pro" and "con." Finding the

"pro" was always easy – all they had to do was call an African-American education specialist or an African-American linguist who was not me. As far as "con" went, however, a media organ who had a white professor question Oakland's policy would of course risk the racist charge. What was thus needed was a black linguist to express an opposing viewpoint, and there turned out to be only one. (McWhorter 2001: 185)

Shortly after the Oakland controversy, the catalyst that elevated McWhorter to even higher realms was the tense atmosphere in the University of California Berkeley campus after the passage of Proposition 209, the voter mandate that outlawed all racial preference programs in California's public higher education institutions and state offices. McWhorter points to this discord on the Berkeley campus as his motivating factor in entering into national discourse as a race spokesperson:

What pushed me over the edge and why I'm sitting here, is when the first class that was admitted to Berkeley without racial preferences was announced...the number of minority students had plummeted drastically. And the campus was festooned with posters, and there seemed to be a rally every day. Various people, including very smart, very seasoned older people, professors, people – Ph.D.'s shouting that we were in danger of resegregation.... This didn't make sense to me because, unfortunately, I had detected a major strain in the African American students that I'd been teaching at Berkeley of lower performance that was not based on poverty.... It seemed to me there was a cultural factor, something that I had observed all of my life, I never thought I would write a book that addressed it. But it was there, and I thought there's a difference between a lot of the black students here and white students. (McWhorter 2003b)

In 2000 The Free Press, a mainstream publishing house with a track record of publishing books by conservatives, released McWhorter's book, *Losing The Race: Self-Sabotage in Black America*. The book received coverage in a number of prominent venues, ranging from the *New York Times*, *Wall Street Journal*, and *Washington Post*, to the various conservative outlets such as the *Weekly Standard*. Not surprisingly given the book's subtitle, *Self-Sabotage in Black America*, it raised eyebrows and attracted attention. McWhorter's perspective, that African Americans needed to take their share of responsibility for continuing to lag behind other groups in the nation, was perceived as "refreshing" given the common and entrenched assumption that African Americans on the whole are uncritically liberal in their outlook, and obsessively fixated on attributing to racism any shortcoming that is applied to them. Of course, there was nothing new about McWhorter's position since many African Americans have put this line of thinking forth for decades. After *Losing the Race*, McWhorter went on to pen two more books that examined race for a general audience, *Authentically Black* and *Winning the Race*. In the preface of *Authentically Black*, McWhorter addressed the critics of his first book about the book's non-academic style:

> Many of the criticisms leveled against *Losing the Race* were predictable. But one that initially took me by surprise was that the book is "not scholarly."... Thus I must make it clear that I never intended *Losing the Race* as a work of scholarship.... I firmly believe that our race dilemma is too urgent for writings on it to serve as fodder for a few graduate students and scholars and then be stashed away on university library shelves, making no difference in the thinking beyond the ivory tower. (McWhorter 2003a: xiv–xv)

As John McWhorter sees it, his writings on race bear no connection to his academic work as a linguist. When he writes about race he is, as he states, "wearing a completely different hat." As a public intellectual he claims to be providing the public with "informed editorials" that may give the readers of his work an "informed common sense" that may "touch the everyday thinking of readers" (McWhorter 2003a: xv). Upon closer examination these "editorials" are not as "informed" as McWhorter would like his readers to believe. For example, in all of his books on race the academic achievement gap between African Americans and other students has been a consistent issue. For McWhorter, as he argued in *Losing the Race*, the causes of underachievement and the struggles of black students have nothing to do with racism, under funding, nor parents' backgrounds. Rather, at the core of the problem is a "truth" that Black Americans have not wanted to grapple with nor have mentioned in open conversations—a cultural defect of anti-intellectualism that runs among African Americans. As McWhorter goes on to explain, many black people are in deep denial, unwilling to believe that their children could be "culturally disinclined" rather than prevented from excelling in school. The reason for this is the pillar of victimology that supports these parents' thinking, which is cultivated by both the media and black Americans themselves (McWhorter 2001: 83).

McWhorter then attempts to logically rule out the familiar reasons given by those on the left (racism, tracking, teacher bias, student confidence, i.e., their vulnerabilities to stereotype threat, etc.). While his critique is worthy of a detailed analysis (see Baker 2008), I want to focus specifically on what he provides as his "evidence" that the problem of underachievement by black students is a cultural problem rather than a structural one. The cultural explanation is the one many Americans, black and non-black, see as a "common sense" truth, especially when black students' academic performance is compared to the performance levels of other students of color such as Asians. McWhorter relies heavily on the common comparison of African American students with Asian American, West Indian, and African students used often to refute the argument that racism is a factor in school performance. This comparison also bolsters the claim that scholastic group differences are due to differences within cultures.[2]

In essence, the cultural problem McWhorter has identified boils down to a disconnect from learning that black children experience as early as kindergarten and that follows them all the way to college and beyond. The source of this feeling of disconnection from learning is the power of being stigmatized by black peers for "acting white": "Namely, the main reason black American students lag behind all others starting in kindergarten and continuing through postgraduate school is that a wariness of books and learning for learning's sake is 'white' has become ingrained in black America culture" (McWhorter 2001: 125). To support his assertion McWhorter borrows from the work of the late anthropologist John Ogbu, who in one study discovered a phenomenon among black children in which those who were excelling in school tended to be castigated by their peers as "acting white." McWhorter relies on Ogbu's discovery as the foundation of his argument, but since many have pointed out that Ogbu's observations are based on students attending schools in inner cities, McWhorter is clear to point out that the "acting white" phenomenon transcends class levels among blacks. He points to instances of this phenomenon among black students attending schools in integrated middle-class suburbs such as Shaker Heights, Ohio and urban middle-class schools such as the Berkeley High School in Berkeley, California. It is important for McWhorter to emphasize that academic underachievement among black students is not just a problem for poor, inner-city students but instead is shared by their middle-class counterparts who live in stable, urban and suburban, middle-class neighborhoods, and go to solid middle-class schools. That fact that academic performance is a problem for black students across the class spectrum becomes McWhorter's trump card to those on the left who want to frame the issue mainly as one that is structural in nature: "Victimology ensures that most discussions of black scholarly performance center upon the obvious and well-known barriers to learning in inner-city neighborhoods; 'black' is tacitly assumed to be shorthand for 'poor' (McWhorter 2001: 101)."

McWhorter wants those who view the academic achievement gap as a structural problem to explain why there is a segment of African American children who have access to the resources necessary for a good education (well-funded schools, stable families and neighborhoods, similar peer networks, etc.) but who, yet still, under perform? For McWhorter, the mere fact that these children come from middle-class families and, unlike their inner-city counterparts, do not attend schools that are dilapidated and resource less, live in war-zone neighborhoods, or have a parent that is incarcerated or incapacitated by substance abuse, illustrates that their families have surmounted the constraints of racism in society and have been able to achieve social mobility, thus putting into question the impact of racism on this problem. If neither poverty nor racism is the main culprit, then as McWhorter sees it, the only logical conclusion must be that there is a defect in African American culture that places a limit on black students' potential. For McWhorter, this cultural defect among the post-civil rights generation of blacks is not the result of harmful actions by whites but instead due to the dominant thinking among blacks that to embrace the power of ideas and the expansion of one's mind is antithetical to what it means to be authentically "black." In his words:

> Anti-intellectualism is not foisted upon black Americans by whites but passed on as a cultural trait. Black kids in suburban middle-class schools are teasing the black 'nerd' as you are reading this not because white people have subjected them to abuse, but because nerdiness is considered external, and even an insult to the culture. (McWhorter 2001: 151)

Therefore anti-intellectualism is not only supported by the pillar of victimology but also gains the support of another problematic pillar-separatism. One strain of separatism fosters the view that anything recognized as most blacks translate "mainstream" as being "white." In fact, the two pillars feed off of each other according to McWhorter, as the "cult of separatism" is produced by the influence of victimology among blacks.

According to McWhorter, victimology shapes the perception of blacks as living in a perpetually hostile white world and thus the need to detach from the hostile white world is motivated by a need of self-preservation.[3]

Six years later in *Winning the Race*, McWhorter revisits the academic achievement gap problem again, making similar arguments as the ones he made in *Losing the Race*. The main difference in this book is that, instead of black students suffering from what McWhorter diagnosed as a "virus of Anti-intellectualism that infects the black community" black students now suffer from what he calls, "therapeutic alienation": "To understand that we are dealing with therapeutic alienation rather than racism brings us to implications for grappling with the black-white achievement gap in the present and future" (McWhorter 2001: 83; 2006: 263). According to McWhorter, therapeutic alienation is the result of the insecurity African Americans feel being black in America, which creates a disproportionate level of alienation but is "maintained because it reinforces one's sense of psychological legitimacy, via defining oneself against an oppressor characterized as eternally depraved" (McWhorter 2006: 5). Another new twist to his argument is that this problem of "therapeutic alienation" did not strike Black Americans until the late sixties; the very decade conservatives like to point to as the beginning of the decline of America. By making a distinction between the pre-civil rights and post-civil rights generations, McWhorter uses a rhetorical ploy that is common in discussions about blacks and racism. This rhetorical ploy creates an African American history in which there is a dichotomy between an idealized, heroic, pre-civil rights generation, and a dysfunctional, confused, post-civil rights generation.

The logic of the argument goes somewhat like this. Given the overt nature of racism in the past, the manner in which it was deeply ensconced in American society as illustrated by the legalized Jim Crow system of the South, it is easy to understand why African Americans would struggle and under perform against their whites peers. Yet, even with these various constraints, the pre-civil rights generation did not stand around and feel pity for themselves. Instead, they showed the determination and courage to work, fight, and even die to have America guarantee them the same privileges and rights as those granted to whites. The fact that blacks still lag behind whites some four decades after the ending of Jim Crow and the passage of both the civil rights and voting rights acts points to the fact that many of the post-civil rights generation were not ready to embrace fully the hard won freedoms earned by their predecessors. For McWhorter the white left and its counterculture is just as much to blame for the spread of therapeutic alienation, for they helped usher in a white mindset of openness toward blacks and a heightening of their awareness to racism. While there is nothing wrong with these developments, the problem emerged, as McWhorter saw it, when the genuine openness of whites to blacks became a form of listening motivated primarily by guilt, which meant that "whites were... ready to nod sagely at almost anything a black person said." This then gave African Americans license to embellish the "evils of the White Man beyond what reality justified." While the alienation the pre-civil rights generation felt in American society spurred them into action, this was not, and continues not to be the case with the post-civil rights generation. Instead, alienation is merely a support used to mask the deep insecurity and psychological damage that plagues African Americans today (McWhorter 2006: 7).

Two aspects of McWhorter's use of a "damage narrative" about African Americans are most telling. First, McWhorter's insertion of the "blacks as a damaged people" narrative parallels and fits the pattern of the conservative co-optation of the ideology of damage often used by liberal social scientists and policy makers. In this broader, historical version of the damage narrative, instead of arguing that slavery was the sole factor in producing the lasting psychological scars on African Americans, conservatives redirect their analysis toward liberal policy, laying the blame on liberalism and liberal social policy such as the Great Society program. In this way they establish arguments that call for the dismantling of the welfare state.[4] McWhorter makes a similar move when he states: "Welfare culture was the product of a system white leftists created that allowed blacks to realize the worst of human nature, in discouraging individual responsibility to make the best of themselves" (McWhorter 2006: 128).

By invoking the rhetoric of damage and the factors that cause it, McWhorter also puts himself in the position of being another black conservative thinker joining the ranks of what legal scholar Ronald Suresh Roberts refers to as the "tough love crowd." Playing the role of the tough critic, McWhorter sees himself as the responsible thinker who expresses a painful but much needed airing of "truths." Like the other "tough love" advocates before him, McWhorter must acknowledge "that their agenda involves bitter medicine" but steadfastly "deny that it departs from their commitment to the dispossessed, claiming that it simply faces truth" (Roberts 1995: 18). In his castigation of those who claim that racism is the main force causing black students to under perform, McWhorter scolds:

> Therapeutic alienation makes the notion of black students held down by racism compelling to many. But this does nothing for the students in question.... Our job is to teach black students to succeed despite bias. Anyone who thinks of that as backward or unenlightened is placing hating whitey over loving black people. You do not love someone whom you distract from coping with obstacles. (McWhorter 2006: 296)

In the practice called "intervention," when concerned relatives and friends confront a substance abuser by revealing in a loving, but forceful manner, their knowledge of the problem and the pain they experience watching the troubled individual engage in self-afflicted suffering, the objective of such a ritual is that the bombardment of "tough love" by relatives and friends who care will force the individual to deal with his or her problem. McWhorter positions himself as the confronting sage performing an intellectual version of an "intervention," to a Black America whom he loves, but who also troubles him because of the self-afflicted wounds she continues to perform on herself. However, by pressing the need to make Black America face up to a "truth" it supposedly has not wanted to deal with squarely, McWhorter ultimately makes arguments that are specious at best and nothing more than articulations of cultural racism at their worst.

Theresa Perry astutely points out that the conclusions Ogbu arrives at in his research, conclusions McWhorter uses to frame his earlier thesis about black students' fear of being stigmatized as "acting white," lead to problematic assumptions about the history of African Americans' relationship to and attitudes toward education:

> What is deeply problematic is Ogbu's reading, knowledge, and interpretation of African American social and educational history and how it has influenced contemporary attitudes. There is simply no evidence to support the claim that African Americans historically developed a deep distrust of school and school people. Ogbu could not have made the assertion that African Americans have not developed an academic tradition if he had known of African Americans' epic struggle for literacy and educational opportunity. (Perry 2003: 62)

The same critique can be made of McWhorter's grand generalization in *Losing the Race* that the denial by whites for centuries of a quality education has led to the passing down of a strain of anti-intellectualism within black culture, which is then reinforced by a practice of blacks distancing themselves from anything that is connected with "whiteness" such as school or books (McWhorter 2001: 83). Within the two chapters he dedicates to anti-intellectualism, McWhorter provides no evidence to indicate that the fear of "acting white" or any other indicator of a black rejection of education was a phenomenon that existed for blacks across centuries.[5] In fact McWhorter is hard pressed in his ability to produce the evidence to his claim because as sociologist Angel Harris insightfully points out, when we look at the history of African Americans in the United States there are various moments, such as during the Jim Crow era, where African Americans demonstrated a deep connection to the value of education and learning.

> Interestingly, during this era of government-legislated racial discrimination-the epitome of barriers to upwardly mobility-historical evidence suggests that blacks attributed more value to schooling than many whites... officials from the Freedmen's Bureau were alarmed by lower-class whites' general apathy toward schooling. In 1869 Louisiana's superintendent wrote that unlike the ex-slaves, "the whites [took] little or no interest in educational matters, even for their own race."[6]

My critique of McWhorter's argument is not focused on whether the "acting white" phenomenon exists. I can attest to the fact that it does and to having been exposed to it myself. The more important point, however is, to what degree does the belief among some black students that being successful in school is "acting white" contribute to an academic achievement gap? Here is where McWhorter cannot provide an adequate answer, and does not make thorough and rigorous connections. Needless to say, learning is a complex and varied process whereby a variety of factors can influence how well or how poorly students do in the classroom. McWhorter provides no definitive evidence illustrating the significance or relevance of such cultural factors as the fear of "acting white" phenomenon in the degree to which it actually contributes to why black students on average have lesser grade point averages and lower scores on standardized tests than white students. The best McWhorter can do is to declare that black students' sense of separation from school is, "like racism, a subtle affair, that students are unaware of it as often as not" (McWhorter 2006: 273).

As, in McWhorter's words, a "quiet habit of the heart," the fear of "acting white" phenomenon is nearly unfeasible to empirically test. As he admits: "It is hardly impossible to fashion tests that reveal that habit of the heart."[7] To make his cultural argument have legs, McWhorter has to point out instead to comparisons between African Americans and other students of color or those within the African diaspora. The successes of African, West Indian, Asian, and Asian American students purportedly illustrate, in McWhorter's argument that an "oppositional" culture is at the heart of the achievement gap for African Americans. As McWhorter states, "Asian immigrants' children take on school as a challenge...helping one another in study groups, refusing to accept anything but their own best efforts" (McWhorter 2001: 129). To further his claim that racism is not the main culprit, McWhorter points to West Indian and African students who, unlike their African American counterparts, "can express feeling besieged by 'racism' while not being hindered by it in any way" (McWhorter 2006: 293). The disproportional numbers of black students on elite campuses, such as Harvard, who have West Indian or African parents, provide McWhorter with further evidence that culture is the problem:

> We must admit that the success of these immigrants' children shows one simple thing: that racism is not a decisive factor in the keeping black students from getting into Harvard. The immigrants' kids managed despite *racism*, which means that what hinders the black American kids is something else. (McWhorter 2006: 293)

In comparing immigrants of color and African Americans, McWhorter is merely dragging out another familiar canard of conservatives, the belief that success is mainly about culture. In McWhorter's narrative West Indians and Africans are the latest groups to join the "model minority" category that Asians, Asians Americans, and Jews already belong to. To McWhorter and other adherents, these groups in the model minority narrative become living proof that the Horatio Alger story comes in all colors. The common trait that these "model minorities" supposedly share is a solid foundation for success established through cultural values such as a propensity to work hard and a persistence that makes it possible to overcome all obstacles.

Three decades ago another black conservative intellectual, the economist Thomas Sowell, proffered the same tenuous argument that West Indians have a cultural compatibility with mainstream American values. McWhorter, like Sowell before him, not only paints a monolithic picture of West Indian life in the US, but also, he obfuscates the complex interaction of a variety factors that influence how well immigrants do once they arrive in the United States. Sociologist Stephen Steinberg has pointed out that selective migration must be considered when attempting to do a comparison between international and native blacks. For example, in one study Steinberg cites, West Indians who migrated to Great Britain versus those who migrated to New York were less successful than their counterparts in New York. Clearly cultural variation cannot be used as an explanation for this disparity as both sets of West Indian immigrants share the same heritage. Instead, upon closer inspection the difference lies in the occupational backgrounds of the two groups, with the West Indians in New York working in higher numbers in professional and other white-collar positions than the West Indians in England (Steinberg 1989: 277).

In addition, this line of argumentation is nothing more than forms of divide and conquer. Asian American legal scholar Frank Wu aptly states, "telling African Americans they ought to be like Asian Americans does a favor to neither group...it only aggravates racial tensions among African Americans and Asian Americans."[8] What the model minority myth also does is through the elevation of groups like Asians, West Indians, or Africans is provide the rationalization of the continued subjugation of African Americans by ultimately resting the blame on their shoulders.[9] In debates around affirmative action in higher education, conservative discourse positions Asians as wrongful victims along side whites. Yet if admissions to universities and colleges were based on an absolute notion of academic merit Asians would obtain higher number of spots than their white counterparts because as a group Asians continue to outpace whites academically.[10] But this point is often overlooked as the focus of blame for conservatives of all racial stripes solely is focused on the masses of so-called "unqualified affirmative action blacks" that benefit from alleged unjust compensatory forms of "social engineering" policies.

Sociologists Alejandro Portes and Ruben Rumbaut also argue that when we take into consideration the educational diversity among immigrants, we must view this issue from two additional perspectives: the differences between nationalities and the differences between individuals. The first perspective takes countries of origin and migration into consideration. The second, the immigration policy and the labor demand of the receiving country must also be considered. When we look at Africans, a group McWhorter uses for comparison, one factor in determining the reasons for their children's educational success lies in the change in the US' immigration policy in 1965. As Portes and Rumbaut note, two criteria used to allow immigrants' entry into the United States was family unification and occupational qualification. Since many Africans did not have families in the US to reunite with, their only option in terms of likelihood of entering the United States was to have high educational and occupational qualifications (Portes and Rumbaut 2006: 72–73). An African immigrant child coming from a home where one or both parents had obtained high levels of education has, the authors argue, higher chances of performing well in US classroom settings. Another common argument used to explain the success of black immigrants experience in the United States focuses on the benefits of being socialized in an all black society. The rationale behind the socialization theory posits that growing up in a society where you are a member of the majority group, like Jamaicans, provides various advantages such as having a wider array of role models that build confidence in one's ability to succeed and curtails any feelings of inferiority in relations to whites thus produces a greater demand for respect from whites in comparison to African Americans. This theory is enticing because of its common sense nature but as sociologist Suzanne Model notes, when a comparison is made between black immigrants who come from a country in the sub-Saharan African region to those originating from South Africa "there is no evidence that the racial composition of the sending country makes a difference in the job outcomes of black immigrants (Model 2009: 114–115)." West Indians and Africans like previous immigrant groups who reached the shores of America, the first racial lesson learned was to distance themselves from African Americans. This distancing can produce contradicting views about themselves and African Americans. For example, on the one hand black immigrants can view themselves as having a superior cultural work ethic to African Americans while at the same time castigating the lack of that work ethic and drive among some of their peers back in their homeland. Or having pride in possessing a low tolerance for racial discrimination while yet critiquing African Americans for "being too quick to cry race" (Model 2009: 152). So black immigrants like West Indians "*need* [emphasis mine] to believe that their work ethic is unusual; they need to believe that theirs is the productive approach to racism. If immigrants cannot influence their destiny, their journey to the United States may have been for naught" (Model 2009: 153). Finally, sociologist Mary Waters provides a more nuanced and complicated picture of West Indian educational achievement in America than the one McWhorter creates. According to Waters, when white, black, and West Indian teachers were asked about the differences between West Indian students and African American students, all three groups of teachers stated that while there may have been some discernible differences in behavior, discipline, and attitudes toward race, none of these differences made the West Indian students better than the African American students (Waters 1999: 270).[11]

The important point that Waters and other sociologists make is that West Indian and other black immigrants' children's success in school has more to do with the interactions of various structural factors than the sole influence of these students cultural backgrounds. Since McWhorter is wedded to legitimizing cultural differences between blacks, and between black and white Americans, no other plausible explanation is acceptable to him. McWhorter dismisses the argument that family wealth may be a factor that influences a student's performance as "illogic," posing instead the trump question: "What about the working-class immigrant kids—many Caribbean and African—who regularly submit such excellent dossiers to top schools, despite their parents rarely having generations-deep stock portfolios to pass on to them or use frills like test preparation classes or fancy private schools? Students like this are rife at Berkeley...no man could miss them" (McWhorter 2006: 287).[12]

In both of his more famous books, McWhorter holds African American parents to the fire for their supposed role in contributing to the achievement gap without, once again, providing any evidence to buttress his claim, beyond anecdotal observation that middle-class black parents do not participate in parent-teacher associations and volunteer organizations in integrated middle-class suburban communities at the same rate as their white counterparts. To McWhorter this is proof positive that education is not a priority in black culture:

In Shaker Heights, while the district is half-black, white parents vastly predominate in parent-teacher organizations and as volunteers at the schools. The black parents are surely deeply committed to their children' well-being, but these discrepancies simply reveal the lower priority that 'the books' have in black culture. (McWhorter 2001: 128)

The logic of this point does not hold as well, since it has been documented that Asian or West Indian parents often assume a more passive relationship with authority figures such as teachers, and they also do not demonstrate the levels of participation in school activities as white parents, yet their children show strong performance in the classroom.

John McWhorter's use of culture alone to explain the differences between immigrants of color and African Americans is problematic for a variety of reasons, but perhaps Portes and Rumbaut state it best in their critique of the cultural explanations given for a related phenomenon—the entrepreneurship of different immigrant groups: "A first problem with culturalistic theories...is that they are always *post factum*; that is, they are invoked once a group has achieved a notable level of business success, but they seldom anticipate which ones will do so (Portes and Rumbaut 2006: 86)." The same could be said regarding immigrants and academic success.

THEMES IN AFRICAN AMERICAN CONSERVATIVE THOUGHT

The Adoption of White Society's Outlook Toward Blacks

A close examination of the dominant themes that make up Black conservative intellectual thought clarifies why this group finds it difficult to have many African Americans readily embracing them as the voice of the Black community. Influenced by the typology used by the late political scientist Ronald Walters on Black conservative thought,[13] I have identified a couple of themes that commonly reoccur in the discourse of Black conservative intellectuals: *The Adoption of White Society's outlook towards Blacks,* and *Support for positions that are often incompatible with Black interests.* In this section, I illustrate how these features are still a continuing component of the contemporary Black conservative intelligentsia and how these themes hinder Black conservative intellectuals ability to be embraced by the majority of African Americans.

In the beginning of *The Content of Our Character,* the book that helped launched Shelby Steele into the national spotlight as a public intellectual, Steele makes it clear that there was much African Americans missed out on during the supposed years of opportunity under President Reagan.

> I believe there was much that Reagan had to offer blacks. His emphasis on traditional American values-individual initiative, self-sufficiency, strong families-offered what I think is the most enduring solution to the demoralization and poverty that continues to widen the gap between blacks and whites in America.[14]

According to Steele, African Americans lost the chance to incorporate values that apparently were foreign to many in the black community. By not giving President Reagan a serious hearing on the importance of, as Steele put it, "American values" African Americans missed the opportunities to do for themselves and raise their status to the level of their white counterparts. Because Reagan took what Steele calls a "posture of innocence" toward race which Blacks saw according to Steele, as preceding a "power move against them" Reagan became a wrongful enemy who's "quite reasonable message seem vindictive."[15] Steele, in essence articulates a common refrain of frustration among whites that see the continued arrested development of African Americans as lying squarely on the shoulders of African Americans themselves. "If they would only adopt the right values, work harder, stop blaming others then success would come to them as it has come to others." In order to justify his point that President Reagan could offer African Americans words of wisdoms by pointing out the advantages of adopting cornerstone values to American success (hard work, entrepreneurial spirit, self-reliance) Steele must conveniently become ahistorical in his analysis. For instance, in Steele's mind there was no such thing as the Black Wall Street of Tulsa, Oklahoma, a space of black entrepreneurship and financial activity so successful that it was one factor that sparked anxiety among whites in the area that culminated with the 1921 race riots, one of the worst race riots in the history of the United States. What Steele fails to comprehend is, it was not Reagan's so-called posture of racial innocence that alienated most African Americans. A more accurate assessment of why President Reagan did not garner much enthusiasm among African Americans points to the various gestures that Reagan took during his campaign for office and while as President that symbolized to African Americans that he was not an ally to Black advancement. Two examples come to mind that illustrate this point. First, Reagan's choice to start his 1980 campaign in Philadelphia, Mississippi, the site where three civil rights activists were murdered, with an arousing speech about the need to restore "States Rights."[16] African Americans, particularly those in the south, were quite familiar with the phrase "states rights" as it was often used by southern white politicians, citizens, and domestic terrorists like the Kl Klux Klan as shorthand for the defense and continuation of formal and informal systemic racism against blacks. The second example was the infamous "welfare queen" narrative Reagan told during campaign speeches and press conferences in 1980 and 1984. To illustrate what is wrong with an expansive government that supposedly produced waste and corruption Reagan told the story how a woman on the south side of Chicago, which implied the woman was African American, was able to take advantage of the largess of governmental programs such as welfare to live a rather comfortable life without ever working, she epitomized the essence of the "welfare queen." With each telling of the story the illustrations of corruption became more pronounced until it reached the point where the accused had bilked the system by using, "80 names, 30 addresses, 12 social security cards," and earning "a tax free income of over $150,000."[17] The story was based on a woman named Linda Taylor who had been charged in 1976 with defrauding the state of Illinois not of $150,000 but $8000. Nevertheless, Reagan's objective had been met which was to send the message to white voters that under his watch government was no longer going to reward the dysfunctional behavior of inner-city Blacks by giving them monies coming from "hard working middle Americans" who were inferred to be white. What these examples taught African Americans was that they could not look toward the White House as being an ally in furthering racial equality or justice. Unfortunately the idea that the poor, particularly African Americans, are more willing to live off the dole than seek employment still persists thirty years after Reagan's invoking of the "welfare queen" mantra. During the 2012 Republican presidential primaries former Pennsylvania senator Rick Santorum stated to a predominately white audience in Iowa "I don't want to make black people's lives better by giving them somebody else's money. I want to give them the opportunity to go out and earn the money and provide for themselves and their families."[18] It was very telling that the individual who garnered the response from Santorum was asking a question about the "problematic foreign influence" in America and not about welfare. Most recently Arizona's Superintendent of Public Instruction John Huppenthal found himself in the center of a controversy for a blog comment he made referring to welfare recipients as "lazy pigs."[19] Yet, perception continues to outweigh facts as according to the Office of Family Assistance, an agency within the U.S. Department of Health and Human Services, in fiscal year 2010 the percentages of African American families receiving Temporary Assistance to Needy Families (TANF) has been decreasing since 2001 to where the percentages between African American (31.9) and white families (31.8) were close to equal Also, in fiscal year 2010 there were more white adult recipients of TANF (37%) than African American adult recipients (33%).[20] It seems, irrespective to what Steele claims, African Americans had good reason for not fully embracing a President who helped continue the dominant stereotype of African Americans as perpetual deadbeat dependents.

Support for Positions That Are Often Incompatible with Black Interests

African American social and economic progress has rested on four important factors: a vibrant economy, enforcement of civil rights legislation, an active government, and strong labor unions. These four structural elements have been vital to African Americans experiencing social mobility in the United States. African American conservatives have differing viewpoints on each of these four factors. For example, according to African American and other conservatives the key to creating and sustaining a strong economy is best done through the reduction of the taxes, particularly for the top class of Americans and corporations (which supposedly will allow for increased capital investments and job creation), the lessening of regulations, shrinkage of government, and weakening of labor unions power.

The caustic attacks on African Americans continuing their established relationship with labor unions or why blacks should support the elimination of a minimum wage has held steady for many decades through the works of Walter Williams, Thomas Sowell and now a more contemporary example, Kevin D. Williamson. Williamson, the most recent African American conservative public intellectual to emerge, is the perfect illustration of a post modernist black conservative intellectual. In the cover photo on the February 2010 issue of the conservative publication National Review Williamson does not look like the typical buttoned down African American conservative intellectual. Instead, Williamson has a wild mane of dread locks, and the look of a young white suburban—x games participant (t-shirt and BMX bicycle that looks ready to do fancy maneuvers off the steps or railings of a municipal building) posing on a New York city street with apartment buildings in the background. Hence, he gives the impression of conservatism's contemporary hipness. Yet even with his hybrid appearance Williamson still puts forth the same arguments around the so-called injurious effects of minimum wage laws and labor unions toward African Americans that have been circulating for over thirty years. For example, Williamson argues that by mandating employers, particularly small businesses, to pay a set bottom wage this in essence locks out African American workers on the margins as they are priced out of the market.[21] The logic being Williamson and other conservatives argue, is employers find their labor cost increased through this piece of legislation which forces them to respond by cutting back on hiring or select a more preferable employee for the job, which in the case of race would be the non-black employee.[22] Williamson adds another twist to the argument against the minimum wage by stating that minimum wage laws not only prevent poor and teenage African Americans from gaining entry into the labor market it also in effects prevents them from having the ability of accumulating social capital that is often important in not only acquiring jobs but also in experiencing job mobility.

What is less often appreciated, though, is the network effect: A guy who's never gotten on the ladder himself cannot give you a hand up. Job-hunting is almost always an exercise in social networking: A friend of your dad helps you get a summer job, an old colleague recommends you for a position with his new firm.[23]

While Williamson is correct in pointing out that social capital is an important component in learning about and acquiring jobs it is the quality of one's social capital that is more important. For example, if an individual is embedded within a social network of people who are also jobless or are in jobs that do not lead to economic and career advancement then that network operates the same as if the individual had no social capital at hand. But Williamson overlooks this point because he is so focused on making minimum wage the target for this situation. The fact remains that is it is not the minimum wage that prevents poor African Americans from gaining the necessary social capital in finding a foothold in the labor economy. Instead, it is the dual impact of race and class segregation that greatly impacts the ability of urban poor African Americans in gaining exposure to the necessary networks needed to achieve job mobility. As sociologist Teresa Gowen insightfully points out, the massive flight of capital from the urban boundary and the wide discrepancies within the educational systems between urban and suburban spaces have a large impact in creating unequal forms of social capital and the closure of paths to meaningful social networks for poor urban African Americans.

Over the last half century, a Bourdieuian conversion process has reproduced the power of St. Louis's white elites *despite* and even *by means of* radical changes in the geographical distribution of black and white, rich and poor, industry and commerce. As the racial order within the city has been challenged both by demands for parity and by rising crime from its disenfranchised African–American population, St. Louis's white middle and upper classes have responded like their counterparts in Detroit, Newark, and other blighted US cities and collectively abandoned the city they had shared, gradually exporting their private, business, and civic lives to a new "St. Louis" outside the city limits. Despite settling into a typically dispersed and privatized suburban way of life they have continued to mobilize SC for their collective interests, converting their social networks into economic capital (especially through tight municipal controls over zoning and property values) and cultural capital (primarily through the educational system).[24]

In addition, most of the jobs that Williamson claims minimum wage laws make unavailable to poor urban African Americans are low-level service occupations that lack decent compensation, benefits, and job mobility—hence the label "dead end job." These are the very type of jobs that do not lead to the accumulation of social capital or a viable social network. Furthermore, while the minimum wage is not the sole solution to assisting an individual out of poverty it does have its benefits. First, it adds meaning and dignity to labor. Second, minimum wage increases help lower reduction in worker absenteeism, less turnover, and create better morale from employees which translates into reduced recruiting and training costs for employers, which allows for higher productivity. Finally, a fair and humane minimum wage is an important first step in the fight to reduce poverty, along with other measures such as greater access to health care, better education, and tax credits. The last point is especially pertinent given that more women than men occupy the lowest wage jobs in the service industry and a third of this female population happens to be either African American or Latina.

The other pillar of Williamson's scorn is labor unions and the continuing presence of racism within them. What Williamson puts forth is a rehash of critiques previously made by others on both the right and left about the racial history of organized labor.[25] Williamson's line of argumentation goes as follows: a main reason why African Americans suffer higher levels of unemployment than other groups is because of the intransigency some sectors of organized labor has toward diversifying. While this intransigency is not of the blatant southern style racism exhibited during the middle of the twentieth century, instead it appears in a softer version of ethnic nepotism with the same end result—African Americans being locked out of possible employment opportunities.

The problem in the labor unions isn't really old-fashioned racism of the white-sheets and Jim Crow variety...What's really happening in the unions is a kind of expansive ethnic nepotism. Unions tend to find good positions and lots of work for people who are friends and family of current unions' members. Indeed, many in the building trades are on the path to union membership early in life. If those unions are dominated by Irish Americans, it's no surprise that a lot of the plums are going to the Kellys and Murphys, and not to the Jacksons and Washingtons... The more blacks are out of work, and the longer they're out of work, the less of a network black job seekers are going to have. And they can't count on the unions to help them out.[26]

The next logical step in Williamson's argument is, if the unions can not or will not change their ways then African Americans need to reconsider their loyalty to organized labor, but this is throwing the baby out with the bathwater approach. There is no denying that racism is still present in segments of organized labor, especially the construction trade, and its continuation portends a grim future for unions as sociologist Kris Paap rightfully points out:

> At the same time, white working-class men appear to be conflating their increasingly precarious economic position with their perceived race and gender-related vulnerabilities in an industry—and unions—that they perceive as privileging white women and people of color. These divisions, which are real and great and show few signs of decreasing, offer dim predictions for the future of the labor movement if they are not addressed. On a most basic level, these divisions clearly prevent the class-based solidarity that will be essential to reviving the American labor movement. White women, white men, and men and women of color must see their interests as unified through the union if they are going to work for the union...These racialized and gendered politics of construction must therefore be recognized as more than just a series of descriptive tales from

the worksite...In doing so, they also illuminate the necessary steps for reversing at least some of labor's decline across industries.[27]

But what Williamson does in his analysis is to infer that because racism is still a nagging problem within the building trades, this is a clear indication that organized labor is not a viable option for African Americans to use to gain employment and social mobility. Statistics show that African Americans have not adopted Williamson's throwing the baby out with the bathwater approach and for good reasons. According to the Bureau of Labor statistics (BLS), in 2010 African Americans had the highest union membership rate (13%) in comparison to whites (12%), Asians (11%), and Hispanics (10%). The BLS summary also reports that among full time wage and salary union workers the median weekly wage was $917 in comparison to $717 for non-union members.[28] Between 2004 and 2007 the median pay rate African American unionized workers received ($17.51) was higher than their non-unionized counterparts ($12.57). African American union workers were also more likely to receive health benefits (75.9%) than African American non-unionized workers (51.1%), and also more likely to have pension plans than their non-unionized counterparts (66–40%).[29] According to the think tank American Progress, workers of color, particularly African Americans, are disproportionately located in lower wage jobs where having union protection is not only necessary but also provides substantial benefits.[30] This claim is supported by the fact that not only do African American union workers in low wage occupations have higher median pay rates than non-union workers ($12.21–$9.45) they also had a sizable advantage in benefits with 51% of unionized African American workers to only 33% non-unionized workers having health benefits. The gap becomes larger when it pertains to pension plans (57%–23%).[31] As the facts clearly illustrate, it would be folly for African Americans to think their economic and employment interests are best served through non-union channels or not supporting minimum wage legislation. The continued support African Americans give to organized labor demonstrates that not only are criticisms of unions and the minimum wage by conservatives such as Williamson falling on deaf ears but also illustrates the recognition by the larger African American community that these criticism are nothing more than a pretext for a much larger agenda of delegitimizing the rights of workers and labor unions.

ALL IS NOT WELL IN PARADISE: A BLACK CONSERVATIVE INTELLECTUAL SCORNED

During the eighties very few African American intellectuals, on the right or left, had as much prominence than that of economist Glenn Loury. Loury's rise fit the hailed trajectory that adherents of American exceptionalism like to point to as proof that America is truly the land of opportunity like no other in the world. Loury grew up in a working-class African American family from the South side of Chicago. Loury's father worked for the Internal Revenue Service and attended law school at nights, Loury's uncle on his mother' side was an assistant state attorney. While Loury was not the street tough like many of his male peers, he did behave like them in certain instances. For example, impregnating his girlfriend not once but twice when they were teenagers. Nevertheless this did not stop Loury from continuing to excel academically. After a brief stint in a technical school, which Loury dropped out of to work in a printing plant to support his girlfriend, who became his wife, and two children, Loury received a scholarship to attend Northwestern. After graduating from Northwestern in 1972 Loury went on to earn his doctorate in economics in 1976 from Massachusetts Institute of Technology (MIT). At both Northwestern and MIT Loury had made a name for himself with his sharp economic acumen. Loury's first academic position was in the economics department at the University of Michigan and it is there where his conservatism was becoming more pronounced. Interestingly it was labor issues not race that brought out Loury's conservatism as it was the late seventies and the nation was in the throes of a deep recession. Loury felt that the overreaching demands by organized labor and too much government interference were just some of what ailed America at the time. Regarding the chronic problems of unemployment, crime, and family disillusion plaguing the inner cities Loury was certain the old stand by approach of the civil rights establishment of pointing to white racism as the culprit and lobbying for more legislation as a solution were no longer effective and useful. Instead, in his opinion, African American leaders needed to urge inner-city African Americans to take responsibility for their actions and return to their religious roots and the ethos of hard work. By the time Harvard hired Loury away from Michigan in 1982 Loury's conservatism had fully come to the fore and so too did his profile as a public intellectual. In addition to publishing in academic journals Loury also put forth his conservatives views on race in such conservative outlets like Commentary magazine.[32] For example, Loury had this to say about the debate around whether it was white racism or the self-destructive behaviors by African Americans that held them back as a group.

> It is absolutely vital that blacks distinguish between the fault, which may be attributed to racism as a cause of the black condition, and the responsibility for relieving that condition. For no people can be genuinely free so long as they look to others for their deliverance...When faced with the ravages of black crime against blacks...the alarming incidence of pregnancy among unwed black teenagers, or the growing dependency of blacks on transfers from an increasingly hostile polity, it is insufficient to respond by saying 'This is the fault of racist America...' such a response dodges the issue of responsibility.[33]

Loury's analysis of what the "true" cause of the continuing problems plaguing African Americans resonated with many on the right and white Americans as Loury's emphasis on African Americans needing to take personal responsibility for their societal ailments was the overwhelming zeitgeist of the eighties. White society was in a period of "civil rights exhaustion," feeling civil rights leaders and white liberals had been asking more than enough from them with the passage of such policies from affirmative action, busing, to minority set-asides programs, it was time that African Americans do what other groups had done and create opportunities for themselves. Ronald Reagan's victory in 1980 was a clear sign that the political winds in the nation were changing; a bolder conservatism was taking hold in America. From a racial standpoint, the prevailing liberal ways of thinking about America's race problem (societal racism as the cause for the racial inequality between African Americans and whites with the solution being the creation and utilization of domestic programs by an activist government) was losing steam and legitimacy. Instead, the focus was on personal responsibility and the new expectation that Americans should expect less *not* more from its government. President elect Reagan made this clear in his 1981 inaugural speech by stating "In this present crisis, government is not the solution to our problem; government is the problem."[34] As discussed in chapter two the incoming Reagan administration made it clear that they were looking to engage with a "new voice" in the African American community. The established civil rights leadership as well as more moderate and liberal African American Republicans were left off of the Reagan administration's radar, instead the administration's focus was directed toward a cadre of conservative African Americans activists, policy analysts, business persons, and academics identified as having "new" and "vibrant" ideas to offer. Out of one meeting with the administration came the creation of the Council for a Black Economic Agenda organization with activist and leader of the organization National Center for Neighborhood Enterprise Robert Woodson selected as the chair.[35] One member of the organization was Glenn Loury, Loury was asked by Woodson to take part because of the "fresh ideas and thoughtful essays" he put forth on issues pertaining to African Americans.[36] While Loury was often outspoken in his criticism of African Americans and the civil rights leadership for their "perceived" unwillingness to look inward for answers to black crime, out of wedlock childbirths, and increased dependency on federal assistance, in a 1982 speech given at a seminar at the conservative Hillsdale College one can see how Loury was trying to straddle that fine line between arguing the continuing significance of racism on African Americans and the need for African Americans to embrace self-sufficiency and take responsibility for their actions. For instance, to those who believed that the melting pot narrative was the premier example of how America worked for all groups Loury responded with, "The standard melting pot story certainly does not do a very good job of describing the experience of blacks in twentieth century America."[37] After presenting reasons for why the melting pot model was not applicable to the African American experience and is not helpful in explaining the struggles of the black poor, Loury answered the question of why can't the black poor do what others have previously done to make it in America, "The answer to the question 'Why don't they pull themselves up the way our parents did when they first came?'..Because they don't face the same structure of economic opportunities, and are burdened with social and psychological encumbrances which your parents did not face."[38] Even though Loury acknowledged racism played and, in some extent, continues to impact the lives of African Americans, ultimately he believed the main problem for African Americans, particularly the black poor, was not the "alleged" racist motives behind the scaling back of domestic programs that African Americans took advantage of or even the mentioning of black crime, or welfare dependency among the black poor instead "the real problem for a minority such as black Americans is not the existence of racism, but its management." The solutions then were African Americans "must starting helping ourselves," and "take unto ourselves more of the responsibility of our collective condition." First step in doing that was African Americans needed to "identify" and cultivate "those personal values promote success."[39] Next, according to Loury, the community needed to "not be afraid to make judgments about faults and failings observed in the community" and "have the courage to voice these judgments."[40] As I mentioned in the previous section the claim by Loury and other African American conservative intellectuals that the problems besieging African Americans comes from a lack of recognition and reverence of mainstream American values and practices is not only false but ahistorical as there are plenty of examples of African Americans wholeheartedly believing in the American Dream and embracing the various values needed to garner success in America,[41] especially poor African Americans. This is particularly important to point out as black conservative intellectuals have garnered plenty of attention and career advancement from asserting that the problem with inner-city African Americans is their lack of values, feeble motivation to succeed, and unwillingness to take responsibility for their own actions and lives. Sociologist Alford Young provides a more nuanced picture of the realities of life for poor urban African American males. According to Young, in the same fashion we view the importance of the accumulation of various forms of capital (human, cultural, social, and financial), as defined by the late French sociologist Pierre Bourdieu, as vital to achieving and maintaining social mobility; within the social worlds of poor urban African American men there is also the processes of capital accumulation taking place. The ways in which poor urban African American males go about accumulating various forms of capital are specific to their social environment. For example, a number of Young's interview subjects spoke about the importance of making the right connections with those in the neighborhood, in essence "Social capital that provides security for and predictability about everyday life has an importance in poor neighborhoods that may not register in the same way as in more privileged communities."[42] So therefore in a community that has strong structures (in tact families, vibrant employment opportunities, and neighborhoods with stable homes values, and high employment and educational levels among its inhabitants) and viable institutions (schools, social service agencies, parks, playgrounds, and other cultural outlets) making connections and creating networks with others for the purpose of using those connections as currency for access to employment or information for opportunities is the traditional motivation for accumulating social capital. Yet, for those living in a community that is void of the strong structures or vibrant institutions that provide stability, learning who is important to know can become a matter of life and death.[43] Young is correct in stating:

> However, the point is not simply that alternative capital matters. In showing how and why it matters, a new cultural depiction of low-income people is produced. The absence of better mobility prospects does not indicate that the men engaged in cultural practice in ways that altogether differ from the more socio-economically secure...Thus, low-income black men, and by extension poor African Americans, are not culturally deficient in terms of the popular value- and norm-centered perspective. Instead, they are capital deficient with respect to certain resources, networks, and schemata of interpretation pertaining to the prospects and possibilities for upward mobility in contemporary American society.[44]

As political scientist Jennifer Hochschild points out the majority of poor African Americans have a strong attachment to the belief that "everyone in America can be successful, that achievement lies within one's own hands, and success is associated with virtue."[45] Regarding education, in Hochschild's study, low-income African Americans with poor educations expressed higher levels of confidence in schools in comparison to other racial and class groups. Even though as Hochschild states, "in light of the horrible conditions in some high schools...and the number of black students thought to be at risk of poor school performance, those results are almost heartbreaking in the degree of faith they reveal."[46] In the same study poor African Americans also expressed a strong belief in the view that learning the value of hard work is the most important life lesson a child can have.[47] In addition, Hochschild found that poor African Americans were more open with their criticism of their own and others "weakness of will than most whites would dare to be out loud."[48] If poor African Americans are not radically different in their views and beliefs than their more affluent counterparts then why can't they turn these beliefs into productive action? As Hochschild points out there are a variety of interconnected factors such as being deficient in knowing things (where to go to develop training skills, etc.) that can lead to success to lacking confidence in the ability to be successful to developing a cynicism and fatalism derived from personal observations and experiences that lead to the realization of a vast difference in the theoretical underpinnings of the American dream and life's realities.[49] Constructions of poor African Americans and their experiences that both Young and Hochschild present challenges to the thinking that Loury and other African American conservative intellectuals posit that first and foremost the struggles of inner-city African Americans comes from a deficit of morals and values. But to provide a more nuanced analysis that incorporates the impact of structure is not a viable approach for a conservative intellectual like Loury because from the conservative perspective the problem of chronic poverty among inner-city African Americans is not from an economic system where the creation of a surplus idle labor pool is a natural by-product (too Marxist) or from a society predicated on a philosophy of white supremacy and privilege (guilty white liberal point of view). As conservatives claim, even with the creation of President Johnson's Great Society programs in the sixties the problems associated with inner-city poverty *increased* instead of decreased illustrating that no amount of government programs alone could solve the problem of poverty. If government is to be a solution it must be first, minimal in its involvement, second it must support more practical and useful solutions such as the creation of enterprise zones in inner cities, and cultivating a support of the practice of marriage among inner-city inhabitants. It was Loury's ability to articulate these and other conservative beliefs in both a rigorous academic manner and sharp public intellectual style that placed Loury in the position of catapulting to grander career heights, which unfortunately were derailed due to some personal missteps. During the President Reagan's second term Loury was nominated in March of 1987 to become under secretary of education to the head of the Education department William Bennett. The night before his confirmation Loury withdrew his nomination citing "personal problems" as the reason. A couple of days later the truth came out about Loury's "personal problems," apparently his young mistress, whose apartment in Boston he was subsidizing, leveled assault charges against him. In addition to being a philanderer it came out Loury was a deadbeat father to his children by his first wife, and also a drug addict hanging out in the very inner-city neighborhoods in Boston and behaving in the manner that as a public figure he forcefully argued was the downfall of poor African Americans.[50] In fact, Loury's personal problems only highlighted his hypocrisy, a hypocrisy not lost on Loury, "I was castigating the moral failings of African American life even as I was deeply caught up in it."[51]

After an arrest for cocaine possession in November of 1987 Loury rebounded, left Harvard for Boston University, became a devout Christian and dedicated family man to his two sons by his second wife, and continued to be a prominent voice for conservatives on the subject of African Americans and race in the United States. By the late nineties Loury was not the same conservative intellectual star he had been a decade earlier, instead, to his conservative loyalists, Loury had transitioned into a different and more problematic intellectual. So it begs the question, what caused Loury to shift his intellectual positions on race? Loury transitioned from the self-help advocate, propagator of "hard truths" African Americans were allegedly resistant in hearing, and anti-racial preference proponent who routinely made such proclamations as "We must let go of the past and take responsibility for our future...embracing the role of victim status...is undignified and demeaning"[52] to an intellectual asserting the centrality of race in producing racial inequality in American society.

> My view is that one cannot think sensibly about social justice issues in a racially divided society if one does not attend to the race-mediated patterns of social intercourse that characterize interpersonal relations in that society. Once the reality of these racially biased interactive patterns is taken into account, race-blindness begins to look much less attractive as a moral position, precisely because of its individualistic, ahistorical, and purely procedural focus.[53]

One factor that hastened Loury's shift away from his previous stances on race was the publications of books on race by conservative thinkers Charles Murray and Dinesh D'Souza. In 1994 *The Bell Curve* was released. One of the arguments put forth in Charles Murray's book, *The Bell Curve*, coauthored with the late Richard Herrnstein, was the argument that both genetic and environmental causes play a role in shaping one's intellect. But it was the book's chapter on racial differences in intelligence that drew the most focus and scrutiny. In that chapter, Murray and Herrnstein argued that racial differences in intelligence were the results of both environmental and *innate* factors. In short Murray and Herrnstein had resurrected what many experts thought had been long invalidated—eugenics and scientific racism. According to the authors, the intellectual "decline" of the United States was due to the fact that populations with lower intelligence were reproducing at higher rates than populations that possed higher levels of intelligence. Therefore it was necessary, the authors asserted, that the welfare state should be disbanded in the interests of the state of the nation. In other words, the government should stop providing programs, like welfare, that encourage poorer "less intelligent" women to reproduce.

The technically precise description of America's fertility policy is that it subsidizes births among poor women, who are also disproportionately at the low end of the intelligence distribution. We urge generally that these policies, represented by the extensive network of cash and services for low-income women who have babies, be ended. The government should stop subsidizing births to anyone rich or poor.[54]

The racial implications of such a suggestion was obvious as Murray and Herrnstein had articulated in a scholarly manner a concern that had been not too far from the surface in America's discourse on race, America was at risk of being inundated with populations of less intelligent and productive peoples of color like African Americans. The following year Dinesh D'Souza's *The End of Racism* was published and while D'Souza did not point to genetic differences as an explanation for the racial inequality between African Americans and whites his culprit was a familiar argument—a deficiency within African American culture that produces the poor choices and actions exhibited by African Americans was what retarded the progress of African Americans as a group. The conservative think tank American Enterprise Institute (AEI) provided support to both Murray and D'Souza while they were working on their books. At the time Loury, and his colleague Robert Woodson, were also fellows there and after the publication of D'Souza's book gave up their fellowship positions with the organization. Almost twenty years later Loury in a critical retrospective piece on the passing of conservative social scientist James Q. Wilson Loury stated that he resigned from AEI because its association with what he thought were "incendiary and what seemed to me borderline racist books."[55] It is interesting that Loury felt D'Souza's book was the proverbial "final straw that broke the camel's back" that influenced his decision to cut ties with the organization when it seems the release of Murray's book one year earlier would have prompted such a move. Perhaps the chilly reception and treatment Loury received from his white counterparts as he broadcast his objections about Murray's *The Bell Curve* was the first sign that he had stepped outside his accepted boundary. As he relayed in a revealing interview in the *Boston Globe* soon after stepping down from AEI, the familiar conservative avenues where his works were readily accepted were not so receptive to his thoughts now.

When I'm cracking on "niggers" there's plenty of space for me in Commentary...When I want to go against their boy—Charles Murray— there's no place for me.[56]

Even though *The Weekly Standard* did publish his critical review of D'Souza's book they also provided D'Souza the opportunity to give an extensive response.[57] In a New York Times op-ed article Loury criticizes his conservative peers for creating a discourse among the right on race that "has largely been reduced to sloganeering, filled with references to black criminality, illegitimacy, and cultural pathology. This talk does not describe a tragedy shared by us all. Instead it denounces a cultural failing said to threaten our civilization."[58] In some ways Loury and his conservative African American intellectual peers played a part in the rise of such discourse as their works prominently featured calls for the civil rights establishment and black community at large to courageously face up to and take responsibility for the very issues he mentions above. It should not be surprising to view books by Murray and D'Souza arguing genetic and cultural inferiority are what prevents African Americans from achieving success in the land of opportunity as a by-product of the construction by black conservative intellectuals of a community hindered by their alleged inability to address personal and moral shortcomings.

The estrangement continued as in 1996 affirmative action was a hot topic in the media and policy circles during President Clinton's second term. President Clinton issued an executive order for the review of all federally based affirmative action programs to see if they were in violations of such things as establishing and or using racial quotas as benchmarks of success under the logic of "mending but not ending" affirmative action. The passage of proposition 209 or formally known as the California Civil Rights Initiative, outlawing the use of race, sex, or ethnicity on the part of public entities in the awarding of contracts, granting admission, or hiring also added to the spotlight on affirmative action. Interestingly fellow African American conservative Ward Connelly played a major role in getting the proposition passed and signed into law. Before the vote on proposition 209 Loury, head of the New Black Leadership association, was strongly urged by fellow members to speak out and mobilize support of the initiative by his colleagues in the organization. With skepticism and concern about the proposition Loury refused and stepped down from his post as chairman.[59]

Before the passage of 209 Loury spoke at a conservative symposium on affirmative action explaining his shifting view of the issue and the need to use affirmative action in integrating schools and police forces. The exchange between Loury and his former white neoconservative allies was heated and sharp. Midge Dector expressing great dismay at Loury changed opinion on the issue, and him retorting, "I say to you we need to think about programs...and you said 'aid and comfort to the enemy.'" Norman Podhoretz exclaimed "You were one of the most eloquent critics of affirmative action...I'm offended by your refusal to see that." Loury responded with "those are my people going down the drain with your no-programs."[60] In reflection, it appears Loury came to a painful realization that other African Americans had perceived about conservatives—when it comes to the plight of African Americans it begins and ends with them.

For all of the eighties and the beginning of the nineties Loury was the heralded conservative African American thinker exalted by the right with praise, exposure, and material support from their vast intellectual infrastructure. When his personal transgressions became public a number of conservatives expressed support for Loury, yet the support and accolades began to evaporate with his breaking ranks on the Murray and D'Souza books and was in full reversal with his shift in his opinion about affirmative action. It is ironic, a movement where personal responsibility and morality are central principles in their ideological makeup, in Loury's case it seemed having an extra-marital affair and substance abuse problem was not as sinful to some conservatives as shifting away from an opposition to affirmative action.

Conclusion

African American conservatives' intellectuals face an uphill battle in winning over the minds and hearts of other African Americans. This is not because African Americans are monolithically liberal in their thinking or naturally drawn to a liberal worldview the presence of African American conservatives disproves this. According to African American conservative intellectuals, there are other nefarious factors at play that prevent them from having their rightful place as leaders and forerunners within their racial group. First, they assert they do not get a fair hearing from the "mainstream media" which is more inclined to present the views of the "established civil rights leadership" than themselves. Instead as

Thomas Sowell once claimed, they are treated as "yokels or fascists."[61] Yet, with the help of an efficient conservative intellectual infrastructure African American conservatives' voices are consistently present in the nation's discourse around racial issues.[62] Some have nationally syndicated newspaper columns (Thomas Sowell), others have fellowships at prominent conservative intellectual think tanks (Shelby Steele, John McWhorter) while others are invited by large cable news outlets such as FOX News and CNN as commentators to propagate their message. Second, African American conservatives argue that the supposedly "civil rights leadership orthodoxy" has a hypnotic and hegemonic control over the African American masses hence rendering them as outsiders.

The problem for the black conservative is more his separation from the *authority* of his racial group than from the actual group. He stands outside a group authority so sharply defined and monolithic that it delivers more than 90% of the black vote to *whichever* Democrat runs for president.[63]

But as legal scholar Ronald Suresh Roberts insightfully states, "They claim to be outsiders even while they are sustained by the culture's most powerful institutions."[64] Case in point, economist Walter Williams has a position at George Mason University funded by the influential conservative Olin foundation and has been a substitute host for Rush Limbaugh's national radio show.[65] Finally, African American conservatives and intellectuals attribute their struggle to be the main voice of African Americans due to the caustic name-calling and challenges to their racial identity by their opponents. As John McWhorter points out, "No one questions the 'blackness' of Redd Foxx or Vanessa Williams, while plenty question the 'blackness' of, for example, Clarence Thomas."[66] But in the guise of being truth tellers who must, for the good of their race, give out harsh but necessary doses of tough love talk as in the form of articles in refereed academic journals, books geared toward both an academic and general public audience, or insight as commentators in print, radio, and television media, the ideas and words of some African American conservative intellectuals ring as callous and cold raising the question do these conservative African American actually like black people?

It is not the work of the so-called liberal bias in the media, the assumed conspiratorial actions of the African American progressive left leadership, or the sometimes crude depictions of African American conservatives by their opponents that is their main barrier to full acceptance by other African Americans. Instead their problem is one that is manifested within the larger conservative movement-persistent racism. As Ramesh Ponnuru points out, "Civil rights are a problem for the American Right: a political problem, an intellectual one, and a moral one."[67] In order to win over hearts and minds African American conservative intellectuals must find a way to strike a delicate balance between their desires to empower African Americans as active individual agents in their own destinies versus the powerful collectivist impulses that fuel African Americans actions to better the welfare of the race. More importantly, for African American conservative intellectuals to make serious inroads within their community they must overcome the stain of racism that has plagued the legacy of American conservatism. One possible manner of overcoming the image problem of being connected to a movement that has a very troubled racial history is, as Glenn Loury did almost two decades ago, is to call the right out on its racism. Their inability to do so continues to make them guilty by association. No matter how many narratives these African American conservative intellectuals tell of their own experiences with racism or the shared histories of growing up in the south and dealing with its brand of "southern racism" if their words and ideas are indistinguishable from the ones white conservatives used to justify the racial status quo that stymied social progress for African Americans their ideas will fall mainly on deaf ears. Until African American conservatives find solutions to these problems these intellectuals will continue to feel like outsiders looking in among their own race.

NOTES

1. Adolph Reed's 1995 Village Voice article "What Are the Drums Saying Booker?: The Curious Role of the Black Public Intellectual" is a classic example of a critical take on the rise of the Black Public Intellectual.
2. McWhorter often makes reference to the purported cultural difference between the different groups of color as evidence that the problem is of a cultural nature. In a later section, I will explain why this utilization of the "model minority" argument is highly problematic.
3. Ibid., 2001, p. 50.
4. As historian Daryl Scott states in his book, *Contempt & Pity*. "Prior to the 1980s, neoconservative damage imagery often assigned the origins of damage among blacks to slavery and caste and faulted black culture for perpetuating it. Since their ascendancy in the 1980s, many conservatives have traced the origins of black pathology to the Great Society rather than to slavery and caste" (Scott 1997: 192).

5. McWhorter tries to counter this in *Winning the Race* when he qualifies that the "acting white" problem among black students came about during the late sixties and was brought on by the settlement of therapeutic alienation within black culture. Though he intersperses his analysis with bits of information about the past legacy of previous generations of African Americans obtaining education by any means, this merely allows him to make the equally specious distinction between pre- and post-civil rights generations. In *Winning the Race* McWhorter also does some backpedaling from his earlier charge that anti-intellectualism has mainly been a problem within African American culture, stating, "Traditionally, anti-intellectualism was distributed in black American culture precisely the way it was in general American culture. In fact, in many ways there was less anti-intellectualism among blacks. During and after the Civil War, blacks were starved for education, and the idea that loving to learn was 'white' was unknown (2006: 268–270)."

6. Angel L. Harris, *Kids Don't Want To Fail: Oppositional Culture and the Black-White Achievement Gap* (Cambridge, MA: Harvard University Press, 2011), p. 50.

7. Since no reasonable student of any racial background would openly admit to not valuing education the only evidence that can be garnered about this problem is from the testimonies of those who have been the object of scorn or by outsiders (teachers, principles,) of the student peer group who either witness or hear testimonies about the stigmatization that takes place. So even though McWhorter has not been able to craft a study, nor cite, more than the one he mentions (Clifton Casteel) in which his interpretation of the results still does not clearly illuminate the severity of the "acting white" problem or this "separation from school" or "habit of the heart" that he refers to, yet he continues to rage on that black kids labeling other black kids as "oreo" or "acting white" is one of the major components of the cultural problem among African Americans that contributes to the academic achievement gap problem.

8. Frank Wu, *Yellow: Race in America Beyond Black and White* (New York: Basic Books, 2002), p. 67.

9. Nancy Chung Allred, "Asian Americans and Affirmative Action: From Yellow Peril to Model Minority and Back Again," *Asian American Law Journal*, vol. 14, no. 1, May 2007, p. 76.

10. Frank Wu, *Yellow*, p. 141. Also see, Jerry Kang, "Negative Action Against Asian Americans: The Internal Instability of Dworkin's Defense of Affirmative Action," *Harvard Civil Rights Law Review*; Jayjia Hsia, "Limits of Affirmative Action: Asian American Asian American Access to Higher Education," *Education Policy*, vol. 2, no. 2, 1988; Thomas J. Espenshade and Alexandria W. Radford, *No Longer Separate, Not*

Yet Equal: Race and Class in Elite College Admission and Campus Life (Princeton, NJ: Princeton University Press, 2009).

11. As Waters elaborates further, the stereotype of the West Indian as the better student was more appropriate during the late 1960s and mid 1970s, but by the early 1990s that picture had dramatically changed due to the change in migration streams. Whereas the earlier wave of West Indians who came to the United States came from middle-class backgrounds in their native homeland, the latter arrivals came from more modest and poorer means, which showed in the range of achievement distribution among West Indian students. This range was, as Waters states, "bipolar" with the West Indian students being "both of the best and the worst students in the school." One explanation Waters provides for why the achievement distribution among West Indian students is bipolar has to do with the differences between the West Indian educational system, modeled after the British system where everyone gets a primary education but only a select group go on to high school and beyond, as opposed to the US system. There are also qualitative differences between the educational systems among the different islands and between the schools in the urban and rural areas of the island, with the quality being better among the urban schools. The upshot of Waters' findings is that the West Indian students McWhorter extols are most likely the "cream of the crop," high-achieving students who were able to move beyond the primary schools back in their homelands, or who may have gotten their foundation back home in the primary schools before coming to the United States (270–277).

12. In contrast, Dalton Conley has persuasively argued that family wealth does matter when it comes to affecting school performance and progress. For example, when race is considered by itself, the gap between African Americans and whites in completing college is quite stark, with only thirty-eight percent of African Americans being as likely to finish college as their white counterparts. When social class is taken into account, however, the difference decreases significantly, with parental educational background being the strongest predictor variable followed by other variables such as equity of parents' primary residence and parents liquid assets (Conley 1999: 72–73).

13. Ronald Walters, *White Nationalism, Black Interests: Conservative Public Policy and the Black Community* (Detroit, MI: Wayne State University Press, 2003), pp. 229–230.

14. Shelby Steele, *The Content of Our Character: A New Vision of Race in America* (New York: Harper Perennial, 1990), p. 9.

15. Ibid.

16. Manning Marable, *Race, Reform, and Rebellion: The Second Reconstruction in Black America*, 1945–1990, 2nd ed. (Jackson: University Press of Mississippi, 1991), pp. 179–180.

17. Duchess Harris, *Black Feminist Politics from Kennedy to Obama* (New York: Palgrave Macmillan, 2009), p. 51.

18. Huma Khan, "What Did Rick Santorum Say? Welfare Comments Scrutinized," January 3, 2012, http://abcnews.go.com/blogs/politics/2012/01/what-did-rick-santorum-say-welfare-comments-scrutinized/, accessed August 19, 2014.

19. The Associated Press, "Emotional John Huppenthal Apologizes for Blog Comment," http://www.nbcnews.com/news/us-news/emotional-john-huppenthal-apologizes-blog-comment-n141281, accessed June 27, 2014. In fact, Huppenthal accused President Obama of enabling the supposedly slothful lifestyle of welfare recipients: "Obama is rewarding the lazy pigs with food stamps (44 million people), air-conditioning, free health care, flat-screen TV's (typical of 'poor' families)".

20. Office of Family Assistance: An office of the administration for Children and Families, "Characteristics and Financial Circumstances of TANF Recipients, Fiscal Year 2010," http://www.acf.hhs.gov/programs/ofa/resource/character/fy2010/fy2010-chap10-ys-final, published August 8, 2012, accessed August 19, 2014.

21. Kevin Williamson, "Keeping Blacks Poor: How the Democratic Party Stands Between Its Most Loyal Constituents and the Jobs They Need," *National Review*, February 8, 2010, p. 32.

22. Economist Walter E. Williams argues that if an employer is faced with two workers who are identical in their productivity and is forced by law to pay a stated wage to whichever employee they hire, the influencing factor will be employers succumbing to their "preference indulgences" as Williams puts it. In other words, if the employer, following Williams' argumentation, must pay both the white worker and black worker the same entry wage the employer will be more inclined to use "noneconomic criteria" such as race in making his selection. According to Williams, there is no economic penalty for the employer to discriminate against the black worker with minimum wage laws in effect, whereas if the black worker was willing to offer his labor at a rate that was cheaper ($5/hr.) than their white counterpart ($8/hr.) the price of the employer's discriminatory decision would be three dollars per hour. Walter E. Williams, *The State Against Blacks* (New York: McGraw-Hill, 1982), p. 42. So in essence according to Williams' logic, in order for low wage black workers to overcome their stigma as undesirable employees they must be willing to subjugate themselves to self exploitation in order to gain employment.

23. Williamson, p. 32.

24. Teresa Gowan, "What's Social Capital Got to Do with It? The Ambiguous (and Overstated) Relationship Between Social Capital and Ghetto Underemployment," *Critical Sociology*, September 2010, p. 61.
25. For a conservative critique to organized labor's racism see Loren A. Smith, "Obstacle to Equal Employment: The Legal Structure of Organized Labor," in *Black America and Organized Labor: A Fair Deal?* By Walter E. Williams, Loren A. Smith, and Wendell W.Gunn (Washington, DC: The Lincoln Institute for Research and Education Publication, 1979). A left of center critique is offered by the late Hebert Hill, "Racial Inequality in Employment: The Patterns of Discrimination," *The Annals of the American Academy of Political and Social Science*, vol. 357, January 1965, pp. 30–47; "Race, Ethnicity and Organized Labor: The Opposition to Affirmative Action," *New Politics*, Winter, 1987.
26. Williamson, pp. 32–33.
27. Kris Paap, "How Good Men of the Union Justify Inequality: Dilemmas of Race and Labor in the Building Trades," *Labor Studies Journal*, December 2008, pp. 388–389.
28. Bureau of Labor Statistics, http://www.bls.gov/news.release/pdf/union2.pdf, posted January 21, 2011, accessed June 16, 2011.
29. John Schmitt, "Unions and Upward Mobility for African-American Workers," April 2008, http://www.cepr.net/index.php/publications/reports/unions-and-upward-mobility-for-african-american-workers/, study released by the Center for Economic Policy and Research, p. 2, accessed June 13, 2011.
30. Folayemi Agbede, "The Importance of Unions for Workers of Color: Unions Offer Protection and Access to the Middle Class," http://www.americanprogress.org/issues/2011/04/importance_unions, posted April 4, 2011, accessed June 13, 2011.
31. John Schmitt, "Unions and Upward Mobility for African-American Workers," p. 5.
32. Robert Boynton, "Loury's Exodus: A Profile of Glenn Loury." *The New Yorker*, May 1, 1995, pp. 33–41.
33. Glenn Loury, "The Moral Quandary of the Black Community," *The Public Interest*, Spring, 1985, p. 11.
34. Ronald Reagan, Transcript of Inaugural Address given on January 20, 1981, http://www.reaganfoundation.org/pdf/SQP012081.pdf, accessed August 18, 2014.
35. Georgia Persons, "The Election of Gary Franks and the Ascendancy of the New Black Conservatives," in *Dilemmas of Black Politics: Issues of Leadership and Strategy*, ed. Georgia Persons (New York: HarperCollins, 1997).

36. Kristin A. Goss, "Harvard Professor, Black Economic Experts Ask for Changes in Administration Policies," January 18, 1985, http://www.the-crimson.com/article/1985/1/18/harvard-professor-black-economic-experts-ask/, accessed August 23, 2014.
37. Glen C. Loury, "Responsibility and Race," *Imprimis*, vol. 12, no. 2, February 1983, p. 1.
38. Ibid., p. 2.
39. Ibid., p. 3.
40. Ibid., p. 4.
41. See Marsha Jean Darling's, "We Have Come This Far by Our Own Hands: A Tradition of African American Self-Help and Philanthropy and the Growth of Corporate Philanthropic Giving to African Americans," in *African Americans and the New Policy Consensus: Retreat of the Liberal State?* eds. Marilyn E. Lashley and Melanie Njeri Jackson (Westport, CT: Greenwood Press, 1994).
42. Alford A. Young, "The (Non) Accumulation of Capital: Explicating the Relationship of Structure and Agency in the Lives of Poor Black Men," *Sociological Theory*, July 1999, p. 224.
43. Ibid.
44. Ibid.
45. Jennifer Hochschild, *Facing Up to the American Dream: Race, Class, and the Soul of the Nation* (Princeton, NJ: Princeton University Press, 1995), p. 159.
46. Ibid., p. 160.
47. Ibid., p. 161.
48. Ibid., p. 176.
49. Ibid.
50. Adam Shatz, "About Face." *The New York Times*, January 20, 2002, p. 21.
51. Ibid., p. 21.
52. Glenn Loury, *One by One from the Inside Out: Essays and Reviews on Race and Responsibility in America* (New York: The Free Press, 1995), pp. 30–31.
53. Glenn Loury, *The Anatomy of Racial Inequality* (Cambridge, MA: Harvard University Press, 2002), p. 113.
54. Charles Murray and Richard Herrnstein, *The Bell Curve: Intelligence and Class Structure in American Life* (New York: The Free Press, 1994), p. 549.
55. Glenn Loury, "Much to Answer For: James Q. Wilson's Legacy." *Boston Review*, May 1, 2012, http://www.bostonreview.net/glenn-loury-much-to-answer-for, accessed September 11, 2014.

56. Wil Haygood, "The Resurrection of Glenn Loury Rising from Public Disgrace, the Conservative Takes a New Look at What the Right Wing Thinks About Blacks," *Boston Globe*, October 26, 1995, accessed from Westlaw data base on September 11, 2014.
57. Adam Shatz, "About Face," p. 22.
58. Glenn C. Loury, "Cast Out by the Right." *The New York Times*, November 30, 1997.
59. Ibid.
60. Jacob Heilbrunn, "Con Games." *The New Republic*, October 20, 1997, p. 18.
61. As quoted in Joseph G. Conti and Brad Stetson, *Challenging the Civil Rights Establishment: Profiles of a New Black Vanguard*, p. 27.
62. For an insider's analysis of the conservative media infrastructure see David Brock's, *The Republican Noise Machine: Right Wing Media and How It Corrupts Democracy* (New York: Three Rivers Press, 2005).
63. Shelby Steele, *A Dream Deferred: The Second Betrayal of Black Freedom in America* (New York: HarperCollins, 1998), p. 6.
64. Ronald Suresh Roberts, *Clarence Thomas and the Tough Love Crowd: Counterfeit Heroes and Unhappy Truths* (New York: New York University Press, 1995), p. 3.
65. David Brock, *The Republican Noise Machine*, p. 108.
66. John McWhorter, *Authentically Black*, pp. 9–10.
67. Ramesh Ponnuru, "The Right's Civil Wrongs: On the Intellectual Roots of a Troubled Legacy," *National Review*, June 21, 2010, p. 16.

REFERENCES

Baker, Houston. *Betrayal: How Black Intellectuals Have Abandoned the Ideals of the Civil Rights Era*. New York, NY: Columbia University Press, 2008.

Conley, Dalton. *Being Black, Living in the Red: Race, Wealth, and Social Policy in America*. Berkeley: University of California Press, 1999.

Herbst, Susan. *Politics at the Margin: Historical Studies of Public Expression Outside the Mainstream*. New York: Cambridge University Press, 1994.

McLemee, Scott, ed. *C. L. R. James on the 'Negro Question.'* Jackson: University Press of Mississippi, 1996.

McWhorter, John. *Losing the Race: Self-Sabotage in Black America*. New York: Perennial, 2001.

———. *Authentically Black: Essays for the Black Silent Majority*. New York: Gotham Books, 2003a.

———. Interview. Brian Lamb. C-Span Book-TV Program, March 2, 2003b. http://www.Booknotes.org.

————. *Winning the Race: Beyond the Crisis in Black America.* New York: Gotham Books, 2006.

Model, Suzanne. *West Indian Immigrants: A Black Success Story?* New York: Russell Sage Foundation Publications, 2009.

Perry, Theresa. "Up from the Parched Earth: Toward a Theory of African-American Achievement." In *Young, Gifted, and Black: Promoting High Achievement Among African-American Students.* Ed. Claude Steele, Theresa Perry, and Asa Hilliard III. Boston, MA: Beacon Press, 2003.

Portes, Alejandro, and Ruben G. Rumbaut. *Immigrant America: A Portrait,* 3rd ed. Berkeley: University of California Press, 2006.

Roberts, Ronald Suresh. *Clarence Thomas and the Tough Love Crowd: Counterfeit Heroes and Unhappy Truths.* New York: New York University Press, 1995.

Scott, Daryl. *Contempt and Pity: Social Policy and the Image of the Damaged Black Psyche, 1880–1996.* Chapel Hill: University of North Carolina Press, 1997.

Steele, Shelby. *A Dream Deferred: The Second Betrayal of Black Freedom in America.* New York: HarperCollins, 1998.

Steinberg, Stephen. *The Ethnic Myth: Race, Ethnicity, and Class in America.* Boston: Beacon Press, 1989.

Waters, Mary C. *Black Identities: West Indian Immigrant Dreams and American Realities.* Cambridge: Harvard University Press, 1999.

Walters, Ronald. "Black Conservatives Failed a Leadership Test." *The New York Beacon,* January 29, 2003: 9.

Wilson, James Q. "Policy Intellectuals and Public Policy." *The Public Interest,* Summer, 1981: 36.

CHAPTER 8

Rolling Rightward: The African American Religious Right

During the 2008 presidential campaign, controversy arose when excerpts from some of the fiery sermons of President Obama's former pastor, Reverend Jeremiah Wright, made their way onto the public Internet site *Youtube* and then eventually the mainstream media. To those unfamiliar with the African American religious community, Wright's caustic criticism of American society's pervasive racism and treatment of African Americans was shocking and off-putting to say the least. However, for African Americans familiar with the Black Church Wright's words were par for the course, a part of the normal discourse one would hear from the pulpit on any given Sunday. Reverend Wright's words sparked a debate over whether Black theology (seen as represented by Wright) was anti-American and racist, and as the media sought to provide a balanced portrayal of African American Christians, their coverage gave some exposure to a segment of the Black church not thought of by many in this discussion—African American conservative Christians.

For the most part, the religious right within the African American community has fallen below the radar of those in the media and academia. Part of the reason why more attention is not paid to the Black religious Right is due to the common associations many have of the "Black Church" and the Black Ministry with the civil rights movement. Both Dr. Martin Luther King Jr.'s legacy and black liberation theology are seen as representing the Black Church's constant and unwavering call for social justice and critique of the injustices of our society. The presence and continuing activism of conservative Black Christians, however,

© The Author(s) 2018

L. G. Prisock, *African Americans in Conservative Movements*,

https://doi.org/10.1007/978-3-319-89351-8_8

not only demonstrates that there is no such thing as a monolithic "Black Church," but also, the Black Church's function as a potential pathway for white conservatives into the black community.

Various factors have made it possible for a developing alliance between the black religious right and their white counterparts, even though this alliance is still quite tenuous, mainly due to possible fractures having to do with race. At the core of the alliance between the conservative segment of the black religious community and the larger conservative movement is the maintenance of an American social structure where capitalism, Christianity and "whiteness" reign supreme as interlinked, institutionalized, discourses. A particular cadre of conservative African American ministers captures the attention of their congregations by welding together spirituality with an emphasis on material prosperity known as the Word of God or prosperity gospel. They use their flashy lifestyles as evidence that by establishing the "proper" relationship with God those in their congregations can enjoy God's blessing of receiving the material fruits available in our capitalist social order. These religious leaders remind their followers that only the love of God and devout faith in Christianity can bring them the salvation they seek, but this salvation is defined as both material and spiritual. They also point out that as a people with a history of surviving the legacy of oppression it is the faith in Christianity that gave the race the strength to endure and move forward. Interspersed throughout their sermons are themes of uplifting the race and adherence to a politics of respectability that does not challenge the continuing supremacy of whiteness but focuses on seeking success and respect within that framework. Given that the context in which these ministers deliver these messages and others is both theatrical and commoditized, they effectively link elements of a black religious culture most of their congregation were raised in with core components of a consumer capitalist ideology.

Those familiar with politics within the African American ministry know that it has never been as monolithic as is commonly assumed. For example, it is no secret that the African American church community has often taken conservative positions on certain issues related to sexuality and gender. Patriarchal and heterosexist norms and customs still flow through many African American churches. As theologian Kelly Brown Douglas points out, "The manner in which Black women are treated in many Black churches reflects the Western Christian tradition's notion of women as evil and its notions of Black women as Jezebels and seducers of men"

(Douglas 1999: 83). To highlight this position, Douglas points to the practice in some Black churches of requiring women to cover their legs with a throw while sitting in the pews so as not to "tempt" the male parishioners. Another example is the treatment of unwed mothers by certain Black churches. At some Black churches, the unwed mother is openly chastised and made to repent publicly to the congregation while the father of the child is often overlooked (Douglas 1999: 83; Townsend Gilkes 2001). The instances of homophobia within African American churches are, sadly, numerous. Just to name a couple of examples, in 1929, prominent minister Adam Clayton Powell, Sr. of the famed Abyssinian Baptist Church led one of the first African American church crusades against homosexuality (Griffin 2006: 60). Homophobia has even penetrated the African American religious music scene, as evidenced when gospel singers Debbie and Angel Winans of the famous African American gospel family released the controversial song, "Its Not Natural," which spoke of the Bible's supposed declaration that homosexuality was an unnatural act in the eyes of God (Griffin 2006: 82).

To see the conservative wing of the Black Church as a marginal segment of the African American religious community would be a mistake, for over the past two decades conservative African American ministers have increasingly gained access and nurtured relationships with those in political power. As they have made inroads in the political world, a number of African American conservative ministers are also making their mark in what I call the "Christian consumerist sphere." To get a clear understanding of the emergence of the African American religious right it is important to examine the social forces that have been influential in their elevation.

FACTORS WITHIN THE RELIGIOUS MOVEMENT THAT HAVE PRODUCED THE BLACK RELIGIOUS RIGHT

The continuing elevation of the Black religious right in the political and social realm can be attributed to a couple of important factors. First, one notes the rise of three, specific, interconnected phenomena: the electric church, super size churches or mega churches, and an entrepreneurial Christianity that places an emphasis on "prosperity gospel." Second, one can also observe the rise of a larger conservative movement greatly aided by its courtship of conservative white Christians. This segment has, in turn, provided a space for the conservative wing of the Black church to thrive.

The Electric Church

While religious broadcasting had been in existence since records, radios, and televisions were first invented, its expansion can be traced back to the sixties when a combination of FCC and radio network policy changes, and the prohibition of liquor and tobacco advertisements on the radio airways, changed the way religious broadcasting was done. Beforehand, religious broadcasters had the option of either purchasing time known as "commercial time" or using what was known as "sustained time." When the FCC mandated that radio stations set aside time slots for religious programming, mainline denominations were mainly reliant on using the "sustained time" provided by the stations. This was not the same for their evangelical counterparts who not only could afford to purchase more of the commercial time, but also, could then spend a good portion of their airtime soliciting for further donations (Hodgson 1997: 173).

There is more to this point than the fact that evangelicals had a better ability to purchase airtime than mainline denominations. In addition, first, many mainline Protestant and Catholic traditions found the act of soliciting or "begging" for monetary contributions over the air troubling and held a deep disdain for the practice. Mainline Protestants and Catholics were also less likely to proselytize as their evangelical brethren, who took very seriously the call to use their position as believers in Jesus to spread his word to others and convert the unconverted (Hadden 1993: 117). Second, the evangelicals' mission to spread the Lord's word and their lack of inhibition in asking their followers to make money contributions to aid in that mission dovetailed perfectly with the free market logic of the broadcasting industry As sociologist Jeffery Hadden notes, "the right to buy air time or sponsorship has been a critical market principle of broadcasting in the United States from nearly the beginning" (Hadden 1993: 116). To the evangelical ministers, their product is Jesus Christ and the airways are God's tools to achieve the circulation of his message. If their viewers and listeners feel spiritually fulfilled and committed as allies in the quest to win the hearts and minds of others to Jesus Christ, their payment to support the broadcast's continuation becomes not just a choice but almost a spiritual obligation.

In a matter of time, with the access provided by their use of commercial time, evangelicals and fundamentalist preachers began to dominate the airways. By the 1980s, close to 90% of religious broadcasting was done by evangelical and fundamentalist ministers (Allitt 2003: 151). In time, many of the evangelical ministers transitioned from radio to television, thereby gaining access to an even larger audience. In 1979, Pat Robertson's Christian Broadcast Network was estimated to be bringing in over fifty-three million dollars in earnings and was broadcast on 154 over the air television stations and eighteen hundred cable stations! (Hodgson 1997: 174). And as white televangelicals were gaining notice for themselves, so too were their black counterparts.[1] One individual credited with being a pioneer amongst contemporary African American televangelists is Bishop Carlton Pearson. Given a context in which there were virtually no outlets for African American televangelists, it is easy to see why Pearson is looked upon as pioneer:

> To understand the significance of Pearson as trailblazer, one must understand the arena of Christian television at the time. White televangelists controlled the airwaves. In the 1980's, Black Entertainment Television was a start up network, and the current stations that direct their programming primarily toward the African American community, like the Word Network, MBC, and TV One, were not yet created. (Walton 2009: 85)

Pearson, a protégé of Oral Roberts, was one of the first African American religious figures to gain access to the emerging religious broadcasting networks. Pearson was the very first African American guest host on the *Praise The Lord* (PTL) television show and the first African American to have his own show on the Trinity Broadcast Network (TBN). The fact that good portion of the audiences who watched the religious shows on these various networks were African Americans was one important factor that helped Pearson penetrate the white televangelical world (Walton 2009). White televangelists, recognizing the advantages of cultivating the African American audience as a solid, potential market for donations, found it increasingly prudent to place diverse faces on the air. Pearson seemed to be a natural choice for the white evangelicals because he was theologically compatible, a proponent of Reaganomics, and possessed a captivating singing voice that made for great entertainment.

Bishop Pearson's success led to two important further developments. Pearson introduced black Pentecostals to powerful figures within the industry such as the Crouch family who owned the TBN. He also paved the way for other African American televangelists such as Bishop T.D. Jakes (Walton 2009: 84–85). No doubt the success of prominent figures within the African American ministry, such as Bishop T.D. Jakes, Reverend Frederick Price, and Pastor Creflo Dollar, to name a few, is influencing many more African American ministers to take to the airways. The size of the audiences of televangelical ministers and their impact on the American political and social landscape is still being debated, but nevertheless, American televangelism has changed the religious landscape here in the United States and shows the potential to do the same in Africa and Latin America. It is clear that the rise of the electronic church gave a number of conservative ministers, both black and white, not only exposure but also the opportunity to expand their following and their marketing base. A complementary relationship has developed between televangelism and large religious communities known as the mega churches, where the influence of one impacts the influence of the other (Bretthauer 1995: 75). Thus, I now direct my analysis toward the impact mega churches have had on the American religious scene and within the African American community.

Mega Churches

During the 2008 presidential campaign, eyebrows were also raised when both Democratic candidate Barack Obama and Republican candidate John McCain agreed to appear together at a sit down session with evangelical minister Rick Warren at the Saddleback Church. At this Civil Forum on the Presidency (as the event came to be known), both men were invited to voice their views separately in front of a live television audience and parishioners in attendance, on a number of issues (ranging from faith to abortion, marriage, and gay rights) raised by Warren. Given that there are thousands of religious leaders in the United States who would have loved to host such an event if the opportunity arose, why was Warren able to get the two politicians together? No doubt a major factor was the fact that Warren is a prominent televangelist and best selling author who pastors a church with a membership estimated to be around twenty thousand.

What exactly constitutes a mega church and what factors have caused a rise in their formation today? According to various sources, a church that has at least a weekly attendance of two thousand people places that church in the mega church category (Chaves 2006: 329; Karnes et al. 2007: 261; Thurman 2005). Churches with large memberships are nothing new, particularly in the African American community where some mega churches were established before the civil war (Townsend Gilkes 1998: 104). In the latter part of the twentieth century, however, particularly during the eighties and nineties, there was an upsurge in the development of mega churches. In one generation (from the early 1970s to the present) the number of mega churches has grown from seventy-four to over twelve hundred (Greenblatt and Powell 2007: 771).[2] At least three important social factors have played a role in the explosion of these religious institutions.

Suburbanization or continued suburban sprawl, made possible by available plots of cheap land, is the first significant contributing factor. Most urban areas are constrained in their ability to provide the large tracts of land needed to build the large building where actual services are conducted, and the various auxiliary buildings that offer a multitude of services (day care services, fitness centers, or shopping malls where Christian products can be purchased). While there are mega churches situated throughout the United States a good number of them are located in the Sunbelt region (southeast and southwest) of the country (Karnes et al. 2007: 262). No doubt the growth of mega churches in this region was related to the economic expansion that occurred in various sun belt urban centers, such as Atlanta, Phoenix, and Orlando to name a few. Because of their size and the various services that mega churches offer, the administrative expenses related to the operation of these institutions are quite costly. Therefore, these churches need to be located in areas where the local economic context is strong and resources are plentiful, as Kimberly Karnes attests to when she states: "While areas of significant economic distress may have the population to support a megachurch, the resource base may be too limited to produce the capital needed to build the necessary structures" (Karnes et al. 2007: 263).

It is also no surprise that a majority of these mega churches are located in suburban areas, not only because the available land provides the space needed for the large configurations of these structures and its satellite buildings, but also, because of the demographic composition of these areas. There is a strong correlation between the median family income of a given suburban area and where a mega church is located. Kimberly Karnes shows that zip code areas within ten miles of a mega church had an average income of more than fifty thousand dollars while other areas had average incomes of less than forty thousand dollars. The median house values in zip code areas ten miles or less were over one hundred and fifty thousand while in other areas the median housing values were under one hundred thousand (Karnes et al. 2007: 265). In addition, then, to plentiful land these mega churches also need parishioners with solid earnings to help cover expenses.

A second contributing factor to the rising popularity of mega churches is the charisma of church leaders and the advancements in technology that further enhance ministers' power, reach and appeal. As mentioned earlier, the relationship between televangelism and mega churches has been of mutual benefit to each. According to sociologist Shayne Lee, "Christian television exposed the country to neo-Pentecostal ideas and practices and influenced middle-class converts and mainliners to join their churches and organizations" (Lee 2005: 37). Television has the power and ability not only to accentuate an individual's level of recognition, but also, to enhance their charisma. Bishop T.D. Jakes' influence provides a good example. Rising up from his humble beginnings in West Virginia to become one of the most influential televangelists today, Jakes received his first major break when Paul Crouch, Christian television baron and founder of the TBN, discovered Jakes after hearing him on Carlton Pearson's television program, delivering part of a sermon the then unknown Jakes gave at a conference. Quite impressed, Crouch soon offered Jakes a full-time spot on his network. After receiving his own show on TBN, Jakes' appeal kept rising with each appearance at conferences, no doubt bolstered by his exposure on Crouch's network (Lee 2005: 54–55).

Some of today's mega churches have become contemporary spiritual arenas with their stadium seating, large LCD jumbotron television screens, advanced lighting and audio systems, large stages for holding both a sizable choir and a full-fledged band, and state-of-the-art production studios. The combination of a talented charismatic preacher, as in the case of T.D. Jakes, and various mechanisms, such as visual aids and lighting effects, with music playing in the background to emphasize a theological point, can transform an ordinary sermon into an emotionally captivating moment: "In a postmodern media age that pays a high premium on style and stimulation, Jakes captivates audiences with riveting sermons, flashy attire, poignant dramatizations, and visual demonstrations to depict key points in his sermons" (Lee 2005: 86).

Spiritual Capitalism

When one adds the minister's charismatic appeal and technological enhancements to the ability to beam these sermons, performed in such a grand theatrical manner, into televisions near and far, not only does a minister's exposure and celebrity grow exponentially, but also, so too does his or her marketing ability. The more captivating one becomes by producing religious theater through sight, sound, and words, the more books, DVD's, and tapes one can sell. As such, several transformations have taken place as the minister transitions into a religious form of the ideal American type of the entrepreneur, with the parishioners and other loyal followers becoming the consumers and the mega church the marketplace. As some white ministers of mega churches, such as Joel Osteen and Rick Warren, have discovered, feeding the soul with God's word is not only good for the spirit but can also be good for the bottom line, and this discovery has not been lost on their black counterparts. Reverend T.D. Jakes has cultivated relationships with large corporations such as Ford and Coca-Cola to sponsor his annual religious festival. Bishop Eddie Long of the New Birth Missionary Baptist Church in Lithonia, GA is comfortable with allowing his parishioners to be a test market for Coca-Cola and McDonald's to distribute free samples of their new products. And in 2006, Chrysler provided test drives of its newest vehicles at the four largest black mega churches in the country. A spokesman for Chrysler justified the automaker's action by saying, "We try to go out to our best prospects in their environment, where they're already engaged…and in the African American community, one of the opportunities is the church" (Greenblatt and Powell 2007: 778).

The blending of capitalism and Christianity does not stop there. At his World Changers Ministries, Reverend Creflo Dollar has a music studio, publishing house, computer graphic design suite, and his own record label. Bishop T.D. Jakes' Potter's House also has its own in-house record label, plus a prison satellite network that broadcasts in over 200 prisons. Bishop Eddie Long's church has a 3-D special effects web page where visitors can receive on demand videos of previous sermons (Kroll 2003: 57). Since Jakes, Long, Dollar, and other black Christian entrepreneurs are quite successful at practicing a spiritual form of black capitalism, one should not expect to hear critiques of capitalism coming from their pulpits anytime soon.

In terms of a final factor contributing to the growth of mega churches, a cultural shift in American religion life that led to more Americans placing less emphasis on denominational identification, concomitant with the decline of the more mainline denominations, has further aided in the growth of large churches. Most mega churches are non-denominational and therefore have more independence in how they conduct their church operations than their more traditional counterparts. From instituting a more relaxed atmosphere in regard to dress code, or modernizing the hymnals with the use of contemporary musical bands, or having the ministers reveal more of their own personal challenges to their congregations thus making them seem more accessible, all of these strategies have touched a chord with many church-going Americans. One member of a mega church described the source of his church's appeal and why he felt at home there: "There were no religious symbols and no 500-year old hymns.... Just an auditorium. The congregation was younger, like me. The pastor wasn't up there in a white robe with tassels and he didn't act like someone who has it all together – he shared his own struggles. It was very real" (Allitt 2003: 227).

This cultural shift represents more than just a movement away from attachments to denominations. It also demonstrates a more individualistic approach to becoming Christians. The leaders of these expanding mega churches have been able to capture the pulse of this cultural change. According to theologian Hudnut-Beumler, James many of these new congregations opening up in the south and southwest were made up of two types of new, migrant, constituencies. One was a religious community comprised of an older generation that settled in the area to begin their golden years and who were accustomed to a form of Protestantism focused on personal salvation and hard work. At the same time, a younger generation was also migrating into the south to go after emerging career opportunities, this group's spirituality was influenced by college campus evangelical groups that placed their spiritual emphasis on the individual developing a personal relationship with Jesus. The churches that recognized this trend and made adjustments to their operations and accommodated both of these groups were the ones that were able to best capitalize on them, and in a number of instances these were the more conservative religious organizations:

> The sum total of this trend was a gain for more conservative congregations that understood the Christian faith and how one got to be a Christian on a more personal and individual basis. The churches that grew most in the Sunbelt were, therefore, churches that catered to the older generation of personal faith retirees or to the generation that sought congregations that most resembled their campus Christian fellowships (such as Campus Crusade, Young Life, Youth for Christ, and Intervarsity. (Hudnet-Beumler 2007: 201)

For African Americans, particularly those in the middle class, attendance at black mega churches went beyond a search for personal spiritual fulfillment to include deeper issues of race and class. For those blacks who had achieved various levels of personal success in their educational and career pursuits, thus taking them further away from other blacks who still lagged behind, the Black Church was the place to regain a validation of what it meant to be black in a society that often and actively devalued it. Social mobility continues to be a tenuous issue for African Americans, due to the continued obstacles many in the black community face in order to achieve it, and the precarious nature of that success once it is attained. A religious narrative has emerged in some of these new black mega churches to offer an explanation for why God chose some blacks to reap rewards and not others. The Word of Faith or prosperity gospel offers the panacea of a religious narrative that provides agency and justification to its followers, encouraging them in the belief that health and material success are there to be claimed precisely because God wants his children to reap the successes of the opportunities He presents them. For proponents of the prosperity gospel, if one has faith and honors God in the "right way," He will ensure that his child receives what He deems appropriate.

There are three main components of the Word of Faith theology. First, there is the idea of "revelation knowledge," a knowledge that comes straight from God and is, therefore, the most reliable form of knowledge, much more so than anything gathered from other sources. The second is the notion of "Identification," that is, the belief that the individual is fully "inhabited by God" and can be thought of as another "incarnation of Jesus." The third is "positive confession," the tenet that holds that the believer has the power to call such things as physical health and material wealth into their life (Posner 2008: 14). The Word of Faith theology thus appears to mark a split from the more familiar doctrine of other black churches where the emphasis is on themes of liberation, perseverance, and community.

In actuality, prosperity gospel has a long and rich history within the African American spiritual community.[3] For more affluent African Americans, "such preaching facilitated psychological relocation and integration in the world of affluence" (Townsend Gilkes 1998: 108). In one way, the philosophy of prosperity gospel can be seen as a way of democratizing affluence. While prosperity gospel offers to those African Americans who are struggling the hope that one day they too will receive their "gifts" of health and wealth from God (as long as they claim and develop the "proper" relationship with the Lord), at the same time it gives to upwardly mobile African Americans "God's blessing" for their material standing (Harrison 2005: 148). However, even if the Word of Faith theology seeks to democratize wealth it leaves intact the existing capitalist social order. As Milmon Harrison states, "The Faith Message encourages *individuals* to be successful *within* the existing economic and social system rather than seeking to overthrow it or reform it to any great degree" (Harrison 2005: 149). To religious black capitalists, such as Dollar, Jakes, and Long, capitalism is their raison d'etre, and they become prominent examples of how the prosperity gospel has worked for them.

Factors Within the Conservative Movement: Political Empowerment

Conservatives' rise to power during the latter part of the twentieth century in the United States would not have been as successful were it not for their ability to forge and cultivate a coalition with evangelical Christians.[4] The right was able to forge this coalition by appealing to the fears and anxieties conservative evangelical and fundamentalist Christians had about society. To conservative Christians, American society's moral foundation was becoming deracinated by the chaos of the sixties and the elevation of secular humanism, a process aided in no small part by the liberal elite's control of various important institutions. Conservative Christians found the evidence for this degradation of society in several Supreme Court rulings, including the outlawing of sponsored prayer and bible study in public schools (Engel v. Vitale 1962, School District of Abington Township v. Schempp 1963) and the legalizing of abortion (Roe v Wade 1973). The involvement of many evangelical Christians in social and cultural battles from the 1970s to the present not only empowered them, but also, it allowed the conservative wing of the Republican Party to acquire political power. Of the many issues that sparked conservative Christians' entry into political activism, there is no question that race was one of them.

In response to the Supreme Court's ruling in Brown v. Board of Education, a number of private, independent, Christian schools appeared throughout the south offering an alternative for white parents who wanted to avoid the soon-to-be desegregated public schools (and retreat from what they saw as an encroaching secular humanism).

These private schools were the solution for parents seeking to provide their children with an education based on evangelical Christian principles that also emphasized traditional moralism. Notwithstanding parents' concerns about providing their children with an upstanding Christian education, race was still a crucial factor. For instance, the reaction to the Brown decision produced a quicker flight of white Christians from public schools than the Court's two rulings about school prayer (Crespino 2008: 95). In addition, many of these conservative Christians mobilized into action when the Internal Revenue Service began to explore removing the tax exempt status from small private academies that carried out racial discrimination in its admissions process. The IRS controversy, as one conservative activist stated, "kicked the sleeping dog. It galvanized the religious right. It was the spark that ignited the religious right's involvement in real politics" (Crespino 2008: 91).

Upon reflection, some within the white religious right have begun to recognize and acknowledge the mistakes white evangelicals made regarding racial equality, African Americans, and the black church. According to Ralph Reed, former leader of the Christian Coalition, the religious right was not only "on the sidelines, but on the wrong side of the most central cause of social justice in this century" (Reed 1996: 68). The religious right made a grave error in being obstructionist toward racial equality, as Reed argues:

> For the past complicity of the white church in the mistreatment of African-Americans and Jews is too large a blot on our history to deny. Tragically, white evangelicals did not merely look the other way as African Americans were denied full equality and participation in American life. They were among the most fiery champions of slavery and later segregation – all the while invoking God's name and quoting the Bible to justify their misdeeds. Why are white evangelicals accorded so little respect in the public square today? Certainly part of the answer lies in our past. (Reed 1994: 236)

The religious right's need to atone for and mend its ways in terms of how it has dealt with race is seen as essential to their success in acquiring both moral and political legitimacy:

> White evangelicals, who now seek a place at the table in political life, remained on the sidelines during the greatest struggle for social justice in this century.... Some criticized the black church for organizing dissent, accusing their ministers of 'politicizing' the gospel, harboring 'outside

agitators,' and 'fomenting discord.' These words have undermined the moral authority of religious conservatives as they have sought to redress other forms of social injustice – abortion, euthanasia, and religious bigotry – in recent times. (Reed 1994: 237)

The consciousness raising produced by Reed and other conservatives has led to the right's courting of African Americans by reaching out to religious figures within the black church and the community at large.

Questions abound over the true motives of the white religious right's outreach to African Americans. Some African Americans see this courtship as a political ploy by white conservatives to utilize African Americans as a form of "window dressing" in a movement that is still racist to its core. Others believe that white conservatives are genuine in their desire to create a multiracial conservative coalition. As the debate continues it should be pointed out that there are several important aspects of this coalition that need to be taken further into account. The rise of a black and white religious right partnership not only provides the veneer of "multiculturalism" or "diversity." The incorporation of conservative black Christians also acts as a counter to an African American theology that has linked spirituality with liberation and used Christian principles to justify and motivate African Americans to fight for social justice. Most importantly, this budding relationship between black and white conservative Christians allows for the possibility of the conservative movement to gain entry into the African American community, a community it has struggled to win to its side historically. In the following section, I examine the different access points that have allowed for the development of a black-white Christian right coalition.

Avenues for the African American Christian Right to Join with Their White Counterparts

Racial Reconciliation Part One: The Southern Baptist Convention's Resolution

In 1988, President Ronald Reagan signed the Civil Liberties Act, the act authorizing the distribution of twenty thousand dollars to each surviving Japanese or Japanese American that was interned at various internment camps in the United States during World War II. President Reagan's successor George H.W. Bush followed this up by signing into law the

Civil Liberties Act Amendments of 1992, which provided an additional four hundred million dollars to ensure that all the surviving internees were given their twenty thousand dollar payout, and also issued a formal apology from the government. The nineties became the decade of what would soon become a global trend, in which both the federal government and private sector institutions sought forgiveness for their complicity in heinous acts committed against particular groups. One particular act of repentance that caught the media's attention was the Southern Baptist Convention's (SBC) issuance of the Racial Reconciliation Resolution of 1995. This was newsworthy because in the history of the SBC race had been a central factor in its existence. As historian Barry Hankins notes, the denomination's origins came about in large part due to the controversy over the morality of slavery with Northern Baptists strongly supporting the abolitionist movement, arguing that slavery was the utmost offensive sin to God, and the Southern Baptists finding justification for the practice through interpretative uses of biblical text (Hankins 2002: 240).

This intradenominational struggle between the two different regions eventually led to southern Baptists breaking off from their northern counterparts and forming a new organization, the SBC, that was independent of the two main Baptist societies. The SBC in many ways represented the intensity and conviction many southern institutions had in their belief in the righteousness of slavery. A good number of the Convention's leaders were outspoken opponents of the Civil Rights movement and while the denomination passed a resolution supporting the Brown decision, many of those who actively resisted the Supreme Court's order to desegregate public schools were Southern Baptists (Hankins 2002: 242–243).

Even though the conservative faction within the SBC was in full command of the denomination's leadership, there was some recognition among some conservatives that something needed to be done to address the race issue. One such individual open to tackling the racist history of the SBC was Richard Land, the executive director of the SBC's Christian Life Commission. Another individual who played a key role in assisting Land was African American minister Reverend Gary Frost, formerly of Youngstown Ohio and now the director of the leadership collaboration for the NYC Leadership Center and senior pastor of Evergreen Baptist Church in Brooklyn NY. Rev. Frost, the first African American Vice President of the SBC, alerted Land to a racial resolution written by other individuals in the denomination a year earlier that had gained no attention. From there the two men began to strategize how to create a resolution that would be more likely to gain support within the denomination.

Through the work of a biracial committee appointed by Land, the official resolution was created and went through the necessary clearing steps to be presented on the floor of the upcoming conference, which was the denomination's one hundred and fiftieth anniversary. Land felt this was the right time to make this gesture, as he stated, "Many of us feel it would be unseemly and terribly wrong to celebrate our sesquicentennial without addressing forthrightly the more unsavory aspects of our past" (Hankins 2002: 244). After the resolution was read, Frost accepted the denomination's apology on behalf of all African Americans. And while the apology by the SBC garnered plenty of media attention given the racist history of the denomination, the reaction to Frost and the conservative-led SBC received mixed responses by other African American Baptists and African Americans in general. A close examination of what the resolution stated sheds light the coolness of the reception among some African Americans.

Of the eighteen statements within the resolution the first five address the denomination's and country's shameful racist past. Statements thirteen and fourteen stated:

> Be it further RESOLVED, that we lament and repudiate historic acts of evil such as slavery from which we continue to reap a bitter harvest, and we recognize that the racism which yet plagues our culture today is inextricably tied to the past;
> Be it further RESOLVED, That we apologize to all African-Americans for condoning and/or perpetuating individual and systemic racism in our lifetime; and we genuinely repent of racism of which we have been guilty, whether consciously (Psalm 19:13) or unconsciously (Leviticus 4:27).[5]

Statements fifteen and sixteen also read as follows:

> Be it further RESOLVED, that we hereby commit ourselves to eradicate racism in all its forms from the Southern Baptist life and ministry;
> Be it RESOLVED, that we commit ourselves to be doers of the Word (James 1:22) by pursuing racial reconciliation in all of our relationships, especially with our brothers and sisters in Christ (1 John 2:6), to the end that our light would so shine before others, that they may see (our) good works and glorify (our) Father in heaven (Matthew 5:16).[6]

The acknowledgments in statements 13 and 14, namely, of the rewards whites still received due to racism, the connection of the past with the present, and the view that racism is something that is both personal and systemic, were all good steps in the right direction. Yet, the general wording of the resolution raised many equally telling questions. Critics asked, what exactly did the SBC have in mind to enact change that would "eradicate racism" that they spoke of in statement 15, and how sincere was the denomination's pursuit of "racial reconciliation" as described in statement 16, or, was there another motive at work?

Some noted that, in light of decreasing white membership in the SBC over time, the creation of the resolution had the appearance of a strategy to make the SBC more attractive to a growing, southern, African American, urban middle class. As one black minister stated, "It was 'ludicrous' for blacks to 'abandon their own conventions...to run after those who historically oppressed and ostracized them. What sense does it make to turn your back on your own institution to make somebody else's stronger?... Black Baptists should not give away their birthright" (Friedland 1998: 243). Would the main objective in "eradicating racism" include focusing on diversifying the leadership and creating a more welcoming climate for Baptists of color within the denomination? To date, almost 15 years since the release of the resolution, the leadership structure of the SBC is still not diverse.

The questions continued—would the SBC go one step further and lobby politicians in Washington on racial equality as vigorously as they had on such social issues as abortion? If so, what types of policies would the SBC push for? Would the SBC push for the passage of a policy that provides reparations to African Americans in the same way that reparation was given to the Japanese and Japanese Americans who were interned during World War II? Or would the SBC, recognizing that racism was also embedded within the infrastructure of America's many systems, demand that those in Washington create redistributive measures that address racial inequality? The conservative direction of the SBC provides the backdrop for, and insight into, some of the conflicts that emerged between the denomination's stated goals as expressed in the resolution, and some of its public policies put in place to address the very issue of racial inequality.

For instance, the use of affirmative action is one area where conflict arises between the philosophical approach of the SBC leadership and what most African Americans see as a necessary policy[7]:

And paradoxically, today's Southern Baptist Convention is the same organization that is supporting the Republicans' cynical attack on affirmative action, and racism still makes affirmative action necessary. If the Southern Baptist are serious about atoning for their historical sins, how can they also join the Republicans in destroying affirmative action – the one federal program that modestly attempts to redress some of the wrongs of discrimination? (Hankins 2002: 249)

Because of the denomination's racist past and the prominent conservatism of its leadership, African Americans who affiliate solely with the SBC and not one of the African American Baptist institutions also, such as the largest and oldest African American religious convention the National Baptist Convention, are viewed with suspicion by other African American Baptists inside and outside of the SBC.

According to Southern Seminary professor T. Vaughn Walker, who is also allied with the National Baptists, the difference between himself and Frost is that, "the black community sees me as one of them here [Southern] and not as a Southern Baptist who happens to be in a black church"(Hankins 2002: 252). Walker's dual alliance sends a signal to other African Americans, especially to his students, that he is not an adherent of the conservatism of the white SBC. This is especially important since, as an African American, he chooses to affiliate with an organization in which one of its members, Rev. Wiley Drake, has openly stated that he is praying for the death of the country's first African American president.[8] Frost's sole identification with the SBC, on the other hand, is seen by some African Americans as analogous to an African American aligning him or herself with the conservative John Birch Society, an organization that was known not only for strident anti-communism but also prominent racism.

Racial Reconciliation Part Two: The Promise Keepers

During the mid-nineties, the state of American masculinity became a national issue as illustrated by Louis Farrakhan's Million Man March, the number of men's movements receiving coverage in the media, and the creation of new ones such as the Promise Keepers. The brainchild of former University of Colorado football coach Bill McCarthy, the Promise Keepers, an evangelical organization, had as its main message the idea that American men and masculinity was in crisis and that the solution to this problem lay in men refocusing their lives back toward God. At the height of the Promise Keepers' existence, the organization was able to fill professional football stadiums with men. Pictures of these men, with their arms rising skyward toward the heavens and tears streaming down their faces as they welcomed Jesus Christ into their lives, were touching and garnered plenty of media attention. One aspect of the Promise Keepers' gatherings that the media took significant notice of was their multiracial appearance. From the racial diversity of the religious figures who spoke about the need for men to embrace racial reconciliation, to the images of white men and men of color in the audience in close embrace, the multiracial nature of these events drew praise from a number of media quarters.

A dedication toward racial reconciliation was one of the organization's seven edicts or "promises." Racial reconciliation was an issue that Promise Keeper founder Bill McCarthy was genuinely committed to, due to his realization of his own racism as it manifested in his reaction to the discovery that his daughter had been impregnated by one of his former black players. McCarthy's sincerity in regard to racial reconciliation was also demonstrated in the composition of the Promise Keepers' board of directors, with 60% (3 out of 5) of the board composed of men of color (Harper 2008: 94). The ministers who participated in Promise Keepers gatherings were also diverse. T.D. Jakes, Wellington Boone, and, Dallas-based minister, Tony Evans, were some notable African American ministers who worked with the organization. While the upper echelon of the organization and its participants were diverse, the audience was mainly comprised of white males. Even with this fact, however, there was still the potential for some significant work to be done in generating racial understanding and a comprehension of the meaning of racial justice.

Unfortunately, upon closer examination of the Promise Keepers' approach toward racial reconciliation it becomes clear why the organization's impact on the issue of race was limited in a number of ways. At the conferences, the emphasis placed on white men and men of color seeking each other out to engage in the process of confession and absolution not only individualized the problem of racism, but also, simultaneously reinforced a discourse of racial homogeneity. In other words, by asking the men to seek each other out based on the skin color, this then became the core factor that defines race. As sociologist John Bartkowski argues further, for the Promise Keepers, "race is indeed reducible to the color of one's skin, for it is only from someone of a decidedly different hue than oneself that forgiveness can be obtained" (Bartkowski 2003: 124).

However, once skin color becomes the main marker of an individual's racial status, that person then becomes a spokesperson for the race to the individual seeking absolution (Bartkowski 2003: 124). Which begs the question, "Is one black man capable of forgiving his white brother's sinful prejudice against the black community?" (Bartkowski 2003: 125).

Hence, the suspicion Reverend Gary Frost of the SBC garnered from other African American Baptists when he spoke for all African Americans in accepting the SBC's apology for their role in supporting slavery and racism. The emphasis on individual prejudice overlooks and downplays the more powerful force of racism embedded in our social structure. By mainly focusing on the individual aspects of racism, the ability to make a meaningful mark on ending it is limited because an individual approach *equalizes* racism's impact. In other words, while both white and African American men can be immorally equal in holding hatred in their hearts toward each other, the power and privilege accrued to each from racism is not equal. By not including in the analysis the ways distribution of resources and accumulation of influence in American society is predicated on the exaltation of whiteness and white supremacy, the Promise Keepers' approach ultimately pictures an imaginary "segregated America in which racial groups are separate but equal" (Bartkowski 2003: 126).

When African American ministers, who in the context of the Promise Keepers garner significant symbolic capital because of their skin color, call on their fellow brothers of color to rid themselves of "the hate that hate produced," but then refuse to call upon the white men in the audience to go back and make their peers and communities aware of the importance of the fight against racism, in both its individual and structural forms, they leave whiteness and white supremacy unchallenged. While strengthening individual relations between men of different races was a fine starting point, when it became the alpha and beta of the Promise Keepers' racial reconciliation mission, the gatherings functioned more as "cathartic events" where racial reconciliation became a "campaign for interpersonal reconciliation" (Harper 2008: 97, 98). And while the African American ministers' participation in the Promise Keepers' program provides some indication of their agreement with the spirit of the organization's notion of racial reconciliation, it is also the case that any expression of difference would most likely have had little impact. Sharon Harper describes what happened to one African American minister who did just that—dared to disagree:

Raleigh Washington was talking about a process that would take the value deeper throughout the PK movement, but his voice was destined to fall on unhearing ears. For he was pressing for the full 'process,' including systemic and structural reconciliation, within a white evangelical organization that conceived of reconciliation using its cultural tools: accountable free will individualism, relationalism, and antistructuralism. (Harper 2008: 101)

The Christian Coalition: Good Samaritans

In the summer of 1996, the nation's attention focused on the south both because of the summer Olympics being held in Atlanta and the rash of racially motivated acts of arson against African American churches. The burning of churches invoked painful memories of a different era when African Americans in the south were under constant assault from domestic, terrorist organizations like the Ku Klux Klan. The church burnings produced outrage and demands from various civil rights organizations and other groups for the federal government to take action in stopping the arsons. One of the organizations that spoke out against the arsons was the Christian Coalition, founded by Pat Robertson and headed by Ralph Reed. Reed held a meeting with African American ministers in Atlanta and out of that meeting came his pledge that the Christian Coalition would pledge one million dollars (in actuality the organization raised close to $750,000) to the effort to rebuild the churches (Marable 1998: 188).

The donation was a part of the Christian Coalition's own racial reconciliation mission, and the centerpiece of that mission was the organization's Samaritan project. Their agenda included a collection of previously advocated right-wing programs aimed at eliminating poverty; federally funded scholarships to allow inner-city children to attend private or parochial schools; empowerment zone programs for inner-city business development; a five hundred dollar tax cut for those participating in volunteer programs aiding the poor; and the removal of restrictions to federal funding to church-based drug rehabilitation programs (Watson 1997: 69). Before the launch of the Samaritan Project the Christian Coalition had been actively mobilizing the African American religious community through various local, grassroots social movements involving pro-life, pro-family, or anti-gambling issues. In its efforts to organize African Americans the Christian Coalition was even willing to jump political boundaries and work with the Democratic party, if this meant furthering their social agenda. This was the case in their efforts to organize thousands of African American Christians in Texas to support African American pro-lifer and former Houston city councilperson, Beverly Clark, in her failed attempt at the Democratic party nomination for Congress (Reed 1996: 221). This was also the case in Reverend Charles Winburn's (of the Kingdom Church) successful run for a seat on Cincinnati's city council. Winburn was the perfect candidate for the Christian Coalition to support because, as Reed states, "Winburn, a registered Democrat, graduated from Christian Coalition training school, and campaigned against gay rights and for welfare reform and school choice" (Reed 1994: 244). In taking on these strategies, Reed recognized that the road to achieving a strong coalition between his socially conservative organization and African American and other communities of color was going to make for a challenging uphill journey, but one worth fighting for:

> If we are truly serious about building bridges to minorities, we must move beyond the white church to make inroads into traditionally Democratic constituencies of color. The liberal and civil rights communities have lost their credibility on virtually every issue, failing to represent the traditionalist view of their constituents on crime, the death penalty, abortion, school choice, and welfare reform. The pro-family movement can compete with the civil rights establishment for minority support if it will make it a priority. (Reed 1994: 241–242)

However, the Christian Coalition did not give up on the idea of trying to incorporate more African American religious leaders and laypersons into the fold of the Republican Party. In 1996, Reverend Earl Jackson, former pastor of the New Cornerstone Exodus Church in Boston Massachusetts, was named the organization's national liaison to African American churches. Jackson, an outspoken black conservative on social issues with his own radio talk show, seemed like the perfect choice, especially since he was also well connected with other socially conservative ministers and had an electronic bully pulpit to propagate his views. Jackson became the front person heading up the Samaritan project, with an additional objective of funneling African Americans into the Republican Party. In the end, Jackson's and the Christian Coalition's efforts to make the Samaritan project successful and usher in blocs of African American voters to the GOP was a complete failure.

The Samaritan Project only lasted one year and the GOP saw very little growth in the numbers of African Americans Republicans. However, the fact that Reverend Jackson's attempt to bring more African Americans into the fold of the Republican Party fell short has not stopped the GOP or other conservative African American ministers from trying.

Reverend Keith Butler of Detroit, Michigan, the head of a Word of Faith mega church that has a membership of over 20,000, is well connected in Republican Party networks.[9] As long as the racial mistrust among African Americans toward the GOP remains, Butler and other black conservative ministers like him will continue to face and fight an uphill battle in shifting African American political loyalties back to the Republican Party.

Faith-Based Policy and Compassionate Conservatism

The Bush administration's proactive efforts to make faith-based programs a staple in American domestic policy is often considered to be the catalyst in the African American faith community's participation in the widening role of the church in social services. As Michael Owens rightfully points out, however, it was Bill Clinton and the passage of his welfare reform act, known as the Personal Responsibility and Work Opportunity Reconciliation Act of 1996 (PRWORA), that played the initial role in opening the door for the African American clergy to take part in delivering social services. According to Owens, the passage of the PRWORA act and enactment of a new group of laws that were part of the act sent a message to the clergy that the government expected them to play a greater role in lowering welfare dependency and poverty in general (Owens 2004: 73). The PRWORA act was part of a larger shift of public functions from the national level to lower levels of the federal system, a process Owens identifies as *devolution*:

> A transformation internal to the state that alters the scale of the activities, redefines government responsibilities for regulating civil society, transfers authority across levels and administrative units of government, redraws the map of government costs and benefits, and changes accessibility and entitlement to government services. (Owens 2004: 74)

It is important to understand the political context in which the PRWORA act was being debated and then enacted. During the mid-nineties, there was a growing sentiment among the public, helped by the advocacy of such social conservatives as Marvin Olasky, that the structure of social welfare programs needed drastic reform in. Olasky, along with other social conservatives, argued that time had shown that the old paradigm of an ever-expanding activist government was ineffective in getting a handle on the problem of chronic poverty. According to the critics, the upward costs of administrating the programs alone were justification for streamlining governmental social welfare practices. Another critique, particularly by Olasky, was that part of the problem with the seeming ineffectiveness of the welfare programs was their lack of a spiritual component. Secular solutions could only go so far in solving the problems of poverty. Instead, more focus needed to be placed on moral, behavioral and spiritual factors, and the lack thereof, that were at play in the causes of those trapped in chronic poverty and perpetual welfare dependency (Owens 2004: 76).

In addition to the criticism of government-based solutions to social problems, urban policy was not on the top of either party's agenda precisely because political support for programs seriously committed to tackling the array of problems besieging urban areas was hard to come by. In fact, race played a central role in the lack of political support for a strong urban agenda, as political scientist Georgia Persons notes, "Urban programs and urban policy had become deeply associated with African Americans and thus were primed for a political backlash" (Persons 2004: 66). Even though President Clinton was a Democrat, he was not one in the reformist liberal mold of Presidents Roosevelt, Kennedy, or Johnson. Instead, Clinton represented the element in the Democratic party that saw the political expediency of both maintaining a "cautious," distant association with African Americans and supporting the agenda of the business sector by loosening the reigns on American capitalism.[10] As Vijay Prashad insightfully points out, Clinton's backing of welfare reform had just as much to do with heeding the business sector's desire for low-cost labor as it did for eliminating the so-called problem of dependency:

> Clinton's feint against welfare freed up the reserve army from its barracks into the battlefield of wage work, where one of the important results was to put pressure on the wages of the service sector. Welfare 'reform' is not the willful result of vicious politicians, but is a condition of globalized capitalism and a failure of nerve among the liberal wing of the mainstream parties to temper the pressure from business for cheap labor. (Prashad 2003: 148–149)

One important provision of the PRWORA act that opened the door to faith-based policies was the Charitable Choice provision. Charitable choice allowed the federal government to provide funding directly to religious organizations that offered social services (Owens 2004). This gave congregations a bigger role in the social service process since under Charitable choice, "states could pay congregations directly with federal funds from the Temporary Assistance for Needy Families (TANF) program, as well as the federal Welfare to Work, Medicaid, supplemental security income, food stamp, Substance Abuse and Mental Health and Community Services Block Grant programs" (Owens 2004: 79). It was the passage of the Charitable Choice provision that influenced George W. Bush to establish the White House Office of Faith-Based and Community Initiatives (WHOFBCI) and to implement such acts as the Charity Aid, Recovery, and Empowerment Act (CARE). Bush's emphasis on incorporating the spiritual community more into the policy fold was an example of what he called "compassionate conservatism," and the major architect behind the crafting of this new conceptual form of conservatism was none other than Marvin Olasky.

A component of compassionate conservatism's philosophy was the inclusion of diverse religious organizations in the handling of poverty, along with a strong belief that the faith-based approach was the most efficient, as argued by Olasky:

> The compassionate conservative goal is to offer a choice of programs: Protestant, Catholic, Jewish, Islamic, Buddhist, atheist.... Judging by the historical record and contemporary testimony, well-managed, faith-based programs are more efficient in fighting poverty, on average, then their nonreligious counterparts.... Faith-based organizations have shown that the best way to teach self-esteem and respect for law is to teach that we are esteemed by a wonderful God who set out for us rules of conduct that benefit society and ourselves.... Therefore, for both pragmatic and philosophical reasons, compassionate conservatives insist that the Bible (or Koran) should not be excluded by judicial fiat from any antipoverty work, including that financed by government, as long as individuals have a choice of programs. (Olasky 2000: 18–19)[11]

It was not lost on Bush and others in the GOP that one group where there could be a positive reception to Bush's faith-based agenda were the African American faith community. As then director of the WHOFBCI,

John DiIulio, stated, "Black Americans are in many ways the most religious people in America" (Black et al. 2004: 103). The response by black religious leaders was varied. Owens ascribes the labels "Advocates, Implementers, and Contestants" to the three stances that some of the black religious leaders took toward charitable choice and other faith-based initiatives.

The group of black ministers that fell into the group of advocates naturally received much attention from the media and among those in policy circles. Proponents of faith-based programs included Pastors T.D. Jakes, Eugene Rivers, Floyd Flake, and Kirbyjohn Caldwell, the latter a close associate of Bush. A couple of months after taking office, and following the contentious 2000 election, Bush had a group of 15 black ministers to the White House to cultivate support for his agenda. As the Rev. Gilbert E. Patterson of Memphis, presiding bishop of the Church of God in Christ stated, "If Bush's program works as intended there would be no reason for Black people to not vote for him four years from now.... We may see the African-American community, for the first time since Abraham Lincoln, supporting a Republican president. The African-American community cannot afford to sit still for four years or eight years with our fingers crossed, waiting for a Democrat. Life goes on" (Thompson 2001: A1).

Even though a sizable number of African American churches are not as active in participating in policy geared toward welfare and poverty, and elect to operate outside of the government-funded social programs, nevertheless there was a critical mass of churches and its leaders who fell into the implementers category (Owens 2004: 89). Two beneficiaries of Bush's faith-based programs were Reverend Herbert Lusk of the Greater Exodus Baptist Church in Philadelphia and Bishop Sedgwick Daniels of Milwaukee. A strong supporter of President Bush, Lusk gave a rousing speech for Bush at the 2000 Republican presidential convention. Lusk's organization then went on to receive over 1 million dollars in federal grants from Bush's faith-based initiative program. Lusk held a support rally for Supreme Court justice Samuel Alito at his church, with other influential members of the Christian right, such as Focus on the Family's James Dobson, Family Research Council's Tony Perkins, and the late Falwell, Jerry in attendance (Edsall 2006: A10). The meeting was the third in a series of meetings dubbed "Justice Sunday" and organized by both the Focus on the Family and Family Research Council organizations to mobilize support for conservative Supreme Court justice nominees. Lusk went on record stating that although he was not familiar with the positions Supreme Court nominee Alito advocated, the fact that he was Bush's selection was enough for him to feel comfortable in endorsing the choice: "I don't know enough about him to say I actually think he's the right man to do the job.... I'm saying I trust a friend of mine who promised me that he would appoint people to the justice system that would be attentive to the needs I care about." (Goodstein 2006: A15). Bishop Daniels, a staunch Democrat who supported both Bill Clinton and Al Gore in previous presidential campaigns, shifted toward President Bush in the 2004 election. Bush aggressively courted Daniels by placing a call to the Bishop and then paying him a visit. Daniels' church received 1.5 million dollars in federal funds; all the while Daniels insisted that it was his commonality with Bush on moral issues and not the money his church received that was the main factor in his switching political alliances (Wallsten and Hamburger 2005: A17).

Bishop Creflo Dollar of Atlanta, Georgia and leader of the Word Changers Church has also been a recipient of President Bush's faith-based initiative. Dollar was awarded a one million dollar grant from the US Administration on Children and Families. Dollar has been a participant in small group discussions with former President Bush along with other influential African American conservative ministers (Posner 2008: 33). The actions of all three of these men, Lusk, Daniels and Dollar, provoke suspicion among some of the black clergy who fall into the third of Owens' categories, the contestants. Some of these latter ministers, such as Reverend Timothy McDonald, president of the African American Ministers Leadership Council, see the flow of federal money to the black churches as a strategy of the Bush administration, "trying to buy the allegiance of the black church." To McDonald this is problematic and helps the wrong people, because it is "to the advantage of the Republican Party, because the black church has been a major thorn in their side" (Prashad 2003: 165). Others worry that the acceptance of money will impact the church's ability to be critical of the administration's future actions and decisions (Owens 2004: 93). And ironically, other forms of criticism articulate strands and themes present in black conservative ideology. One minister saw participation in the faith-based programs as a direct violation of a major component in African American self-help ideology—the value of collective responsibility: "How can we say we're free and independent of white folks...if we go begging to government for relief? We must do for ourselves, with our own money, even if it means we don't solve all of our problems. We must maintain our dignity" (Owens 2004: 93).

The likelihood that African American churches alone could solve the myriad problems facing many of those living in marginal inner-city areas is virtually zero (Owens and Smith 2005: 331).[12] Critics of the Bush administration's faith-based programs worry that the government is asking the church community to do more than it is capable of. In addition, the contestants say the focus on churches is a strategy to redirect responsibility for America's social problems away from the government. Reverend Herb Lusk's church is located in North Philadelphia, one of the city's poorest sections, an area that has suffered greatly from the structural dislocation of deindustrialization and practices of institutional racism such as redlining and discriminatory lending by banks. A wholesale advocacy of shifting responsibility to institutions such as the church overlooks the role the government must play in ameliorating the problems it played a role in producing. Although George W. Bush's tenure in the White House has ended, the black ministers who participated in the faith-based programs have no need to worry. President Barack Obama has decided to continue the operation of faith-based programs with Reverend Joshua DuBois at the helm. The philosophy DuBois and Obama stress in their operation of the program is one of cooperation across party lines, as Obama recently stated: "I don't care if you're a conservative evangelical who's never voted for a Democrat before; we're going to sit down with you and find areas to work together"(Gordy 2009: 84). Only time will tell, but Obama's decision does seem to indicate that when it comes to passing the buck for urban social problems to the churches, neither party is putting up much of a fuss about reducing that aspect of governmental responsibility.

Grassroots Activism in the Culture Wars

Of all of the avenues previously mentioned, none provides religious and nonreligious conservatives with a better chance of establishing a connection with the African American community than working with African Americans at the grassroots level on various social issues. Ever since the 1980s, when those wanting to have society uphold and honor traditional values were viewed as mainly white social and religious conservatives, contestation over such issues as education, pornography, entertainment content, abortion, and gay rights have fallen under the rubric of the "culture wars." As these wars progressed into the 1990s, the traditional values movement seemed to diversify and a number of African Americans began adding their voices to the social conservative movement. In reality, African American voices, particularly those from the black church, had always been active and present in these discussions, as evidenced by the long history of the black anti-abortion movement trying to mobilize African Americans against abortion. And as Reverend Johnny Hunter of North Carolina, the founder and leader of the largest African American anti-abortion organization (Life Education and Resources Network, i.e., L.E.A.R.N.) continues to assert:

> In reaching the African American community and the traditional black church...the primary goal of LEARN is to facilitate a strong, viable grassroots network of African American and minority pro-life and pro-family advocates who are motivated by their love for Jesus Christ and their neighbors, and by the devastating impact abortion has on mothers and their children. (Prisock 2003: 6–7)

Rev Hunter has also taken on the role of attempting to mobilize African Americans into the Republican Party. And like his counterpart Rev Earl Jackson, Hunter has seen little success for his efforts. But even with the continued inability to translate social conservatism among African Americans into political conservatism doesn't mean the opportunities are not there for the formation of a black-white conservative coalition.

THE ENTREPRENEURIAL MINISTER ON A MISSION: THE REV. FLOYD FLAKE

The educational realm is another area in which a black-white conservative coalition could form, as public school systems comprised of black and brown children in many urban areas continue to become poorer and the urgency to find solutions to their structural problems grows with each passing day. Another minister, Reverend Floyd H. Flake, the senior pastor of the mega church (with a membership of over 22,000) Greater Allen African Methodist Episcopal Cathedral in Jamaica, Queens, has taken up the call to push educational reform through the use of school choice programs. Rev. Flake is also the president of Wilberforce University and a former member of the United States House of Representatives.

Raised by a family with a strong belief in self-reliance, the power of education and Christian morality, Flake has taken these values gleaned from his upbringing and applied them to his broader, spiritual philosophy of life. In 2000, Flake authored the book, *The Way of the Bootstrapper: Nine Action Steps for Achieving Your Dreams*, a treatise that blends the philosophies of personal responsibility, economic self-sufficiency, patriotism, respect for elders and cooperative action. Reverend Floyd Flake's involvement in education stems from his time as the director of student affairs at the historically black Lincoln University, through his tenure as Dean of Students at Boston University, to his presidency of his alma mater, Wilberforce University in Wilberforce, Ohio, also a historically black institution. Flake's decade-long term as a New York Democratic congressman came to an end when he stepped down to focus more of his energies toward leadership of his church. Greater Allen African Methodist Episcopal Cathedral, has an annual budget of more than twenty million, which not only takes care of church expenses but also funds a nursing home, housing complexes, various strip malls, real estate properties, and an independent Christian school (Morken and Formicola 1999).

In many ways Rev. Flake is the epitome of the traditional black minister, as Morken and Formicola describe:

> Historically, they have been the religious and political leaders of their communities. At times they have been at the forefront in the battles for freedom, equality, and moral righteousness in the United States. Until recently they have been the best-educated and most respected members of their often-marginalized societies. They have connections to the white members of their towns and state power structures. They serve as liaisons and buffers between black and white constituencies in local politics. (Morken and Formicola 1999: 210)

However, Flake has made it clear that in his mind, he and other ministers like him are not of the mold of the traditional African American ministers in terms of how they think they can best serve the black community. Whereas the traditional ministers, according to Flake, focused on the working toward social justice and political power, he and his peers see the black community's interest as best served by focusing on developing a strong pulse for entrepreneurship among African Americans: "We've realized that the political-social model we've been operating on in the last 30 years is bankrupt" (Harrison 2005: 139). During Flake's time in office he became adept at crossing over political lines. Due to his advocacy of entrepreneurship, his socially conservative beliefs, and his support for school choice, Flake has often joined alliances with conservatives. During former Governor George Pataki's re-election bid Flake appeared on television with the governor to announce Pataki's support for charter schools (Harrison 2005: 211). Flake also supported Republican mayors Rudy Giuliani and Michael Bloomberg in their campaigns for mayor of New York City, and Ken Blackwell's unsuccessful bid to be governor of Ohio.[13] Currently, he is a senior fellow at the conservative think tank the Manhattan Institute where he writes on issues relating to school choice. However, Reverend Flake's political affiliation as a Democratic, his conservative views on social issues, and his community activism also place him within both the advocate and implementer roles that Michael Owens has laid out in his typology (Owens 2004: 88). When asked about his connections with conservatives and Republicans Flake explains his desire not to be bound by political labels by stating:

> I don't think God is Republican or Democrat. I think God is apolitical, and so we have to become apolitical enough to be strong and important leaders in the communities we are part of, and when we do that, government then will seek us out and want to partner with us, so that 'faith-based' does not become just rhetoric, but becomes a reality.[14]

THE FUTURE OF THE WHITE AND BLACK RELIGIOUS RIGHT COALITION

Whether the issue is how to provide quality education to African American children, or how to uphold the sanctity of the institution of marriage, these and other sociocultural issues will continue to provide avenues for the development of a coalition of white and black Christian conservatives. It remains to be seen what social, ideological, and political effects these contemporary stirrings of such a coalition among the leaders of the black religious right will have on the future. On the one hand, the possibilities for future alliances looks strong if the foundation of the coalition is centered on continuing the cultural wars that took place during the 1980s and 1990s. There seems to be no shortage of African American conservative ministers who are outspoken about their opposition to gay rights, gay marriage, abortion, or laws banning prayer in public schools. The strident promotion of American capitalism—whether in the form of Rev. Floyd Flake's call to develop black entrepreneurial infrastructures in black communities, or in the advocacy of a spiritual version of capitalism conveyed through the preaching of the prosperity gospel—is another area of unification for the two sides of white conservatives and the black religious right.[15]

Those African American ministers who advocate the benefits of the prosperity gospel seem to be as comfortable calling the Republican Party their political home as do their white counterparts. One such example is Reverend Keith Butler, both a preacher of the prosperity gospel and a strident Republican Party activist and former Detroit city councilman (the first Republican councilman elected since before World War II) who lost in the GOP's primary for the senate race.[16] Claiming the Republican Party for their political identity is not strictly for black ministers who preach prosperity however. Others find the Republican Party the best political option for carrying out the true mission of Christianity. It is this belief, fed by conservative organizers and black preachers, that could lay the groundwork for an even broader and more long-lasting social conservatism amongst African Americans based on the coming together of Christian values, black identity, and conservative ideology. During the historical presidential campaign and eventual election of the nation's first African American president, a number of black conservative ministers were not as enthusiastic about the prospect of Barack Obama winning the White House. Bishop Gilbert Coleman, pastor of the 1000-member Freedom Christian Fellowship in Philadelphia, felt that African Americans were not evaluating then-senator Obama on his merits as a Christian: "Some of the basic tenets of the Christian faith he does not hold to. The homosexual agenda, abortion and things he's said about the economy are unsettling. He does not take a true position as it relates to his own Christianity" (Duin 2008). While these sentiments were not powerful enough to override the historic importance of Obama's election for African American voters, they do have the potential to shape the parameters of what Obama or any other progressive politician feels they can stand for in an increasingly Christianized and conservative public sphere.

Those black conservative ministers whose views support the legitimacy of whiteness and white supremacy in American society will also strengthen the relationship between the black and white religious right. The Reverend Jessie Lee Peterson of Los Angeles and founder of the conservative community-based organization, The Brotherhood Organization of A New Destiny (BOND), has garnered much media exposure in his appearances on Fox News and on his nationally syndicated radio show, which is now heard also online. Peterson is no stranger to controversy since he is known for regularly making comments about African Americans that are more denigrating than supportive. Peterson described the African Americans left behind during the wake of Hurricane Katrina in New Orleans as, "primarily immoral, welfare-pampered blacks that stayed behind and waited for the government to bail them out" (Peterson 2005a). In a follow-up article, Peterson related the positive feedback he received from his previous article about hurricane Katrina, explaining further that the validation he was receiving was in part due to the fact that he, "said what white Americans know to be true, but are afraid to say.... *Everyone* knows most of black America is screwed up – immoral, dependent, weak – but so few are able to say so" (Peterson 2005b).

Other adept ministers support whiteness and white supremacy even within the context of reaffirming African Americans. For example, in one of his sermons, Rev. Herb Lusk exalted those African Americans who made inroads into the American mainstream economically and occupationally. While encouraging his congregation to acknowledge the sacrifices that were made by previous generations of African Americans, Lusk also introduced his congregation to the current president of the Focus on the Family organization, who happened to be sitting in the audience. Lusk announced: "Listen to me, folks, a house divided against itself cannot stand. And what your pastor's trying to do is to build bridges, not walls but bridges; there are people on the other side that love Jesus just as much as we do" (Bradley Hagerty 2006). The "people on the other side" whom Lusk is referring to may love their vision of Jesus and Christianity, but Focus on the Family has no history of fighting for racial justice and equality. In fact, the organization has been outspoken in its opposition to various actions taken by the government to eradicate the racial status quo in America, one that continues to support the supremacy of whiteness. As scholar Paul Apostolidis points out, Focus on the Family founder James Dobson has gone on record to state that since there is still "anger and hostility" between the races even with the passage of government programs such as affirmative action, this is the evidence that such "governmental programs" are unable to "solve the problem" of racial discrimination (Apostolidis 2000: 215).

On the other hand, the relationship between white and black conservative Christians has also had its difficult moments. Race continues to be the proverbial match that could send this coalition up in flames. In the late 1990s, Rev. Fred Price made headlines with his declaration condemning American Christianity for its racism. Price stated, "Religion has been the most flagrant perpetrator of racism in the world.... In particular, the Christian church in America has been the leader of racism in the world and particularly in America" (Graham 1999: 44). Price's disgust with the church came after he heard a tape of a sermon given by the son of his mentor, the late Kenneth Hagin Sr., in which Hagin Jr. preached against interracial marriage. Along similar lines, Reverend Kirbyjohn Caldwell established a website named "James Dobson doesn't speak for me" in response to a radio broadcast by James Dobson where he provided a critical examination of a speech on faith and public policy by then presidential candidate Obama addressed to an evangelical organization. Dobson's critique of Obama's speech called his declaration of his Christian faith into question, but it was the mere fact that Dobson would think he could decide best the legitimacy of Obama's faith, more so than Obama himself, which outraged Caldwell: "I think it's a crime and a shame that Senator Obama has had to explain the fact that he's a Christian.... Criticize his politics. Criticize his stance on whatever, but don't question his faith. Never in the history of American politics has someone said that he is a Christian and someone came back to say, 'No you're not.'" The questioning of President Obama's faith went beyond whether his views on social issues fell in line with those of social conservatives such as Dobson. There was also an anti-Islamic and xenophobic component to the suspicion among those on the right. One theory circulating within conservative networks is that President Obama is a Muslim with a hidden agenda to destroy America, and that he is not an actual American citizen. In terms of the latter, queries about the authenticity of President Obama's birth certificate in Hawaii have been growing since Obama took office.

There are many instances in which the attacks on President Obama by those in the Christian right have been racist in tone. One occurred at an annual Value Voters Summit meeting sponsored by the Family Research Council, a group that has gone into black communities to mobilize black ministers against gay marriage. At one of the exhibits two entrepreneurs with strong connections to Christian right organizations were selling boxes of waffle mix with a depiction Obama on the cover that was reminiscent of the stereotypical image of Aunt Jemima. On the top flap of the box was a cartoon of Obama "in a turban, next to an arrow printed with the text: Point box toward Mecca for tastier waffles."

The Christian right's differing views on race, and persistent racism at its worst, continues to raise the question of how effective it can be in integrating ordinary African Americans into its fold. Connections with prominent African American religious leaders have yet to yield a significant show of support or expressions of acceptance among their congregations. In their study of African American participation in a white missionary organization, Marla F. McGlathery and Traci Griffin point out that cultural differences within the organization, the stigma of the organization within the African American community, and the influence of race in shaping the organization's relationship to political conservatism, all combined to complicate the integration and full acceptance of African Americans (McGlathery and Griffin 2007). Sociologists Michael Emerson and Christian Smith argue that the challenge facing the white Christian right will be its ability to adopt a different cultural understanding of race:

> White evangelicals' cultural tools and racial isolation direct them to see the world individualistically and as a series of discrete incidents. They also direct them to desire a color-blind society. Black evangelicals tend to see the racial world very differently. Ironically, evangelicalism's cultural tools lead people in different social and geographical realities to assess the race problem in divergent and non-reconciliatory ways. (Emerson and Smith 2000: 91)

Political scientist Carrin Robinson sums it up best by stating, "social conservatism alone does not appear to be able to bridge the divide that remains" between the white Christian right and African Americans. And yet, even with the present challenges the emergence of an active and vocal conservative segment of the African American faith community should not be taken lightly or dismissively, particularly given the central role the church as an institution within the African American community. Historically the black church has been both "a preserver of African American heritage and an agent for reform." The extent of the impact of an increasingly visible and well-funded African American conservative Christians, both for the social betterment of the African American community and in the influence of conservative ideologies in American society at large, remains to be seen.

NOTES

1. As theologian Jonathan Walton documents, African American participation in religious broadcasting has a long and rich history dating back
   to the religious race records of the early twentieth century and the first
   religious radio broadcasts by African American ministers such as Elder
   Solomon Lightfoot Michaux during the late 1920s. For a concise discussion of this history see pages 33–41 in Walton (2009).
2. Bill Hybels is often credited with sparking the growth of mega churches
   in the United States when he opened his mega church, Willow Creek
   Community Church of Great Barrington, IL, in 1975. Before founding
   his church Hybels went door to door and asked residents to name various factors that were keeping them away from attending church regularly.
   Hybels then organized his church around the data he collected, for example, instituting a casual dress code, modernizing the music, and using
   theatrics in his sermons.
3. According to Milmon F. Harrison, while many view Frederick Price
   of Los Angeles as the main figure to introduce the African American
   faith community to prosperity gospel, in fact there were two other figures before Price that can be credited with this introduction, Reverend
   Johnnie Coleman and Frederick Eikerenkoetter, otherwise known as
   Reverend Ike (Harrison 2005: 134–137).
4. See *With God On Our Side*, William Martin's impressive sociological
   examination of the rise of the Religious right (1996).
5. As quoted at http://www.sbc.net/resolutions.
6. Ibid.
7. The SBC has been a strong supporter of the Republican Party's positions on a variety of issues, including the Republican Right's central idea
   concerning the need for a diminishing of the role of government. This
   directly conflicts with African Americans' sense that racial progress has
   resulted not only through the combination of hard work and sacrifice on
   the part of African Americans, but also, an activism that has pressured the
   government to enact policies and create laws aimed to end racism and
   lessen racial inequality.
8. James Wright, "Southern Baptist Minister Prays for Obama's Death."
   Baltimore Afro-American, June 21, 2009, http://www.afro.com/
   SearchIndexer/tabid/461/itemid/3937/Default.aspx. According to
   Wright, Rev. Drake was quoted on a Fox News radio program as stating:
   "If he does not turn to God and does not turn his life around, I am asking God to enforce imprecatory prayers that are throughout the Scripture
   that would cause him death."

9. For a detailed summary of Butler's history with the Republican Party (see Posner 2008: 31–32).

10. By describing Clinton as maintaining a "cautious" distance from African Americans I am essentially speaking to the manner in which he was able to make several symbolic gestures and overtures to his African American constituents to keep their support (the appointment of several African Americans to his cabinet, his speaking out against racism when the time called for it or commissioning panels to hold national discussions about race, even his willingness to appear on entertainment venues with African American hosts), while on the other hand, sending the message to whites that he was not beholden to blacks (for example, with his criticism of Sister Soulja in comments made during a speech given to Rev. Jessie Jackson's PUSH organization, and his entertaining the idea that race based social policies such as affirmative action were not "untouchable," which he captured with the ambiguous phrase "mend it don't end it."

11. According to Olasky, compassionate conservatism has seven major principles. One of the bedrock principles is the focus on returning to the basics. According to principle number two—Basic, "compassionate conservatives choose the most basic means of bringing help to those who need it the most." This is in essence a call for a return to a more traditionalist form of conservatism where the emphasis is placed on the utilization of alternative institutions to solve the various social problems that arise in modern society. Instead of working from a top down, governmental approach, the opposite should be used: a bottom-up approach that begins with seeking help from within the family, and if not there then from social networks within one's community or organizations in the community, and if outside organizations are needed they would operate with significant input from members of the community being served. The government should only be brought in as a last resort and, if so, it too should start at the local level and work up to the federal (Olasky 2000: 17).

12. As Owens and Smith elaborate, "Congregations in low-income neighborhoods, as we observed in the public housing neighborhoods, do not provide social services in areas that directly increase self-sufficiency among the residents of impoverished places…. [T]he social services of congregations in low-income may not help people 'get ahead', even if they help them 'get by'" (331).

13. Both Blackwell and Flake share a devout social and religious conservatism that has brought criticism to both men from other African American political and community leaders.

14. As quoted in a profile of Floyd Flake, September 24, 2004, Episode no. 804, www.pbs.org/wnet/religionandethics/week804/profile.htm.

15. According to theologian Robert M. Franklin, the ministers who preach prosperity gospel are nothing more than spiritual entrepreneurs that, through their advocacy of this philosophy, transform Christianity into an "investment" when done properly that provides "yield" in material wealth (Franklin 2007: 119).

16. As journalist Sarah Posner points out, the Republican Party has courted prosperity gospel preachers because they have "huge followings and are therefore worth cultivating for votes" (Posner 2008: 13).

REFERENCES

Allitt, Patrick. *Religion in America Since 1945: A History.* New York: Columbia University Press, 2003.

Apostolidis, Paul. *Stations of the Cross: Adorno and Christian Right Radio.* Durham, NC: Duke University Press, 2000.

Bartkowski, John. *The Promise Keepers: Servants, Soldiers, and Godly Men.* New Brunswick, NJ: Rutgers University Press, 2003.

Black, Amy E., Douglas L. Loopman, and David K. Ryden. *Of Little Faith: The Politics of George W. Bush's Faith-Based Initiatives.* Washington, DC: Georgetown University Press, 2004.

Bradley Hagerty, Barbara. "Conservative Black Clergy Make Waves from Pulpit." Transcript of Broadcast on NPR *All Things Considered* Broadcast, April 6, 2006, www.npr.org.

Bretthauer, Berit. "The Challenge of Televangelism." *Peace Review*, vol. 7, no. 1, 1995.

Chaves, Mark. "All Creatures Great and Small: Megachurches in Context." *Review of Religious Research*, June 2006.

Crespino, Joseph. "Civil Rights and the Religious Right." In *Rightward Bound: Making America Conservative in the 1970s.* Eds. Bruce J. Schulman and Julian E. Zelizer. Cambridge, MA: Harvard University Press, 2008.

Douglas, Kelly Brown. *Sexuality and the Black Church: A Womanist Perspective.* Maryknoll, NY: Orbis Books, 1999.

Duin, Julia. "Pro-life Black Pastors Wary of Obama." *Washington Times*, July 4, 2008, www.washingtontimes.com/news/2008/jul/04/black-pastors-wary-of-obama/6.

Edsall, Thomas B. "Christian Right Mobilizes for Judge." *Washington Post*, January 9, 2006: A10.

Emerson, Michael O., and Christian Smith. *Divided by Faith: Evangelical Religion and the Problem of Race in America.* New York, NY: Oxford University Press, 2000.

Franklin, Robert M. *Crisis in the Village: Restoring Hope in African American Communities*. Minneapolis, MN: Fortress Press, 2007.

Friedland, Michael B. *Lift Up Your Voice Like a Trumpet: White Clergy and the Civil Rights and Antiwar Movements, 1954–1973*. Chapel Hill: University of North Carolina Press, 1998.

Goodstein, Laurie. "Minister, a Bush Ally, Gives Church as Site for Alito Rally." *The New York Times*, January 5, 2006: A15.

Gordy, Cynthia. "Where Church and State Meet." *Essence*, August 2009: 84.

Graham, Rhonda B. "Holy War: Rev. Fred Price is Fighting the Church Over the Racism." *Emerge Magazine*, January 1999.

Greenblatt, Alan, and Tracie Powell. "Rise of the Megachurches." In *CQ Researcher: Rise of the Megachurches: Are They Straying Too Far from Their Mission?* September 21, 2007.

Griffin, Horace L. *Their Own Receive Them Not: African American Lesbians & Gays in Black Churches*. Cleveland, OH: The Pilgrim Press, 2006.

Hadden, Jeffrey K. "The Rise and Fall of American Televangelism." *Annals of the American Academy of Political and Social Science*, vol. 527, Religion in the Nineties, May 1993.

Hankins, Barry. *Uneasy in Babylon: Southern Baptist Conservatives and American Culture*. Tuscaloosa: The University of Alabama Press, 2002.

Harper, Lisa Sharon. *Evangelical≠ Republican…or Democrat*. New York, NY: The New Press, 2008.

Harrison, Milmon F. *Righteous Riches: The Word of Faith Movement in Contemporary African American Religion*. New York, NY: Oxford University Press, 2005.

Hodgson, Godfrey. *The World Turned Right Side Up: A History of the Conservative Ascendancy in America*. Boston, MA: Mariner Books, 1997.

Hudnet-Beumler, James. *In Pursuit of the Almighty Dollar: A History of Money and American Protestantism*. Chapel Hill: University of North Carolina Press, 2007.

Karnes, Kimberly, Wayne McIntosh, Irwin L. Morris, and Shanna Pearson-Merkowitz. "Mighty Fortress: Explaining the Spatial Distribution of American Megachurches." *Journal for the Scientific Study of Religion*, vol. 46, no. 2, 2007: 261–268.

Kroll, Luisa. "Christian Capitalism: Megachurches, Megabusinesses." *Forbes*, September 17, 2003.

Lee, Shayne. *T.D. Jakes: America's New Preacher*. New York: New York University Press, 2005.

Marable, Manning. *Black Liberation in Conservative America*. Boston, MA: South End Press, 1998.

Martin, William. *With God on Our Side: The Rise of the Religious Right in America*. New York: Broadway Books, 1996.

McGlathery, Marla Frederick, and Traci Griffin. "Becoming Conservative, Becoming White?: Black Evangelicals and the Para-Church Movement." In *This Side of Heaven: Race, Ethnicity, and Christian Faith*. Eds. Robert J. Priest and Alvaro L. Nieves. New York, NY: Oxford University Press, 2007.

Morken, Hubert, and Jo Renee Formicola. *The Politics of School Choice*. Lanham, MD: Rowman and Littlefield, 1999.

Olasky, Marvin. *Compassionate Conservatism: What It Is, What It Does, and How It Can Transform America*. New York: The Free Press, 2000.

Owens, Michael Leo. "Contestant, Advocate, Implementer: Social Services and the Policy Roles of African American Churches." In *Long March Ahead: African American Churches and Public Policy in Post-civil Rights America, The Public Influences of African American Churches, Volume II*. Ed. R. Drew Smith. Durham, NC: Duke University Press, 2004.

Owens, Michael Leo, and R. Drew Smith. "Congregations in Low-Income Neighborhoods and the Implications for Social Welfare Policy Research." *Nonprofit and Voluntary Sector Quarterly*, vol. 3, no. 35, 2005.

Persons, Georgia A. "National Politics and Charitable Choice as Urban Policy for Community Development." *The Annals of the American Academy*, vol. 594, July 2004.

Peterson, Jessie Lee. "Moral Poverty Cost Blacks in New Orleans." September 21, 2005a, www.worldnetdaily.com.

———. "Truth: Solution to Black America's Moral Poverty."October 7, 2005b, www.worldnetdaily.com.

Posner, Sarah. *God's Profits: Faith, Fraud, and the Republican Crusade for Values Voters*. Sausalito, CA: PoliPoint Press, 2008.

Prashad, Vijay. *Keeping Up with the Dow Joneses: Debt, Prison, Workfare*. Boston, MA: South End Press, 2003.

Prisock, Louis G. "If You Love Children, Say So: The African American Anti-Abortion Movement." *The Public Eye*, Fall 2003.

Reed, Ralph. *Politically Incorrect: The Emerging Faith Factor in American Politics*. Dallas, TX: Word Publishing, 1994.

———. *Active Faith: How Christians Are Changing the Soul of American Politics*. New York: The Free Press, 1996.

Thompson, Azure. "Bush Meets with Black Clergy." *Afro-American Red Star*. Washington, DC, March 24, 2001: A1.

Thurman, Scott. "United States Has More Megachurches Than Previously Thought." *Hartford Seminary*, 2005. Web report, http://www.hartsem.edu/events/news_mega.htm.

Townsend Gilkes, Cheryl. *If It Wasn't for the Women: Black Women's Experience and Womanist Culture in Church and Community*. Maryknoll, NY: Orbis Books, 2001.

————. "Plenty of Good Room: Adaptation in a Changing Black Church." *Annals of the American Academy of Political and Social Science*, vol. 558, Americans and Religions in the Twenty-First Century, July 1998.

Wallsten, Peter, and Tom Hamburger. "Bush Rewarded by Black Pastors' Faith." *Los Angeles Times*, January 18, 2005: A17.

Walton, Jonathan L. *Watch This: The Ethics and Aesthetics of Black Televangelism.* New York: New York University Press, 2009.

Watson, Justin. *The Christian Coalition: Dreams of Restoration, Demands for Recognition.* New York: St. Martin's Press, 1997.

CHAPTER 9

Epilogue—Looking Back, Looking Forward: The Future of Black Conservatism in the Twenty-First Century

When I was writing the introduction to this book the country was in the midst of the 2016 presidential election, businessman, reality star, Donald Trump was confounding experts with his continued status as the front-runner for the Republican Party's nomination. Even as Trump captured the GOP nomination the majority of analysts and media pundits predicted his Democratic Party counterpart Hillary Clinton would win the general election handily. In Truman like fashion Donald Trump pulled a major upset by defeating Hillary Clinton to become the 45th president of the United States. In addition to capturing the White House the GOP went on to become the majority in both the Senate and Congress giving them all three branches of government. Even so, this development did not quell the concern among conservatives who opposed President Trump's candidacy from the start and for good reason. The potential crisis with North Korea where President Trump and North Korean leader Kim Jong-un exchanged insults and threats of using their nation's nuclear weapons on each other, the investigation of Russia's interference in the 2016 election and Trump's alleged connection to Russia, his continued use of Twitter castigating anyone or anything that provoked his ire making him look less and less presidential, and of course his problematic response to the violence in Charlottesville Virginia that took place between white supremacists and anti-racist protestors where white nationalist James Fields drove his car into a crowd killing anti-racist protestor Heather Heyer. Many were disturbed with President Trump attributing blame to both sides and stating that there was some

© The Author(s) 2018
L. G. Prisock, *African Americans in Conservative Movements*,
https://doi.org/10.1007/978-3-319-89351-8_9

"very fine people" among the white nationalists. President Trump's appearance of providing cover for white supremacy has been a major concern for some conservatives who want conservatism to move beyond its problematic racial history and fear that the outspokenness of a radical white nationalist branch of conservatism known as the Alt-Right, establishes the impression that conservatism has reverted back to the "bad old days of the 1950s." For African American conservatives, especially those that support President Trump, the question remains how can they grow their ranks within the black community, especially if many of their African American peers equate support of President Trump and or his policies with embracing white supremacy?

One discovery I had as I finished this project was how apt that timeless adage "the more things change the more they stay the same" is. The African American pro-life movement lost its foundational leader when Mildred Jefferson passed away in 2010. In spite of the loss of their pioneer the African American pro-life movement continues working toward stopping, in their words, the "black genocide" that is taking place in the black communities across the nation and bringing more African Americans to their cause. Dr. Day Gardner, Star Parker, and Dr. Alveda King continue to be visible figures of the movement along with Reverend Johnny Hunter and his organization L.E.A.R.N. Kay Cole James has gone on to make history by becoming the first African American woman to head a conservative think tank. In December of 2017, James was named president of the Heritage Foundation, one of the "big four"[1] conservative think tanks. In fact, James is the first African American to lead a conservative think tank. James comes in on the heels of turmoil at Heritage under the leadership of her predecessor James DeMint. While James' expanding profile within the Right signals the increasing diversification of the conservative movement, she still has some concerns, and doubts, about conservatives ability to accept the growing demographical changes taking place in the country.

> I am extremely concerned about the inability of the Christian community, the conservative community, and the Republican Party to deal with the browning of America. We tend as conservatives to stay right in our communities, to hold rallies where we get ourselves energized. (Olasky 2013)

James acknowledges, "Overt racism in America is gone" but she is clear that doesn't mean racism has disappeared altogether as "covert racism is alive and well. I see it every day in subtle ways" (Olasky 2013).

Meanwhile, activists like Star Parker and others are paying close attention to what the pulse is at the grassroots level as evident by their appropriation of the phrase "black lives matter" to "black women matter" and "black children matter." As Parker states, "Many are now starting to connect the dots, that it's not just the police that have it out for African Americans in poor communities…It's also abortionists" (Cunningham 2015). Parker's equating abortion to the material conditions of the inner city African Americans within a conspiratorial context is a common rhetorical strategy among African American conservative social activists. Unfortunately, race continues to be a problem within the anti-abortion movement as the movement is still segregated. One white pro-life leader acknowledged that it is still a challenge to get white organizations and its members to support and appear at rallies organized by African American groups. As well, rallies by white pro-life groups tend to be attended mainly by whites with very few African Americans present. Structurally, the anti-abortion movement is definitely separate but not equal as some of the white organizations, like the National Right To Life, bring in close to seven million dollars annually, the same cannot be said for African American organizations. Only a few African American organizations are registered as 501(c) 3 non-profits and none raise enough money to be required to report their collection. To be eligible to file a regular 990-disclosure form with the Internal Revenue System an organization must bring in yearly a minimum of two hundred thousand dollars. African American pro-lifers identify several factors that contribute to their difficulty in marshaling significant contributions (Cunningham 2015). First, they point to the difficulty in getting many of their peers to provide money due to the continued negative image some blacks have of the anti-abortion movement as one that is both violent and racist. Second, black pro-lifers claim because white activists and pro-lifer supporters know African Americans tend to vote overwhelmingly for the Democratic party they assume African Americans are more liberal on social issues like abortion and therefore are less inclined to view the African American pro-life organizations as a worthy investment of time and money. Finally, some black pro-lifers feel the larger predominately white organization could do a better job of working with them; such as helping black pro-life organizations get more exposure to larger white activist audiences (Cunningham 2015).

Like the black pro-life movement the black school voucher movement lost its pioneering leader when Annette "Polly" Williams died in 2014. Williams helped establish school choice programs in her hometown of Milwaukee and other cities across the nation. While Williams was at one point the darling of her white conservative peers over time she became a steady thorn in their side with her continuing critique of their racism and questioning the genuineness of their concern for inner city black children. By the time Williams retired from the political scene she had become deeply alienated by the direction the school choice movement was taking. The advocacy by white activists and politicians to make school choice programs universal was what Williams suspected would happen, meaning whites were using improving poor black children educational opportunities as a front for their real motive—keeping their children out of schools that had black children. After Williams retired her protégé Howard Fuller took over the leadership role that she had once occupied, the transition was not a smooth one as tensions developed between the two with Williams accusing Fuller of becoming the white conservatives next black token and Fuller firing back that Williams was just bitter and jealous. Before Williams's death the two managed to get back on speaking terms and after Williams passed Fuller spoke highly of his mentor and all of her valuable contributions. Fuller continues to be the face of the black school choice movement, although his organization the Black Alliance for Educational Options (BAEO) had to close its doors after 18 years in operation due to insolvency. BAEO's closing is significant in two ways, first, it was the only group at the national level exclusively focused on expanding school choice for poor and working-class African American families through voucher programs or charter schools. Second, and more importantly, it had functioned as a pipeline for developing up and coming black school choice activists. Fuller attributed his organization's troubles to the increasing competition for funding and visibility (Prothero 2017). Nevertheless given the consistent support from African Americans for charter schools and choice programs Fuller and other black school advocates will continue to have a voice in the debate over what's the best option for black families in providing quality education to their children.

When the Supreme Court on June 26, 2015 ruled that same sex marriage was legal in all fifty states that seemed to be the death knell for the anti-LGBTQ rights movement. But for activists like Bishop Harry Jackson, pastor of a mega church in Maryland, there is too much at stake to stop fighting- the survival of the black family. According to Jackson, his mission to keep protecting traditional marriage is "in part simply an acknowledgment of the concern that redefinition of marriage will further undermine the structure of families in our community in which more than 7 out of 10 children are born out of marriage" (Jackson 2015). Ironically, while Jackson and other black anti-LGBTQ rights activists continue to view their cause through a raced lens, they continue to not acknowledge nor care that their actions hurts one segment of the community-African American LGBTQ individuals. In fact, Jackson and others must keep the LGBTQ portion of the black community invisible so as to legitimize their claim they are fighting for the best interest of *all* blacks in the community.

The recent presidential election again showed the Republican Party's inability to attract African American voters at the national level. President Trump like his GOP presidential predecessors garnered less than ten percent of the African American vote and with African Americans feeling more alienated from the GOP with Trump at the helm, the task of African American Republicans to increase the numbers of African Americans has become more daunting. As sociologist Corey Fields states while there is a desire from Republican leaders to attract more African Americans to the party the inability of the GOP to move away from the entrenched racial thought paradigm about African Americans continues to hinder any major progress:

> The leadership of the Republican Party has made it very clear that they want more people who identify as black among their ranks...and it has dedicated time and money to outreach efforts. At the same time, Republicans stubbornly stick to a very particular set of ideas about black people. Representatives of the party have consistently been linked to events that reflect an anti-black sentiment, to racist statements, and to ideas about black pathology. (Fields 2016: 196)

The tasks of convincing more African Americans to invest their political capital toward the Republican Party and their agenda is even more difficult for those African American Republicans who eschew a color blind philosophy for a more race-conscious approach. As Fields notes, race conscious African American Republicans tended to have a "much more contentious relations with white Republican leaders" (Fields 2016: 197). So long as there is a favoring of color blind African American Republicans over the black Republicans who believe race advocacy and conservatism do not have to be mutually exclusive, more time and money poured into outreach efforts will yield very little improvement over what has already been garnered. Somehow the leadership of the

GOP must come to realize that the two approaches: color blindness and race consciousness can have a place in the big tent if Republicans hope to have more African Americans walk into it.

Present African American conservative intellectuals will continue to be beneficiaries of the intellectual largesse the larger conservative movement can provide them with the well-established and efficient infrastructure that is in place. There will be more black conservative intellectuals to come, contributing their voices to the conservative African American intellectual project as have Thomas Sowell, Shelby Steele, and John McWhorter to name a few. The very talented African American conservative intellectuals will quickly be identified and processed through the conservative intellectual infrastructure where they will become public intellectuals contributing to the national and contentious debate between themselves and black liberal left intellectuals on the state of African Americans in the United States and the severity of America's continuing race problem. It seems the number of African American conservative male intellectuals are endless but the situation for women is vastly different. There are some female black conservative women who are pundits and writers, such as Angela McGlowan and Star Parker. These women are in a sense Gramscian organic intellectuals in that they do not have the training or background as social scientists, academics, or even journalists but they write books, have paper and online columns, and are called upon to provide their opinions by the media to issues pertaining to African Americans. On the other hand, there is a paucity of prominent female conservative African American academic public intellectuals. As of now political scientist Carol Swain at Vanderbilt University is the most recognizable. The paucity of recognizable conservative black female academics is not an indication of a lack of talent; one can only speculate that the smallness of this group could be attributed to a lack of mentorship and support that their male counterparts receive. African American conservative intellectuals of all stripes should view Glenn Loury's experience as a cautionary tale of the potential dangers that can come upon them if they are deemed to have veered too far away from the "acceptable perspectives" conservatives have on issues of race and racism.

The African American Christian Right will continue to be a force in the African American community. With access to large audiences and plentiful resources at their mega churches, religious figures like Reverend T.D. Jakes, Bishop Harry Jackson, Reverends Floyd Flake, and Fred Price will continue to command the attention of their black parishioners with their uplifting and guiding spiritual messages. These and other conservative black ministers will continue to sell the possibility of material and spiritual comfort their prosperity gospel sermons offer while also calling on their parishioners to support conservative agendas like protecting traditional marriage, or warning against the ever dangerous progress of the LGBTQ community. Black women will be reminded that they are the key to the stability of the black family by being good "helpmates" while black men will be told that they must be the protectors, providers, and leaders of the family. The Black Christian right will continue to find it challenging to marshal the social conservatism of their followers into wide spread support for a political conservative agenda as a number of conservative African American ministers have close ties to the Republican Party but are as ineffective as black Republicans in increasing African American support for the GOP. A strength of the conservative African American Christian right is its ability to weather controversies as illustrated by the one involving the late Bishop Eddie Long. Long was the pastor of the New Birth Missionary Baptist Church, a mega church located in Lithonia, Georgia and a staunch opponent of homosexuality. Long's opposition to homosexuality went beyond the pulpit; it included coordinating a rally in Atlanta against same sex marriage (Georgia Voice Editors 2010). Long was known for wearing suits that displayed his muscular frame and putting forth a brawny bravado all of which helped him reinforce his heterosexual masculinity. So when four young African American males from his church accused Long of taking advantage of them sexually the black Christian community was stunned, eyebrows were raised when Long decided to settle out of court with the four young men but Long explained he did so to protect himself, family, and church (Uwumarogie 2016). In the end, the once strapping minister looked weak and gaunt as cancer ravished his body and worst yet, appeared to be a hypocrite that put into question, for some of his followers, the authenticity of his beliefs. The Long controversy raised questions and debates about the merits of the black Christian Right ministers and their philosophy but as before the black Christian Right survived the storm and continued on. One important question is, can the Black Christian Right and white Christian right establish a solid relationship between themselves and the religious communities they answer to? White conservatives feel building alliances with African American conservative Christians can be the access point into cultivating support amongst blacks. Because of the historical racism the white Christian Right has shown toward African Americans the relations between the two camps has been tenuous at best and contentious at worst. For the past twenty-five years attempts have been made to foster a more harmonious racial relationship through racial reconciliation summits or organizations like the Promise Keepers. So far each of these strategies have yielded limited results. For example, Bill McCarthy, founder of the Promise Keepers organization was earnest in his attempt to get men of different racial backgrounds to form bonds around their common identity as male Christians. Unfortunately of the variety of issues raised at Promise Keepers events, race received the least amount enthusiasm from the mainly white male audiences. Race will continue to be the fault line within the conservative Christian community posing the potential of creating a deep fissure under the right circumstances.

Of the four areas this book has examined I believe the social movements realm offers the best opportunity for African Americans conservatives to gain support among its peers due to the continued ability of activists to connect concerns and issues of everyday African Americans with their agenda is what keeps the social movement arena as the one that shows the most potential for African American conservatives. It will be imperative that African American conservatives find ways to provide messages that do not sound like they are parroting their white counterparts. This is not a call for them to shy away from critiques of black leadership and its citizens but instead a challenge for them to offer nuanced visions and solutions to the many problems that face African Americans. For example, through her interviews with everyday black Americans political scientist Angela Lewis illustrates the nuanced ways African Americans who identify as conservatives think. According to Lewis, blacks that identify as conservatives differ from their white peers in that they "are not overtly critical of an active government" (Lewis 2013: 139). Therefore arguments that demonize government are more likely to fall on deaf ears because of the relationship blacks have had with the state. For instance, the public sector has always been an area that provided more employment opportunities for African Americans than the private sector. Accusing African Americans of being "enslaved on the Democratic Party's plantation" will not do much in convincing blacks that it is in their best interest to join the Republican Party, especially when the GOP has shown little progress in making it a hospitable home for blacks. While African Americans realize the Democratic Party often falls short in working toward their best interests they are more often to choose the devil they know over the devil they despise.

Even self identified black conservatives when asked what is the best political strategy for blacks did not suggest working with Republicans but instead forming an independent political party (Lewis 2013: 139). Black conservative critiques of black poverty and the social disarray present in many inner city neighborhoods that are indistinguishable from the ones made by white racists will not command a hearing among fellow blacks, the tough love discourse may win respect and accolades from their white counterparts but not significant support from many African Americans. Being a black conservative and critiquing the continued racism experienced by African Americans do not have to be mutually exclusive, the two can co-exist. In fact, African American conservatism could possibly gain more of a hearing among blacks if *black conscious* conservatives[2] (believers in the power of the collective as in the concept of a linked fate, support traditional family values, self-help philosophy, hard work, self-reliance, and acknowledge the continuing presence of racism) received more exposure in the media and from the larger conservative movement than those who Lewis labels *individualist conservatives* (blacks who strongly believe in individualism, dislike being connected to the black community, and like their white counterparts have an intense distaste for liberal policies such as affirmative action and welfare) (Lewis 2013: 136). In the end, I believe African American conservatives will be able to escape the racial rock and hard place position they find themselves in when American conservatives do the following: first dedicate themselves to minimizing anti-black racism within their ranks and resisting the temptations of using anti-black racism for political or social gain. Second, come to the realization that the key toward a real post-racial society will not come from hiding behind the mirage of color blindness but instead understanding that escaping race calls for a continual focus on how to dismantle all systems of race privileging, that mainly benefits whites, and replacing them with systems that emphasize true equality of opportunity.

NOTES

1. There are many conservative think tanks in the United States but four of them are seen as being in a class by themselves: Heritage Foundation, American Enterprise Institute, Hoover Institute, and the Manhattan Institute.
2. While Lewis calls this group of black conservatives Afrocentric conservatives I prefer the term black conscious as it helps avoid any confusion with blacks that adhere to the more academic definition of Afrocentrism.

L. G. PRISOCK

References

Cunningham, Paige Winfield. "'Black babies matter': The black anti-abortion movement's political problems." *Washington Examiner*, September 28, 2015, https://www.washingtonexaminer.com/black-babies-matter-the-black-antiabortion-movementspoliticalproblems.

Fields, Corey. *Black Elephants in the Room: The Unexpected Politics of African American Republicans*. Berkeley: University of California Press, 2016.

Georgia Voice Editors. "Flashback: Bishop Eddie Long's Anti-gay March Through Atlanta." *The Georgia Voice*, uploaded September 24, 2010, https://thegavoice.com/flashback-bishop-eddie-longs-anti-gay-march-through-atlanta/, accessed February 24, 2018.

Jackson, Harry. "Bishop Harry Jackson: The Supreme Court Just Declared War on the Church." *Charisma News*, uploaded July 1, 2015, https://www.charismanews.com/opinion/50362-bishop-harry-jackson-supremecourt-just-declared-war-on-the-church, accessed February 23, 2018.

Lewis, Angela. *Conservatism in the Black Community: To the Right and Misunderstood*. New York: Routledge, 2013.

Olasky, Marvin. "'The cavalry is not coming' The conservative movement and the GOP, says Kay Coles James, have given up on the black community." *World News*, Feburary 8, 2013, https://world.wngorg/2013/02the_cavalry_is_not_coming.

Prothero, Arianna. "The Only National Black School Choice Advocacy Group Is Folding." *Education Week*, uploaded October 25, 2017, http://blogs.edweek.org/edweek/charterschoice/2017/10/the_only_national_black_school_choice_advocacy_group_is_closing.html, accessed February 23, 2018.

Uwumarogie, Victoria. "Bishop Eddie Long on Considering Suicide During Sexual Misconduct Allegations and Saving His Marriage." *Madamenoire*, uploaded May 25, 2016, http://madamenoire.com/698895/bishop-eddie-long, accessed February 24, 2018.

Bibliography

Abraham, Ken. *Who Are the Promise Keepers?: Understanding the Christian Men's Movement.* New York, NY: Doubleday, 1997.

African American Life Alliance. April 25, 2007, http://www.aala.org.

Allitt, Patrick. *Religion in America Since 1945: A History.* New York: Columbia University Press, 2003.

———. *The Conservatives: Ideas and Personalities Throughout American History.* New Haven, CT: Yale University Press, 2009.

American Life League, Culture of Life Studies Program, Mildred Fay Jefferson, uploaded February 6, 2016, http://cultureoflifestudies.com/newsletter/dr-mildred-fay-jefferson/, accessed February 23, 2018.

Anderson, Faye M. "The Value of Black GOP Activists." *Washington Afro-American,* vol. 106, June 12, 1998: A5.

———. "The Republicans' Illusion of Inclusion." *The New York Times,* August 1, 2000a.

———. "Why I Left." *The Capital Report,* July 8, 2000b: 1, http://www.politicallyblack.com.

———. "Do Some Serious Spring-Cleaning in Your Big Tent…The Stench Has Become Intolerable—Letter of Resignation from the Republican Party." *The Capital Report,* July 8, 2000c: 2, http://www.politicallyblack.com.

Ansell, Amy Elizabeth. *New Right, New Racism: Race and Reaction in the United States and Britain.* New York: New York University Press, 1997.

———. "The Color of America's Culture Wars." In *Unraveling the Right: The New Conservatism in American Politics.* Ed. Amy E. Ansell. Boulder, CO: Westview Press, 1998.

Apostolidis, Paul. *Stations of the Cross: Adorno and Christian Right Radio.* Durham, NC: Duke University Press, 2000.

© The Editor(s) (if applicable) and The Author(s) 2018   349
L. G. Prisock, *African Americans in Conservative Movements,*
https://doi.org/10.1007/978-3-319-89351-8

Asadullah, Samad A. "Between the Lines: Racism in the Church; the Price Is Right." *Los Angeles Sentinel*, April 8, 1998: A7.

Association of American Physicians and Surgeons Newsletter. "AAPS Members Run for Congress," vol. 50, no. 5, May 1994.

Baker, Houston. *Betrayal: How Black Intellectuals Have Abandoned the Ideals of the Civil Rights Era.* New York, NY: Columbia University Press, 2008.

Banerjee, Neela. "Black Churches Struggle Over Their Role in Politics." *New York Times*, March 6, 2005: 15.

Barnes, Fred. "InventaNegro, INC." *The New Republic*, April 15, 1985.

Bartkowski, John. *The Promise Keepers: Servants, Soldiers, and Godly Men.* New Brunswick, NJ: Rutgers University Press, 2003.

Bartlett, Bruce. *Wrong on Race: The Democratic Party's Buried Past.* New York, NY: St. Martin's Press, 2008.

Bartlett Pack, Juluette. "Abortion: The Black Woman's Voice." Pamphlet. Texas Black Americans for Life, 1995.

Benson, Rusty. "Black Community Waking to Most Basic Civil Right: African American Pastors Are New Abolitionists." *American Family Association Journal*, January 2001.

Berlet, Chip. "Following the Threads." In *Unraveling the Right.* Ed. Amy Ansell. Boulder, CO: Westview Press, 1998a.

———. "Who Is Mediating the Storm? Right-Wing Alternative Information Networks." In *Media, Culture, and Religious Right.* Eds. Linda Kintz and Julie Lesage. Minneapolis: University of Minnesota Press, 1998b.

Berlet, Chip, and Matthew N. Lyons. *Right Wing Populism in America: Too Close for Comfort.* New York: Guilford Publisher, 2000.

Billingsley, Andrew. *Climbing Jacob's Ladder: The Enduring Legacy of African American Families.* New York, NY: Simon and Schuster, 1992, p. 6.

Black Americans for Life Newsletter. "1999 Congressional Black Caucus Continues toDeliver Pro-Abortion Votes." *Black Americans for Life Newsletter*, Fall 1999: 1.

"Black Republicans Say 'Party Can No Longer Be Lily White.'" *The Atlanta Inquirer*, February 8, 2003.

"Black Baptist Pastor Speaks at Catholic Interparish Council." Library Section, *African American Life Alliance*, April 25, 2007: 1, http://www.afamforlife.org.

Black, Earl, and Merle Black. *The Rise of Southern Republicanism.* Cambridge, MA: Harvard University Press, 2002.

Black, Amy E., Douglas L. Loopman, and David K. Ryden. *Of Little Faith: The Politics of George W. Bush's Faith-Based Initiatives.* Washington, DC: Georgetown University Press, 2004.

Blumenthal, Sidney. *The Rise of the Counter-Establishment: From Conservative Ideology to Political Power.* New York: Times Books, 1986.

Bolce, Louis, et. al. "The 1992 Republican 'Tent': No Blacks Walked In." *Political Science Quarterly*, vol. 108, no. 2, 1993: 255–270.

Bonilla-Silva, Eduardo. *Racism Without Racists: Color-Blind Racism and the Persistence of Racial Inequality in the United States.* Lanham, MD: Rowman and Littlefield, 2006.

Bositis, David A. *African Americans and the Republican Party.* Washington, DC: The Joint Center for Political and Economic Studies, 1996.

———. *2000 Joint Center for Political and Economic Studies National Opinion Poll.* Washington, DC: Joint Center for Political and Economic Studies, 2000.

———. *Diverging Generations: The Transformation of African American Views.* Washington, DC: The Joint Center for Political and Economic Studies, 2001.

———. *Blacks and the 2008 Republican National Convention.* Washington, DC: The Joint Center for Political and Economic Studies, 2008.

Bracey, Christopher Alan. *Saviors or Sellouts: The Promise and Peril of Black Conservatism, from Booker T. Washington to Condoleezza Rice.* Boston, MA: Beacon Press, 2008.

Bradley Hagerty, Barbara. "Conservative Black Clergy Make Waves from Pulpit." Transcript of Broadcast on NPR *All Things Considered* Broadcast, April 6, 2006, http://www.npr.org.

Brennan, Mary C. *Turning Right in the Sixties: The Conservative Capture of the GOP.* Chapel Hill: The University of North Carolina Press, 1995.

Bretthauer, Berit. "The Challenge of Televangelism." *Peace Review*, vol. 7, no. 1, 1995.

Brooks Hodge, Sharon. "Pregnant Women Seek Help from Pro-life Groups." *Headway*, August 31, 1997: 26.

Brown, Tony. *Black Lies, White Lies: The Truth According to Tony Brown.* New York: William Morrow, 1995.

Brown Jenkins, Elaine. *Jumping Double Dutch: A New Agenda for Blacks and the Republican Party.* Silver Spring, MD: Beckham Publishers, 1996.

Brown, Joseph. "Conspiracy Theories Blind Us to Real Problems, Solutions." *Headway*, June 30, 1996: 27.

Buckley, William F. Jr. *Up from Liberalism.* New York: McDowell, Obolensky Publishers, 1959.

Carlson, Jody. *George C. Wallace and the Politics of Powerlessness: The Wallace Campaigns for the Presidency, 1964–1976.* Edison, NJ: Transaction Publishers, 1981.

Carroll, Joe. "Abortion Remains a Divisive Issue in the Presidential Race." *Irish Times*, January 29, 2000.

Carter, Dan T. *The Politics of Rage: George Wallace, the Origins of the New Conservatism, and the Transformation of American Politics.* Baton Rouge: Louisiana State University Press, 1995.

———. *From George Wallace to Newt Gingrich: Race in the Conservative Counterrevolution 1963–1994.* Baton Rouge: Louisiana State University Press, 1996.

Carter, Stephen. *Reflections of an Affirmative Action Baby*. New York, NY: Basic Books, 1991.

Chamberlain, Pam, and Jean Hardisty. "Reproducing Patriarchy: Reproductive Rights Under Siege." *The Public Eye*, Spring 2000: 14.

Champion, Jackson R. *Blacks in the Republican Party? The Story of a Revolutionary Conservative Black Republican*. Washington, DC: LenChamps Publishers, 1976.

Chattanoga, W.W. "Speaking Truth to Obliviousness," uploaded June 24, 2015, http://www.economist.com/blogs/democracyinamerica/2015/06/ben-carson-race, accessed July 14, 2016.

Chaves, Mark. "All Creatures Great and Small: Megachurches in Context." *Review of Religious Research*, June 2006.

Cho, Sumo. "Redeeming Whiteness in the Shadow of Interment: Earl Warren, Brown, and a Theory of Racial Redemption." *Boston College Third World Law Journal*, vol. 19, no. 1, 1998: 73–170.

Chumley, Cheryl K. "Ben Carson Likens Abortion in America to 'Human Sacrifice' of Paganists," uploaded July 2, 2014, https://www.washingtontimes.com/news/2014/jul/2/ben-carson-likens-abortion-america-human-sacrifice/, accessed June 15, 2016.

"CIA-Drug Accusations Revive Fears of Conspiracy." *The Philadelphia Tribune*, October 8, 1996: 8A.

Clarkson, Frederick. *Eternal Hostility: The Struggle Between Theocracy and Democracy*. Monroe, ME: Common Courage Press, 1997, p. 2.

Clawson, Dan. "Editor's Note." *Contemporary Sociology: A Journal of Reviews*, vol. 24, no. 2, March 1995.

Clawson, Dan, and Mary Ann Clawson. "Reagan or Business? Foundations of the New Conservatism." In *The Business Elite as a Ruling Class*. Ed. Michael Schwartz. New York: Holmes & Meier, 1987, pp. 201–217.

Clawson, Dan, Alan Neustadtl, and Denise Scott. *Money Talks: Corporate PACs and Political Influence*. New York, NY: Basic Books, 1992.

Collins, Sharon. *Black Corporate Executives: The Making and Breaking of a Black Middle Class*. Philadelphia, PA: Temple University Press, 1997.

Conley, Dalton. *Being Black, Living in the Red: Race, Wealth, and Social Policy in America*. Berkeley: University of California Press, 1999.

Coulter, Ann. "Another Damascus Road Conversion." August 18, 2000, http://www.townhall.com/columnists/anncoulter.

Crenshaw, Kimberlé. "Mapping the Margins: Intersectionality, Identity Politics, and Violence Against Women of Color." In *The Public Nature of Private Violence: The Discovery of Domestic Abuse*. Eds. Martha Albertson Fineman and Roxanne Mykitiuk. New York, NY: Routledge, 1994.

———. "Demarginalizing the Intersection of Race and Sex: A Black Feminist Critique of Antidiscrimination Doctrine, Feminist Theory and Antiracist Politics." In *The Black Feminist Reader*. Eds. Joy James and T. Denean Sharpley-Whiting. Malden, MA: Blackwell, 2001, pp. 208–238.

Crespino, Joseph. "Civil Rights and the Religious Right." In *Rightward Bound: Making America Conservative in the 1970s*. Eds. Bruce J. Schulman and Julian E. Zelizer. Cambridge, MA: Harvard University Press, 2008.

Critchlow, Donald T., and Nancy MacLean. *Debating the American Conservative Movement: 1945 to the Present*. Lanham, MD: Rowman and Littlefield, 2009.

"Cynthia McKinney's Honorable Defeat: The Hard Right's New Black Strategy Rolls On." *The Black Commentator*, September 5, 2002, http://www.black-commentator.com.

Davis, Angela. "Slaying the Dream: The Black Family and the Crisis of Capitalism." *Black Scholar*, September/October 1986: 3.

———. "Racism, Birth Control, and Reproductive Rights." In *From Abortion to Reproductive Rights: Transforming a Movement*. Ed. Marlene Fried. Boston: South End Press, 1990, p. 3.

Davis, R.D. "Could Someone Please Tell Me Why?" *New Visions Commentary*, The National Center for Public Policy Research, July 1996: 1.

Dawson, Michael. "African American Political Opinion: Volatility in the Reagan-Bush Era." In *African American Power and Politics: The Political Context Variable*. Ed. Hanes Walton, Jr. New York: Columbia University Press, 1997.

Decter, Midge. *The New Chastity and Other Arguments Against Women's Liberation*. New York: Coward, McCann & Geoghegan, 1972.

———. "Boys on the Beach." *Commentary*, 1980.

———. *An Old Wife's Tale: My Seven Decades in Love and War*. New York: Regan Books, 2001.

Dent, David J. *In Search of Black America: Discovering the American Dream*. New York: Simon and Schuster, 2000.

DeVeaux, Stuart. "Young, Black, and Republican." In *Black and Right: The Bold New Voice of Black Conservatives in America*. Eds. Stan Faryna, Brad Stetson, and Joseph G. Conti. Westport, CT: Praeger, 1997.

Diamond, Sara. *Roads to Dominion: Right-Wing Movements and Political Power in the United States*. New York: The Guilford Press, 1995.

———. *Not By Politics Alone: The Enduring Influence of the Christian Right*. New York: The Guilford Press, 1998.

Dixon, Bruce. "Muzzling the African American Agenda with Black Help: The DLC's Corporate Dollars of Destruction." *The Black Commentator*, June 12, 2003, http://www.blackcommentator.com.

Dorrien, Gary. *The Neoconservative Mind: Politics, Culture, and the War of Ideology*. Philadelphia, PA: Temple University Press, 1993.

———. "Inventing an American Conservatism: The Neoconservative Episode." In *Unraveling the Right*. Ed. Amy Ansell. Boulder, CO: Westview Press, 1998.

Douglas, Kelly Brown. *Sexuality and the Black Church: A Womanist Perspective*. Maryknoll, NY: Orbis Books, 1999.

Dugger, Karen. "Race Differences in the Determinants of Support for Legalized Abortion." *Social Science Quarterly*, September 1991.

Duin, Julia. "Pastor's Crusade Aims to Halt Wave of Black Abortions, 'It's Killed More Than Ku Klux Klan.'" *The Washington Times*, January 10, 1997: B7.

———. "Pro-life Black Pastors Wary of Obama." *Washington Times*, July 4, 2008, http://www.washingtontimes.com/news/2008/jul/04/black-pastors-wary-of-obama/6.

Edsall, Thomas B. "Christian Right Mobilizes for Judge." *Washington Post*, January 9, 2006: A10.

Edsall, Thomas Byrne, and Mary D. Edsall. *Chain Reaction: The Impact of Race, Rights, and Taxes on American Politics*. New York: W. W. Norton, 1992.

Edwards, Lee. *Goldwater: The Man Who Made a Revolution*. Washington, DC: Regnery, 1995.

———. *The Conservative Revolution: The Movement That Remade America*. New York: The Free Press, 1999.

Emerson, Michael O., and Christian Smith. *Divided by Faith: Evangelical Religion and the Problem of Race in America*. New York, NY: Oxford University Press, 2000.

Escoffier, Jeffrey. "Pessimism of the Mind: Intellectuals, Universities and the Left." *Socialist Review*, vol. 18, no. 1, January–March 1988.

Faludi, Susan. *Backlash: The Undeclared War Against American Women*. New York: Crown Publishers, 1991.

Falwell, Jerry. *Listen, America!* New York: Doubleday, 1980.

Farrington, Brendan. "Obama Inspires Black Republicans to Switch Parties." *Associated Press*, August 21, 2008.

Fauntroy, Michael K. *Republicans and the Black Vote*. Boulder, CO: Lynne Rienner, 2007.

Fields, Corey. *Black Elephants in the Room: The Unexpected Politics of African American Republicans*. Berkeley: University of California Press, 2016.

Felsenthal, Carol. *The Sweetheart of the Silent Majority: The Biography of Phyllis Schlafly*. New York: Doubleday, 1981.

Flake, Floyd H. *The Way of the Bootstrapper: Nine Action Steps for Achieving Your Dreams*. New York, NY: Harper, 2000.

Francis, Samuel. *Beautiful Loser: Essays on the Failure of American Conservatism*. Columbia: University of Missouri Press, 1993.

Franklin, Robert M. *Crisis in the Village: Restoring Hope in African American Communities*. Minneapolis, MN: Fortress Press, 2007.

Franks, Gary. *Searching for the Promised Land: An African American's Optimistic Odyssey*. New York: Regan Books, 1996.

Freedman, Samuel G. *The Inheritance: How Three Families and America Moved from Roosevelt to Reagan and Beyond*. New York: Simon and Schuster, 1996.

Fried, Marlene. "Abortion in the United States-Legal But Inaccessible." In *Abortion Wars: A Half Century of Struggle, 1950–2000.* Ed. Rickie Solinger. Berkeley: University of California Press, 1998.

Friedland, Michael B. *Lift Up Your Voice Like a Trumpet: White Clergy and the Civil Rights and Antiwar Movements, 1954–1973.* Chapel Hill: University of North Carolina Press, 1998.

Frommer, Frederick J. "Black Conservatives Conflicted on Obama Campaign." *Associated Press,* June 14, 2008: 1.

"Fruit of the Poisoned Tree: The Hard Right's Plan to Capture Newark NJ." *The Black Commentator,* April 5, 2002, http://www.blackcommentator.com.

Frum, David. *Dead Right: "A New Republican Era Has Dawned...Or Has It? Will the Right Do What It Must to Shrink Government and Strengthen Family Values?"* New York: Basic Books, 1994.

Frymer, Paul. *Uneasy Alliances: Race and Party Competition in America.* Princeton, NJ: Princeton University Press, 1999.

Furlow, Akua. "African-Americans and Induced Abortion." *Newsletter of the Association for Interdisciplinary Research in Values and Social Change,* vol. 6, no. 1, November/December 1993.

Gateway. April 25, 2007, http://www.gateway.org/content/learn.htm.

Genovese, Eugene. *The Southern Tradition: The Achievement and Limitations of an American Conservatism.* Cambridge, MA: Harvard University Press, 1994.

George, Susan. "How to Win the War of Ideas." *Dissent Magazine,* Summer 1997: 48.

Georgia Voice Editors. "Flashback: Bishop Eddie Long's Anti-gay March Through Atlanta." *Georgia Voice,* uploaded September 24, 2010, https://thegavoice.com/flashback-bishop-eddie-longs-anti-gay-march-through-atlanta/, accessed February 24, 2018.

Gerson, Mark. *The Neoconservative Vision: From the Cold War to the Culture Wars.* Lanham, MD: Madison Books, 1996.

Glazer, Nathan. "In Defense of Preference." *The New Republic,* vol. 218, no. 14, pp. 18–25.

Goldberg, Robert Alan. *Barry Goldwater.* New Haven, CT: Yale University Press, 1995.

Goldfarb, Jeffrey. *The Cynical Society: The Culture of Politics and the Politics of Culture in American Life.* Chicago, IL: The University of Chicago Press, 1991.

Goldwater, Barry. *The Conscience of a Conservative.* Shepherdsville, KY: Victor Publishing, 1960.

Goodstein, Laurie. "Minister, a Bush Ally, Gives Church as Site for Alito Rally." *The New York Times,* January 5, 2006: A15.

"GOP Outreach: Fact or Fiction? A Roundtable Discussion." *Headway,* March 31, 1998.

"GOP Woos Minorities." *Oakland Post*, March 4, 1998: 2.

Gordon, Linda. *Woman's Body, Woman's Right: Birth Control in America*. New York: Penguin Book, 1990.

Gordy, Cynthia. "Where Church and State Meet." *Essence*, August 2009: 84.

Gorney, Cynthia. *Article of Faith: A Frontline History of the Abortion Wars*. New York: Simon and Schuster, 1998.

Gottfried, Paul. *The Conservative Movement*. Rev. ed. New York: Twayne Publishers, 1993.

Gouldner, Alvin. *The Future of Intellectuals and the Rise of the New Class*. New York: Macmillan Press, 1979.

Graham, Rhonda B. "Holy War: Rev. Fred Price Is Fighting the Church Over the Racism." *Emerge Magazine*, January 1999.

Gramsci, Antonio. *An Antonio Gramsci Reader: Selected Writings, 1916–1935*. Ed. David Forgacs. New York: Schocken Books, 1988.

Greenberg, Stanley B. *Middle Class Dreams: The Politics and Power of the New American Majority*. New Haven, CT: Yale University, 1996.

Greenblatt, Alan, and Tracie Powell. "Rise of the Megachurches." In *CQ Researcher: Rise of the Megachurches: Are They Straying Too Far from Their Mission?* September 21, 2007.

Greenhaw, Wayne. *Watch Out for George Wallace*. Englewood Cliffs, NJ: Prentice-Hall, 1976.

Griffin, Horace L. *Their Own Receive Them Not: African American Lesbians & Gays in Black Churches*. Cleveland, OH: The Pilgrim Press, 2006.

Grossman, James R. "Traditional Politics or the Politics of Tradition." *Reviews in American History*, vol. 21, 1993: 533–538.

Hadden, Jeffrey K. "The Rise and Fall of American Televangelism." *Annals of the American Academy of Political and Social Science*, vol. 527. Religion in the Nineties, May 1993.

Hamblin, Ken. *Pick a Better Country: An Unassuming Colored Guy Speaks His Mind About America*. New York: Touchtone Books, 1997.

Haney, David Paul. *The Americanization of Social Science: Intellectuals and Public Responsibility in the Postwar United States*. Philadelphia: Temple University Press, 2008.

Hankins, Barry. *Uneasy in Babylon: Southern Baptist Conservatives and American Culture*. Tuscaloosa: The University of Alabama Press, 2002.

Hardisty, Jean. *Mobilizing Resentment: Conservative Resurgence from the John Birch Society to the Promise Keepers*. Boston, MA: Beacon Press, 1999.

Harper, Lisa Sharon. *Evangelical≠Republican...or Democrat*. New York, NY: The New Press, 2008.

Harries, Owen. "A Primer for Polemicists." *Commentary*, September 1984: 58.

Harrison, Milmon F. *Righteous Riches: The Word of Faith Movement in Contemporary African American Religion*. New York, NY: Oxford University Press, 2005.

Heilbrunn, Jacob. "Con Games." *The New Republic*, October 20, 1997: 18.

Herbst, Susan. *Politics at the Margin: Historical Studies of Public Expression Outside the Mainstream*. New York: Cambridge University Press, 1994.

Heritage Foundation. April 25, 2007, http://www.heritage.org/staff/james. html.

Herrmann, Andrew. "Anti-welfare Stance Makes Her Star of Right." *Chicago Sun-Times*, December 17, 1994: 23.

Herrnstein, Richard, and Charles J. Murray. *The Bell Curve: Intelligence and Class Structure in American Life*. New York, NY: The Free Press, 1995.

Hilgers, T.W., and D.J. Horan eds. *Abortion and Social Justice*. New York: Sheed & Ward, 1972.

Hill, Herbert. "Black-Jewish Conflict in the Labor Context." In *African Americans and Jews in the Twentieth Century: Studies in Convergence and Conflict*. Eds. V.P. Franklin, et al. Columbia: University of Missouri Press, 1998.

Hill Collins, Patricia. "Will the 'Real' Mother Stand Up?: The Logics of Eugenics and American National Family Planning." In *Revisiting Women, Health, and Healing: Feminist, Cultural, and Technoscience Perspectives*. Eds. Adele E. Clarke and Virginia L. Olesen. New York: Routledge, 1999.

———. *Black Feminist Thought: Knowledge, Consciousness and the Politics of Empowerment*. New York, NY: Routledge, 2000.

Himmelstein, Jerome. *To the Right: The Transformation of American Conservatism*. Berkeley: The University of California Press, 1990.

Hixon, William B. *Search for the American Right Wing: An Analysis of the Social Science Record, 1955–1987*. Princeton, NJ: Princeton University Press, 1992.

Hodgson, Godfrey. *The World Turned Right Side Up: A History of the Conservative Ascendancy in America*. Boston, MA: Mariner Books, 1997.

Hofstader, Richard. *The Paranoid Style in American Politics and Other Essays*. New York: Alfred A. Knopf, 1964.

Holmes, Steven A. "Re-Rethinking Affirmative Action." *The New York Times*, April 5, 1998: 5.

Hudnet-Beumler, James. *In Pursuit of the Almighty Dollar: A History of Money and American Protestantism*. Chapel Hill: University of North Carolina Press, 2007.

Hunter, Johnny. Rev. Interview. "African Americans for Life: Black Baptist Pastor Speaks at Catholic Interparish Council." *Gulf Coast Christian Newspaper*, 1996: 3.

Hurston, Zora Neale. *Dust Tracks on a Road: An Autobiography*. New York: Harper Perennial Modern Classics, 1942.

Ingraham, Laura, and Stephen P. Vaughn. "Powell Is Bad for the G.O.P." *The New York Times*, September 20, 1995: 21.

Ireland, Doug. "Back to the Future GOP Revives Anti-gay Marriage Campaign for '06." *Public Eye*, Summer 2006: 6.

Jackson, Michele. "Should Pro-life Black Americans Work Separately or Join NRLC?" *National Right to Life News*, vol. 14, no. 3, April 22, 1997.

———. "End the Ignorance Now!" *National Right to Life News*, vol. 24, no. 3, August 12, 1998.

———. "Should We Allow Denial of Our Right to Informed Consent About Abortion?" *Black Americans for Life Newsletter*, Spring 1999: 1.

Jackson, Derrick Z. "Barbour Campaign Shows GOP's Racist Side." *The Boston Globe*, October 29, 2003: 27.

Jackson, Harry. "Bishop Harry Jackson: The Supreme Court Just Declared War on the Church." *Charisma News*, uploaded July 1, 2015, https://www.charismanews.com/opinion/50362-bishop-harry-jackson-supremecourt-just-declared-war-on-the-church, accessed February 23, 2018.

Jacobson, Matthew Frye. *Whiteness of a Different Color: European Immigrants and the Alchemy of Race*. Cambridge, MA: Harvard University Press, 1999.

James, Kay Cole. *Never Forget: The Riveting Story of One's Woman's Journey from Public Housing to the Corridors of Power*. Grand Rapids, MI: Zondervan Publishing House, 1992.

———. "Abortion Is a Form of Discrimination," uploaded January 18, 2018, https://twitter.com/KayColesJames/status/954430209176100866, accessed February 23, 2018.

Jeansonne, Glen. *Gerald L.K. Smith: The Minister of Hate*. New Haven, CT: Yale University Press, 1988.

Jones, Reginald. *Black Americans for Life Newsletter*, Spring 1999: 3.

Jones, Rhett, "Black Creole Cultures: The Eighteenth Century Origins of African American Conservatism." In *Dimensions of Black Conservatism in the United States: Made in America*. Eds. Gayle T. Tate and Lewis A. Randolph. New York: Palgrave Press, 2002.

Karabel, Jerome. "Towards a Theory of Intellectuals and Politics." *Theory and Society*, vol. 25, no. 2, April 1996: 205–233.

Karnes, Kimberly, Wayne McIntosh, Irwin L. Morris, and Shanna Pearson-Merkowitz. "Mighty Fortress: Explaining the Spatial Distribution of American Megachurches." *Journal for the Scientific Study of Religion*, vol. 46, no. 2, 2007: 261–268.

Kazin, Michael, and Maurice Isserman. *America Divided: The Civil War of the 1960s*. New York: Oxford University Press, 2000.

Kilson, Martin. "A Letter from Harvard: The Black Trojan Horse." *The Black Commentator*, May 8, 2002: 1, http://www.blackcommentator.com.

King, Deborah K. "Multiple Jeopardy, Multiple Consciousness: The Context of a Black Feminist Ideology." *Signs*, vol. 14, no. 1, Autumn 1988: 42–72.

Kintz, Linda. *Between Jesus and the Market: The Emotions That Matter in Right-Wing America*. Durham, NC: Duke University Press, 1997.

Klinkner, Philip A., and Rogers M. Smith. *The Unsteady March: The Rise and Decline of Racial Equality.* Chicago, IL: The University of Chicago Press, 1999.

Krickus, Richard. *Pursuing the American Dream: White Ethnics and the New Populism.* Bloomington: Indiana University Press, 1976.

Kristol, Irving. *Neoconservatism: The Autobiography of an Idea.* New York: The Free Press, 1995.

Kroll, Luisa. "Christian Capitalism: Megachurches, Megabusinesses." *Forbes,* September 17, 2003.

Kurzman, Charles, and Lynn Owens. "The Sociology of Intellectuals." *Annual Review of Sociology,* vol. 28, 2002: 63–90.

Lee, Shayne. *T.D. Jakes: America's New Preacher.* New York: New York University Press, 2005.

Lehner, Peggy. "Abortion and the African-American Community." *Newsletter. Crisis Pregnancy Ministry–Focus on the Family,* November 2001.

Lewis, Angela. *Conservatism in the Black Community: To the Right and Misunderstood.* New York: Routledge, 2013.

Lewis, Matt. "Twitter's Right-Wing Civil War: For a Not-Insignificant Portion of the Online Right, a New Form of White Nationalism Is Taking Root— And It Coincides with the Rise of Donald Trump," uploaded July 28, 2015, http://www.thedailybeast.com/articles/2015/07/28/twitter-s-right-wing-civil-war.html, accessed September 4, 2015.

Lieberman, Trudy. *Slanting the Story: The Forces That Shape the News.* New York: The New Press, 2000.

Life Education and Resources Network. April 25, 2007, http://www.learninc.org.

Lind, Michael. *Up from Conservatism: Why the Right Is Wrong for America.* New York: The Free Press, 1996.

Lipset, Seymour Martin, and Earl Raab. The Politics of Unreason: Right Wing Extremism in America, 1790–1970. New York, NY: Harper and Row, 1970.

Lipsitz, George. *The Possessive Investment in Whiteness: How White People Profit from Identity Politics.* Philadelphia, PA: Temple University Press, 2006.

Lopez, Ian Haney. *Dog Whistle Politics: How Coded Racial Appeals Have Reinvented Racism and Wrecked the Middle Class.* New York: Oxford University Press, 2014.

Luker, Kristen. *Abortion & the Politics of Motherhood.* Berkeley: The University of California Press, 1984.

Macek, Steve. *Urban Nightmares: The Media, the Right, and the Moral Panic Over the City.* Minneapolis: University of Minnesota Press, 2006.

Malveaux, Julianne. "Why Are the Black Conservatives All Men?" *Ms. Magazine,* March/April 1991.

Mann, Brian. *Welcome to the Homeland: A Journey to the Rural Heart of America's Conservative Revolution.* Hanover, NH: Steerforth Press, 2006.

Marable, Manning. *Black Liberation in Conservative America.* Boston, MA: South End Press, 1998.

Martin, William. *With God on Our Side: The Rise of the Religious Right in America.* New York: Broadway Books, 1996.

Marx, Karl, and Frederick Engels. *The German Ideology: Parts I & III.* New York: International, 1947.

Mayer, Jeremy D. *Running on Race: Racial Politics in Presidential Campaigns, 1960–2000.* New York: Random House, 2002.

McClarey, Donald R. "Mildred Fay Jefferson, Requiescat in Pace." *The American Catholic,* uploaded October 18 2010, https://www.issues4life.org/blast/2011080.html, accessed February 23, 2018.

McCarthy, Jean. "Dr. Day Gardner on Abortionist's 'Ugly Black Babies' Remark: She's Heard Before." *LifeSite,* uploaded August 7, 2012, https://www.lifesitenews.com/news/dr.-day-gardner-on-abortionists-ugly-black-babies-remark-shes-heard-it-befo, accessed February 23, 2018.

McGirr, Lisa. *Suburban Warriors: The Origins of the New American Right.* Princeton, NJ: Princeton University Press, 2001.

McGlathery, Marla Frederick, and Traci Griffin. "Becoming Conservative, Becoming White?: Black Evangelicals and the Para-Church Movement." In *This Side of Heaven: Race, Ethnicity, and Christian Faith.* Eds. Robert J. Priest and Alvaro L. Nieves. New York, NY: Oxford University Press, 2007.

McGlowan, Angela. *Bamboozled: How Americans Are Being Exploited by the Lies of the Liberal Agenda.* Nashville, TN: Thomas Nelson, 2007.

McIntosh, Peggy. *White Privilege: Unpacking the Invisible Knapsack.* s.n., 1989.

McLemee, Scott. ed. *C. L. R. James on the 'Negro Question'.* Jackson, MI: University Press of Mississippi, 1996.

McWhorter, John. *Losing the Race: Self-Sabotage in Black America.* New York: Perennial, 2001.

———. *Authentically Black: Essays for the Black Silent Majority.* New York: Gotham Books, 2003a.

———. Interview. Brian Lamb. C-Span Book-TV Program. March 2, 2003b, http://www.Booknotes.org.

———. *Winning the Race: Beyond the Crisis in Black America.* New York: Gotham Books, 2006.

Melich, Tanya. *The Republican War Against Women: An Insider's Report from Behind the Lines.* New York: Bantam, 1996.

Mendelberg, Tali. *The Race Card: Campaign Strategy, Implicit Messages, and the Norm of Equality.* Princeton, NJ: Princeton University, 2001.

Mills, C. Wright. *The Sociological Imagination.* New York: Oxford University Press, 2000.

Monroe, Ann. "Race to the Right." *Mother Jones*, May/June 1997.

Montgomery, Peter. "Point Man for the Wedge Strategy: Harry Jackson Is the Face of the Religious Right's Outreach to African American Christians," http://www.pfaw.org/site/...harry_jackson_point.

Moore, Jimmy. "Fiery Black Conservative Running for Congress in North Carolina." *Talon News*, October 10, 2003: 3, http://www.gopusa.com.

Morken, Hubert, and Jo Renee Formicola. *The Politics of School Choice*. Lanham, MD: Rowman and Littlefield, 1999.

Morris, Aldon. *The Origins of the Civil Rights Movement: Black Communities Organizing for Change*. New York: The Free Press, 1984.

Mullings, Leith. "Households Headed by Women: The Politics of Race, Class, and Gender." In *Conceiving the New World Order: The Global Politics of Reproduction*. Eds. Faye D. Ginsburg and Rayna Rapp. Berkeley: University of California Press, 1995.

Murakami, Keri. "Christian Coalition Trying to Reach Out–African Americans, Rabbi Are Speakers." *The Seattle Times*, June 25, 1995: B1.

Murray, Charles. *Losing Ground: American Social Policy, 1950–1980*. New York, NY: Basic Books, 1994.

Obama, Barack. *The Audacity of Hope: Thoughts on Reclaiming the American Dream*. New York, NY: Crown Publishers, 2006.

O'Conner, Alice. *Social Science for What?: Philanthropy and the Social Question in a World Turned Right Side Up*. New York: Russell Sage, 2007.

Olasky, Marvin. *Compassionate Conservatism: What It Is, What It Does, and How It Can Transform America*. New York: The Free Press, 2000.

O'Reilly, Kenneth. *Nixon's Piano: Presidents and Racial Politics from Washington to Clinton*. New York: The Free Press, 1995.

Owens, Michael Leo. "Contestant, Advocate, Implementer: Social Services and the Policy Roles of African American Churches." In *Long March Ahead: African American Churches and Public Policy in Post-civil Rights America, the Public Influences of African American Churches, Volume II*. Ed. R. Drew Smith. Durham, NC: Duke University Press, 2004.

Owens, Michael Leo, and R. Drew Smith. "Congregations in Low-Income Neighborhoods and the Implications for Social Welfare Policy Research." *Nonprofit and Voluntary Sector Quarterly*, vol. 3, no. 35, 2005.

Pack, Juliette Bartlett. "Abortion: The Black Woman's Voice." Pamphlet. Texas Black Americans for Life, 1995.

Paget, Karen M. "Lessons of Right-Wing Philanthropy." *The American Prospect*, September–October 1998.

———. "The Big Chill: Foundations and Political Passion." *The American Prospect*, May–June 1999: 28–33.

Paige, Connie. *The Right to Lifers: Who They Are, How They Operate, Where Do They Get Their Money*. New York: Summit Books, 1983.

————. "Watch on the Right: The Amazing Rise of Beverly LaHaye." *Ms Magazine*, February 1987: 26.

Parker, Star. *Pimps, Whores and Welfare Brats: The Stunning Conservative Transformation of a Former Welfare Queen*. New York: Pocket Books, 1997.

————. "GOP Can't Get It Right with Black Outreach." *The Philadelphia Tribune*, May 4, 2001: 7A.

Peele, Gillian. *Revival and Reaction: The Right in Contemporary America*. New York: Oxford University Press, 1984.

Perlstein, Rick. *Before the Storm: Barry Goldwater and the Unmaking of the American Consensus*. New York: Hill and Wang, 2001.

Perry, Theresa. "Up from the Parched Earth: Toward a Theory of African-American Achievement." In *Young, Gifted, and Black: Promoting High Achievement Among African-American Students*. Eds. Claude Steele, Theresa Perry, and Asa Hilliard III. Boston, MA: Beacon Press, 2003.

Persons, Georgia A. "National Politics and Charitable Choice as Urban Policy for Community Development." *The Annals of the American Academy*, vol. 594, July 2004.

Peterson, Jessie Lee. "Moral Poverty Cost Blacks in New Orleans." September 21, 2005a, http://www.worldnetdaily.com.

————. "Truth: Solution to Black America's Moral Poverty." October 7, 2005b, http://www.worldnetdaily.com.

Phillips, Kevin. *The Emerging Republican Majority*. New Rochelle, NY: Arlington House, 1969.

Pollack Petchesky, Rosalind. *Abortion and Woman's Choice: The State, Sexuality, and Reproductive Freedom*. New York: Longman, 1984.

Portes, Alejandro, and Ruben G. Rumbaut. *Immigrant America: A Portrait*, 3rd ed. Berkeley: University of California Press, 2006.

Posner, Sarah. *God's Profits: Faith, Fraud, and the Republican Crusade for Values Voters*. Sausalito, CA: Polipoint Press, 2008.

Prashad, Vijay. *Keeping Up with the Dow Joneses: Debt, Prison, Workfare*. Boston, MA: South End Press, 2003.

Prisock, Louis G. "If You Love Children, Say So: The African American Anti-Abortion Movement." *The Public Eye*, Fall 2003.

Pro-life Action League. "Scheidlers Cheer Black Americans for Life Honorees," uploaded August 14, 2005, https://prolifeaction.org/2005/2005v24n-2bafl/, accessed February 23, 2018.

Prothero, Arianna. "The Only National Black School Choice Advocacy Group Is Folding." *Education Week*, uploaded October 25, 2017, http://blogs.edweek.org/edweek/charterschoice/2017/10/the_only_national_black_school_choice_advocacy_group_is_closing.html, accessed February 23, 2018.

Rae, Nicole. *The Decline and Fall of the Liberal Republicans: From 1952 to the Present*. New York: Oxford University Press, 1989.

Reed, Adolph. "The Descent of Black Conservatism." *The Progressive*, October 1997: 18–20.

Reed, Adolph, and Julian Bond. "Equality: Why We Can't Wait." *The Nation*, December 9, 1991.

Reed, Ralph. *Politically Incorrect: The Emerging Faith Factor in American Politics*. Dallas, TX: Word Publishing, 1994.

———. *Active Faith: How Christians Are Changing the Soul of American Politics*. New York: The Free Press, 1996.

Rees, Matthew. *From the Deck to the Sea: Blacks and the Republican Party*. Wakefield, NH: Longwood Academic, 1991.

Religious News Services. "Enlisting Blacks in the Battle Against Abortion." *Christianity Today*, October 1994.

Reuter, Theodore. "The New Black Conservatives." In *The Politics of Race: African Americans and the Political System*. Ed. Theodore Reuter. Armonk, NY: M. E. Sharpe, 1995.

Ricci, David M. *The Transformation of American Politics: The New Washington and the Rise of Think Tanks*. New Haven, CT: Yale University Press, 1994.

Ridgeway, James. "Heritage on the Hill: The Right's Pre-eminent P.R. Machine." *The Nation*, December 22, 1997: 16.

Rieder, Jonathan. *Canarsie: The Jews and Italians of Brooklyn Against Liberalism*. Cambridge, MA: Harvard University Press, 1985.

Roberts, Ronald Suresh. *Clarence Thomas and the Tough Love Crowd: Counterfeit Heroes and Unhappy Truths*. New York: New York University Press, 1995.

Roberts, Dorothy. *Killing the Black Body: Race, Reproduction, and the Meaning of Liberty*. New York: Pantheon, 1997.

Robinson, Pearl. "Whither the Future of Blacks in the Republican Party?" *Political Science Quarterly*, vol. 97, Summer 1982.

Robinson, Carrin. "From Every Tribe and Nation?: Blacks and the Christian Right." *Social Science Quarterly*, September 2006.

Roediger, David. *Working Toward Whiteness: How America's Immigrants Became White*. New York, NY: Basic Books, 2006.

———. *The Wages of Whiteness: Race and the Making of the American Working Class*. New York, NY: Verso, 2007.

Roseboro, Paulette. "The Rape of Black America." Speech. Charles County Community College, March 1999.

Ross, Loretta. "African-American Women and Abortion: 1800–1970." In *Theorizing Black Feminisms: The Visionary Pragmatism of Black Women*. Eds. Stanlie M. James and Abena P.A. Busia. New York: Routledge, 1994.

———. "African American Women and Abortion." In *Abortion Wars: A Half Century of Struggle, 1950–2000*. Ed. Rickie Solinger. Berkeley: University of California Press, 1998.

Rossiter, Clinton. *Conservatism in America: The Thankless Persuasion*, 2nd ed. New York: Alfred A. Knopf, 1962.

Scott, Daryl. *Contempt and Pity: Social Policy and the Image of the Damaged Black Psyche, 1880–1996*. Chapel Hill: University of North Carolina Press, 1997.

Shapiro, Walter. "Jack Kemp's Race Card." *Esquire*, November 1996.

Sherman, Richard B. *The Republican Party and Black America from McKinley to Hoover: 1896–1933*. Charlottesville: University of Virginia Press, 1973.

Simpson, Andrea Y. *The Tie That Binds: Identity and Political Attitudes in the Post-civil Rights Generation*. New York: New York University Press, 1998.

"Slavery and Abortion: The Parallel." Pamphlet. Blacks For Life.

Sleeper, Jim. *Closest of Strangers*. New York: W. W. Norton, 1997.

Smith Jr., J. Clay. "A Black Lawyer's Response to the Fairmont Papers." *Howard Law Journal*, vol. 23, 1983: 195.

Smith, James A. *The Idea Brokers: Think Tanks and the Rise of the New Policy Elite*. New York: The Free Press, 1991.

Smith, Barbara. "Blacks & Gays: Healing the Great Divide." In *Eyes Right: Challenging the Right Wing Backlash*. Ed. Chip Berlet. Boston, MA: South End Press, 1995.

Snow, David, E. Burke Rockford Jr., Steven K. Worden, and Robert D. Benford. "Frame Alignment Processes, Micromobilization, and Movement Participation." *American Sociological Review*, August 1986.

Solinger, Rickie. *Beggars and Choosers: How the Politics of Choice Shapes Adoption, Abortion, and Welfare in the United States*. New York: Hill and Wang, 2001.

Song, Jaymes. "Hawaii Again Declares Obama Birth Certificate Real." *Associate Press*, July 28, 2009, http://www.yahoo.com/news.

Sowell, Thomas. "Politics and Opportunity: The Background." In *The Fairmont Papers: Black Alternatives Conference December 1980*. San Francisco, CA: Institute for Contemporary Studies, 1980.

Squitieri, Tom. "Keyes Says He'll Leave Party If GOP Softens on Abortion, Constitution Party Says Candidate Is Welcome to Join." *USA Today*, May 22, 2000: 17A.

Stan, Adele. "Christian Right Voter Summit Sells Racist Obama Waffles." September 15, 2008, http://www.alternet.org/.../christian_right_voter_summit_sells_racist_'obama_waffles'.

Staub, Michael E. "'Negroes Are Not Jews': Race, Holocaust Consciousness, and the Rise of Jewish Neoconservatism." *Radical History Review*, vol. 75, 1999: 3–27.

Steele, Shelby. *The Content of Our Character: A New Vision of Race in America*. New York: HarperCollins, 1991.

———. *A Dream Deferred: The Second Betrayal of Black Freedom in America*. New York: HarperCollins, 1998.

Stefancic, Jean, and Richard Delgado. *No Mercy: How Conservative Think Tanks and Foundations Changed America's Social Agenda*. Philadelphia, PA: Temple University Press, 1996.

Steinberg, Stephen. *The Ethnic Myth: Race, Ethnicity, and Class in America*. Boston: Beacon Press, 1989.

Steinfels, Peter. *The Neoconservatives: Men Who Are Changing America's Politics*. New York: Simon and Schuster, 1979.

Stoesz, David. "Packaging the Conservative Revolution." *Social Epistemology*, vol. 2, no. 2, 1988.

Stone, Deborah. "Empty Nest Politics." *The Nation*, vol. 51, June 12, 2000.

Sugrue, Thomas. *The Origins of the Urban Crisis: Race and Inequality in Postwar Detroit*. Princeton, NJ: Princeton University Press, 1996.

Szelenyi, Ivan. "Gouldner's Theory of Intellectuals as a Flawed Universal Class." *Theory and Society*, vol. 11, no. 6, November 1982: 779–798.

Szelenyi, Ivan, and Bill Martin. "The Three Waves of New Class Theories." *Theory and Society*, vol. 17, no. 5, September 1988: 645–667.

Tafel, Richard. *Party Crasher: A Gay Republican Challenges Politics as Usual*. New York: Simon and Schuster, 1999.

Taylor, April J. "High-Tech, Pop-A-Pill Culture: New Forms of Social Control for Black Women." In *Dangerous Intersections: Feminist Perspectives on Population, Environment, and Development*. Eds. Jael Silliman and Ynestra King. Cambridge, MA: South End Press, 1999.

The Philadelphia Tribune. "CIA-Drug Accusations Revive Fears of Conspiracy." In *The Philadelphia Tribune*, October 8, 1996: 8A.

Thompson, Azure. "Bush Meets with Black Clergy." *Afro-American Red Star*. Washington, DC, March 24, 2001: A1.

Thurman, Scott. "United States Has More Megachurches Than Previously Thought." *Hartford Seminary*, 2005. Web report www.hartsem.edu/events/news_mega.htm.

Toler, Deborah. "Black Conservatives." In *Eyes Right!: Challenging the Right Wing Backlash*. Ed. Chip Berlet. Boston, MA: South End Press, 1995.

Townsend Gilkes, Cheryl. "Plenty of Good Room: Adaptation in a Changing Black Church." *Annals of the American Academy of Political and Social Science*, vol. 558, Americans and Religions in the Twenty-First Century, July 1998.

———. *If It Wasn't for the Women: Black Women's Experience and Womanist Culture in Church and Community*. Maryknoll, NY: Orbis Books, 2001.

Townsley, Eleanor. "A History of Intellectuals and the Demise of the New Class Academics and the U.S. Government in the 1960s." *Theory and Society*, vol. 29, no. 6, December 2000: 739–784.

Tyler, Raven. "Rising Stars in the Party of Lincoln." *The Philadelphia Tribune*, August 1, 2000: 7E.

Uwumarogie, Victoria. "Bishop Eddie Long on Considering Suicide During Sexual Misconduct Allegations and Saving His Marriage." *Madamenoire*, uploaded May 25, 2016, http://madamenoire.com/698895/bishop-eddie-long, accessed February 24, 2018.

Viguerie, Richard A. *The New Right: We're Ready to Lead.* Falls Church, VA: Caroline House Publishers, 1981.

Wald, Alan M. *The New York Intellectuals: The Rise and Decline of the Anti-Stalinist Left From the 1930s to the 1980s.* Chapel Hill: The University of North Carolina Press, 1987.

Wallsten Peter, and Tom Hamburger. "Bush Rewarded by Black Pastors' Faith." *Los Angeles Times*, January 18, 2005: A17.

Walters, Ronald. "Black Conservatives Failed a Leadership Test." *The New York Beacon*, January 29, 2003: 9.

Walton Jr., Hanes. *Black Republicans: The Politics of the Black and Tans.* Metuchen, NJ: The Scarecrow Press, 1975.

———. ed. *African American Power and Politics: The Political Context Variable.* New York: Columbia University Press, 1997.

Walton, Jonathan L. *Watch This: The Ethics and Aesthetics of Black Televangelism.* New York: New York University Press, 2009.

Warren, Donald I. *The Radical Center: Middle Americans and the Politics of Alienation.* Notre Dame: University of Notre Dame Press, 1976.

Washington, Booker T. *Up from Slavery: An Autobiography.* New York: Doubleday, 1904.

Waters, Mary C. *Black Identities: West Indian Immigrant Dreams and American Realities.* Cambridge: Harvard University Press, 1999.

Watkins, Vincent B. "Black or White, the Issue Must Be Life." *National Right to Life News*, August 12, 1998.

Watson, Justin. *The Christian Coalition: Dreams of Restoration, Demands for Recognition.* New York: St. Martin's Press, 1997.

Watts, J.C. Jr. *What Color Is a Conservative? My Life and My Politics.* New York: HarperCollins, 2002.

Weisbord, Robert G. *Genocide?: Birth Control and the Black American.* New York: Greenwood Press, 1975.

Weiss, Nancy J. *Farewell to the Party of Lincoln: Black Politics in the Age of FDR.* Princeton, NJ: Princeton University Press, 1983.

Weiss, Rick. "New Status for Embryos in Research." *Washington Post*, October 30, 2002: AO1.

Welhouwer, Peter W. "Releasing the Fetters: Parties and the Mobilization of the African-American Electorate." *The Journal of Politics*, vol. 62, February 2000: 206–222.

Weyrich, Paul. "Blue Collar or Blue Blood?: The New Right Compared with the Old Right." In *The New Right Papers*. Ed. Robert W. Whitaker. New York: St. Martin's Press, 1982.

White, Richard. *'It's Your Misfortune and None of My Own': A History of the American West.* Norman: University of Oklahoma Press, 1991.

Wilcox, Clyde. *Onward Christian Soldiers: The Religious Right in American Politics*, 2nd ed. Boulder, CO: Westview Press, 2000.

Williams, Juan. "Bush Shouldn't Write Off the Black Vote." *The New York Times*, June 16, 2004.

Williams, Oscar. *George S. Schuyler: Portrait of a Black Conservative.* Knoxville: The University of Tennessee Press, 2007.

Williams, Krissah. "Bush Pastor Launches Pro-Obama Web Site," June 27, 2008, www.washingtonpost.com.

Willke, J.C. *Abortion and Slavery: History Repeats.* Cincinnati, OH: Hayes Publishing, 1984.

Wills, Christopher. "Obama Tells Black Fathers to Engage Their Children." *Associated Press*, June 17, 2008: 1.

Wilson, James Q. "Policy Intellectuals and Public Policy." *The Public Interest*, Summer 1981: 36.

Wright, James. "Southern Baptist Minister Prays for Obama's Death." *Baltimore Afro-American*, June 21, 2009, http://www.afro.com/SearchIndexer/tabid/461/itemid/3937/Default.aspx.

Wypijewski, JoAnn. "The De-alignment of America." *The Nation*, October 28, 1996.

Index

Organization of the Petroleum
Exporting Companies (OPEC),
80
Osteen, Joel, 305
Owens, Doug, 214
Owens, Michael, 319, 327, 333n12

P
Paap, Kris, 276
Pack, Juliette Bartlett, 120
paleoconservatives, 67–68
Palin, Sarah, 230–31
Parents of New York United, 87n5
Parker, Star, 104–6, 135nn14–15,
175, 186–87, 235n16, 340–41,
344
Parker, Wendy, 158
Pataki, George, 327
patriarchy, 133, 298. See also gender
Patrick, Deval, 49
Patriot Movement, 100, 134n6
Patterson, Gilbert E., 322
Patterson, John, 34
Patterson, Robert B., 19–20
Pearson, Carlton, 301, 304
Peele, Gillian, 50
People for the American Way, 147
People United to Save Humanity
(PUSH), 333n10
perceptional segregation, 209–10
performance of blackness, 85, 260–70,
290n5, 290n7
Perkins, Tony, 147, 322
Perlstein, Rick, 43n7
Perry, Rick, 205–211
Perry, Theresa, 264
Personal Responsibility and Work
Opportunity Reconciliation Act
(PRWORA), 319–21
Persons, Georgia, 320
persuasive simplification, 256–70

Peterson, Jessie Lee, 328–29
Pettigrew, Thomas, 43n9
Phelps, Fred, 151, 167n9
Phelps, Nate, 167n9
Phelps-Roper, Shirley, 150–51, 167n9
Phillips, Howard, 51, 90n21
Phillips, Joseph, 224–25
Phillips, Kevin, 39
Phoenix Urban League, 29
Pickett, Justin T., 216
Pimps, Whores, and Welfare Brats
(Parker), 104
pioneer pressure, 202–203
Pittsburgh Courier, 124
plain folk Americanism, 80–82. See also
conservative populism
Planned Parenthood, 100, 107, 109,
118–20, 123, 132
Plessy v. Ferguson, 19, 61, 154
Podhoretz, Norman, 57–59, 62–63,
87n10, 88n13, 89n14, 287
Ponnuru, Ramesh, 289
population control, 98, 102, 121,
137n30. See also eugenics
populism. See conservative populism
Portes, Alejandro, 267–70
Posner, Sarah, 334n16
Potter's House, 305
Powell, Adam Clayton, Sr., 299
Powell, Colin, 183
Praise The Lord (PTL), 301
Prashad, Vijay, 320
presidential election of 1948, 12–14
presidential election of 1952, 14–15,
17
presidential election of 1956, 18
presidential election of 1960, 26, 37,
42n3, 180
presidential election of 1964, 18,
27–34, 37, 180, 235n15
presidential election of 1968, 17–18,
37–39, 83